Lecture Notes in Computer Science 7270

Commenced Publication in 1973
Founding and Former Series Editors:
Gerhard Goos, Juris Hartmanis, and Jan van Leeuwen

W0192943

Ngoc Thanh Nguyen (Ed.)

Transactions on Computational Collective Intelligence VII

 Springer

Volume Editor

Ngoc Thanh Nguyen
Wroclaw University of Technology
Wyb. Wyspiańskiego 27
50-370 Wroclaw, Poland
E-mail: ngoc-thanh.nguyen@pwr.edu.pl

ISSN 0302-9743 (LNCS)   e-ISSN 1611-3349 (LNCS)
ISSN 2190-9288 (TCCI)
ISBN 978-3-642-32065-1   e-ISBN 978-3-642-32066-8
DOI 10.1007/978-3-642-32066-8

Springer Heidelberg Dordrecht London New York

Library of Congress Control Number: 2012942489

CR Subject Classification (1998):
I.2.11, H.3.4, I.2.6, H.3, H.4, H.5, I.2, D.2, K.4.4, G.1.2, F.1.1

Typesetting: Camera-ready by author, data conversion by Scientific Publishing Services, Chennai, India

Printed on acid-free paper

Springer is part of Springer Science+Business Media (www.springer.com)

Transactions on Computational Collective Intelligence VII

Preface

Welcome to the seventh volume of *Transactions on Computational Collective Intelligence* (TCCI). This is the second issue in 2012.

As a journal, TCCI is indexed by major databases such as ISI Web of Science, EI Engineering Index, ACM Digital Library, DBLP, and Scopus. Moreover, we are pleased to report that TCCI has been selected to be included in the Excellence in Research for Australia (ERA) 2012 Journal List, Australian Research Council.

This volume of TCCI includes ten interesting and original papers that have been selected after a peer-review process.

The first paper, entitled "The Process of Reaching Agreement in Meaning Negotiation" by Elisa Burato and Matteo Cristani, presents an approach for the problem of defining a general framework that can be used to formalize the steps that brings a group of agents to reach an agreement about the meaning of a set of terms. In particular, the authors worked out an algorithm which automates the meaning negotiation process.

In the second paper, "Formalizing Emotional E-Commerce Agents for a Simple Negotiation Protocol," the authors, Veronica Jascanu, Nicolae Jascanu and Severin Bumbaru, address the emotional e-commerce problem. They built a platform for its solution by formalizing the customer, supplier and community agents. A simple negotiation protocol as a proof of concept is also presented.

The next paper, "Engineering Multi-Agent Systems Through Statecharts-Based JADE Agents and Tools" by Giancarlo Fortino, Francesco Rango and Wilma Russo, includes a framework and a related tool supporting a Statecharts-based development of JADE-based MAS. In particular, a model for programming JADE behaviors through a variant of the Statecharts, named Distilled StateCharts (DSCs), has been developed by enhancing the JADE add-on HSM Behavior.

In the fourth paper entitled "Fleet Organization Models for Online Vehicle Routing Problems" the authors, Mahdi Zargayouna and Besma Zeddini, address online vehicle routing problems with time windows. They proposed two agent-oriented models which enable a particular dynamic organization of the vehicles with the objective to minimize the appearance of such areas. The first model deals with a spatial representation of the agents' action zones, and the second is grounded on the space-time representation of these zones.

In "Neural Smooth Function Approximation and Prediction with Adaptive Learning Rate" by Villèvo Adanhounmè, Théophile K. Dagba, and Sèmiyou A. Adédjouma, an algebraic approach for representing multidimensional and non-linear functions by feedforward neural networks implemented for the approximation of smooth batch data containing the input–output of hidden neurons and the final neural output of the network is presented and discussed.

The next paper entitled "A Multi-Classifier Approach to Dialogue Act Classification Using Function Words," by James O'Shea, Zuhair Bandar and Keeley Crockett, presents a novel technique for the classification of sentences as dialogue acts, which is based on structural information contained in function words. The experiments performed by the authors on classifying questions in the presence of a mix of straightforward and "difficult" non-questions gave very promising results, with classification accuracy equal to almost 90%.

In the seventh paper, "Building Group Recommendations in E-learning Systems" Danuta Zakrzewska presents an agent-based recommender system, which is capable of suggesting to a new student a group of similar profiles and consequently of proposing suitable learning resources for him. The author has performed several tests for real data of different groups of similar students as well as of individual learners.

The next paper, "Individual Semiosis in Multi-agent Systems" by Wojciech Lorkiewicz, Radoslaw Katarzyniak, and Ryszard Kowalczyk presents research studies on the dynamics of the knowledge alignment processes in multi-agent environments, depending on the internal behavior of agents and the dynamics of the observed phase transition in the alignment process.

The ninth paper entitled "Evaluation of Multi-Agent Systems: Proposal and Validation of a Metric Plan," by Pierpaolo Di Bitonto, Maria Laterza, Teresa Roselli, Veronica Rossano, presents a method for evaluating static multi-agent systems and its validation. The originality of the method is based on the possibility of the MAS to be evaluated in the context of the environment in which it will operate, and its adequacy for the environment to be judged from the viewpoints of both the designer and the evaluator.

In the last paper, "Egress Modeling Through Cellular Automata-Based Multi-Agent Systems," Jarosław Wąs presents an analysis of evacuation models based on a multi-agent approaches. This analysis is based on several evacuation experiments carried out by the author and on a practical approach toward the creation of computer simulations using cellular automata-based multi-agent systems.

TCCI is a peer-reviewed and authoritative journal dealing with the working potential of CCI methodologies and applications, as well as emerging issues of interest to academics and practitioners. The research area of CCI has been growing significantly in recent years and we are very thankful to everyone within the CCI research community who has supported the *Transactions on Computational Collective Intelligence* and its affiliated events including the *International*

Conferences on Computational Collective Intelligence (ICCCI). ICCCI 2012 will be held in Ho Chi Minh city, Vietnam, in November 2012. After each event of ICCCI we invite authors of selected papers to extend them and submit for publication in TCCI.

We would like to thank all the authors, Editorial Board members, and the reviewers for their contributions to TCCI. Finally, we would also like to express our gratitude to the LNCS editorial staff of Springer led by Alfred Hofmann for supporting the TCCI journal.

April 2012   Ngoc Thanh Nguyen

Transactions on Computational Collective Intelligence

This Springer journal focuses on research in applications of the computer-based methods of computational collective intelligence (CCI) and their applications in a wide range of fields such as the Semantic Web, social networks and multi-agent systems. It aims to provide a forum for the presentation of scientific research and technological achievements accomplished by the international community.

The topics addressed by this journal include all solutions of real-life problems for which it is necessary to use CCI technologies to achieve effective results. The emphasis of the papers published is on novel and original research and technological advancements. Special features on specific topics are welcome.

Editor-in-Chief

Table of Contents

The Process of Reaching Agreement
in Meaning Negotiation

Elisa Burato and Matteo Cristani

Dipartimento di Informatica, Università di Verona,
Cà Vignal 2, Strada Le Grazie 15, I-37134 Verona
{elisa.burato,matteo.cristani}@univr.it

Abstract. The process of reaching an agreement about the meaning of
a set of terms is known as *Meaning Negotiation*. The problem of representing this process contains some sub-problems: to represent the knowledge of the agents about the meaning of the negotiating set of terms, to
model the behaviour of the agents involved and to define the agreement
and disagreement conditions.

Although a large attention from many diverse communities has been
driven to this theme in the recent literature of Artificial Intelligence and
Knowledge Representation, the results of these investigations depend
upon the number of the involved agents. The mechanism of reaching an
agreement has been largely studied in the Game Theory community, but
only for *quantitative* objects to be negotiated.

In this paper we approach the problem of defining a general framework
that can be used to formalise the steps that brings two agents in one case
or a group of more than two agents in the other one to reach an agreement
about the meaning of a set of terms. In particular, once we have defined a
logical framework to represent the situation of two agents that negotiate
we define an algorithm automating the Meaning Negotiation process and
study its computational properties. We then extend the algorithm to a
framework in which negotiating agents are more than two.

1 Introduction and Motivations

In recent years it became clear that computer systems do not work in isolation.
Rather, computer systems are increasingly acting as elements in a complex, distributed community of people and systems. In order to fulfill their tasks, computer systems must cooperate and coordinate their activities and communicate
with other systems and with people. Cooperation and coordination are needed
almost everywhere computers are used. Examples include health institutions,
electricity networks, electronic commerce, robotic systems, digital libraries, mil-
itary units etc.

Problems of coordination and cooperation are not unique to automated systems. They exist at multiple levels of activity in a wide range of populations.
People achieve their own goals through communication and cooperation with
other people or machines. The main difficulty in agent cooperation and communication, is *mutual understanding*. People and, in general, *intelligent agents*

N.T. Nguyen (Ed.): Transactions on CCI VII, LNCS 7270, pp. 1–42, 2012.

come from different organisations and individuals and thus they have different backgrounds and, maybe, different expression languages. Since we aim at designing agents that can be defined intelligent, we need to provide them with the ability of managing conflicts, misunderstanding and disagreements.

Intelligent agents are developed for a wide number of reasons and applications, that is in all the situations in which people can delegate their interests to somebody else. In fact the word *intelligent* refers to the ability to behave, to reason and to perceive situations and the environment the agents are in, as humans do, or equivalently in terms of rationality.

In all the applications of intelligent agents, a basic mechanism of agreement is required: information agent, electronic commerce agent, e-learning systems and automated legal reasoning technologies have to know the meaning of all the information they receive from the user. In all the situations in which a misunderstanding arises, the system does not work as the user's expectations and it produces negative or wrong outcomes.

Negotiation is one of the main mechanisms for reaching an agreement among entities, i.e. computer systems or humans or a mix of them. It consists in reaching an agreement about something when the negotiators begin the discussion starting from different viewpoints about the sharing object. Differently from quantitative negotiations, in meaning negotiation the proposals are pieces of knowledge, i.e. the expressions of what an agent knows about the negotiated terms, and they may be accepted or rejected. In particular, *Meaning Negotiation* (henceforth MN) is a negotiation process in which the sharing object is the meaning of a set of terms. To negotiate the meaning of a set of terms means to propose definitions, properties, typical memberships of the terms' definitions, and/or to accept or to reject definitions.

The participants of a MN may disagree in many ways:

- The properties used to define the terms are inconsistent and contradictory;
- The relevant properties for an agent are more/less than those expressed by another agent or different ones;
- Some agents do not know the properties used by someone in the community.

Example 1. As a running example, consider the negotiation about the meaning of the term "vehicle". Let Alice and Bob be two agents participating to the negotiation. Suppose that Alice thinks that a vehicle always has two, three, four or six wheels; a handlebar or a steering wheel; a motor, or two or four bicycle pedals, or a tow bar. On the other hand, Bob thinks that it always has two, three or four wheels; a handlebar or a steering wheel; a motor, or two or four bicycle pedals. Alice and Bob are in disagreement because Bob does not know if a vehicle has a tow bar or not.   □

In the above example, the MN depends upon the relevance of the terms the agents use. Alice and Bob define "vehicle" in different ways and with different terms. In fact, Alice uses "tow bar" and Bob does not. Bob does not say anything about the tow bar (maybe he does not know what a tow bar is), or maybe he does not consider as relevant the properties about the tow bar. In this paper we assume that the agents make assertions only about the properties they consider as relevant.

The aim of the paper is to give a general model to represent the process of reaching agreement in MN. The negotiation process has already been dealt in terms of games but, to the best of our knowledge, only quantitative negotiation were studied. MN is not quantitative thus one of the main problem in dealing with it is the identification of the agreement and disagreement situations, i.e. the mutual evaluation of the proposals of the players. The purpose of the paper is to extend the current literature with the formalisation of the MN problem as a game, and by defining the exact conditions for reaching an agreement. Our work starts with the study of the representation of the knowledge of the agents in a MN, and in particular the representation of the properties the agents consider as necessary and unforgivable in defining the meaning of the set of terms they are negotiating and, viceversa, which are the facultative ones, because these properties identify the negotiation space between agents. We call the first one the stubborn knowledge of the agent and flexible knowledge the second one.

The *first contribution* of the paper is the definition of the meaning negotiating agent in terms of her stubborn and flexible knowledge.

One important issue in MN is the evaluation of a received proposal. Agents make proposal and evaluate the opponents' one. The evaluation mechanism is not trivial when the negotiation is not quantitative. When is one definition of a set of terms better than another one? When are two or more definitions equivalent? Here, we study how a proposal is evaluated with respect to the knowledge of an agent. The *second contribution* of the paper is the study of the agreement and disagreement situations between the agents and the definition of the different ways in which they may be in disagreement (absolute, relative, essence and compatibility).

Another important point in MN (as well as in Multiple Agent Systems research, MAS), is the strategical component in the definition of negotiating agent. In this paper we do not give any definition of strategy of agents but we assume that whenever an agent has to choose the next move, she has a way to do it. In general, in MAS literature there are two main ways, called attitudes, in which the agents behave: collaborative and competitive. A collaborative agent always chooses the move that improves the welfare of the MAS she is in, whereas a competitive agent moves in order to achieve her goals and, possibly, to impede the other ones. The study of the strategies in MN process needs the definition of MAS welfare and goals, and of the attainment of a goal.

This paper follows an incremental approach. Initially we focus upon the MN between only two players and then to more than one. The paper is organised as follow: Section 2 discusses the current approaches of MN in Artificial Intelligence literature and in Section 3 we present the games representing negotiation processes, Section 4 formalises the definition of agent and of subjective hierarchy, and Section 5 presents a formalisation of the MN process by Game Theory for a bilateral scenario and Section 6 for a more than two agents one. The paper ends with the summary of the contributions of our paper (Section 7).

2   Discussion and Related Work

The Meaning Negotiation problem has received ample attention in the Artificial Intelligence community. Two are the most general approaches to the problem of finding shared knowledge from many different and possibly inconsistent ones. The first way to model the MN process is by viewing it as a conflict resolution. The participants of a negotiation litigate about how to share something and they may disagree in many ways [22]. In this context, the methods used to persuade the audience, potentially over the counterpart alone, is *argumentative*, in the sense that it considers valid the assertions and provides a reasonable way to argue that they are true.

Argumentation theory is the interdisciplinary study of how humans should, can, and do reach conclusions through logical reasoning, founding the conclusions on the previous claims, and on the premises, even when the process itself is inconsistent or paraconsistent. In other terms an argumentation is a logical proof of a given claim that is not necessarily derived from unquestionable premises. It includes the arts and sciences of civil debate, dialogue, conversation, and persuasion. It studies rules of inference, logic, and procedural rules in both artificial and real world settings.

Argumentation includes debate and negotiation which are concerned with reaching mutually acceptable conclusions [29,35,1,42]. It also encompasses *eristic* dialogue, the branch of social debate in which victory over an opponent is the primary goal. This art and science is often the means by which people protect their beliefs or self-interests in rational dialogue, in common parlance, and during the process of arguing.

The main approaches to the Argumentation theory are: the pragma-dialectical theory and the argumentative schemes.

In pragma-dialectical theory, the argumentation is viewed as a critical discussion about the resolution of a conflicts. In this ideal model of a critical discussion, four discussion stages are distinguished that the discussion parties have to go through to resolve their difference of opinion (see [46] pp.85-88; [47], pp.34-35; [48], pp.59-62):

1. the confrontation stage: the interlocutors establish that they have a difference of opinion;
2. opening stage: they decide to resolve this difference of opinion. The interlocutors determine their points of departure: they agree upon the rules of the discussion and establish which propositions they can use in their argumentation;
3. argumentation stage: the protagonist defends his/her standpoint by putting forward arguments to counter the antagonists objections or doubt;
4. concluding stage: the discussion parties evaluate to what extent their initial difference of opinion has been resolved and in whose favor.

The ideal model stipulates ten rules (see [45], pp.182-183) that apply to an argumentative discussion. Violations of the discussion rules are said to frustrate the reasonable resolution of the difference of opinion and they are therefore considered as fallacies.

The representation of *Argumentative schemes* constitutes one of the central topics in current argumentation theory and these represent common patterns of reasoning used in everyday conversational discourse. Important contributions to the study of argument schemes have been also made by Douglas Walton [10,38,11,12,38]. As considered by him, argument schemes technically have the form of an inference rule: an argument scheme has a set of premises and a conclusion.

The argumentation schemes approach is based upon the Toulmin model of the argumentation [44].

The process of resolving conflicts among agents by argumentation involves not only a negotiation dialogue, but also a *persuasion* one [51]. The participants in a negotiation by argumentation propose arguments to the opponents and make counterproposals in two way: by rebutting and or by undercutting the proposals of the opponents. Rebuttal of a rule claiming c, is made by a rule in which the claim is the negation of c. A rule r undercuts a rule r' if the claim of r is the negation of some of the premises of r'[1].

When no undercut and rebuttal rules are available, an agent can accept the argument posted by someone else in the system in two ways [14]:

- *skeptical*: the argument is acceptable until somebody else claims the contrary;
- *credulous*: the argument is wholeheartedly accepted.

In [13] the author explores the mechanisms humans use in argumentation to state the correctness, the appropriateness and the acceptability of arguments.

To persuade the opponents about the validity of the argument she proposes, the proponent has to *justify* it [36,37,50,40,26,43] or to have its proof. Recent investigations have dealt with the problem about who has the burden of proving a claim and which argument produces a burden of proof [15,49,39,34,18]. In [23] a complete survey of the logical models of arguments is presented.

Argumentation is largely used in legal reasoning to model the interactions according to the legal debate rules [9,19,3,28]. In particular, in [2], the authors formalise an argumentation framework in order to model the definitions of *objectively* and *subjectively acceptable*, and *indefensible* argument. The definition of the above degrees of acceptance of an argument is based upon a value given to the arguments and a form of preference between them that the agents have.

In [32], the authors present a brief survey of argumentation in multi-agent systems. It is not only brief, but rather idiosyncratic, and focuses on the areas of research of belief revision, agent communication and reasoning.

---

[1] Note that, since it is not assumed that the rules are consistent and classical, it does not follow an equivalence of the two arguments, since an undercut can remove a premise that is not proved to be true, and a rebuttal can remove a conclusion that is not derived in a deductive way from the premises.

The second way to model MN is as a set of operations on the beliefs' sets of the agents involved. The scope is to construct a commonly accepted knowledge as the process of merging information becoming from different sources. The problem of how the merging has to be done was approached in two steps:

- how the different sources have inconsistent beliefs and how they are mutually reliable;
- how and when beliefs causing conflicts have to be merged into the knowledge base.

The first point was studied by the *information fusion* researchers and the second by the *belief revision* ones.

In [21] the author makes a survey of the contributions from the artificial intelligence research literature about logic-based information fusion. The assumption made by the early approaches were:

- Information sources are mutually independent;
- All sources exhibit the same level of importance;
- The level of information importance is also constant.

The main assumption regards the completely reliance of all the information sources as in [5]. More realistic approaches suppose that the information sources are not equally reliable and that some source is to be preferred with respect to the other available ones. In [20] the reliability of the information sources is defined as a preference order. Another precedent approach assume a weight applied to the beliefs for each source by which they come [31].

In the situations in which the information sources are equally reliable, the merging is said *non-prioritized* otherwise a degree of certainty or plausibility is given to the belief [16].

When the beliefs coming from the different sources, they have to be merged in order to *minimally change* the initial knowledge base. The operation needed to add new information into a knowledge base is known as *revision* and it involves only conflicting beliefs during a negotiation process. The general approach of *maximal adjustment* is to remove the present belief causing the conflict and adding the new one. In [4] the author present a *disjunctive maximal adjustment* in which the belief are weighted and thus not always removed or simply added into the knowledge base.

The merging[2] of beliefs was defined by two operators [30]: *majority* and *arbitration*. Both make assumptions upon the information sources. The former revises the knowledge base by belief belonging to the majority number of

---

[2] One can be tempted to assume that arbitration and majority operators can be fruitfully employed to solve any admissible problem of negotiation. However, negotiation is the process of reaching agreements not the underlying semantic theory about the models. Therefore, although we can model the resulting theory by the theory of belief revision, negotiation processes are out of scope in these theories.

information sources. The latter revises the knowledge bases by the beliefs belonging to the most reliable information sources[3].

In [27] the author defines the postulates regulating the merging operators by assuming that there are *integrity constraints* to assure.

Thus, in belief merging and information fusion literature, the negotiation is modeled as a two stage process: contraction of the beliefs causing the conflict and expansions by the new knowledge [5]. In [53] the author define a way to formalise the negotiation process as a function and he proposes a set of postulates, similar to the AGM ones for revision for the negotiation function.

3   Negotiation Games

In general, the current Artificial Intelligence and Game Theory literature deals with the problem of Negotiation by modeling it depending on the number of the players, whether two or more.

There are, in fact, many different models of games. In particular, Bargaining [24], Pleadings [17], and Divorce are games in which the players are two. A technical investigation about the protocol problems in pairwise negotiation models based on two-players games has been carried out in [41]. English Auction is a well-known model of multiple parties auction, as well as Dutch Auction, First-price sealed-bid auction and Vickrey auction. As a general reference look at [52].

We are not interested in every game setting, but only in two fundamental ones: Bargaining, and the English Auction. In these game models we have a full representation of the real-world negotiation attitude, that indeed consists in a tradeoff between the tension onto obtaining the best result, in an individual perspective and the desire to obtain an agreement.

In the Bargainig game, two agents discuss how to share one dollar. The agents make in turn a request that is the part of one dollar they want. The Bargaining Game develops in two stages: the demand stage and the war of attrition one. In the first stage both agent make simultaneously a proposal and if the two proposal are *compatible* in the sense that their sum is less then one dollar, the game end in positive. Agents has the part of one dollar they asked for and moreover they receive half of the remaining part. If the first two proposals is not compatible, then the second stage begins. In the war of attrition stage each agent continues to make in turn a proposal until a pair of compatible ones is found. The Bargaining Game may be infinite. It is not a violation that agents make always the same proposals. To limit the length of the game, a timestamp and a maximal number of proposals are introduced as parameter of the game.

---

[3] The notion of reliability introduced here does not overlap fully with the notion of importance given in Information Fusion approaches. In fact a source may be important but unreliable, though is unlikely that unimportant sources result reliable, generally speaking.

In a more than two negotiating agents scenario, the modelisation of the MN depends also on the role of the involved agents. Having $n + 1$ agents in the negotiation, the possible role distinctions are:

- 1-n: one seller and many buyers;
- n-1: many sellers and one buyer;
- n_1-n_2: many sellers and many buyers.

In the first case (1-n), the agents behave like in an auction. Before entering the auction, the seller establishes a maximal price for the item. The seller begins the game by making the initial request that is the *reservation price*. The auction develops by *beats*. A beat consists of:

1. the seller makes a request;
2. each buyer proposes a counteroffer or accepts the seller's proposal.

No more beat begins if the maximal price is reached or if the buying agents do not make new proposals. In auction scenarios, a proposal is also called a *bid*. The end of the auction is established by the seller, i.e. by the auctioneer. In general, in an auction there is only one winner, i.e. only one agent buys the item.

There are many types of auction that differ how the agents make their bids, the number of proposals the players do and the order with respect wo which, each agent makes a bid. We only consider here the English Auction model. This is the most commonly known type of auction. The auction begins by a proposal of the auctioneer that is the *reservation price* (which may be 0) of the good in negotiation. The agents alternate by making proposal and their bid have to be more then the current highest bid. All the agents can see the bids being made, and are able to participate to the bid if they so desire. When no agent is willing to make a new bid, then the good is allocated to the agent that has made the current highest bid, and the price they pay for the good is the amount of this bid.

4   Terminology and Definitions

In this section we give a formal definition of negotiating agent and of disagreement and agreement conditions. An agent participating into a MN process distinguishes from other agents in the language she uses to represent her knowledge about the world and, presumably, in her beliefs. Therefore, the agents may have different expression languages and different point of view about the subject under negotiation. Suppose a group of agents are speaking about the meaning of the word *fiera*. The correct use of the word *fiera* is linked to the language in which it has a meaning. Agents express themselves in their language and they use only the terms they know and they think as relevant with respect to the MN they are involved in. Moreover, since the MN is contextual, the set of the beliefs constituting the knowledge of the agents changes in different MN processes.

The same for the unquestionable knowledge of the agent; basic information about a concept changes when the context does. Suppose that the MN is about the word *fiera* again: if the context of the term is "animals" then the unquestionable knowledge of the agent may be "a *fiera* is a wild beast with sharp teeth", otherwise if the context is "events" then the unquestionable knowledge may be "*fiera* is a trade event".

Definition 1 formalises the agent as en entity characterised by an expression language and a set of beliefs with some unquestionable information about the object in negotiation.

Definition 1. *An* agent, *indicated by* ag, *is defined as a triple* $(\mathcal{L}_{ag}, Ax_{ag}, Stub_{ag})$ *where:*

- $\mathcal{L}_{ag}$ *is the expression language of* ag;
- Ax_{ag} *is the axioms' set establishing her initial point of view about the world;*
- $Stub_{ag}$ *is a subset of* Ax_{ag} *and it represents the unquestionable knowledge of* ag.

By Definition 1, the agents are characterised by a behavioral nature representing their negotiation power. We assume that each agent has at least one axiom and that she has at least one element in her stubbornness set.

The limit case is represented by those agents with empty stubbornness set. Agents with no unquestionable knowledge have no negotiation power and she is always inclined to give up her beliefs in order to meet the opponents' ones. Such an agent is called of *absolute flexibility*. Conversely, an agent is in *absolute stubbornness* when all her axioms are stubborn ones. An absolutely stubborn agent has high negotiation power and she never gives up her beliefs. If an agent is nor absolutely flexible nor absolutely stubborn she is *imperfectly committed*.

Example 2. Let Alice be an agent negotiating the term "vehicle" as in Example 1. Alice thinks that a vehicle has two, three, four or six wheels; a handlebar or a steering wheel; a motor, or two or four bicycle pedals, or a tow bar. Suppose that:

1. Alice thinks that these properties have always to be true. The formal definition of Alice is $(\mathcal{L}_A, Ax_A, Stub_A)$ where:

$$\mathcal{L}_A = \{\, 2wheels, 3wheels, 4wheels, 6wheels, Handlebar, SteeringWheel, Motor,$$
$$2bicyclePedals, 4bicyclePedals, TowBar \}$$

$$Ax_A = \{ (2wheels \vee 3wheels \vee 4wheels \vee 6wheels)^{(\sharp 1)},$$
$$(Handlebar \vee SteeringWheel)^{(\sharp 2)},$$
$$(Motor \vee 2bicyclePedals \vee 4bicyclePedals \vee TowBar)^{(\sharp 3)} \}$$

$Stub_A = Ax_A$.

Alice is absolutely stubborn because her stubbornness knowledge is equivalent to her beliefs' set. Otherwise, suppose that

2. Alice also thinks that the properties have not necessarily to be true. Thus, $Stub_A = \emptyset$ and Alice is absolutely flexible. Finally, suppose that
3. Alice thinks that a "vehicle" may be defined only as a car, then having four wheels, a steering wheel, and a motor; or also as a bicycle, then having two wheels, a handlebar and two bicycle pedals. Thus:

$$Ax_A = \{(2wheels \lor 3wheels \lor 4wheels \lor 6wheels)^{(\sharp 1)},$$
$$(Handlebar \lor SteeringWheel)^{(\sharp 2)},$$
$$(Motor \lor 2bicyclePedals \lor 4bicyclePedals \lor TowBar)^{(\sharp 3)},$$
$$4wheels^{(\sharp 4)}, SteeringWheel^{(\sharp 5)}, Motor^{(\sharp 6)},$$
$$(3wheels \lor 4wheels)^{(\sharp 7)},$$
$$(2bicyclePedals \lor Motor)^{(\sharp 8)}\}$$

$$Stub_A = \{(2wheels \lor 3wheels \lor 4wheels \lor 6wheels)^{(\sharp 1)},$$
$$(Handlebar \lor SteeringWheel)^{(\sharp 2)},$$
$$(Motor \lor 2bicyclePedals \lor 4bicyclePedals \lor TowBar)^{(\sharp 3)}\}$$

Alice is imperfectly committed because $Stub_A \subset Ax_A$.

□

Note that, in the above example, each formula in the axioms' set is numbered by ($\sharp n$). We use this notation to make the presentation of the following examples briefer.

The following proposition is a direct consequence of the definition of absolutely flexible agent.

Proposition 1. *When in a 1-1 MN process, at least one agent is of absolute flexibility the outcome of the process is the opponent's first proposal.*

Proof. Consider two agents ag_1 and ag_2 and suppose that ag_1 is of absolute flexibility, and that it is ag_2's turn to start. Whatsoever the most specific theory ag_2 is proposing, ag_1 will accept it, otherwise, there would be at least one incompatible axiom for ag_2, in ag_1's most specific theory. This is contradictory with the assumption that ag_1 is of absolute flexibility. ∎

The above proposition states that an absolutely flexible agent is not a powerful negotiating one because she has not unquestionable beliefs about the world and she always accepts the other's theory.

Agents express themselves in a formal language, that is a language built by well-formed formulas. In this paper we limit ourselves in studying models based on propositional logic or in first-order logic. Starting from a language, an axioms' set and a set of inference rules (Δ), an agent builds her own theory about the world. Given $ag = (\mathcal{L}_{ag}, Ax_{ag}, Stub_{ag})$ and a set of the inference rules Δ, T_{ag} is the set of theorems built by Ax_{ag} applying a finite number of inference rules in Δ. $T_{ag} = \{\phi|(Ax_{ag}) \vdash^* \phi\}$ is the theory about the world of the agent ag and ag is identified by it.

During the negotiation the agents make proposals that are "pieces" of their knowledge and they choose the next proposal in some way, but, in general, when Alice chooses x as the next proposal then she prefers it to all her feasible proposals. As said above, in this paper we do not investigate the ways in which an agent chooses the next move to perform but we assume that each agent has a preference relation between her feasible proposals that leads to the next move.

The preference relation helps the agent in choosing the next proposal to perform in the MN; typically human people first ask for the most preferred thing and if no positive concession is received then a new request for a less preferred thing is done. In negotiation, participants typically ask more then how they expect because it increases the probability of having the expected outcome. For instance, suppose that Alice wants to sell her red skirt and she hopes to gain almost 20\$; Bob is interested in buying the red skirt and he asks to Alice the purchase price. Alice may behave in two different ways:

1. Alice request 20\$ to Bob;
2. Alice request 30\$ to Bob.

In the former case Alice has less chances of selling the skirt to Bob than in the latter case. Bob may be annoyed of Alice's behaviour of not lowering her start price, and he may think she is not friendly. Viceversa, in the latter case Alice seems to be condescending and picks at Bob in negotiating for the skirt. Moreover, if Bob offers 25\$, Alice obviously accept and gains more than what she expected.

In MN, the proposals of the agents are definitions of the contending term and in general, the preference relation between proposals is coherent with the degree of the exhaustiveness of the definition proposed. Usually, a more exhaustive definition is preferred to a less exhaustive one. The proposals the agents make in negotiation are logical theories and exhaustive relation between proposals translate in *restriction* (or *generalisation*) relation between logical theories. A theory T_1 is a restriction of a theory T_2, and T_2 is a generalisation of T_1, if

$$T_2 \vdash \bigwedge_{\phi \in T_1} \phi \text{ and } T_1 \nvdash \bigwedge_{\psi \in T_2} \psi$$

Suppose, $T_1 = p \wedge q$ and $T_2 = p$ then T_1 is a restriction of T_2.

The generalisation of a theory is the result of a weakening operation on its formulas. There are many ways in which a theory can be generalised. In this thesis, we assume that each agent participating into a MN process has a *finite* number of "partial" point of views that are generalisations of her initial one, T_{ag}. At each step of the negotiation process, the agent takes a node of the subjective hierarchy as her *current viewpoint*. The nodes of the subjective hierarchy are acceptable world representations, i.e. acceptable outcomes of the negotiation.

Moreover, here we do not care about how the agents weaken the formulas of their beliefs. We assume that if an agent think that a theory can be generalised then she also knows how the generalisation is done.

Henceforth, we use the symbol $\prec$ for the preference relation and by $T_1 \prec T_2$ we mean that T_1 is a restriction of T_2.

The preference order between the beliefs of the agent, produces the graph we call *subjective hierarchy*. In Definition 2 the subjective hierarchy structure is formalised.

Definition 2. *Given* T_{ag}, *an agent theory, based on a set of axioms* Ax_{ag}, *the subjective hierarchy of* ag *is a finite graph* TheoryTree$_{ag}$ = $\langle V, E \rangle$ *where:*

i) $T_{ag}^0 = Ax_{ag}^*$ *is the head;*

ii) $V \subseteq \{T_{ag}^i\}$ *where for every* T_{ag}^i, $T_{ag}^i \succ T_{ag}^0$;

iii) $E \subseteq \{(T_{ag}^i, T_{ag}^j)\}$, *where both* T_{ag}^i *and* T_{ag}^j *are in* V *and* $T_{ag}^i \prec T_{ag}^j$;

iv) *there's only one leaf,* $\emptyset$, *representing a theory of the stubbornness axioms, then* $T_{ag}^{\perp} = (Stub_{ag})^*$

v) *The relation* E *is antitransitive.*

The last property of antitransitivity is settled because the represented relation is a partial order, therefore transitive. The transitive closure of the graph is the preference relation. This settling makes the model most compact. The structure of the subjective hierarchy depends on the negotiation power of the agent. Figure 1 shows the different structures of Alice of Example 2. An absolutely flexible agent (Figure 1(a)) has two nodes: the root is her initial viewpoint and the leaf is the empty set. An absolutely stubborn agent (Figure 1(c)) has only one node that is both her initial and her stubbornness point of view. The imperfectly committed agent (Figure 1(b)) has many intermediate nodes that are her acceptable viewpoints, i.e. acceptable outcomes for the negotiation process.

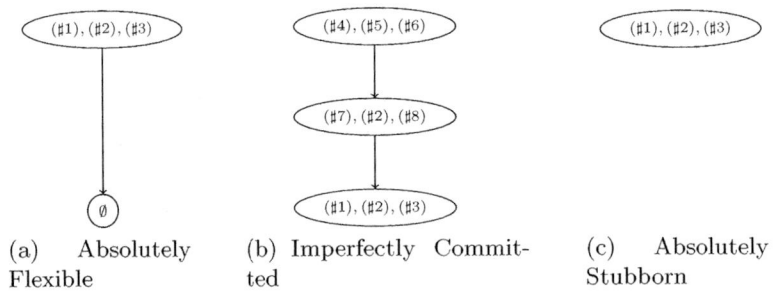

(a)   Absolutely Flexible

(b) Imperfectly Committed

(c)   Absolutely Stubborn

Fig. 1. Subjective hierarchies of Alice of Example 2 when she is the absolutely flexible (a), imperfectly committed (b), and absolutely stubborn (c). The numbers inside the nodes belong to Example 2.

A straightforward consequence of the definition of subjective hierarchy and of the relation $\prec$ is the following proposition.

Proposition 2. *A subjective hierarchy* TheoryTree$_{ag}$ = $\langle V, E \rangle$ *is a directed acyclic graph.*

Proof. Straightforward consequence of the definition of subjective hierarchy. ■

In general, apart for absolutely flexible agents, there are unquestionable axioms agents always defend. The negotiating agents choose the proposal to perform in the negotiation by keeping a node in their subjective hierarchy and the choose depends on the attitudes of the agents. As said in Section 1, the attitudes are the guidelines for behaving in multiple agent contexts. The agency of the agents depends on their goals and on what they think about each other. The main attitudes, collaborative and competitive, call for community welfare, in the former case, and for personal advantage in the latter one. Different attitudes cause different ways to visit the subjective hierarchy.

Agents in a MN, have four feasible actions: propose, receive, accept or reject.

The receiving, accepting and rejecting actions are performed when the negotiation continues for at least another step, in the first case, when the received proposal is in some sense a *good* compromise for the agent, in the second case, and when the received proposal is not *acceptable* for the agent, in the last case.

The acceptability or the goodness of a proposal depends on the generalisation or restriction relation between the current point of view of the agent and her received proposal which is the current viewpoint of another agent in the system. The viewpoints of the agents relation are pairwise. Let ag_1 and ag_2 two negotiating agents, and T_{ag_1} and T_{ag_2} their current point of views; the relation between T_{ag_1} and T_{ag_2} are:

equivalence: if $T_{ag_1} \vdash \bigwedge_{\phi \in T_{ag_2}} \phi$ and $T_{ag_2} \vdash \bigwedge_{\phi \in T_{ag_1}} \phi$ and $T_{ag_1} \wedge T_{ag_2} \not\vdash \bot$
   then theories are *equivalent* denoted with $T_{ag_1} \sim T_{ag_2}$;
restriction: if $T_{ag_1} \vdash \bigwedge_{\phi \in T_{ag_2}} \phi$ and $T_2 \not\vdash \bigwedge_{\phi \in T_1} \phi$ and $T_{ag_1} \wedge T_{ag_2} \not\vdash \bot$ then
   T_{ag_1} is *limited* or *restricted* with respect to T_{ag_2}; we denote this with $T_{ag_1} \prec T_{ag_2}$;
compatibility: if $T_{ag_1} \not\vdash \bigwedge_{\phi \in T_{ag_2}} \phi$ and $T_{ag_2} \not\vdash \bigwedge_{\phi \in T_{ag_1}} \phi$ and $T_{ag_1} \wedge T_{ag_2} \not\vdash \bot$
   then theories are consistent but not comparable. In this case we say that the
   theories are *compatible* and denote it with $T_{ag_1} \bowtie T_{ag_2}$;
inconsistence: if $T_{ag_1} \wedge T_{ag_2} \vdash \bot$ the theories are inconsistent; we denote this
   with $T_{ag_1} \dashv\vdash T_{ag_2}$.

The above relations are tested when agents receive proposal. Because of the expression language in the definition of the agent, the test of the relation between theories have to use a translation function from the sending language to the receiver one. If ag_1 is the receiver and τ_{ag_1,ag_2} is the translation function from the ag_2's language to the ag_1's one, in the description of the relation above, $\tau_{ag_1,ag_2}(T_{ag_2})$ is instead of T_{ag_2}.

A received proposal is obviously acceptable when it is equivalent to one of the nodes of the subjective hierarchy of the receiver. Sometimes a proposal may be considered good or acceptable also when it is not equivalent to a node of the subjective hierarchy, but there is a pair of nodes that bound it, i.e. the former node is a restriction of the proposal and the latter is a generalisation.

The former definition of acceptability is *skeptical* and the latter is *credulous*. In both definition, the acceptability of an offer depends on its position in the subjective hierarchy. Definition 3 defines the acceptability of a received proposal for a credulous agent.

Definition 3. *Let* $ag_1 = (\mathcal{L}_{ag_1}, Ax_{ag_1}, Stub_{ag_1})$ *be a credulous agent and* TheoryTree$_{ag_1} = \langle V, E \rangle$ *her subjective hierarchy, and* T *a received proposal.* T *is* good, *or* acceptable, *for* ag_1 *iff*

- *T is equivalent to a node of the subjective hierarchy of* ag_1, TheoryTree$_{ag_1}$; *or*
- *T is a generalisation of a node of* TheoryTree$_{ag_1}$ *and it is not a generalisation of* $T^{\perp}_{ag_1}$;
- *T is a restriction of a node of* TheoryTree$_{ag_1}$ *and it is not a restriction of the source node of* TheoryTree$_{ag_1}$, $T^0_{ag_1}$.

A skeptical agent considers acceptable a proposal when only the first point is satisfied.

Figure 2 shows a graphical representation of a good offer with respect to a subjective hierarchy. When the last made proposal is good for all the agents in the

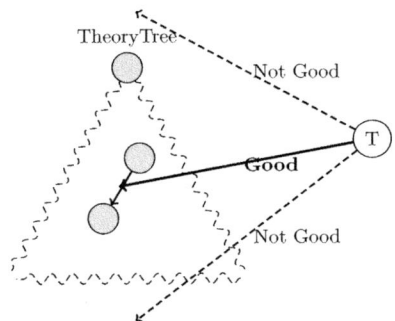

Fig. 2. Credulous acceptability of a proposal received by one agent during the negotiation. Dashed curved lines represent the structure of the subjective hierarchy of the receiving agent. Gray nodes are admissible viewpoints of the agent and the white node is the received proposal T. T is good if it maps into the subjective hierarchy of the agent.

MAS receiving it, the MN ends with a positive outcome, i.e. the shared theory. Otherwise, the MN development depends on how an offer is not acceptable. In Figure 2, there are two dashed arrows of the mapping of T into the subjective hierarchy TheoryTree.

An agent cannot accept a too restricted offer because in a MN context "restriction" means "more features". As said above, the agent characterised a concept definition with the features she considers relevant and which she knows. A restricted definitions involve more terms then a less restricted one or add

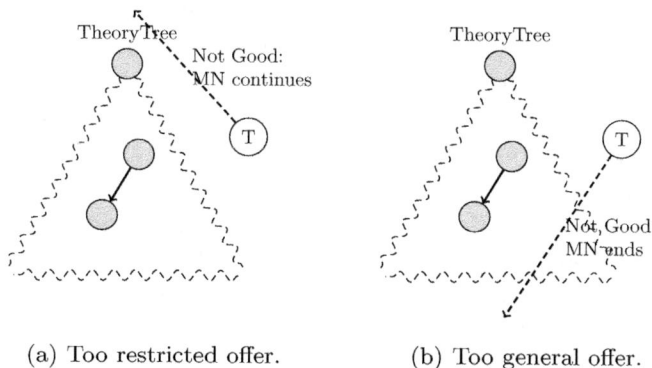

(a) Too restricted offer.   (b) Too general offer.

Fig. 3. Different not good offers. The MN proceeds in the first case (a) and ends in the second case (b).

properties. Such a scenario is depicted in Figure 3(a). The MN process continues for at least one step more in which the receiver hopes a generalisation of the sender's viewpoint.

A proposal is again not acceptable when it is too general, i.e. it does not include all the properties that the receiver considers as necessary. Accepting a too general proposal means that the receiver has no more to consider the beliefs she has in her stubbornness set. However it violates the definition of agent we gave in Definition 1. When the received offer is too general the MN process ends with a negative outcome. Figure 3(b) shows the collocation of a too general proposal in the subjective hierarchy of the receiver.

5   MN by Bargaining Game

5.1   Introduction

In this section we exhibit a formalisation of 1-1 MN by the Bargaining Game. The scenario in which two agents negotiate in order to obtain an acceptable common view of a domain, is similar to the problem of finding how to split 1$ between two requesting players. We model MN by the Bargaining game in which the agents make proposal in turns until an agreement is found. In this section we first present the Bargaining Game (Section 5.2) and then we formalise the MN in terms of it (Section 5.3).

5.2   The Bargaining Game

"A two-person bargaining situation involves two individuals who have the opportunity to collaborate for mutual benefit in more than one way." [33].

In the Bargaining Game agents play in order to share one dollar. The negotiation process is by *bootstrap*, i.e. the players begin the bargaining by simultaneously proposing a share to each other. The goal of the players is to find a pair of shares that are *compatible*, i.e. the sum of the demands is less than one dollar. Therefore, if the agents i and j demand x and y respectively, they end the bargaining in a positive way if $x + y \leq 1$. When the initial proposals are not compatible, the players have to continue the bargaining by changing or reiterating the share they ask.

The game is two stage.

1. *Demand Stage*: In the first stage each agent demands her share x and thus offers to the opponent the remaining $1 - x$; if the demands are compatible the game ends positively, otherwise the second stage begins.
2. *The "war of attrition" Stage*: the agents make their demands in turns in order to find a pair of compatible demands.

The game develops by agents making proposals representing the part of one dollar they ask to exit the bargaining.

In [25], the author models the bargaining game with imperfect commitment. In this paper, the key assumption is that, with small probability, the players commit themselves to their initial demands before the war of attrition stage starts. The committed player is called *stubborn* and the not-committed one is called *flexible*. The commitment of an agent with respect to her initial position represents the *negotiation power* of the agent. "To cease or not to cease" are negotiation actions and the agent chooses whether to cease or not depending on her negotiation power. A stubborn agent commits herself to her initial demand and waits until her opponent accepts it; thus a stubborn agent perpetually makes the same proposal during the bargaining and accepts the opponent's one iff it is equivalent to her own.

The outcomes of a bargaining game are:

- *agreement*: if a pair of compatible proposals was performed by the agents, i.e. the two players agree on how the share of one dollar has to be;
- *disagreement*: otherwise.

The agreement outcome is reached by testing the compatibility relation between the proposal made by agents. Conversely, there is not a simple condition to say the bargaining ends negatively, thus in disagreement. The disagreement is the running condition of the bargaining and of the negotiation process because the involved agents continue in performing proposals until an agreement is found, so that a new proposal is made if the agents do not agree.

Perpetual disagreement is the limit case representing the never-ending negotiation; when the two players are stubborn there is no possibility to incur agreement. In [25] author asserts that a flexible agent gradually accepts the opponent's offer by choosing the timing acceptance randomly. He calls *potentially exhaustive time* the time needed for the flexible agent to accept the opponent's share. A stubborn agent has the same exhaustive time of her opponent because she never accepts until her opponent does.

At the beginning of the bargaining game, the agents do not know the negotiation power of the opponent. If the "war of attrition" stage begins, a player may *abduce* whether the opponent is committed to her initial demand or not. An agent can only perceive the negotiation power of her opponent through the negotiation proposal's sequence. Uncertainty about the opponent's negotiation power leads the bargaining in having multiple endings, positive or negative.

The necessary but not sufficient condition to find an equilibrium is that at least one of the two playing agent is flexible, as claimed in the following theorem.

Theorem 1 (Kambe, [25]). *If all agents playing in a Bargaining Game are stubborn, then the game has a perpetual disagreement.*

In the Theory of Games, the agents may change their negotiation power in an unique and irreversible fashion: flexible agents become stubborn. This happens when an agent has reached her minimum acceptable offer, under which the loss is perceived as excessive.

The main assumption in our framework is that all players are committed with respect to their initial proposals in different ways and with different degrees. Therefore, the commitment is a *preference* the agent has with respect to the set of her feasible demands. In the next section we formalise the MN problem by the Bargaining Game.

5.3   The Bargaining Framework

In this section we give a formalisation of the steps of a pairwise MN process with the Bargaining Game guidelines. We first discuss the multiple agent system configurations, i.e. players, actions and etc., and then show how the "demand" and "the war of attrition" stages develop.

The multiple agent system in a 1-1 MN consists of two agents, named Alice $= (\mathcal{L}_A, Ax_A, Stub_A)$ and Bob $= (\mathcal{L}_B, Ax_B, Stub_B)$. Initially, we suppose that the agents express themselves in the same language, $\mathcal{L}_A = \mathcal{L}_B$ thus no translation function is needed and no misunderstandings occur.

The set of the feasible actions of the agents are: propose, receive, accept and reject. Agents in negotiation play in turns when entering in "the war of attrition" stage, thus if Alice sends a proposal to Bob, Bob makes a receive action and Alice makes a propose one.

Moreover, in this framework we do not take care of the agent attitudes and we only assume that the involved agents choose the proposal to put forward in some way.

The current proposal of each agent represents her current point of view, i.e. an admissible positive outcome of the process and a good definition of the item in negotiation. As said in the previous section, the agents change beliefs during the negotiation. Even if the initial set of beliefs is a parameter in agent definition and it is constant during the process, the agent changes the current beliefs' set. The initial knowledge of the agent can be called as *viewpoint* and the current set of beliefs as the *current angle*. A viewpoint has many angles and the agents negotiate them. Therefore the first proposal an agent makes is her viewpoint and the next ones are angles. Let T be an angle for the agent ag, then ag puts it forward by the logical formula φ_T:

$$\varphi_T = \bigwedge_{\phi \in T} \phi$$

As direct consequence of the definition of subjective hierarchy, each node of the graph has a logical formula.

Henceforth, we use the symbol T^{Cur}_{ag} to denote the current angle of the agent ag and $\varphi_{T^{Cur}_{ag}}$ as its logical formula representation, the symbol, $\varphi_{T^0_{ag}}$ is the initial knowledge of the agents, i.e. her viewpoint.

Demand Stage. In the first stage of the MN by Bargaining, the agents propose simultaneously their viewpoints. The simultaneity of the first stage of the negotiation is not problematic because the agents may propose in two different times and then synchronise them: the result is the same as the simultaneous proposing actions.

After proposing and thus receiving the opponent's viewpoint each agent knows whether they are in agreement or not.

The relation between the viewpoints is evaluated by both agents. Let ag_i and ag_j be the two players and ag_i the referring agent, each of the players perform the following tests in order:

1. "is my viewpoint the same as the opponent's one?" : $\vdash (\varphi_{T^0_{ag_i}} \leftrightarrow \varphi_{T^0_{ag_j}})$;
2. "is my viewpoint a restriction of the opponent's one?" : $\vdash (\varphi_{T^0_{ag_i}} \to \varphi_{T^0_{ag_j}})$ and $\nvdash (\varphi_{T^0_{ag_j}} \to \varphi_{T^0_{ag_i}})$;
3. "is my viewpoint a generalisation of the opponent's one?" : $\vdash (\varphi_{T^0_{ag_j}} \to \varphi_{T^0_{ag_i}})$ and $\nvdash (\varphi_{T^0_{ag_i}} \to \varphi_{T^0_{ag_j}})$;
4. "is my viewpoint only consistent with respect to the opponent's one?" : $(\varphi_{T^0_{ag_i}} \wedge \varphi_{T^0_{ag_j}}) \nvdash \perp$ and $\nvdash (\varphi_{T^0_{ag_i}} \to \varphi_{T^0_{ag_j}})$ and $\nvdash (\varphi_{T^0_{ag_j}} \to \varphi_{T^0_{ag_i}})$;
5. "is my viewpoint inconsistent with respect to the opponent's one?" : $(\varphi_{T^0_{ag_i}} \wedge \varphi_{T^0_{ag_j}}) \vdash \perp$.

The above evaluation tests have to be done in order and the positive answers of the questions state the relations between agents. The relations between the agents with respect to the above tests are:

1) agreement;
2) (and 3) for credulous agent) relative disagreement;
4) compatibility;
5) absolute disagreement.

The Demand stage and MN ends with a positive outcome if the agents are in agreement relation, otherwise the next stage begins.

Figure 4 shows a simple graphical representation of the exchanging message of the agents in the demand stage.

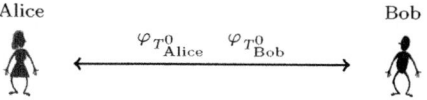

Fig. 4. Demand Stage: Alice and Bob simultaneously propose their viewpoints

The War of Attrition Stage. In the second stage of the MN by Bargaining, the agents continue to propose until an agreement is found. Differently from the demand stage, in the war of attrition one it is needed an order of game between agents. The negotiation power of the agents makes an important role in the development and in the ending of the MN process. In the case that both the agents are absolutely stubborn, the process cannot ends in positive because of the current not-agreement condition between and of the non-existence of new proposals. In all the other combinations of negotiation powers of the players, the MN outcome depends on the relation between the stubbornness angles of the agents. Alice does not know which is the unquestionable knowledge of Bob and viceversa. Therefore, the eventual positive (or negative) outcome of the MN is explored and searched by agents into their subjective hierarchies. If each agent reaches her stubbornness node and not an agreement is checked, then MN ends negatively. The finiteness of the nodes of the subjective hierarchy leads to the finiteness of the MN.

Figure 5 depicts the exchanging messages between agents during the war of attrition stage.

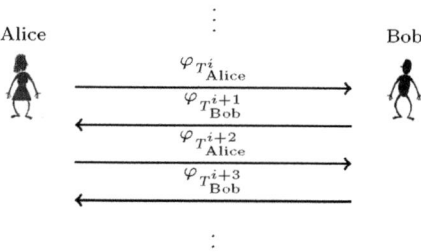

Fig. 5. "The war of attrition" stage: Alice and Bob propose their viewpoints in turns

Let Alice be the next proposing agent. Alice knows her last offer, $\varphi_{T^i_{Alice}}$, and the counterproposal of Bob, $\varphi_{T^{i+1}_{Bob}}$. Alice has two ways in choosing the current angle and thus the next proposal to make:

- weakening her last offer and assume a less exhaustive definition as her new current angle (Figure 6(b));
- change her last offer with a different one with the same degree of exhaustiveness as her current angle (Figure 6(c)).

A weakening proposal is the result of a visit in depth from the current angle, instead the changing angle action corresponds to a step of visiting in breadth. As shown in Figure 6, the new current angle is related in some way to the last one and the choice of the best node to take as current angle depends on the attitudes of the agent and of her strategy. There are many available weakened and shifted angles for each current node. The agent chooses among the available nodes in dependence on the relation they are with respect to the last received offer and on her attitude. Table 1 shows how all the relations among the last proposal, the received offer and the new current angle and which is the visit way that causes it. Let me explain all the cases in Table 1.

Table 1. Relations among the last proposal, the received offer and the new proposal

$T_A^i \; ? \; T_B^{i+1}$	$T_A^{i+2} \; ? \; T_B^{i+1}$	Weakening (W) or Changing (C)
	$\sim$	W
	$\succ$	W
$\prec$	$\succ$	C/W
	$\bowtie$	C
	$+\!\!\vdash$	C
	$\succ$	C
$\succ$	$\bowtie$	C
	$+\!\!\vdash$	C
	$\sim$	C
	$\succ$	C/W
$\bowtie$	$\prec$	C
	$\bowtie$	C/W
	$+\!\!\vdash$	C/W
	$\sim$	C
	$\succ$	C
$+\!\!\vdash$	$\prec$	C
	$\bowtie$	C
	$+\!\!\vdash$	C

$T_A^i \prec T_B^{i+1}$: by definition of $\prec$, $T_A^i \prec T_B^{i+1}$ iff $\varphi_{T_A^i} \to \varphi_{T_B^{i+1}}$.

- Suppose Alice makes a weakening, $\varphi_{T_A^i} \to \varphi_{T_A^{i+2}}$. Then

  1. if $\varphi_{T_A^{i+2}} \to \varphi_{T_B^{i+1}}$ then $T_A^{i+2} \prec T_B^{i+1}$;
  2. if $\varphi_{T_A^{i+2}} \leftrightarrow \varphi_{T_B^{i+1}}$ then $T_A^{i+2} \sim T_B^{i+1}$;
  3. if $\varphi_{T_A^{i+2}} \leftarrow \varphi_{T_B^{i+1}}$ then $T_A^{i+2} \succ T_B^{i+1}$;

- Suppose Alice makes a change, $(\varphi_{T_A^i} \vee \varphi_{T_A^{i+2}}) \wedge \neg(\varphi_{T_A^i} \to \varphi_{T_A^{i+2}}) \wedge \neg(\varphi_{T_A^i} \leftarrow \varphi_{T_A^{i+2}})$. Then

  1. if $\varphi_{T_A^{i+2}} \to \varphi_{T_B^{i+1}}$ then $T_A^{i+2} \prec T_B^{i+1}$;
  2. if $(\varphi_{T_A^{i+2}} \wedge \varphi_{T_B^{i+1}}) \wedge \neg(\varphi_{T_A^{i+2}} \to \varphi_{T_B^{i+1}}) \wedge \neg(\varphi_{T_A^{i+2}} \leftarrow \varphi_{T_B^{i+1}})$ then $T_A^{i+2} \bowtie T_B^{i+1}$;
  3. if $\neg(\varphi_{T_A^{i+2}} \wedge \varphi_{T_B^{i+1}})$ then $T_A^{i+2} +\!\!\vdash T_B^{i+1}$;

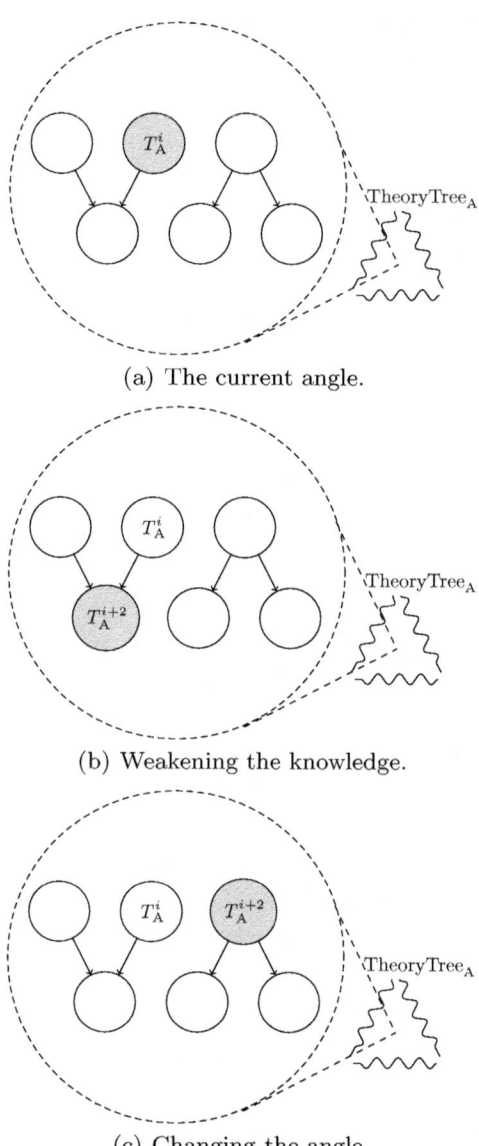

(a) The current angle.

(b) Weakening the knowledge.

(c) Changing the angle.

Fig. 6. Choosing a new proposal. The figures show extracts from the subjective hierarchy of the agent Alice. The gray nodes represents current angles. The weakening proposal is a child node of the last one (from (a) to (b)). Changing angle means to choose a "brother" node in the subjective hierarchy (from (a) to (c)).

$T_A^i \succ T_B^{i+1}$: by definition of $\succ$, $T_A^i \succ T_B^{i+1}$ iff $\varphi_{T_A^i} \leftarrow \varphi_{T_B^{i+1}}$. Alice may perform a weakening action but the situation between the players does not change. Suppose Alice makes a changing action, $(\varphi_{T_A^i} \vee \varphi_{T_A^{i+2}}) \wedge \neg(\varphi_{T_A^i} \rightarrow \varphi_{T_A^{i+2}}) \wedge \neg(\varphi_{T_A^i} \leftarrow \varphi_{T_A^{i+2}})$. Then

1. if $\varphi_{T_A^{i+2}} \leftarrow \varphi_{T_B^{i+1}}$ then $T_A^{i+2} \succ T_B^{i+1}$;
2. if $(\varphi_{T_A^{i+2}} \wedge \varphi_{T_B^{i+1}}) \wedge \neg(\varphi_{T_A^{i+2}} \rightarrow \varphi_{T_B^{i+1}}) \wedge \neg(\varphi_{T_A^{i+2}} \leftarrow \varphi_{T_B^{i+1}})$ then $T_A^{i+2} \bowtie T_B^{i+1}$;
3. if $\neg(\varphi_{T_A^{i+2}} \vee \varphi_{T_B^{i+1}})$ then $T_A^{i+2} \dashv\vdash T_B^{i+1}$;

$T_A^i \bowtie T_B^{i+1}$: by definition of $\bowtie$, $T_A^i \bowtie T_B^{i+1}$ iff $(\varphi_{T_A^i} \wedge \varphi_{T_B^{i+1}}) \wedge \neg(\varphi_{T_A^i} \rightarrow \varphi_{T_B^{i+1}}) \wedge \neg(\varphi_{T_A^i} \leftarrow \varphi_{T_B^{i+1}})$.

– Suppose Alice makes a weakening, $\varphi_{T_A^i} \rightarrow \varphi_{T_A^{i+2}}$. Then

1. if $\varphi_{T_A^{i+2}} \leftarrow \varphi_{T_B^{i+1}}$ then $T_A^{i+2} \succ T_B^{i+1}$;
2. if $(\varphi_{T_A^{i+2}} \vee \varphi_{T_B^{i+1}}) \wedge \neg(\varphi_{T_A^{i+2}} \rightarrow \varphi_{T_B^{i+1}}) \wedge \neg(\varphi_{T_A^{i+2}} \leftarrow \varphi_{T_B^{i+1}})$ then $T_A^{i+2} \bowtie T_B^{i+1}$;
3. if $\neg(\varphi_{T_A^{i+2}} \wedge \varphi_{T_B^{i+1}})$ then $T_A^{i+2} \dashv\vdash T_B^{i+1}$;

– Suppose Alice makes a change, $(\varphi_{T_A^i} \wedge \varphi_{T_A^{i+2}}) \wedge \neg(\varphi_{T_A^i} \rightarrow \varphi_{T_A^{i+2}}) \wedge \neg(\varphi_{T_A^i} \leftarrow \varphi_{T_A^{i+2}})$. Then

1. if $\varphi_{T_A^{i+2}} \leftrightarrow \varphi_{T_B^{i+1}}$ then $T_A^{i+2} \sim T_B^{i+1}$;
2. if $\varphi_{T_A^{i+2}} \leftarrow \varphi_{T_B^{i+1}}$ then $T_A^{i+2} \succ T_B^{i+1}$;
3. if $\varphi_{T_A^{i+2}} \rightarrow \varphi_{T_B^{i+1}}$ then $T_A^{i+2} \prec T_B^{i+1}$;
4. if $(\varphi_{T_A^{i+2}} \wedge \varphi_{T_B^{i+1}}) \wedge \neg(\varphi_{T_A^{i+2}} \rightarrow \varphi_{T_B^{i+1}}) \wedge \neg(\varphi_{T_A^{i+2}} \leftarrow \varphi_{T_B^{i+1}})$ then $T_A^{i+2} \bowtie T_B^{i+1}$;
5. if $\neg(\varphi_{T_A^{i+2}} \wedge \varphi_{T_B^{i+1}})$ then $T_A^{i+2} \dashv\vdash T_B^{i+1}$;

$T_A^i \dashv\vdash T_B^{i+1}$: by definition of $\dashv\vdash$, $T_A^i \dashv\vdash TB^{i+1}$ iff $\neg(\varphi_{T_A^i} \wedge \varphi_{T_B^{i+1}})$. Whenever Alice makes a weakening action the absolute disagreement between Alice and Bob does not change because they do not share any generalisation of their viewpoints. Suppose Alice makes a changing action, $(\varphi_{T_A^i} \wedge \varphi_{T_A^{i+2}}) \wedge \neg(\varphi_{T_A^i} \rightarrow \varphi_{T_A^{i+2}}) \wedge \neg(\varphi_{T_A^i} \leftarrow \varphi_{T_A^{i+2}})$. Then

1. if $\varphi_{T_A^{i+2}} \leftrightarrow \varphi_{T_B^{i+1}}$ then $T_A^{i+2} \sim T_B^{i+1}$;
2. if $\varphi_{T_A^{i+2}} \rightarrow \varphi_{T_B^{i+1}}$ then $T_A^{i+2} \prec T_B^{i+1}$;
3. if $\varphi_{T_A^{i+2}} \leftarrow \varphi_{T_B^{i+1}}$ then $T_A^{i+2} \succ T_B^{i+1}$;
4. if $(\varphi_{T_A^{i+2}} \wedge \varphi_{T_B^{i+1}}) \wedge \neg(\varphi_{T_A^{i+2}} \rightarrow \varphi_{T_B^{i+1}}) \wedge \neg(\varphi_{T_A^{i+2}} \leftarrow \varphi_{T_B^{i+1}})$ then $T_A^{i+2} \bowtie T_B^{i+1}$;
5. if $\neg(\varphi_{T_A^{i+2}} \wedge \varphi_{T_B^{i+1}})$ then $T_A^{i+2} \dashv\vdash T_B^{i+1}$.

Algorithm 1 implements the MN by the Bargaining Game.

Algorithm 1. A credulous MN algorithm by Bargaining.

Input : Two agents and their subjective hierarchies, ag_1, ag_2, TheoryTree$_{ag_1}$ and TheoryTree$_{ag_2}$

Output: A negotiated theory, if possible, otherwise $\bot$

```
   /* initialisation                                                    */
1  stub₁ = stub₂ = false;
2  T^cur_ag₁ = T^0_ag₁ ;
3  T^cur_ag₂ = T^0_ag₂ ;
4  φ_T^cur_ag₁ = ⋀_{α∈T^cur_ag₁} α ;
5  φ_T^cur_ag₂ = ⋀_{β∈T^cur_ag₂} β ;
   /* Demand Stage                                                      */
6  ag₁ proposes φ_T^cur_ag₁ to ag₂, ag₂ receives φ_T^cur_ag₁ from ag₁ ;
7  ag₂ proposes φ_T^cur_ag₂ to ag₁, ag₁ receives φ_T^cur_ag₂ from ag₂ ;
8  if (φ_T^cur_agᵢ ↔ φ_T^cur_agⱼ) then
9  |    return T^cur_ag₁                                    // Agreement
10 else
      /* ''The War of Attrition'' stage                                 */
11 |  i = 1, j = 2; // ag₁ is the receiver and ag₂ is the sender
12 |  while not(φ_T^cur_agᵢ ↔ φ_T^cur_agⱼ) or (¬stubᵢ ∨ ¬stubⱼ) do
13 |  |    if (T^cur_agᵢ ∼ T^⊥_agᵢ) then
              /* agᵢ is in stubbornness set                             */
14 |  |    |    stubᵢ = true ;
15 |  |    end
16 |  |    T = visit(agᵢ, TheoryTree_agᵢ, T^cur_agᵢ) ;
17 |  |    T^cur_agᵢ = T;
18 |  |    φ_T^cur_agᵢ = ⋀_{α∈T^cur_ag₁} α ;
19 |  |    if (φ_T^cur_agⱼ → φ_T^cur_agᵢ) then
20 |  |    |    T^cur_agᵢ = T^cur_agⱼ, φ_T^cur_agᵢ = φ_T^cur_agⱼ ;
21 |  |    end
22 |  |    agᵢ proposes φ_T^cur_agᵢ to agⱼ, agⱼ receives φ_T^cur_agᵢ from agᵢ ;
23 |  |    temp = j;
24 |  |    j = i;
25 |  |    i = temp;
26 |  end
27 end
28 if (φ_T^cur_agᵢ ↔ φ_T^cur_agⱼ) or (φ_T^cur_agⱼ → φ_T^cur_agᵢ)) then
29 |    return T^cur_agⱼ                                    // Agreement
30 else
31 |    return ⊥                                            // Disagreement
32 end
```

The main phases of the algorithm are:

1. *initialisation*:
   the system keeps the initial viewpoints of the agents as their current angles
   $(T^{cur}_{ag_1} = T^0_{ag_1}, \; T^{cur}_{ag_2} = T^0_{ag_2})$ and the logical formulas for each of them
   $(\varphi_{T^{cur}_{ag_1}} = \bigwedge_{\alpha \in T^{cur}_{ag_1}} \alpha, \; \varphi_{T^{cur}_{ag_2}} = \bigwedge_{\beta \in T^{cur}_{ag_2}} \beta)$. Two boolean variables are used
   to keep under control the stubbornness of the agents ($stub_1$ and $stub_2$).
   At the beginning of the MN the agents are assumed to be not absolutely
   stubborn ($stub_1 = stub_2 = \texttt{false}$);
2. *demand stage*:
   each agent sends her viewpoint and receives the opponent's one; the system evaluates the exchanged messages to find if an agreement is reached.
   If it is the case, the MN ends with a positive outcome that is $T^0_{ag_1}$ or $T^0_{ag_2}$
   indifferently;
3. *the war of attrition stage*:
   at the beginning of the war of attrition stage a proposing order between
   agents is established ($i = 1, j = 2$) and the stubbornness condition of
   the proposing agent is tested. The proposing agent chooses the next angle
   $(T = \text{visit}(ag_i, \text{TheoryTree}_{ag_i}, T^{cur}_{ag_i}))$. The new node T is reached by weakening, changing action or by renewing the last proposal. The strategy of the
   agent makes deterministic the choice of T. Having T as the new proposal, ag_i
   tests if it is a generalisation of the ag_j's last offer and in this case, she accepts
   it and puts it as her new proposal. At the end of a war of attrition turn,
   the proposing agent ag_i sends $T^{cur}_{ag_i}$ to ag_j and a new turn begins with ag_j
   as proposing agent ($temp = j, \; j = i, \; i = temp$). The war of attrition stage
   ends when an agreement is found or when both agents are in stubbornness.

The following example shows how the algorithm works.

Example 3. Let Alice and Bob be two agents negotiating the meaning of "vehicle". Suppose Alice is defined as in Example 2.
   Let Bob be defined as $(\mathcal{L}_B, Ax_B, Stub_B)$ where:

$$\mathcal{L}_B = \{ \textit{2wheels, 3wheels, 4wheels, Handlebar, SteeringWheel, Motor,}$$
$$\textit{2bicyclePedals, 4bicyclePedals} \}$$

$$Ax_B = \{ (\textit{2wheels} \lor \textit{3wheels} \lor \textit{4wheels})^{(\sharp 9)}, (\textit{Handlebar} \lor \textit{SteeringWheel})^{(\sharp 2)},$$
$$(\textit{Motor} \lor \textit{2bicyclePedals} \lor \textit{4bicyclePedals})^{(\sharp 10)},$$
$$\textit{2wheels}^{(\sharp 11)}, \textit{Handlebar}^{(\sharp 12)}, \textit{2bicyclePedals}^{(\sharp 13)} (\textit{2wheels} \lor \textit{3wheels})^{(\sharp 14)},$$
$$(\textit{2bicyclePedals} \lor \textit{4bicyclePedals})^{(\sharp 15)} \}$$

$$Stub_B = \{ (\textit{2wheels} \lor \textit{3wheels} \lor \textit{4wheels})^{(\sharp 9)}, (\textit{Handlebar} \lor \textit{SteeringWheel})^{(\sharp 2)},$$
$$(\textit{Motor} \lor \textit{2bicyclePedals} \lor \textit{4bicyclePedals})^{(\sharp 10)} \}$$

Both the agents are imperfectly committed and their subjective hierarchies are as in Figure 7.

Let Alice be the first bidding agent.

- The demand stage begins and Alice proposes $\varphi_{T_A^{cur}} = (\sharp 4) \wedge (\sharp 5) \wedge (\sharp 6)$ to Bob and he receives it (Step 6).
- Bob proposes $\varphi_{T_B^{cur}} = (\sharp 11) \wedge (\sharp 12) \wedge (\sharp 13)$ to Alice and she receives it (Step 7).
- The war of attrition stage begins because $\varphi_{T_A^{cur}}$ and $\varphi_{T_B^{cur}}$ are not equivalent.
- Alice is not in stubbornness ($T_A^{cur} \not\sim T_A^{\perp}$) thus she chooses a new proposal, i.e. a node in her subjective hierarchy (Step 16).
- Let $T_A^{cur} = \{(\sharp 7), (\sharp 2), (\sharp 8)\}$ (Step 17) that is the result of a weakening action to the previous node, and $\varphi_{T_A^{cur}} = (\sharp 7) \wedge (\sharp 2) \wedge (\sharp 8)$ (Step 18). $\varphi_{T_B^{cur}} \not\rightarrow \varphi_{T_A^{cur}}$ (Step 19) then
- Alice proposes $\varphi_{T_A^{cur}}$ to Bob and he receives it.
- Bob is not in stubbornness ($T_B^{cur} \not\sim T_B^{\perp}$) thus he chooses a new proposal, i.e. a node in his subjective hierarchy (Step 16).
- Let $T_B^{cur} = \{(\sharp 14), (\sharp 2), (\sharp 13)\}$ (Step 17) that is the result of a weakening action to the previous node, and $\varphi_{T_B^{cur}} = (\sharp 14) \wedge (\sharp 2) \wedge (\sharp 13)$ (Step 18).
- $\varphi_{T_A^{cur}} \not\rightarrow \varphi_{T_B^{cur}}$ (Step 19) then Bob proposes $\varphi_{T_B^{cur}}$ to Alice and she receives it.
- Alice is not in stubbornness ($T_A^{cur} \not\sim T_A^{\perp}$) thus she chooses a new proposal, i.e. a node in her subjective hierarchy (Step 16).
- Let $T_A^{cur} = \{(\sharp 1), (\sharp 2), (\sharp 3)\}$ (Step 17) that is the result of a weakening action to the previous node, and $\varphi_{T_A^{cur}} = (\sharp 1) \wedge (\sharp 2) \wedge (\sharp 3)$ (Step 18).
- $\varphi_{T_B^{cur}} \rightarrow \varphi_{T_A^{cur}}$ (Step 19) then Alice assumes Bob's current angle as her one ($T_A^{cur} = T_B^{cur}$).
- Alice proposes $\varphi_{T_A^{cur}}$ to Bob and he receives it.
- The condition ($\varphi_{T_B^{cur}} \leftrightarrow \varphi_{T_A^{cur}}$) is true.
- The MN ends positively with a shared point of view, $T_B^{cur} = \{(\sharp 14), (\sharp 2), (\sharp 13)\}$.

$\square$

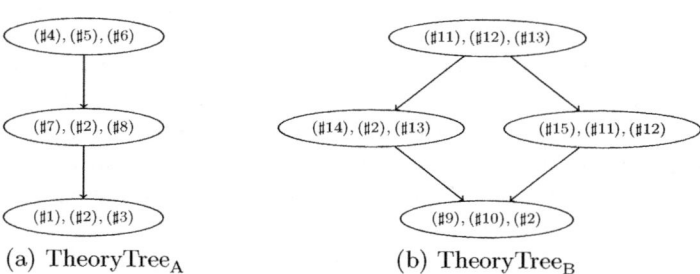

(a) TheoryTree$_A$ (b) TheoryTree$_B$

Fig. 7. Subjective hierarchies of Alice (a) and of Bob (b) of Example 3

5.4   Theoretical Results

In this section, we present some results obtained by our formalisation. We show that the MN algorithm is correct and complete by Theorem 3.

We can now derive a theoretical decidability result, regarding the problem defined for one pair of agents that negotiate propositional theories in subjective hierarchies. Given two agents ag_1 and ag_2 that possess one subjective hierarchy each, the problem of performing a negotiation process of the hierarchies between those agents is named *MN problem*.

Theorem 2. *The MN problem is decidable iff the theories of the agents are propositional.*

Proof. ($\Rightarrow$) Suppose that MN is fully decidable, i.e. there exists an algorithm that computes the shared theory between agents. The main test of the MN problem is to check if the logical formula for the theory of agent ag_i is logically equivalent to the logical formula for the theory f agent ag_j, where $ag_i, ag_j \in Ag$. This test translates in "is φ_{ag_i} in T_{ag_j}?". The membership of a formula to a propositional logical theory is decidable only for propositional theories. Therefore, all the theories of the agents are propositional.

($\Leftarrow$) Suppose that T_{ag_i} is propositional for all $ag_i \in Ag$, i.e. that there exists an algorithm computing the membership of a formula to their logical theories. The membership test is he main point of the MN problem. In fact the test $(\varphi_{ag_i} \leftrightarrow \varphi_{ag_j})$ is equivalent to test if $\varphi_{ag_i} \in T_{ag_j}$ and $\varphi_{ag_j} \in T_{ag_2}$. The two test are decidable because both T_{ag_i} and T_{ag_j} are decidable then MN is decidable. ∎

In particular, Algorithm 1 is able to process MN problems. The following theorem proves that if there is a positive outcome then the algorithm finds it (completeness) and that if the algorithm produces a positive outcome then it is a shared viewpoint for the agents (correctness).

Theorem 3. *Algorithm 1 is correct and complete.*

Proof. Suppose that there is not a possible positive outcome, that is the agents cannot share a point of view. In such a case, agent ag_i, after visiting all nodes of her $TheoryTree_i$, reaches one leaf node that constitutes her current theory. The same happens for her opponent player. Each agent tests that the two theories are not compatible and that she cannot propose another theory because she is at a leaf node and has already visited all the nodes having an edge connecting them to the leaf one. By construction the agents go to step 10 and then the negotiation fails. Suppose that two theories exist, one per agent, that are equivalent. Suppose that the process starts with the proposal of ag_1; she continues to compare the theory she received with the theory she is currently assuming as current one, so to make a new proposal until the current theory of the opponent is compatible with her current one. When this situation is reached then also ag_2 thinks that the two theories are compatible. The process ends positively with agents sharing a theory about the world. ∎

The complexity of Algorithm 1 is obtained in Theorem 4.

Theorem 4. *Algorithm 1 solves the MN Problem in* $\mathbf{O}(h \times \mathbf{C})$ *where h is the maximum number of nodes in the agents' hierarchies and* $\mathbf{C}$ *is the computational cost of the relationship test between theories of the agents.*

Proof. Consider the case in which there is no possible shared theory. Since the stubbornness sets of the two agents are incompatible, we shall visit all the nodes of both subjective hierarchies in turn, in order to reach the conclusion that no common shared theory can be negotiated. Moreover, if such a common shared theory can be found the process necessarily terminates before. Therefore the case of incompatible stubbornness sets is the worst complexity case.

Suppose $ag_1 = (\mathcal{L}ag_1, Ax_{ag_1}, Stub_{ag_1})$ and $ag_2 = (\mathcal{L}ag_2, Ax_{ag_2}, Stub_{ag_2})$. Let be n_i the number of nodes ag_i can negotiate. Each subjective hierarchy TheoryTree$_i$ of ag_i has h_i number of vertices. By construction, Algorithm 1 visits all the vertices. Then such algorithm makes $max\{h_1, h_2\}$ steps in the worst case and for each step it makes a test of the relationship between theories that costs $\mathbf{C}$. ∎

In particular, when the theories of the agents are propositional, the computational cost of the algorithm is $\mathbf{O}(h \times m \times 2^l)$ where h is the maximum number of nodes in the subjective hierarchies, m is the maximum number of logical formulas in each theories of agents, and l is the maximum number of occurring symbols.

An interesting special case occurs when the subjective hierarchies cannot reach a final agreement about the negotiated meaning. The following theorem establishes when this is the case.

Theorem 5. *If* $(Stub_{ag_1})^* \not\sim (Stub_{ag_2})^*$ *then the MN process fails.*

Proof. By construction, $(Stub_{ag_1})^*$ is the unique leaf node of subjective hierarchy TheoryTree$_{ag_i}$ of the agent ag_i and it represents the most general theory ag_i can assume. If the most general theories of agents are not identical then no other less general ones are. ∎

There are other special cases in MN process: when at least one agent is of absolute flexibility (see 1) and when both agents are of absolute stubbornness. The first case is enunciated in proposition 1. The last case is established by Theorem 6[4].

Theorem 6. *If both agents in a MN process are absolutely stubborn then the complexity of the process is* $O(m \times l)$ *where n is the maximum number of theorems in agents' theory and l is the maximum number of symbols occurring in a theorem.*

---

[4] We assume here that the underlying theory is propositional logic. However analogous proofs can be exhibited for different logical models, so that the computed complexity is parametric in the underlying theory. For first-order logic we can derive a corresponding theorem, that is omitted and left to the reader.

Proof. Suppose ag_1 and ag_2 are absolutely stubborn then $T_{ag_i} = (Stub_{ag_i})^*$ $\forall i \in \{1, 2\}$. Suppose the MN process starts with ag_2 sending $ThCur_2 = T_{ag_2}$ to ag_1. If $T_{ag_1} \vdash \varphi(T_{ag_2})'$ then agreement is reached otherwise the process fails. The process complexity depends on the complexity of theorem proving in propositional logic. Without loss of generality we can assume that the axioms are expressed in Clausal Normal Form, so we can use the resolution principle (see [8]) to prove the relevant theorems. Resolution principle implementations are linear in the number of symbols occurring in formulas and in the number of formulas. ∎

6   MN by English Auction

6.1   Introduction

In this section we show how we formalise 1-n MN by the English Auction Game. 1-n MN takes place when there are more than two people that want to share something. In general, the first agent making a proposal is the one that evaluates the opponents' offers and that states when the involved agents agree. Therefore, the first *bidding* agent behaves like a referee in an English Auction scenario. In fact, as said above, the agents negotiate by ceasing, if possible, or by rebidding the previous proposal if they strategically think it is the best action to perform.

We first present the English Auction Game (Section 6.2) and then formalise the MN in terms of it (Section 6.3).

6.2   The English Auction Game

English Auction is the most common game in the modelisation of negotiation processes in which more than two agents are involved. As said above, the game begins by the proposal of the auctioneer that is called *reservation price* and it is the minimum price the agents have to pay to win the auction. In the next step of the English Auction, each player makes her offer by incrementing the last bidden one, i.e. the auctioneer's proposal. There is not a fixed number of turns for agents' bidding, instead the game continues until no more bids are performed. The game ends with a winner that is the agent who bids the highest offer.

In a MN perspective, the English Auction game is slightly different in outcome. The goal of the negotiation is to obtain that the agents share a viewpoint. Therefore the positive ending condition of the game is that all the agents make the same bid and the bidden proposal is the representation of their viewpoints.

There are MN contexts in which it is sufficient a "major" part of the agents in agreeing about something to consider positive the negotiation. In general "major part" means that a number of agents, typically more then 50% , but it may mean that a part of the most trustworthy agents are in agreement. The latter case prevails when there are specialists about the negotiation subject into the multiple agent system and their opinion is more relevant then the opponents' ones. In this paper, the trustworthiness of the agent is not specifically considered because it is represented inside the definition of an agent. When participating to a negotiation process, the agents assume a viewpoint and many admissible angles of it. A specialist knows more about the negotiation subject than a less expert agent and her negotiation behaviour will be to make concessions as few as possible. Conversely, if a no expert agent knows that an agent in the MAS is a specialist, then she trusts the specialist and probably makes concessions with respect to the proposals of the specialist. Therefore, the degree of knowledge of an agent translates into the trustworthiness with respect to herself, thus into her negotiation attitude.

In the former case, the minimum number of agreeing agents is a parameter of the game: suppose α is the chosen number for "major part", the MN continues until at least α agents agree about a common angle. The minimum number of agreing agents is called *degree of sharing*. A MN process for more than two agents has two positive ending conditions and two types of positive outcomes, if a positive outcome exists:

partially positive : when the degree of sharing is less than the number of the participants;

totally positive : when the degree of sharing is equal to the number of the negotiating agents.

The role of the auctioneer is to monitor the game in order to understand when it ends and whether this happens in a positive or a negative way. In general, the auctioneer is the first bidding agent but in a negotiation perspective she may play in two ways: active or passive. An active referee is a participant of the negotiation and the reservation price is her viewpoint. Moreover, an active referee makes herself proposals during the auction as all the other agents and she is considered in the agreement test. A passive auctioneer does not affect the negotiation. She only tests the process and makes only one bid, the first one for the reservation price.

6.3   The English Auction Framework

In this section we formalise the MN problem as an English Auction game. The framework we present models the MN process by assuming that there are at least three agents involved and that one of them is nominated the *auctioneer* (referee) namely the agent who controls and decides the process development. The existence of a referee is relevant but not a constraint to our model because, generally the first bidding agent is the one that regulates the game for every type of auction. The negotiation is performed by a dialogue among the agents involved: bids and accepting or rejecting proposals are send as messages to the agents.

The main assumption is that only the referee receives the proposals of the players. The auctioneer broadcasts her proposal and the participants make counteroffers and send them only to the auctioneer. The evaluation of the counterproposals is left to the referee. This way avoids that the agents evaluate and propose at the same time. The result is n, where n is the number of the agents involved, parallel sessions of MN by Bargaining in which one of the player is the auctioneer and the other is one among the agents. Figure 8 depicts the configuration of the multiple agent system for our formalism. The agents negotiate one-to-one with the auctioneer who is involved in n bargaining negotiations. The

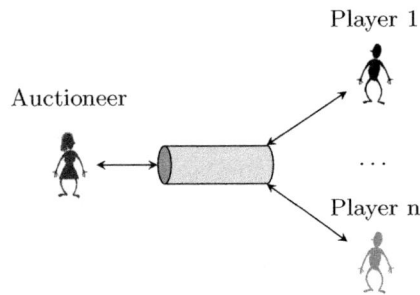

Fig. 8. MN by English Auction configuration

auctioneer has to make the same proposal for each of the bargaining negotiations in order to synchronise all the 1-1 negotiations as a single 1-n one and find a common viewpoint, i.e. the same outcome for the 1-1 negotiations.

We formalise MN by viewing it as a sequence of *beats*. Every beat is started by the auctioneer and participated by all the other agents in the game. Because the MN process works to build shared knowledge among a set of negotiating agents, we assume that the referee allows the *degree of sharing* she wants to obtain in front of the auction. The degree establishes the minimum number of agreeing agents the auctioneer admits to consider the MN positive: if n is the number of negotiating agents, the degree of sharing α is such that $0 < \alpha \le n$. The case in which $\alpha = 1$ is clearly degenerated, being possible in this situation, an outcome in which the auctioneer is the only agreeing agent.

Suppose that n is the number of the negotiating agents. A *beat* is a set of n pairs of (auctioneer proposal, agent counterproposal). As in the framework above (Section 5.3), the proposals and the counterproposals of the agents in MN represent viewpoints and angles. The current proposal of each agent represents her current point of view, i.e. an admissible positive outcome of the process and a good definition of the item in negotiation. As said in the previous section, the agents change beliefs during the negotiation. Even if the initial set of beliefs is a parameter in agent definition and it is constant during the process, the agent changes the current beliefs set. The initial knowledge of the agent can be called a *viewpoint* and the current set of beliefs a the *current angle*. A viewpoint has many angles and the agents negotiate them. Therefore the first proposal an agent makes is her viewpoint and the next ones are angles. Let T be an angle for the agent ag, then ag puts it forward by its logical formula φ_T:

$$\varphi_T = \bigwedge_{\phi \in T} \phi$$

As direct consequence of the definition of subjective hierarchy, each node of the graph has a logical formula.

Henceforth, we use the symbol T_{ag}^{Cur} to denote the current angle of the agent ag and $\varphi_{T_{ag}^{Cur}}$ as its logical formula representation, the symbol, $\varphi_{T_{ag}^{0}}$ is the initial knowledge of the agents, i.e. her viewpoint.

The negotiation develops by *beats* that are sessions of 1-1 negotiation between the auctioneer and a player. In the following subsections we describe a beat, and the behaviours of the auctioneer and of each agent.

Beat. A beat consists of a set of MN by Bargaining rounds in which the auctioneer makes a proposal and receives the opponents' ones. Let ag_a the auctioneer and ag_i an agent involved in the negotiation, the steps of a beat are the following:

1. The auctioneer broadcasts her current angle as the logical formula $\varphi_{T_{ag_a}^{cur}}$;
2. Each player ag_i receives the proposal of the auctioneer and evaluates it with respect to her own current angle in order to test if it is good;
3. Suppose ag_i thinks $T_{ag_a}^{cur}$ is not good, then ag_i makes a counteroffer and chooses it into her subjective hierarchy;
4. Each agent ag_i makes a counteroffer to the auctioneer;
5. The auctioneer ag_a receives the proposals from the agents;
6. ag_a controls the MN situation by checking if a viewpoint exists that is shared by at least α agents where α is the degree of sharing.
7. If a shared viewpoint exists then the auctioneer ends the MN with a positive outcome, i.e. the shared theory;
8. otherwise the negotiation continues and a new beat begins.

At the beginning of a beat every agent adopts an angle of her initial viewpoint that is a theory belonging to her subjective hierarchy defined in Definition 2.

At the end of each beat the referee controls the state of the MN process that is whether an agreement is reached or no possible shared point of view exists and thus the negotiation ends negatively. The auctioneer is able to state if the process is positively, whether partially or totally, or negatively ending or if a new beat has to start with a new proposal of the referee.

Bidding Agent. A negotiating agent behaves like a Bargaining player: she receives an offer and she may accept, reject it or she may make a counteroffer.

The acceptability and the rejection of a received offer depend upon its *goodness*. In all the situations in which the auctioneer proposal is not good, the agent chooses a new proposal to perform among the nodes of her subjective hierarchy by visiting it in some way. The choice depends on the attitude of the agent.

Auctioneer. The role of the auctioneer is of supervising the negotiation process to state if and how it ends. The actions of the referee for each beat is of three stages:

Proposal. The auctioneer makes a proposal and sends it to each agent, and receives the negotiating agents' proposals.

Test. The auctioneer tests if any ending conditions is reached with respect to the last proposals received by the negotiating agents.

Elaboration. The auctioneer has to perform a new proposal whenever the agreement has not been reached. She does so by visiting her subjective hierarchy in some way depending on her attitude.

The proposal that the referee asserts during a beat is the same for each negotiating agent. The auctioneer chooses the next proposal to make in a way that is related to her attitude and to the trustworthiness with respect to the opponents. The referee makes assertions that support the agents she considers more reliable, more trustworthy, more friendly etc. than others, i.e. that she prefers in some way.

Only the referee knows the opponents' proposal and she is the only agent involved which is able to check if the MN is positive or negative ending. A MN process is considered *positive* when the auctioneer asserts that a commonly accepted theory is found (*total* agreement) or that an acceptable number α of agreeing agents exist on that theory (*partial* agreement), as *negative* if there is not a common viewpoint shared by all the negotiating agents or by an acceptable number of them. We represent these possible MN outcomes as ending conditions the referee checks at the end of every beat.

Definition 4 (MN Ending Conditions). *Suppose that $T_{ag_a}^{cur}$ is the last theory the auctioneer advanced and α is the degree of sharing that she assumes. Then she may test the following MN ending conditions:*

Total. *T_{win} is the least general theory with respect to Th bidden by a negotiating agent and it is good for all the other negotiating agents;*

Partial. *T_{win} is the least general theory with respect to Th bidden by a negotiating agent ag_{win} such that it is good for at least α negotiating agents;*

Negative. *there is not a theory shared by at least α negotiating agents and the auctioneer is stubborn.*

The MN process closes positively iff the total or partial ending conditions are eventually tested, otherwise it closes negatively.

When at the end of a beat the auctioneer controls the MN state, she checks the existence of a winning theory among those proposed by the agents and checks if there are other proposals she may perform. The referee is the only one able to decide and state how the MN ends because no other agent knows what the others proposed.

If there are only two agents involved in the auction, a referee and a negotiated agent, the MN process automated by Algorithm 2 computes in the same way as Algorithm 1.

The following example shows how Algorithm 2 works: depending on the sharing degree the MN ends in positive (first case) or in negative way (second case).

Algorithm 2. A credulous MN algorithm by English Auction (MNEA)

Input : n subjective hierarchies, ag_a the auctioneer, α the degree of sharing
Output: A negotiated theory, if possible

```
 1  m = 0, b_win = ⊥                          // Initialisation;
 2  count[] = array of (n+1) integers;
 3  forall the i ∈ Ag ∪ {ag_a} do
 4  |    T_i^cur = T_i^0, φ_{T_i^cur} = ⋀_{α∈T_i^cur};
 5  |    stub_i = false;
 6  end
 7  while ((b_win = ⊥) or (α ≥ m)) or ⋁_{i∈Ag∪{ag_a}} ¬stub_i do
 8  |    ag_a broadcasts φ_{T_{ag_a}^cur}         // Beat beginning;
 9  |    forall the i ∈ Ag do
10  |    |    if T_i^cur ∼ T_i^⊥ then
11  |    |    |    stub_i = true;
12  |    |    end
13  |    |    if ¬(φ_{T_i^cur} ↔ φ_{T_{ag_a}^cur}) then
14  |    |    |    T_{ag_i}^cur = visit(i, TheoryTree_i, T_i^cur) ;
15  |    |    |    φ_{T_{ag_i}^cur} = ⋀_{φ∈T_{ag_i}^cur} φ ;
16  |    |    |    if (φ_{T_{ag_a}^cur} → φ_{T_i^cur}) then
17  |    |    |    |    T_i^cur = T_{ag_a}^cur, φ_{T_i^cur} = φ_{T_{ag_a}^cur} ;
18  |    |    |    end
19  |    |    end
20  |    |    i proposes φ_{T_i^cur} to ag_a;
21  |    end
22  |    ag_a receives the bids of the agents bids = [φ_{T_{ag_a}^cur}, φ_{T_{ag_1}^cur}, φ_{T_{ag_2}^cur} ..., φ_{T_{ag_n}^cur}];
23  |    for i = 0 to n − 1 do
24  |    |    count[i] = 0;
25  |    |    for j = i + 1 to n do
26  |    |    |    if bids[i] ↔ bids[j] then
27  |    |    |    |    count[i] + +;
28  |    |    |    end
29  |    |    end
30  |    end
31  |    m = max(count), win = indexOf(m, count);
32  |    if T_{ag_a}^cur ∼ T_{ag_a}^⊥ then
33  |    |    stub_{ag_a} = true;
34  |    end
35  |    T_{ag_a}^cur = visit(ag_a, TheoryTree_{ag_a}, T_{ag_a}^cur);
36  |    if there is ag_i such that (φ_{T_{ag_i}^cur} → φ_{T_{ag_a}^cur}) then
37  |    |    T_{ag_a}^cur = T_{ag_i}^cur, φ_{T_{ag_a}^cur} = φ_{T_{ag_i}^cur} ;
38  |    end
39  |    else
40  |    |    φ_{T_{ag_a}^cur} = ⋀_{φ∈T_{ag_a}^cur} φ           // Beat ending
41  |    end
42  end
43  if (bids[win] ≠ ⊥) and (α ≤ m) then
44  |    return bids[win]                        // Agreement
45  end
46  else
47  |    return ⊥                                // Disagreement
48  end
```

Example 4. Let Alice, Bob and Charles be three agents negotiating the meaning of "vehicle". Suppose Alice and Bob are defined as in Example 3. Let Charles be defined as $(\mathcal{L}_C, Ax_C, Stub_C)$ where:

$$\mathcal{L}_C = \{4wheels, Handlebar, Steering Wheel, Motor, TowBar\}$$

$$Ax_C = \{4wheels^{(\sharp 4)}, (Handlebar \vee Steering Wheel)^{(\sharp 2)},$$
$$TowBar^{(\sharp 16)}, Steering Wheel^{(\sharp 5)}, (TowBar \vee Motor)^{(\sharp 17)}\}$$

$$Stub_C = \{4wheels^{(\sharp 4)}, (Handlebar \vee Steering Wheel)^{(\sharp 2)}, (TowBar \vee Motor)^{(\sharp 17)}\}$$

The agents are all imperfectly committed and their subjective hierarchies are as in Figure 9.

Let Alice be the first bidding agent and she is nominated the referee of the MN.

(First case) Suppose that the sharing degree of the MN is two so that at least two agents have to agree with a shared viewpoint.
- The MN begins with the initialisation of the variables (Step 1-7): $T_A^{cur} = \{(\sharp 4), (\sharp 5), (\sharp 6)\}$, $T_B^{cur} = \{(\sharp 11), (\sharp 12), (\sharp 13)\}$ and $T_C^{cur} = \{(\sharp 4), (\sharp 5), (\sharp 16)\}$.
- Alice proposes $\varphi_{T_A^{cur}} = (\sharp 4) \wedge (\sharp 5) \wedge (\sharp 6)$ to Bob and Charles.
- Bob is not stubborn and $\neg(T_A^{cur} \leftrightarrow T_B^{cur})$. Bob chooses a proposal and changes T_B^{cur} by $T_B^{cur} = \{(\sharp 14), (\sharp 2), (\sharp 13)\}$ and he proposes it to Alice.
- Charles is not stubborn and $\neg(T_A^{cur} \leftrightarrow T_C^{cur})$. Charles chooses a proposal and changes T_C^{cur} by $T_C^{cur} = \{(\sharp 4), (\sharp 2), (\sharp 17)\}$. $(\varphi_{T_A^{cur}} \rightarrow \varphi_{T_C^{cur}})$ is true and Charles accepts the proposal of Alice by $T_C^{cur} = T_A^{cur}$ and $\varphi_{T_C^{cur}} = \varphi_{T_A^{cur}}$ and he proposes it to Alice.
- Alice receives the proposals of Bob and Charles: $bids = [\varphi_{T_A^{cur}}, \varphi_{T_B^{cur}}, \varphi_{T_C^{cur}}]$, $count = [2, 0, 2]$, $m = 2$, $win = 0$.
- Alice checks if she is in stubborn and searches a new feasible proposal. Thus, $T_A^{cur} = \{(\sharp 7), (\sharp 2), (\sharp 8)\}$ and $\varphi_{T_A^{cur}} = (\sharp 7) \wedge (\sharp 2) \wedge (\sharp 8)$.
- At Step 7, α is equal to m. The MN closes in Step 38 with $\{(\sharp 4), (\sharp 5), (\sharp 6)\}$ as the partial positive outcome.

(Second case) Suppose that the sharing degree was three.
- The MN continues and Alice proposes $\varphi_{T_A^{cur}}$ to Bob and Charles.
- Bob is not stubborn and $\neg(T_A^{cur} \leftrightarrow T_B^{cur})$. Bob chooses a proposal and changes T_B^{cur} by $T_B^{cur} = \{(\sharp 15), (\sharp 11), (\sharp 12)\}$. and he proposes it to Alice.
- Charles is not stubborn and $\neg(T_A^{cur} \leftrightarrow T_C^{cur})$. Charles chooses a proposal and changes T_C^{cur} by $T_C^{cur} = \{(\sharp 4), (\sharp 2), (\sharp 17)\}$ and he proposes it to Alice.
- Alice receives the proposals of Bob and Charles: $bids = [\varphi_{T_A^{cur}}, \varphi_{T_B^{cur}}, \varphi_{T_C^{cur}}]$, $count = [0, 0, 0]$, $m = 0$, $win = -1$.
- Alice checks if she is in stubborn and searches a new feasible proposal. Thus, $T_A^{cur} = \{(\sharp 1), (\sharp 2), (\sharp 3)\}$ and $\varphi_{T_A^{cur}} = (\sharp 1) \wedge (\sharp 2) \wedge (\sharp 3)$.

- The MN continues because the sharing degree is not reached and Alice proposes $\varphi_{T_A^{cur}}$ to Bob and Charles.
- Bob is not stubborn and $\neg(T_A^{cur} \leftrightarrow T_B^{cur})$. Bob chooses a proposal and changes T_B^{cur} by $T_B^{cur} = \{(\sharp 9), (\sharp 10), (\sharp 2)\}$ and he proposes it to Alice.
- Charles is stubborn and $\neg(T_A^{cur} \leftrightarrow T_C^{cur})$. Charles remakes the last proposal to Alice.
- Alice receives the proposals of Bob and Charles: $bids = [\varphi_{T_A^{cur}}, \varphi_{T_B^{cur}}, \varphi_{T_C^{cur}}]$, $count = [0, 0, 0]$, $m = 0$, $win = -1$.
- Alice is in stubborn.
- The MN continues because the sharing degree is not reached and Bob is not stubborn. Alice puts forward again $\varphi_{T_A^{cur}}$ to Bob and Charles.
- Bob is stubborn and $\neg(T_A^{cur} \leftrightarrow T_B^{cur})$. Bob remakes the last proposal to Alice and the same thing for Charles.
- Alice receives the proposals of Bob and Charles: $bids = [\varphi_{T_A^{cur}}, \varphi_{T_B^{cur}}, \varphi_{T_C^{cur}}]$, $count = [0, 0, 0]$, $m = 0$, $win = -1$.
- Alice is in stubborn thus the MN closes in disagreement because no shared viewpoint is found.

□

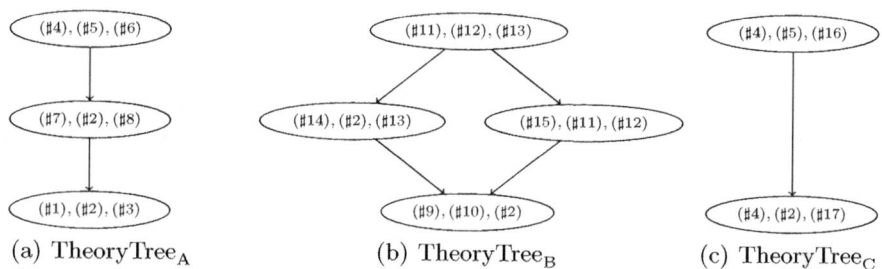

(a) TheoryTree$_A$ (b) TheoryTree$_B$ (c) TheoryTree$_C$

Fig. 9. Subjective hierarchies of Alice (a), Bob (b) and Charles (c) of Example 4

6.4 Theoretical Results

we now provide some theorems about the correctness (Theorem 7) and the completeness (Theorem 8) of Algorithm 2 (called henceforth MNEA). Assuming some restrictions to the representation of the agents viewpoints we finally show that the algorithm is polynomially decidable (Theorem 9).

The aim of this presentation is to prove that the proposed framework can be applied in practice. Nonetheless, some more investigation is needed to say the last word upon the presented formalism. In particular, we still do not have a proof that the obtained computational result is a lower bound, although we conjecture that the obtained upper bound result is also a lower bound. We start by showing that the MN algorithm we formalise is correct, namely the theory it outputs is the one at least α negotiating agents consider *good*, where α is the degree of sharing input.

First of all we claim soundness and completeness of the Algorithm MNEA.

Theorem 7. *If T is the theory that Algorithm MNEA outputs then T is the least general theory with respect to the one advanced by the auctioneer and which is shared by at least α agents where α is the degree of sharing assumed by the referee.*

Proof. Let be Ag $= \{ag_1, ag_2, \ldots, ag_n, ag_a\}$ the set of the agents involved in a MN process in which one of them is reserved to be a referee (ag_a), and T the theory MNEA outcomes. Suppose by contradiction that T is either not the least generalisation of an auctioneer theory or that T is not good for at least α agents, then:

T $\npreceq$ T$_a$: if T is not a generalisation of the auctioneer's theory then the algorithm has passed *Step 2.5* or *2.6* and it goes to *Step 11* stopping in negative outcome.

T is not shared by at least α agents: when the algorithm computes *Step 8* it fails and goes to *Step 9*. If no other proposal can be made by ag_a because she is in stubbornness then the algorithm performs *Step 5.1, 5.2* and goes to *Step 11* and it stops in negative outcome.

Therefore the claim is proven.   ∎

The next theorem proves that the algorithm is able to outputs the right MN theory if it exists.

Theorem 8. *Let T be the theory which is the least generalisation among those the negotiating agents may admit. MNEA with the the $n+1$ subjective hierarchies $\{\mathcal{H}_1, \mathcal{H}_2, \ldots, \mathcal{H}_n, \mathcal{H}_a\}$ in input, computes the MN problem and outputs T.*

Proof. To prove that the algorithm is complete we have to show that it preserve MN theory's properties in computing. The outcome of a MN process is a theory T which is:

1. $T_a \preceq T$, where T_a is the last theory the auctioneer advanced: this is guaranteed by *Steps 2.1-2.4*;
2. $\alpha \leq |\{\mathcal{H}_i : \exists S \in \mathcal{H}_i.T \preceq S$ where $i \in [1, n]\}|$: the number of the negotiating agents assuming T as *good* is at least α, namely the degree of sharing. This is guaranteed by *Steps 5-10*.

                                                                        ∎

The complexity of the algorithm automating the MN problem depends on the representation of the agents' points of views. Henceforth we assume that establishing if a theory is good for an agent is a decidable problem.

Theorem 9. *If n is the number of the negotiating agents and h the maximum number of nodes among those of the subjective hierarchies of the negotiating agents, then MNEA computes the MN process in $\mathbf{O}(h^2 \times n \times \mathbf{C})$ where $\mathbf{C}$ is the computational cost of the relationship test among the theories advanced by agents during the MN.*

Proof. The worst case occurs when no theory can be shared by the MN players. In this situation the auctioneer performs at most h proposals and for each proposal every negotiating agent tests if she considers good the received theory: no negotiating agent establishes that the proposal received is good and she does so by visiting all her subjective hierarchy's nodes (h) and by testing the relationship between the node she visited and the theory proposed by the auctioneer. Then, for each bid the auctioneer advances at most h bids to all the n agents, who check if it is good by relating it with respect to all the nodes in their subjective hierarchies (at most h nodes per graph). If the cost of the relationship test is $\mathbf{C}$, the MNEA algorithm computes this case in $h \times n \times h \times \mathbf{C}$ steps.   ∎

If we assume that the agent knowledge bases are CPL or FOL formulae without identity, we can prove that Algorithm MNEA computes in polynomial time with respect to negotiating agents, number of theories involved, and number of axioms in the theories. This is claimed in the following theorem.

Theorem 10. *Let n be the number of the negotiating agents, h the maximum number of nodes among those of the subjective hierarchies of the negotiating agents. If m is the maximum number of the axioms in the agents knowledge bases and l the maximum number of symbols occurring in an axiom, then MNEA computes the MN process in $\mathbf{O}(h^2 \times n \times m \times 2^l)$.*

Proof. Suppose that the relationship among the theories bidden by agents is computed by resolution principle. The implementation of the resolution principle are linear in the number of formulas and exponential in the number of occurring symbols.   ∎

A nondeterministic version of the algorithm, based upon linear resolution can be easily built so that we can inherit the computational properties of this approach. Based on this approach we can prove that MN with English Auction is an NP problem[5].

Lemma 1. *The nondeterministic version of Algorithm MNEA computes the MN problem in polynomial time with respect to the number of symbols in the involved theories.*

Proof. Consider a nondeterministic version of MNEA obtained by associating to the deterministic version of MNEA an oracle engine that computes in polynomial time the consistency of a set of clauses in CPL or FOL by linear resolution. Such an engine can be easily defined, as proved in several papers about Mechanical Theorem Proving. Since every deterministic algorithm that calls an oracle engine to compute in polynomial time the solution of the problem is nondeterministically polynomial, proved that the procedure ends in a nondeterministic polynomial time as well, by Theorem 10. Therefore the claim is proved.   ∎

A straightforward consequence of the above results is the following theorem. From Lemma 1 we can derive the following theorem, that poses practical modality of MNEA in nondeterministic version.

---

[5] We omit this part of the investigation and we leave it to future works.

Theorem 11. *MN problem with at least three parties and subjective hierarchies in FOL is in NP.*

7   Conclusions

In this paper we presented a formalisation of the Meaning Negotiation problem in a game-theoretic perspective. MN is largely studied in Artificial Intelligence community and, in particular, by Knowledge Representation researches. However, only a little attention has been given to the automation of the process in a way that may result independent of the number of involved agents and of their expression language. Moreover, the main part of the current approaches deals with the problem of the MN as the definition of an agent communication language and of a communication protocol, and only a minor effort is devoted to the mechanism that allows the involved agents to reach an agreement.

Here, we focused upon the MN problem in terms of knowledge representation and of automatic mechanism for reaching an agreement and the formalisation we gave is derived in subsequent steps. First, we defined a negotiating agent by two set of knowledge: stubborn and flexible. The stubborn knowledge of the agent is the unquestionable one and it represents the necessary properties to define the meaning of the set of terms the agent is negotiating. Instead, the flexible knowledge is the representation of the properties that the agent value as not necessary, but useful, to define the negotiating terms. A negotiating agent is willing to cede with respect to non necessary properties.

After the definition of an agent and of her knowledge, we defined the agreement condition as the situation in which all the agent or an acceptable part of them value as *good* the same proposal. Otherwise agents are in disagreement.

We identified four ways in which agents are in disagreement: absolute, essence, relative disagreement or compatibility. The disagreement relation is binary because it depends upon the relation between the knowledge of the agents, thus, for instance, Alice may have inconsistent knowledge with respect to the knowledge of Bob (absolute disagreement) and she may have a consistent but not generalised or restricted knowledge with respect to the knowledge of Charles (compatibility). The types of disagreement are useful for agents to understand why they are not in agreement and, maybe, in choosing the next proposal to perform. For instance, in a bilateral MN when both agents recognise that they are in absolute disagreement then the MN situation is that of Theorem 1 and no actions can improve the outcome of the negotiation, i.e. disagreement.

We focused upon the MN automation in an incremental way because we initially gave an algorithm for bilateral MN by Bargaining game and then for multiple parties MN by English Auction. We proved that both algorithm are correct and complete and we examine their computational costs.

The investigation we carried out can be extended by strategical rules in the definition of agents' behavior. Here, we assumed that each negotiating agent has a way to choose the next proposal to perform but no choosing function are defined. The strategy of the agents are important to analyse the development of the MN process and to the identification of the optimum result. In Game Theory literature, the negotiation process has optimal, maximal and minimal outcomes and researchers have studied the equilibrium condition to find them. To the best of our knowledge, in the current Artificial Intelligence literature there are no definitions of optimality, maximality and minimality of MN outcomes. These definitions are difficult to find because the non quantitative nature of the MN proposals. Someone may consider optimal for an agent her initial angle, and maximal any proposal with minimal "differences" with respect to the optimal one. A measure of distance between proposals may be necessary in order to identify a set of thresholds. With a measure of distance, we may consider maximal the proposals having the distance with respect to the optimum that is less than the correspondent threshold. Even more difficult to obtain is the notion of minimality. A proposal may be minimum when it corresponds to the stubborn set of axioms. Minimal would mean closest to the minimum. In general the difficulties with distances is that although a proposal that is acceptable for both agent would not minimal (or maximal or optimal) for one, it can have those properties for another agent. Therefore it would be nice to provide a method to employ the notion of distance between proposals to isolate proposals that result optimal, maximal or minimal from a "collective viewpoint. In our modelisation it is not possible to define when the outcome of the MN is optimal, or when it is maximal or minimal, since the strategy of the agents is not represented in the model.

This paper can also be extended by logical rules to represent the reasoning mechanism of the agent when they have to evaluate a received proposal and to make a new one.

Acknowledgments. We are indebted with Luca Viganò for general discussion, specific useful hints and suggestions. He also revised and suggested partly the running example. We also thank Leon van der Torre, Guido Governatori and Antonino Rotolo who read and commented an earlier version of the paper. This work has been partially developed starting from the PhD thesis of Elisa Burato *Meaning Negotiation in Multiple Agent System: an automated reasoning approach* and it is a generalisation and extension of previously published papers [6,7].

References

1. Atkinson, K., Bench-Capon, T.J.M., McBurney, P.: Arguing about cases as practical reasoning. In: ICAIL 2005: Proceedings of the 10th International Conference on Artificial Intelligence and Law, pp. 35–44 (2005)
2. Bench-Capon, T., Atkinson, K., Chorley, A.: Persuasion and value in legal argument. J. Logic and Computation 15(6), 1075–1097 (2005)
3. Bench-Capon, T.J.M.: Argument in artificial intelligence and law. Artif. Intell. Law 5(4), 249–261 (1997)
4. Benferhat, S., Kaci, S., Le Berre, D., Williams, M.-A.: Weakening conflicting information for iterated revision and knowledge integration. Artif. Intell. 153(1-2), 339–371 (2004)

5. Booth, R.: Social contraction and belief negotiation. Inf. Fusion 7(1), 19–34 (2006)
6. Burato, E., Cristani, M.: Contract clause negotiation by game theory. In: ICAIL, pp. 71–80. ACM (2007)
7. Burato, E., Cristani, M.: Learning as Meaning Negotiation: A Model Based on English Auction. In: Håkansson, A., Nguyen, N.T., Hartung, R.L., Howlett, R.J., Jain, L.C. (eds.) KES-AMSTA 2009. LNCS, vol. 5559, pp. 60–69. Springer, Heidelberg (2009)
8. Chang, C.-L., Lee, R.C.-T.: Symbolic Logic and Mechanical Theorem Proving. Academic Press (1987)
9. Daskalopulu, A., Sergot, M.: The representation of legal contracts. AI and Society 11(1/2), 6–17 (1997)
10. Douglas, W. (ed.): Argumentation Schemes for Presumptive Reasoning. Routledge (1996)
11. Douglas, W. (ed.): Argumentation Methods for Artificial Intelligence in Law. Cambridge University Press (2005)
12. Douglas, W., Christopher, R., Fabrizio, M. (eds.): Argumentation Schemes. Springer (2008)
13. Dung, P.M.: On the acceptability of arguments and its fundamental role in nonmonotonic reasoning, logic programming and n-person games. Artificial Intelligence 77(2), 321–357 (1995)
14. Dung, P.M., Mancarella, P., Toni, F.: Computing ideal sceptical argumentation. Artif. Intell. 171(10-15), 642–674 (2007)
15. Farley, A.M., Freeman, K.: Burden of proof in legal argumentation. In: ICAIL 1995: Proceedings of the 5th International Conference on Artificial Intelligence and Law, pp. 156–164. ACM, New York (1995)
16. Fermé, E., Rott, H.: Revision by comparison. Artif. Intell. 157(1-2), 5–47 (2004)
17. Gordon, T.F.: The pleadings game: formalizing procedural justice. In: ICAIL 1993: Proceedings of the 4th International Conference on Artificial Intelligence and Law, pp. 10–19. ACM, New York (1993)
18. Gordon, T.F., Prakken, H., Walton, D.: The carneades model of argument and burden of proof. Artificial Intelligence 171(10-15), 875–896 (2007)
19. Gordon, T.F., Walton, D.: Legal reasoning with argumentation schemes. In: ICAIL 2009: Proceedings of the 12th International Conference on Artificial Intelligence and Law, pp. 137–146. ACM, New York (2009)
20. Grégoire, E.: An unbiased approach to iterated fusion by weakening. Inf. Fusion 7(1), 35–40 (2006)
21. Grégoire, E., Konieczny, S.: Logic-based approaches to information fusion. Inf. Fusion 7(1), 4–18 (2006)
22. Hunter, A., Summerton, R.: A knowledge-based approach to merging information. Knowledge-Based Systems 19(8), 647–674 (2006)
23. Iván, C.C., Maguitman, A.G., Loui, R.P.: Logical models of argument. ACM Comput. Surv. 32(4), 337–383 (2000)
24. Kambe, S.: Bargaining with imperfect commitment. Games and Economic Behavior 28(2), 217–237 (1995)
25. Kambe, S.: Bargaining with imperfect commitment. Games and Economic Behavior 28(2), 217–237 (1995)
26. McBurney, P., Atkinson, K., Bench-Capon, T.: Justifying practical reasoning. In: Proceedings of the Fourth Workshop on Computational Models of Natural Argument (CMNA 2004), pp. 87–90 (2004)
27. Konieczny, S.: On the difference between merging knowledge bases and combining them. In: KR, pp. 135–144 (2000)

28. Kowalski, R.A., Toni, F.: Abstract argumentation. Artificial Intelligence and Law 4, 275–296 (1996)
29. Kraus, S., Sycara, K., Evenchik, A.: Reaching agreements through argumentation: a logical model and implementation. Artificial Intelligence 104(1-2), 1–69 (1998)
30. Liberatore, P., Schaerf, M.: Arbitration (or how to merge knowledge bases). IEEE Trans. on Knowl. and Data Eng. 10(1), 76–90 (1998)
31. Lin, J.: Integration of weighted knowledge bases. Artificial Intelligence 83(2), 363–378 (1996)
32. Maudet, N., Parsons, S., Rahwan, I.: Argumentation in Multi-Agent Systems: Context and Recent Developments. In: Maudet, N., Parsons, S., Rahwan, I. (eds.) ArgMAS 2006. LNCS (LNAI), vol. 4766, pp. 1–16. Springer, Heidelberg (2007)
33. Nash, J.: The bargaining problem. Econometrica 18(2), 155–162 (1950)
34. Oren, N., Norman, T.J., Preece, A.: Subjective logic and arguing with evidence. Artificial Intelligence 171(10-15), 838–854 (2007)
35. Parsons, S., Sierra, C., Jennings, N.: Agents that reason and negotiate by arguing. J. Logic and Computation 8(3), 261–292 (1998)
36. Pollock, J.L.: Justification and defeat. Artificial Intelligence 67(2), 377–407 (1994)
37. Pollock, J.L.: Defeasible reasoning with variable degrees of justification. Artificial Intelligence 133(1-2), 233–282 (2001)
38. Prakken, H., Reed, C., Walton, D.: Argumentation schemes and generalisations in reasoning about evidence. In: ICAIL 2003: Proceedings of the 9th International Conference on Artificial Intelligence and Law, pp. 32–41. ACM Press, New York (2003)
39. Prakken, H., Reed, C., Walton, D.: Dialogues about the burden of proof. In: ICAIL 2005: Proceedings of the 10th International Conference on Artificial Intelligence and Law, pp. 115–124. ACM, New York (2005)
40. Rubinelli, S.: Let me tell you why! when argumentation in doctor-patient interaction makes a difference. Argumentation 20(3), 353–375 (2006)
41. Rubinstein, A.: Perfect equilibrium in a bargaining model. Econometrica 50(1), 97–110 (1982)
42. Schroeder, M., Schweimeier, R.: Arguments and misunderstandings: Fuzzy unification for negotiating agents. Electronic Notes in Theoretical Computer Science 70(5), 1–19 (2002)
43. Thakur, S.S., Governatori, G., Padmanabhan, V., Eriksson Lundström, J.: Dialogue Games in Defeasible Logic. In: Orgun, M.A., Thornton, J. (eds.) AI 2007. LNCS (LNAI), vol. 4830, pp. 497–506. Springer, Heidelberg (2007)
44. Toulmin, S.: The Uses of Argument. Cambrigde University Press (2003)
45. van Eemeren, F.H. (ed.): Advances in pragma-dialectics. SicSat / Newport News, Vale Press, Amsterdam, VA (2002)
46. van Eemeren, F.H., Grootendorst, R. (eds.): Speech acts in argumentative discussions: A theoretical model for the analysis of discussions directed towards solving conflicts of opinion. Floris Publications, Dordrecht (1984)
47. van Eemeren, F.H., Grootendorst, R. (eds.): Argumentation, communication, and fallacies: a pragma-dialectical perspective. Erlbaum, Hillsdale (1992)
48. van Eemerena, F.H., Grootendorst, R. (eds.): A systematic theory of argumentation: The pragma-dialectical approach. Cambridge University Press, Cambridge (2004)
49. Walton, D.: Is there a burden of questioning? Artif. Intell. Law 11(1), 1–43 (2003)
50. Walton, D.: Justification of argument schemes. The Australasian Journal of Logic 3, 1–13 (2005)

51. Walton, D., Krabbe, E.: Commitment in Dialogue. State University of New York Press (1995)
52. Wurman, P., Wellman, M., Walsh, W.: A parametrization of the auction design space. Games and Economic Behavior 35(1-2), 304–338 (2001)
53. Zhang, D., Foo, N., Meyer, T., Kwok, R.: Negotiation as mutual belief revision. In: AAAI 2004: Proceedings of the 19th National Conference on Artificial Intelligence, pp. 317–322. AAAI Press / The MIT Press (2004)

Formalizing Emotional E-Commerce Agents for a Simple Negotiation Protocol

Veronica Jascanu, Nicolae Jascanu, and Severin Bumbaru

Department of Computer Science at University Dunarea de Jos of Galati Romania
{veronica.jascanu,nicolae.jascanu,severin.bumbaru}@ugal.ro

Abstract. Electronic commerce has become a central pillar of the Internet. Easy access, mobile devices with permanent connection, social networks and the real-time conversation streams have a big influence over B2C and C2C commerce. Currently, e-commerce becomes a social commerce, much closer to the traditional paradigm. The inclusion of emotional components in the act of trading complies with the current social trends and further approaches the electronic commerce to the traditional one. This paper continues the work on an emotional e-commerce platform by formalizing the customer, supplier and community agents. We present a simple negotiation protocol as a proof of concept.

Keywords: multi-agent systems, negotiation, e-commerce, affective computing.

1   Introduction

In recent years, e-commerce has gained a key role in modern society. Currently, online e-commerce includes many directions like advertising and marketing, payment mechanisms, security and privacy, reputation and trust, contracting and economic legislation, business management, distribution, sale and purchase of goods and services [1]. Huge amount of products and services offered online and the scenarios in which trading occur electronically, requires the development of automatic tools. The goal is to understand the user and to give what he wants or what he needs at the right time. Using a multi-agent system to represent the various entities participating at the act of commerce is a proven method for addressing the complexity of the system. In recent years, research on electronic commerce shaped around intelligent agents [2].

The goal for service providers is to understand the customer and give appropriate products and services. All major service providers have specific methods for monitoring and identification of consumer preferences. Amazon is the representative service that, based on the history of interactions between products and customers, is able to recommend similar products that may be useful in the given context. Over 60% of customers of the Netflix movie rental service are using automatic recommendations for choosing the movies. The emergence of social communities has a major impact on e-commerce. Many online commerce services have begun to include social elements to attract a greater number of clients. Opportunity to express your opinion, to talk about a product or service, to influence the others view

N.T. Nguyen (Ed.): Transactions on CCI VII, LNCS 7270, pp. 43–60, 2012.

represents a natural evolution of the online trading. There are studies about the dynamics of information flow in social groups and the influence of the online interactions over the real life. As electronic commerce becomes a permanent part of our contemporary society, the need to use intelligent and automated systems to facilitate various operations becomes more pressing. Intelligent agents may have significant contributions in several areas like necessity identification, products and suppliers brokering, social interactions, negotiations, payment, delivery, and after sales services.

Emotion is a fundamental aspect of life. Extensive research in psychology shows that even a random emotion, triggered by unrelated events can have a major influence over the decision. Incorporating emotions in decision-making system is necessary for solving complex problems and better understanding the decisions. Today, emotional theories are a multi-disciplinary research area, which includes cognitive psychology, neurology, genetics etc. One of the leaders in emotional research is the European project FP6 HUMAINE (Human-Machine Interaction Network on Emotion) [3], which bring together over 33 partners from 14 European countries. Emotional research has taken such a magnitude that the W3C consortium is seeking to define a markup emotional language EmotionML that standardizes the description of emotional knowledge [4].

We should treat emotions as knowledge in order to integrate them in a system. Various emotional models such as discrete models, in which each response to an action is associated to a distinct emotion, could represent the emotional knowledge. We could also represent the emotional knowledge by using dimensional models. The circumplex model is a powerful theoretical tool, which describes the relations between emotions, and predicts the effects on behavior and knowledge. The structural model assumes that emotional states, depending on intensity are positive, zero or negative correlated. Russell's circumplex is a two-dimensional model with the following axes: pleasant-unpleasant or valence and aroused-relaxed axis or excitation [5]. Russell's circumplex model proved over decades that it could represent an impressive number of distinct emotional terms. The model is currently being used in a variety of areas, from customer satisfaction analysis and extraction of qualitative knowledge related to products or services, to mobile applications and interactive games [6], [7].

Since the early 90's, emotional theories began to be used in the field of intelligent agents. Picard [8] separates the human emotion from the one of a software agent. For the agents, emotion is just a label that describes a certain state and the corresponding action. Many psychologists have developed emotional theories in such a way that researchers in artificial intelligence can easily assimilate them [9].

Electronic commerce should finally meet the client and his style of doing trades. Traditional trade has a history of thousands of years and the online version must take into account the many subtleties of human nature.

In this paper, we continue our work on a multi-agent system for electronic commerce that integrates emotional models for each one of the three agents: the customer, the supplier and the community [10]. Using the formalism proposed by Parsons and Sabater [11], [12], we formalize each agent for a simple negotiation protocol.

2   A Brief Presentation of the Emotional E-Commerce Platform

The platform has three agents: the customer, the supplier and the community. The community agent has a supportive role during negotiation for both customer and supplier agents (Figure 1). At its turn, each agent is specified as a multi-agent system using the formalism of Parsons and Sabater.

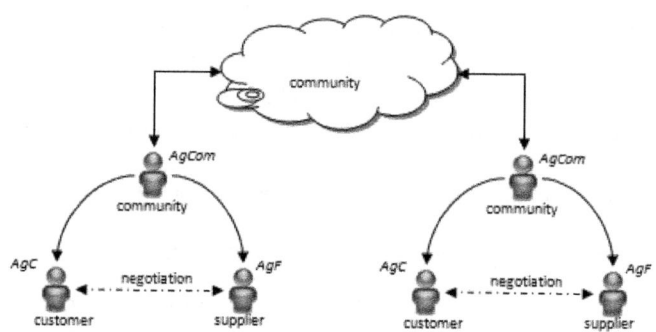

Fig. 1. The three agents of the multi-agent platform: AgC - customer agent, AgF - supplier agent and AgCom - community agent

Each agent has an emotional component and a specific knowledge acquisition method. Each agent uses the Russell's circumplex model of emotion in a slightly different way. The knowledge is acquired directly from the human partner whenever the system does not know details on the subject of negotiation.

2.1   The Customer Agent

It is not easy to know what we like or what we want. Considering the vast amount of easy accessible choices offered through internet, this becomes cumbersome. There are so many similar products and services that the selection process is difficult. Even for exactly the same merchandise, we have to decide between suppliers, after-sales services, delivery costs, warranties etc. Moreover, for humans, choosing is far from being an algorithmic process. It depends on personal experiences, taste, education, emotional state, current needs, desires, hopes etc. The choosing process is a trade-off between rational and emotional issues.

We are using the circumplex to gather the emotional aspects of the negotiation act. The system is able to capture the fine aspects of emotional-rational conflict inherent in any negotiation process.

Let us say, we want to have a vacation in a Caribbean resort. For a long time we wished for a vacation in Caribbean islands. Even if it is expensive and we have little available time, this year we will take our vacation. Of course, money and time are not the only issues. The resort should be near the beach, very quiet and have positive reviews regarding the existing services. We are willing to pay a little more for our dream, but if the price is too high, we will refuse the offer. However, if we find that the services are of poor quality during that period, the weather is bad, and there are not many tourists, it is possible for the rational to win.

It is hard to translate in words our trade-offs between all of this issues. Maybe we will accept a higher price and a not so quiet resort, but a twenty minutes time to the beach will make the offer inacceptable. What will happen if the time to the beach is ten minutes or five minutes? Considering that our dream was a resort situated on the beach, five minutes are still acceptable but for ten minutes, we should think twice.

Deciding which value is more important is not easy. When the product or service has more than two or three characteristics, it becomes difficult for a human to explain why it prefers one combination of values to other. Our intuition is that in the process of choosing are involved rational and emotional components, past experiences, intuition, desires and hopes.

Our work is based on the following three propositions[13]:

Proposition 1. The result of choice process is an emotional state.

Considering that the result is an emotional state, the knowledge acquisition problem is a little bit simplified. We could use several instruments and theories about emotions from psychology in order to capture and interpret that emotional state. We choose to use the circumplex theory, for emotional knowledge acquisition and representation. The circumplex model of affect is a continuous model, so the customer does not need to express the emotional state explicitly by choosing a word or a category. The customer should translate the emotional state in terms of pleasure and arousal, which is far simpler.

Proposition 2. When the customer marks an emotional reference on the circumplex, it considers that the other characteristics have at least good values.

The second proposition states that the customer should focus only on the value of one characteristic. For example, the customer will mark on circumplex his emotional state when the time to beach is ten minutes considering that the price and number of days are good. It is obvious that, if the time to beach is big, like twenty or twenty-five minutes, the other characteristics should be very good for the customer to accept the offer. We think that this process of focusing just on a single characteristic at each time mimics brain mechanisms when we face a complex decision.

Proposition 3. There is an order between emotional references from the commerce point of view.

Between two products or services, it is commonsense to choose the one that makes a greater pleasure or makes you feel better. Between twenty-five minutes and three minutes time to beach, for sure we will choose the last one. The pleasure degree is not the only one that influences our decision. The arousal level has also a strong influence in the final decision.

Figure 2 shows a negotiation configuration for a trip to the sea, with the following characteristics: price, number of days, time from the hotel to the beach. The system is able to decide between any sets of values for characteristics:

[B = 1000 $, G = 9 days, L = 10 min] and [B = 1000 $, O = 7 days, P = 6 min]

where B, G, L, O and P are represented on figure 2.

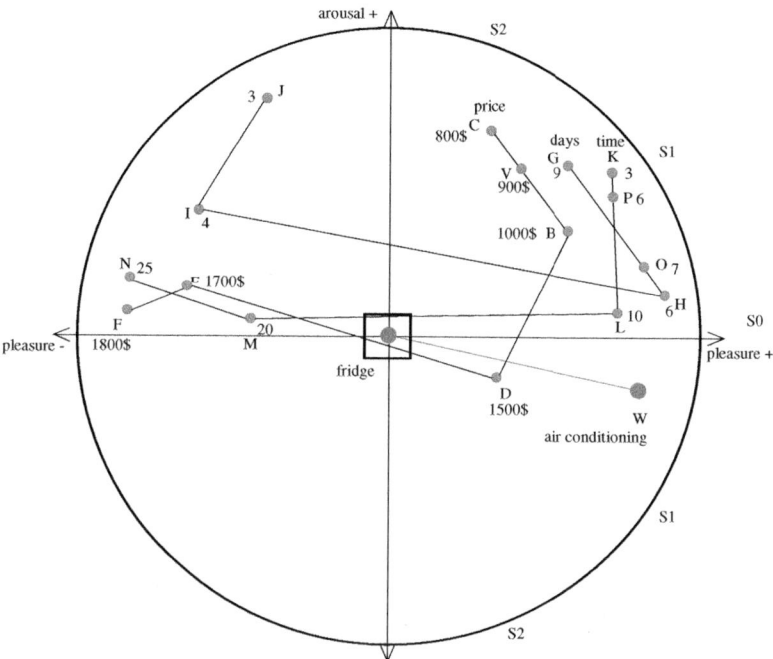

Fig. 2. The customer agent configuration for negotiating a sea trip. There are five characteristics: price, number of days, time to reach the beach, air conditioning unit and fridge.

Our purpose is to create a method that takes such an emotional configuration and transforms it into an algorithm able to decide between any two configurations of real values. In other words, we need an algorithm that calculates a cost between two successive values of the same characteristic. A first step is to order the emotional references. We call this step the quantitative inference.

The second step consists in finding the cost between the current emotional reference and the next one. The cost depends on many factors. Practically we move from one emotion to other and somehow we must capture this in the algorithm. We call this step the qualitative inference.

The *cost* value for the [B, G, L] configuration is 1.33 and for [B, O, P] of 1.36. In conclusion, the system will choose the configuration with a lower cost, namely [B, G, L]. To select between various configurations of negotiation, the system performs the quantitative analysis that provides an order for the emotional references on a characteristic (e.g. the ordering for the characteristic *price* is C, V, B, D, E and F) and the qualitative analysis that sets a *cost* for each segment separately. The order of the emotional moments is deduced by using a geometric surface and the cost is determined through a fuzzy inference system. With a sort and a cost per segment, the system can decide and choose between any configurations simultaneously. Explanations that are more detailed are presented in Jascanu's PhD Summary [14].

In Figure 3 there are several configurations and the corresponding costs.

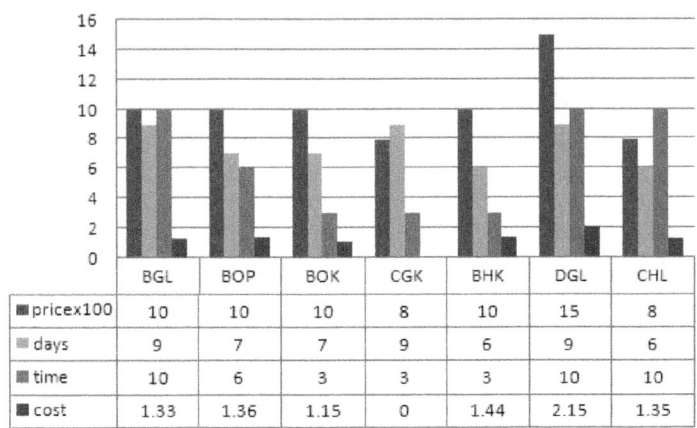

	BGL	BOP	BOK	CGK	BHK	DGL	CHL
■ pricex100	10	10	10	8	10	15	8
▨ days	9	7	7	9	6	9	6
■ time	10	6	3	3	3	10	10
■ cost	1.33	1.36	1.15	0	1.44	2.15	1.35

Fig. 3. Several configurations with the associated costs

The best combination of emotional references is C, G and K, which have a zero total cost, and the worst is F, J and N with a total cost of 7.15. In figure 3, we present several possible combinations and associated cost of each one. Let us take for example BGL = 1000$, 9 days, 10 min and DGL = 1500$, 9 days, 10 min. It is obvious that the BGL combination is preferred because of the smallest price. Between BGL = 1000$, 9 days, 10 min and BHK = 1000$, 6 days, 3 min we prefer BGL because 6 days are a too short vacation at a price of 1000$. The 3 minutes time to beach is very appealing, but a 6 days' vacation is too short for the price of 1000$. Interesting comparisons are between BGL, BOP and CHL. It is very difficult even for a human to tradeoff between price, days and time.

As an observation, if someone does not agree with the order of combinations, we must remember that this is the emotional configuration. The best person to analyze the results is the person who configured the circumplex. If the person is satisfied with the inference results than the model is valid.

2.2   The Supplier Agent

The supplier's agent specification can be easily adapted to any system already in production. In essence, the supplier sets a list of products and services, each entry having associated an order. The order represents the supplier's preferences for selling those products. Only the supplier knows the list in its entirety. The list is minimally exposed during negotiations.

The emotional component of the supplier agent is a step forward for the B2C and C2C commerce. For instance, during off-season it is more beneficial to negotiate the price for an accommodation than to impose a fixed one. Whenever it is hard to decide over rental details, it is better to use an emotional configuration and let the system to negotiate. The supplier uses the same model described for the customer agent, such as the system is consistent in representation. Table 1 shows a fragment from the supplier negotiation configuration. The last entry in table has two emotional characteristics defined using the circumplex model. The formalism used in table 1 was developed in order to be able to represent domain values for characteristics. A number of 10 to 12 persons is represented as $[\![\{10...12\}]\!]$ and a number of more than 15 persons as $[\![15\!\mapsto]\!]$. If there is a non-smoker room, we use the $[\![\|]\!]$ symbol. If the room has a fridge or any other feature, we use the $[\![\{\}]\!]$ symbol. The formalism is detailed in [13] and [14].

Table 1. The negotiation configuration for the supplier agent. The formalism is similar with the one at the customer agent.

!	* no. pers.	* price	* days	time	* smoker	A/C	fridge
$[\![\{9\}]\!]$	$[\![\{10...12\}]\!]$	$[\![\{350\}]\!]$	$[\![\{5\}]\!]$	$[\![\{4...6\}]\!]$	$[\![\|]\!]$	$[\![\{\}]\!]$	$[\![\{\}]\!]$
$[\![\{10\}]\!]$	$[\![15\!\mapsto]\!]$	$[\![\{280\}]\!]$	$[\![\{5...9\}]\!]$	$[\![\{4...6\}]\!]$	$[\![\|]\!]$	$[\![\{\}]\!]$	$[\![\{\}]\!]$
$[\![\{15\}]\!]$	*cplx*	*cplx*	$[\![\{3\}\!\mapsto]\!]$	$[\![\{4...6\}]\!]$	$[\![\|]\!]$	$[\![\{\}]\!]$	$[\![\{\}]\!]$

Each record of the table represents a negotiation configuration. Each configuration has several characteristics. The characteristic of selling priority (!) is one necessary characteristic for each configuration. We choose to use the term priority over profit because there are situations when the profit is not easy to be calculated or makes no sense. By using priorities the systems becomes very flexible. Depending on the sales, we could adjust the priority for a product or services.

Apart from the priority characteristic, the negotiation configuration could have other three types of characteristics:

1. *simple* – these are characteristics with values. The definition of the domain and the formalism used are identical with the one from the customer agent.
2. *non-negotiable* – this are mandatory characteristics for a customer. The configuration of the customer agent must have this characteristic. The values are not important, but the characteristic must exist. The supplier also uses the non-negotiable characteristics to force age, behavior or any other kind of restriction it may want. The customer should respect all conditions before the negotiation process starts.
3. *negotiable* – let us consider the following scenario: during high season, the supplier rents its resort only for groups of ten to fifteen persons at a fixed price. At the end of the season, it accepts also smaller groups of five to ten persons at a smaller fixed price. During off-season, the supplier is open to negotiations and accepts even groups of two or three persons. The inference engine using the circumplex model of affect could implement such a

situation in a similar way as the one from the customer agent. The supplier defines what is its emotional states regarding, for example, price and number of persons and the inference engine will negotiate using also this emotional characteristics.

2.3   The Community Agent

The community has a consultative role for both customer and supplier agents. E-commerce systems have solved the problem of facilitating search and selection of products and services, but they created another problem, namely: information over-loading. There are so many e-commerce stores, that the user hardly finds what he needs. The selection of a product even by a single parameter, the *price*, proves to be a laborious job. Furthermore, if you do not know exactly what or where to look it is even more difficult to choose from the huge available supplies. Let us say that we look for supplementary information regarding our vacation to Caribbean islands. Many travel websites lists the opinions of the tourists about their visited places. The opinion is stored as a textual description along with a rate. The textual description is the most helpful source of information for us. Here, the tourists describe at their best the experiences. They tell what they liked or not, what was funny, interesting or boring. They reveal how they were treated, what was the quality of services, what was bad or what was wrong. On the other side, the rating system is very inflexible. There are several very general fields and the tourist tries to convert his or her experience to a five star grade. Then, the system aggregates all this ratings showing the final rates for each field. The idea of showing an overview is very good but the rating system cannot capture the subtleties of the felt experience. On the other hand, reading hundreds of textual descriptions is very confusing.

Table 2 represents the structure of the recording for an emotional opinion.

Table 2. The negotiation configuration for the supplier agent. The formalism is similar with the one at the customer agent.

Context	Keywords: holiday, Greece, room-service, landscape
Resource link: image, video, text, internet	
Default fields	
Timestamp	
Location	
User profile	
Emotional opinion	
Keywords	Cleanness, service quality, quietness
EmotionML	Will be used EmotionML to represent the emotion
Comments	Comments and descriptions
Resource link: image, video, text, internet	
Emotional opinion	
.....	
Emotional opinion	
.....	

The knowledge base of the community agent is an emotional one. Instead of writing a textual description with your feelings about a place or event, you could place an emotional reference on the circumplex. We describe the emotional references using a set of keywords as in the figure 4. Therefore, the keywords are associated with a feeling. Therefore, you are able to express your feelings at that moment. During a vacation, you will easily express tenths of emotional references. All this references could easily replace the textual description. Moreover, the references are already rated in a very intuitive and flexible system. The system will aggregate all the information even there are many opinions. An overview for a vacation to the Caribbean islands will show what is exciting, boring or relaxing.

The circumplex model is used to acquire emotional impressions on any topic or experience. The emotional opinions are indexed and can be interrogated in various ways. The emotional opinions are qualitative parameters of products and services. Thus, a customer agent that has no previous experience in a specific negotiation could use the information provided by the community. Such qualitative knowledge is extremely useful during negotiation, and can significantly influence the choices of both agents. In addition, for the supplier agent, the community plays a major role. The agent will better understand the product or service and will change the negotiation parameters appropriately.

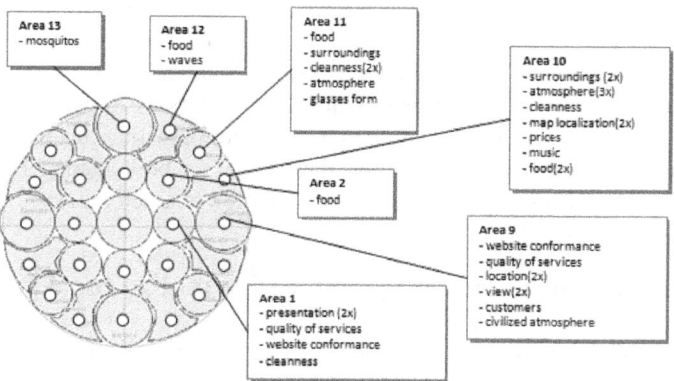

Fig. 4. The emotional knowledge acquired during a practical experiment. The subjects expressed feelings about a touristic location. The figure shows information only for the first quadrant.

3   A Simple Negotiation Protocol

The customer agent is able to analyze and sort out any number of negotiation instances received from the supplier. The negotiation starts with customer agent sending the most favorable configuration: the one with a zero cost (figure 5). In our case, the best configuration is [800$, 9 days, 3 min]. The supplier agent receives this configuration, and for each characteristic it tries to find the best offer around the

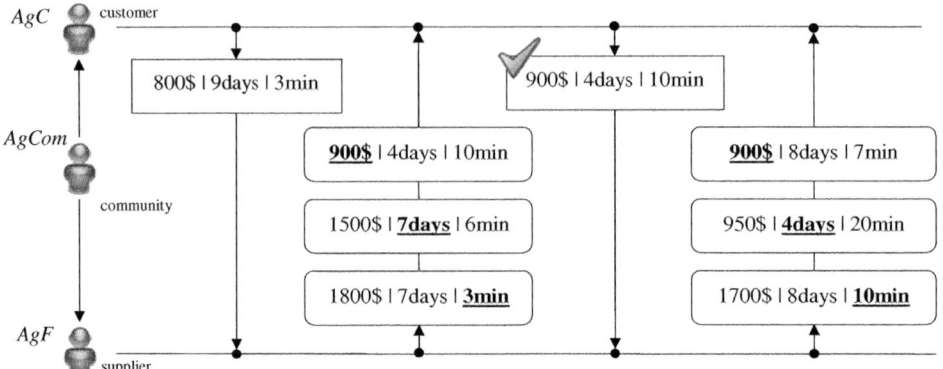

Fig. 5. The sequence diagram of a simple negotiation protocol between customer and supplier agents

specified value. Therefore, the supplier will generate three offers. The customer agent calculates the offers and selects the one with the minimal cost. In this case, the selected offer is [900$, 4 days, 10 min]. The agent sends this negotiation instance to the supplier agent. The costs of the newly generated offers are bigger so that the negotiation is over.

We keep the protocol very simple as a proof of concept. The ability of customer agent to sort out any number of negotiation instances is essential for our algorithm. Therefore, we cut down many negotiation steps between the customer and supplier agents. The community agent has a consultative role for both agents. The information from community acts as a weight over the negotiation characteristics.

4   Using a Multi-context System to Formalize the Agents

In order to implement a practical platform, we have formalized the customer, supplier and community agents using the multi-context approach of Parsons and Sabater. The customer agent is a multi-agent system with the following entities (figure 6):

- GM (Goal Manager) - generates the necessary goals to solve a situation and monitor their status;
- PM (Plan Manager) - it is a repository of plans to accomplish each goal;
- CM (Configuration Manager) - represents the active negotiation configuration;
- IM (Instance Manager) - it is a store for the negotiation instances received from the supplier;
- IE (Inference Engine) - it calculates the cost of each received instance and selects the one with the smallest cost;
- SM (Social Manager) - it is the communication node between internal and external entities.

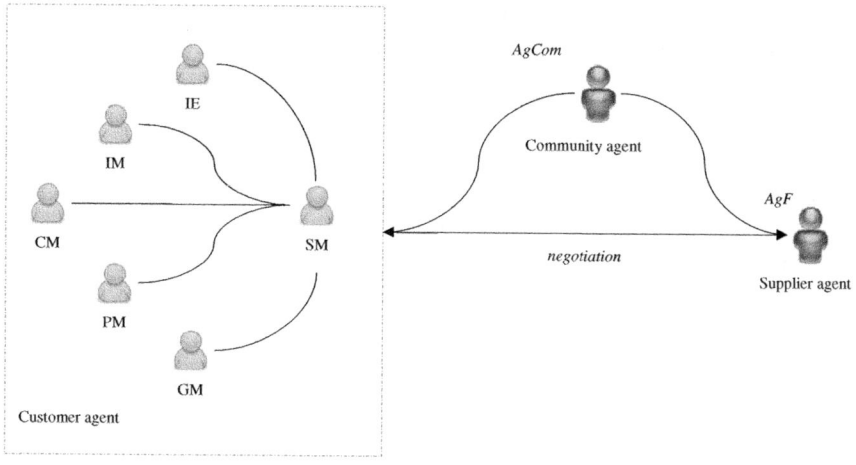

Fig. 6. The functional schema of the customer agent

The Goal Manager has the following internal units (figure 7):

- CU (Communication Unit) - receives and sends messages;
- G (Goals) - it is a repository of goals;
- C/CR (Community opinions and costs storage) - it is a storage unit for the community opinions and the calculated costs of negotiation instances;
- P - it is a storage for plans

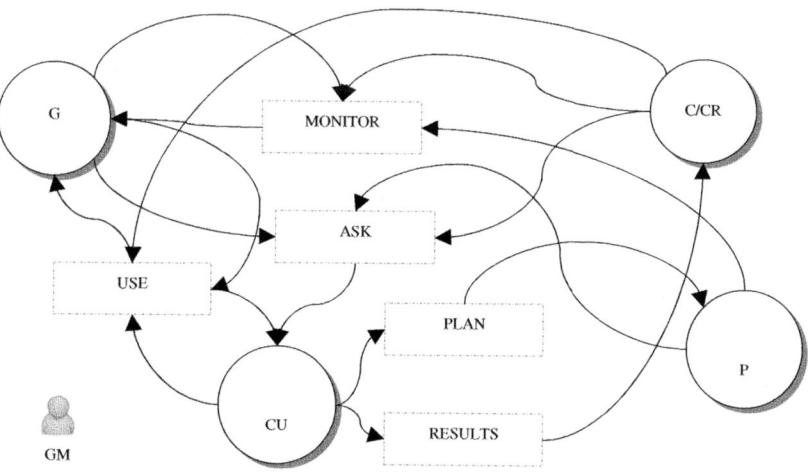

Fig. 7. GM (Goal Manger) - generates the necessary goals to solve a situation

We define a *negotiation offer* as the sets of values sent by the supplier agent. The *negotiation instance* represents the set of values received by the supplier agent.

$$O_F = \{[id_{ch1},(ch_1,val),(ch_2,val),.......]...\}$$
$$I_C = \{[(ch_1,val),(ch_2,val),.......]\}$$
$$\tag{1}$$

where ch is the characteristic and val is the value.

For each entity with have bridge rules that relates formulae in different units. When the communication unit CU receives an *ask* message from the social manager agent SM to analyze the supplier's *offer*, the USE bridge generates the analyze goal G.

$$USE = \frac{CU > ask(^{AgC}\!/_{SM},{}^{AgC}\!/_{GM},offer(AgC,AgF,O_F),\{\})}{G:goal(analyze(O_F))} . \tag{2}$$

If the functional unit G has fulfilled its goals (*done*) and the computation was not yet flagged as finished, and we have the *result* at the C/CR unit, the CU unit may send the *answer* to the IM agent.

$$USE = \frac{\begin{array}{l} G:done(community(O_F)) \\ G:done(analyzeEach(O_F)) \\ G:not(done(analyze(O_F))) \\ C/CR:result(analyzeEach(O_F),\{I_C\}) \end{array}}{CU:answer(^{AgC}\!/_{GM},{}^{AgC}\!/_{IM},result(O_F,I_C))} . \tag{3}$$
$$G:done(analyze(O_F))$$

When there is a new analyze goal in the functional unit G, the MONITOR bridge will verify if there is a specific plan at functional unit P. If there isn't one, this will be flagged at unit G.

$$. \; MONITOR = \frac{\begin{array}{l} G:goal(analyze(O_F)) \\ P:not(plan(O_F)) \end{array}}{G:not(done(analyze(O_F)))} \tag{4}$$

As soon as the plan exists at unit P, the bridge MONITOR will generate the new goals accordingly. The *community* and *analyzeEach* commands are explained for the plan agent PM.

$$. \; MONITOR = \frac{\begin{array}{l} P:plan(O_F,P)) \\ G:not(done(analyze(O_F))) \end{array}}{\begin{array}{l} G:goal(community(O_F)) \\ G:goal(analyzeEach(O_F)) \end{array}} \tag{5}$$

If the bridge MONITOR detects that the community opinions and the cost for each offer are not present at the functional unit C/CR, will flag this.

$$MONITOR = \frac{\begin{array}{l} G:goal(community(O_F)) \\ C\,/\,CR:not(result(community(O_F),\{\})) \end{array}}{G:not(done(community(O_F)))}$$

$$MONITOR = \frac{\begin{array}{l} G:goal(analyzeEach(O_F)) \\ C\,/\,CR:not(result(analyzeEach(O_F),\{\})) \end{array}}{G:not(done(analyzeEach(O_F)))}$$

(6)

When the bridge unit MONITOR has the results, it flags the goals as done.

$$MONITOR = \frac{\begin{array}{l} G:not(done(community(O_F))) \\ C\,/\,CR:result(community(O_F),\{R\}) \end{array}}{G:done(community(O_F))}$$

$$MONITOR = \frac{\begin{array}{l} G:not(done(analyzeEach(O_F))) \\ C\,/\,CR:result(analyzeEach(O_F),\{I_C\}) \end{array}}{G:done(analyzeEach(O_F))}$$

(7)

If the bridge unit ASK, detects that there is a goal and it is not flagged as done because there is no plan for this, it will make a request to the PM agent to get the corresponding plan.

$$ASK = \frac{\begin{array}{l} G:goal(analyze(O_F)) \\ G:not(done(analyze(O_F))) \\ P:not(plan(O_F)) \end{array}}{CU:ask(^{AgC}\!/\!_{GM},{}^{AgC}\!/\!_{PM},goal(analyze(O_F)),\{\})}.$$

(8)

If ASK unit detects that for *community* and *analyzeEach* there are no results, it will send a request for results to the CM agent.

$$ASK = \frac{\begin{array}{l} G:not(done(community(O_F))) \\ C\,/\,CR:not(result(community(O_F),\{\})) \end{array}}{CU:ask(^{AgC}\!/\!_{GM},{}^{AgC}\!/\!_{CM},community(O_F))}$$

$$ASK = \frac{\begin{array}{l} G:not(done(analyzeEach(O_F))) \\ C\,/\,CR:not(result(analyzeEach(O_F),\{\})) \end{array}}{CU:ask(^{AgC}\!/\!_{GM},{}^{AgC}\!/\!_{CM},analyzeEach(O_F))}$$

(9)

The bridge unit PLAN get the plans through the CU unit from the PM agent.

$$PLAN = \frac{CU>answer(^{AgC}\!/\!_{PM},{}^{AgC}\!/\!_{GM},goal(analyze(O_F)),\{P\})}{P:plan(O_F,P)}.$$

(10)

The bridge unit RESULTS gets the result and store it at the C/CR agent.

$$RESULTS = \frac{CU > answer(^{AgC}\!/\!_{CM}, ^{AgC}\!/\!_{GM}, result(community(O_F),\{R\}))}{C/CR : result(community(O_F),\{R\})} \tag{11}$$

$$RESULTS = \frac{CU > answer(^{AgC}\!/\!_{IE}, ^{AgC}\!/\!_{GM}, result(analyzeEach(O_F),\{I_C\}))}{C/CR : result(analyzeEach(O_F),\{I_C\})}$$

The plans manager agent PM is a repository of plans for goals. The plans are delivered through the functional communication unit CU. The functional unit P is the repository.

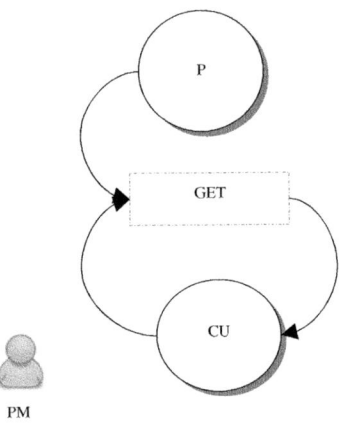

Fig. 8. PM - Plan Manger – store the plans

When a request for plan from agent G comes, the bridge unit GET will verify the repository and will send the corresponding plan through the Cu unit.

$$GET = \frac{\begin{array}{c} CU > ask(^{AgC}\!/\!_{GM}, ^{AgC}\!/\!_{PM}, goal(analyze(O_F)),\{\}), \\ P : plan(analyze(O_F)) \end{array}}{\begin{array}{c} CU : answer(^{AgC}\!/\!_{PM}, ^{AgC}\!/\!_{GM}, goal(analyze(O_F)), \\ \{community(O_F) \wedge analyzeEach(O_F)\}) \end{array}} \tag{12}$$

The configuration manager agent CM stores the current negotiation configuration at the functional unit CNeg and the community opinion on the negotiation configuration at the functional unit Cmnty. The community agent will be consulted only once during the negation, because the community opinion is highly probable to remain the same.

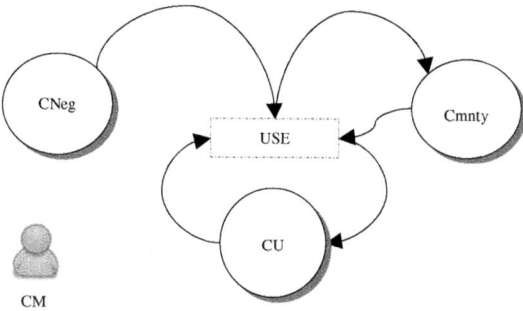

Fig. 9. CM – Configuration Manager – repository of negotiation configurations

When an ASK request comes from GM agent, the bridge unit USE will verify if the functional unit CMNTY already has the information regarding the community opinion. If such an information does not exist, a request is send to the community agent.

$$USE = \frac{CU > ask(^{AgC}\!/\!_{GM}, ^{AgC}\!/\!_{CM}, community(O_F))}{Cmnty : not(result(community(O_F), \{\}))} \frac{CNeg : configuration(X)}{CU : ask(^{AgC}\!/\!_{CM}, ^{AgC}\!/\!_{SM}, seek(AgCom, AgC, X))}. \tag{13}$$

When the response comes from the community agent, the bridge unit USE will refresh the information from the CMNTY unit.

$$USE = \frac{CU > answer(^{AgC}\!/\!_{SM}, ^{AgC}\!/\!_{CM}, result(AgCom, AgC, X, R))}{Cmnty : result(community(O_F), R)}. \tag{14}$$

The community opinion will be transmitted to the agent GM

$$USE = \frac{Cmnty : result(community(O_F), \{R\})}{CU : answer(^{AgC}\!/\!_{CM}, ^{AgC}\!/\!_{GM}, result(community(O_F), \{R\}))}. \tag{15}$$

If the functional unit CU receives an *analyzeEach* request, this request will be transmitted to the IE inference engine agent that will calculate the cost. Alongside the offer, the agent will transmit also the negotiation configuration X and the community opinion R.

$$USE = \frac{CU > ask(^{AgC}\!/\!_{GM}, ^{AgC}\!/\!_{CM}, analyzeEach(O_F))}{CU : ask(^{AgC}\!/\!_{CM}, ^{AgC}\!/\!_{IE}, analyze(X, O_F, R))}. \tag{16}$$

The IE inference engine agent receives requests for cost calculations for an instance of the negotiation configuration.

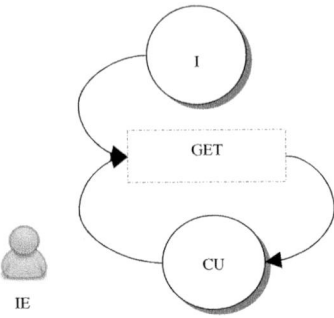

Fig. 10. IE – inference engine agent

The bridge unit GET sends to the functional unit I the request for cost calculation.

$$GET = \frac{CU > ask(^{AgC}/_{CM}, {^{AgC}}/_{IE}, analyze(X, O_F, R))}{I : analyze(X, O_F, R)}. \tag{17}$$

When the cost is calculated, the CU unit will send the result directly at the GM agent.

$$GET = \frac{I : result(analyze(X, O_F, R), \{I_C\})}{CU : answer(^{AgC}/_{IE}, {^{AgC}}/_{GM}, result(analyzeEach(O_F), \{I_C\}))}. \tag{18}$$

The IM agent updates its knowledge base and sends the instance to the SM agent.

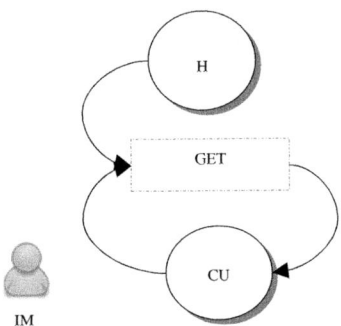

Fig. 11. IM – instance manager repository agent

The results are stored at the functional unit H. The response is transmitted to the supplier agent through the SM social manager agent.

$$USE = \frac{CU > answer(^{AgC}/_{GM}, {^{AgC}}/_{IM}, result(O_F, I_C))}{H : update(result(O_F, I_C))}$$

$$USE = \frac{H : update(result(O_F, I_C))}{CU : answer(^{AgC}/_{IM}, {^{AgC}}/_{SM}, check(AgF, AgC, I_C), \{\})} \tag{19}$$

The SM social manager agent is a communication router that translates messages from and to the supplier agent and routes the messages internally.

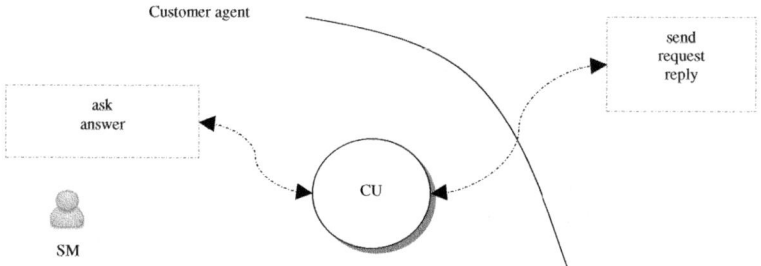

Fig. 12. SM (Social Manger) - routes the messages internally and externally

The *send* messages from the supplier agent are transformed in internal ASK messages while the *answer* ones are transformed in external *send* messages.

$$send(AgF, {}^{AgC}\!\big/\!_{SM}, offer(AgC, AgF, O_F))$$
$$\rightarrow ask({}^{AgC}\!\big/\!_{SM}, {}^{AgC}\!\big/\!_{GM}, offer(AgC, AgF, O_F), \{\})$$

$$answer({}^{AgC}\!\big/\!_{IM}, {}^{AgC}\!\big/\!_{SM}, check(AgF, AgC, I_C), \{\})$$
$$\rightarrow send(AgC, {}^{AgF}\!\big/\!_{SM}, check(AgF, AgC, I_C))$$

$$(20)$$

5   Conclusion

In this paper, we briefly presented a simple negotiation protocol and the formalism for agents to accomplish it. Using the formalism of Parsons and Sabater, we have formalized completely each agent. At present time, we have implemented a prototype using the JADE multi-agent platform. Regarding the community agent, we have an Android mobile application that gathers emotional knowledge in different experiments. Further research will augment the negotiation protocol with an argumentation framework that deals with the defined emotional aspects. We think that this is a natural step forward for a more human-like experience for the retail area of electronic commerce.

References

1. Sierra, C., Dignum, F.P.M.: Agent-Mediated Electronic Commerce: Scientific and Technological Roadmap. In: Sierra, C., Dignum, F.P.M. (eds.) AgentLink 2000. LNCS (LNAI), vol. 1991, pp. 1–8. Springer, Heidelberg (2001)

2. Fatima, S.S., Wooldridge, M.J., Jennings, N.R.: On Efficient Procedures for Multi-issue Negotiation. In: Fasli, M., Shehory, O. (eds.) TADA/AMEC 2006. LNCS (LNAI), vol. 4452, pp. 31–45. Springer, Heidelberg (2007)
3. Humaine Network of Excellence, IST FP6 (2004), http://www.emotion-research.net
4. Emotion Markup Language EmotionML, World Wide Web Consortium W3C (2008), http://www.w3.org/2005/Incubator/emotion/XGR-emotionml-20081120/
5. Russell, J.: A circumplex model of affect. In: Judd, C., Simpson, J., King, L. (eds.) Journal of Personality and Social Psychology, vol. 39(6), pp. 1161–1178 (1980)
6. Stahl, A.: Designing for Emotional Expressivity. Licentiate Thesis. Institute of Design, Umea University, Sweden (2006)
7. Adam, C.: The Emotions: From Psychological Theories to Logical Formalization and Implementation in a BDI agent. PhD Thesis, Institut de Recherche en Informatique de Toulouse - IRIT, France (2007)
8. Picard, R.W.: Affective Computing. MIT Press, 55 Hayward Street, Cambridge, MA 02142-1493, USA (1997) ISBN 0-262-16170-2
9. Ortony, A., Clore, G.L., Collins, A.: The cognitive structure of emotions. Cambridge University Press, Trumpington Street, NY 10011-4211, USA (1988) ISBN 0-521-35364-5
10. Jascanu, N., Jascanu, V., Bumbaru, S.: Toward Emotional E-Commerce: The Customer Agent. In: Lovrek, I., Howlett, R.J., Jain, L.C. (eds.) KES 2008, Part I. LNCS (LNAI), vol. 5177, pp. 202–209. Springer, Heidelberg (2008)
11. Parsons, S., Jennings, N.R., Sabater, J., Sierra, C.: Agent Specification Using Multi-context Systems. In: d'Inverno, M., Luck, M., Fisher, M., Preist, C. (eds.) UKMAS Workshops 1996-2000. LNCS (LNAI), vol. 2403, pp. 205–226. Springer, Heidelberg (2002)
12. Sabater, J., Sierra, C., Parsons, S., Jennings, N.R.: Using Multi-context Systems to Engineer Executable Agents. In: Jennings, N.R., Lesperance, Y. (eds.) ATAL 1999. LNCS, vol. 1757, pp. 260–276. Springer, Heidelberg (2000)
13. Jascanu, N., Jascanu, V., Bumbaru, S.: Toward Emotional E-Commerce. In: Hâkansson, A., Hartung, R., Nguyen, N.T. (eds.) Agent and Multi-agent Technology for Internet and Enterprise Systems. SCI, vol. 289, pp. 293–321. Springer, Heidelberg (2010)
14. Jascanu, N.: Intelligent software agents for electronic commerce. Contributions. PhD Summary, supervisor Prof.dr.ing. Severin Bumbaru, Department of Computer Science, University Dunarea de Jos of Galati (2009), http://wwww.ugal.ro/doc/Rezumat_teza_doctorat_Jascanu_Nicolae.pdf (available in Romanian)

Engineering Multi-Agent Systems
through Statecharts-Based JADE Agents and Tools

Giancarlo Fortino, Francesco Rango, and Wilma Russo

Dept. of Electronics, Informatics and Systems (DEIS) – University of Calabria,
Via P. Bucci, cubo 41C, 87036 Rende (CS), Italy
{g.fortino,w.russo}@unical.it, frango@si.deis.unical.it

Abstract. The JADE framework, which is one of the most used in the AOSE
community to program and execute multi-agent systems (MASs), still needs to
be further supported by methods and tools for enabling a more effective
modeling and prototyping of JADE-based MASs. In this paper we propose a
framework and a related tool supporting a Statecharts-based development of
JADE-based MAS with the purpose of providing an effective approach for
engineering multi-agent systems and leveraging agent-oriented development
methodologies and processes adopting JADE as target agent platform. In
particular, a framework for programming JADE behaviors through a variant of
the Statecharts, named Distilled StateCharts (DSCs), has been first developed
by enhancing the JADE add-on HSMBehaviour. Then, to enable rapid
prototyping of JADE agents, a visual tool for DSCs has been extended with
translation rules based on the developed framework that allows to automatically
translate DSC specifications into DSC-based JADE behaviors. The proposed
approach is exemplified through a case study concerning an agent-based
meeting organization system.

Keywords: Statecharts, Software agents, JADE, Visual programming, Automatic
code generation, CASE tool.

1   Introduction

In the last decade the agent oriented software engineering (AOSE) research area has
produced a rich set of methodologies and tools that can be actually exploited for the
development of complex software systems in terms of multi-agent systems (MASs)
[1]. In parallel with AOSE, the mainstream software engineering area has driven
UML 2.0 [2] along with related methodologies and tools to become the *de facto*
standard for the development of software systems. In particular, the UML state
machines, derived from the Harel's Statecharts [3], are an effective and widely
adopted formalism for the specification of active component behaviors and protocols
in general-purpose and real-time systems. It is widely recognized that the benefits
provided by Statecharts for engineering complex software systems are mainly visual
programming, executable specifications, protocol-oriented specifications, and a set of
CASE tools facilitating software development. In this context, to effectively develop

N.T. Nguyen (Ed.): Transactions on CCI VII, LNCS 7270, pp. 61–81, 2012.
© Springer-Verlag Berlin Heidelberg 2012

multi-agent systems (MAS), models, frameworks and tools are needed to support flexible and rigorous specifications and subsequent implementations of agent behaviors and agent-to-agent interaction protocols [4]. Thus the use of Statecharts-based models, frameworks and tools for the development of MASs could provide the same benefits in the AOSE research area as those provided in the context of traditional software engineering. However, in the AOSE research area, Statecharts are still under-used to specify agent behaviors and protocols even though some proposed agent models founded on different types of state machines are available [5, 6, 7, 8, 9, 10, 12].

In this paper we propose programming frameworks and techniques supporting a Statecharts-based development of JADE-based MASs. The main contribution of this paper is twofold: (i) the integration of Statecharts and MASs to deliver the same important benefits provided by Statecharts for the engineering of traditional software systems; (ii) the definition of a Statecharts-driven development method for the JADE platform which is one of the most used agent platform in the agent community. Moreover, the proposed approach can be fruitfully exploited to leverage already existing agent-oriented development methodologies and processes adopting JADE as target agent platform (e.g. INGENIAS [16], PASSI [17], MESSAGE [18]). In particular, a framework for programming JADE behaviors through the Distilled StateCharts (DSCs) formalism, named DistilledStateChartBehaviour, has been developed by enhancing the JADE HSMBehaviour. To enable rapid prototyping of JADE agents, a CASE tool obtained by enhancing the ELDATool with a new component based on the DistilledStateChartBehaviour for automatic code generation of DSC-based behaviors into JADE code, is made available. The proposed approach is exemplified through a case study regarding an agent-based meeting organization system.

The rest of this paper is organized as follows. Section 2 discusses and compares related work. In section 3, after an introduction of the basic concepts of the Distilled StateCharts formalism, the JADE DistilledStateChartBehaviour is described. In section 4 a CASE tool-driven approach for engineering JADE-based MAS from modeling to implementation, is presented. Section 5 details a case study exemplifying the proposed Statecharts-based approach and provides an experimental evaluation of the scalability of the developed MAS. Finally, conclusions are drawn and on-going work delineated.

2   Related Work

To date several proposals are available which provide frameworks based on state machines to design and implement agent behaviors and interactions. Among such proposals, the most known and interesting ones are the JADE FSMBehaviour [5], the SmartAgent framework [6], the ELDA agent model [7], and the Bond agent framework [8]. In particular, the JADE framework [5], one of the most used agent-oriented framework in academy and industry, provides the FSMBehaviour [9] for the modeling of agent behaviors based on finite state machines (FSMs). However agent behavior programming is not flexible as it does not rely on ECA (Event-Condition-Action)-rule based transitions, and does not provide important mechanisms for reducing behavior complexity such as well-structured OR-decomposition and history entrances. In particular, although states of the FSMBehaviour can be FSMBehaviours or other behaviors, mechanisms for handling this induced state hierarchy are not provided. The SmartAgent model [10, 6] extends the JADE CompositeBehaviour and provides a behavior based on hierarchical state machines driven by ECA rules, named HSMBehaviour. However, the HSMBehaviour does not even support shallow and deep history entrance mechanisms, useful for reducing behavior complexity even further and for transparently archiving agent states. In addition, although visual modeling and emulation of HSMBehaviour agents can be done with the provided HSMEditor [11], automatic translation of modeled agents into JADE code is not supported. The ELDA (Event-driven Lightweight Distilled Statecharts-based Agents) agent model [7] is based on a Statecharts-like machine, providing or-decomposition and history entrance mechanisms, named Distilled StateCharts [12] suitable for the modeling of lightweight agents for distributed computing. Moreover, they can be effectively modeled through the ELDATool, a graphical tool for visual specification, automatic code translation and simulation of ELDA-based systems [13]. However, an ELDA-based execution platform is not yet available so confining the use of ELDA agents in the MAS simulation domain. The behavior of the Bond agents [8] is based on a multi-plane state machine where each plane is modeled as an FSM. However, the Bond agent model does not offer the state hierarchy, history mechanisms, and tools for automating agent prototyping. Finally other previous agent frameworks are ZEUS [14], which provides an execution subsystem for non-hierarchical state machine-based agents, and the JACKAL conversation engine that also uses a state machine model [15]. In Table 1 a comparison in terms of behavioral, interaction and mobility models among the aforementioned frameworks is provided. In particular, the differences about behavioral models are those discussed above whereas, with respect to the interaction models, they are mainly based on messages apart from Bond and ELDA which rely on multiple coordination models (not only messages but also tuple spaces and publish/subscribe); moreover, the mobility model is of the weak type apart from ELDA which allows for coarse-grain strong mobility [7].

Table 1. Comparison among state machine oriented frameworks

FRAMEWORKS/MODELS	BEHAVIOURAL	INTERACTION	MOBILITY
Jade	flat finite state machines (FSMBehaviour)	Message passing	Weak
SmartAgent	hierarchical finite state machines (HSMBehaviour)	Message passing	Weak
Bond	multi-plane state machine: each plane is an FSM	Message passing, TSpace and P/S	Weak
Actors	active objects with state variables and action methods	Message passing	Weak
ZEUS	flat finite state machines	Message passing	Weak
JACKAL	flat finite state machines	Message passing	Weak
ELDA	Distilled StateCharts	Multi-coordination	Coarse-grain Strong

3   Statecharts-Based JADE Agents

In this section, the DSC formalism, which provides a powerful and rich set of modeling concepts enabling an effective specification of agent behavior, is overviewed. Then, the proposed framework for programming DSC-based JADE agents, which enhances JADE with the benefits deriving from Statecharts, is described.

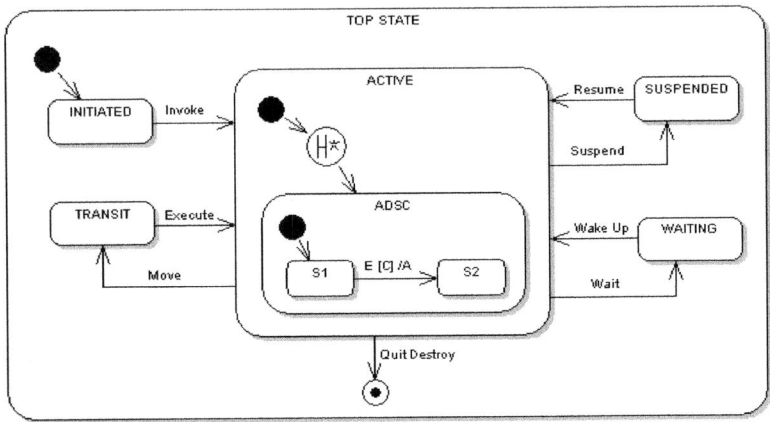

Fig. 1. A FIPA compliant DSC-based agent behavior

3.1   The Distilled StateCharts Model

The Distilled StateCharts (DSCs) formalism [12] is derived from the Harel's Statecharts through a distillation process, purposely carried out for the modeling of lightweight mobile agent behavior, which led to the following structural/semantics differences between Statecharts and DSCs:

- State entry and exit actions as well as activities are empty so actions can be only hooked to transitions;
- Each composite state has a pseudo initial state from which the default entrance of the composite state originates;
- Transitions (apart from default entrances and default history entrances) are always labeled by an event;
- Default entrance and default history entrances can only be labeled with an action;
- And-decomposition of states and related synchronization modeling constructs are not used as DSCs were introduced for supporting the behavioral modeling of single-threaded agents;
- Run-to-completion step semantics, defined according to the UML state machines semantics [19], are adopted.

A DSC-based agent behavior relies on an enhanced basic template built according to the FIPA agent lifecycle [20] which JADE agents are compliant with (see Figure 1). In particular, the ACTIVE state, in which an agent carries out its goal-oriented tasks, is always entered through a deep history entrance (H*) whose default history entrance targets the active DSC (ADSC) state, which actually models the active agent behavior. The default entrance of ACTIVE targeting H* allows restoring the agent execution state after agent migration and, in general, after agent suspension.

3.2   A Framework for Programming DSC-Based JADE Agents

A new JADE behavior, named DistilledStateChartBehaviour, has been defined to program JADE agents through the DSC formalism. In particular, the DistilledStateChartBehaviour, which is defined by enhancing the HSMBehaviour [10, 6] with the DSC mechanisms, specifically implements the history mechanisms that allow a partial (through shallow history H) or full (through deep history H*) recovery of the state history when re-entering into any state previously exited.

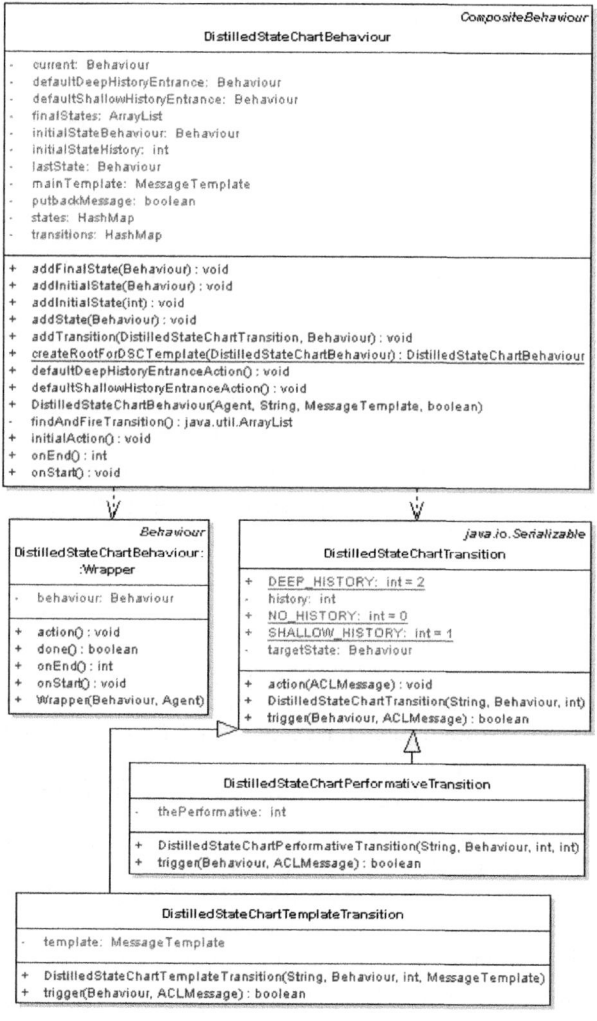

Fig. 2. Simplified class diagram of the JADE DistilledStateChartBehaviour

Figure 2 shows a simplified UML class diagram of the DistilledStateChartBehaviour. In particular, the DistilledStateChartBehaviour inherits from the JADE CompositeBehaviour and includes both a set of nested DistilledStateChartBehaviours and other Behaviours, which represent the *states* of the DSC. It maintains the list of *transitions*, represented by the DistilledStateChartTransition class, and handles the event-driven mechanism for transition firing which also determines the *current* state of the DSC state machine at run-time. As it is shown in Figure 3, an event E, instance of the ACLMessage class, is fetched from the JADE event queue by the dispatcher component of the DistilledStateChartBehaviour and delivered to the DSC current state (S1) so triggering a state transition to a new state (S2) if the guard C holds.

In the following a detailed description of the main mechanisms (state management, behavior scheduling, event handling, transition firing and history entrances) of the DistilledStateChartBehaviour is presented.

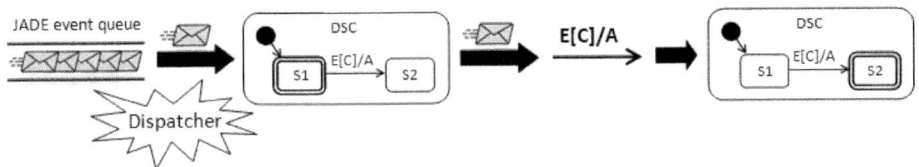

Fig. 3. The event handling scheme

State Management. Any type of JADE behavior can be added as simple, initial or final state to the DistilledStatechartsBehaviour through the methods *addState*, *addInitialState* and *addFinalState*, respectively. The *createRootForDSCTemplate* method automatically builds the root of the DistilledStatechartsBehaviour that allows entering into the active state through the deep history entrance (see Figure 1). The *initialAction* method allows inserting an initial action on the default entrance. The methods *onEnd*, *onStart* and *action* should be kept empty.

Behaviour Scheduling. The DistilledStateChartBehaviour receives the thread of control from the JADE run-time system through the invocation of the *action* method according to the cooperative concurrency mechanism of JADE. The *action* method of the DistilledStateChartBehaviour, in turn, invokes the *action* method of the current state; the DistilledStateChartBehaviour starts executing the initial state, activates other states by following the fired transitions and, finally, terminates when enters into one of its final states. On the invocation of the *action* method of the current behavior, the Wrapper object, which encapsulates each simple state, allows checking all transitions outcoming from the current state and executing the fireable transitions (through the *findAndFireTransition* method). This mechanism allows implementing the UML state machine rule: "as soon as a transition is able to fire, it does". Indeed, the actual implementation is based on the single-threaded model of JADE, which does not support preemption of an action execution.

Event Handling. An important feature of the DSC state machines is the event driven mechanism for triggering transitions. An event can be represented as a regular JADE ACLMessage so enabling the reuse of the message queuing mechanism of JADE (see Figure 3): when the DistilledStateChartBehaviour is checking for a transition firing, the *receive* method of JADE is invoked to fetch the first message in the queue, which is then passed to the transitions to check if one of them can be fired. The main issue of such mechanism is the integration of behaviors as states. In particular, as an event message in queue is fetched through the *receive* method, if this method is invoked inside the *action* method, it can interfere with the transition firing mechanism. Moreover, if a message/event is received in a state in which the event is not expected, the two following options, which can be set in the DistilledStateChartBehaviour constructor are possible: the event is re-inserted into the queue (*putbackMessage*=true) so that it could be fetched by another state that is able to handle it, or it is discharged (*putbackMessage*=false). The same event handling mechanism can be also used when an agent has multiple behaviors for the purpose of avoiding important event losses. In this case, the message template mechanism based on selective filters for events can be used. In particular, each behavior performs a *receive* operation with a different message template so as to fetch only the events it is able to handle.

Transition Firing. A transition is represented by the DistilledStateChartTransition class and is added through the *addTransition* method which takes as parameters the transition to be added and the source state. The target state is defined at DistilledStateChartTransition creation and can be at any level of the hierarchy so supporting the specification of inter-level state transitions. The DistilledStateChartTransition unifies the mechanisms of trigger event and guard into the *trigger(Behaviour source, ACLMessage event)* method, where *source* is the transition source state and *event* is the transition triggering event. The *trigger* method checks for the transition firing and, if the check is successful, the *action* method of DistilledStateChartTransition, which can contain the action hooked to the transition, is invoked. The check based on both the *trigger* and *findAndFireTransition* methods not only involves the current state but also all the states, from the inner to the outer, encapsulating it. The DistilledStateChartPerformativeTransition and DistilledStateChartTemplateTransition classes extend DistilledStateChartTransition providing a new version of the *trigger* method that allows to check respectively if the received event respects a specific performative or MessageTemplate.

History Entrances. The DistilledStateChartBehaviour includes the *defaultDeepHistoryEntrance* and the *defaultShallowHistoryEntrance* referring to the states (or behaviors) associated to the deep and shallow history entrances, respectively. To restore the state history, the *lastState* variable of a composite state of the DistilledStateChartBehaviour type, which stores a reference to the last visited state before exiting the composite state, is used. Moreover, the DistilledStateChartTransition includes the two constants *DEEP_HISTORY* and *SHALLOW_HISTORY* that indicate that the target composite state is to be entered through the deep or shallow history.

4   CASE Tool-Driven Development of DSC-Based JADE Agents

The development of DSC-based JADE agents relies on the process reported in Figure 4 which is organized in the following three phases:

- The *Modeling* phase produces the DSC-based MAS Model on the basis of the High-Level System Design which can be defined either ad-hoc or by means of other methodologies which also support the analysis and high-level design phases [17, 18, 16]. In particular, the DSC-based MAS Model is specified through the DSC formalism and the JADE API.
- The *Coding* phase works out the DSC-based MAS Model and automatically produces the JADE MAS code according to the DistilledStateChartBehaviour.
- The *Deployment and Execution* phase is fully supported by the JADE Platform to run the developed MAS. A careful evaluation of the obtained Testing Results (e.g. execution traces, performance indices, etc) with respect to the functional and non-functional requirements could lead to a further iteration step which starts from a new (re)modeling activity.

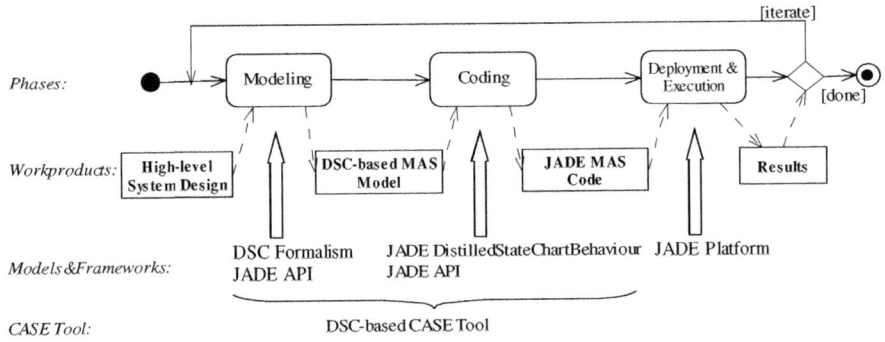

Fig. 4. The CASE-driven development process

The first two phases are fully supported by the DSC-based CASE tool that makes it available (i) the visual modeling of the DSC-based behavior of the agents composing the MAS under-development and (ii) the automatic translation of the modeled agent behaviors into ready-to-be-executed JADE code according to the DistilledStatechartsBehaviour framework.

The CASE tool is obtained by enhancing the ELDATool [7], a graphical tool for visual specification, automatic code translation and simulation of ELDA-based systems, with a new component named CodeGeneratorForJADE embedded into the ELDAEditor plug-in. This important facility, which is not offered by the HSMBehaviour graphical tools [11], makes the programming of Statecharts-based JADE agents easier than manual programming of the HSMBehaviour and DistilledStateChartBehaviour based on complex programming patterns.

As the ELDATool is based on the ELDA agent model [7], the specific event types, exploitable for the modeling phase, are: (i) the ELDAEventMSG, which represents asynchronous messages; (ii) the ELDAEventInternal, which represents self-triggering events. Both kinds of events derive from the ELDAEvent class and are inserted into an ACLMessage as message content. Moreover it is worth noting that the specification of state variables, actions, guards, events and functions is based on the Java language and the JADE API.

5   A Case Study: An Agent-Based Meeting Organization System

In this section the DSC-based development of an agent-based meeting organization system, in which agents coordinate to arrange meetings, is proposed. The developed MAS is derived from a case study based on a meeting participant protocol proposed in [21, 11]. In particular, the MAS is based on three types of agents (see Figure 5): (i) MeetingRequester (MRA), which is the meeting organizer; (ii) MeetingBroker (MBA), which arranges meetings on the basis of the MRA requests; (iii) MeetingParticipant (MPA), which represents a meeting participant.

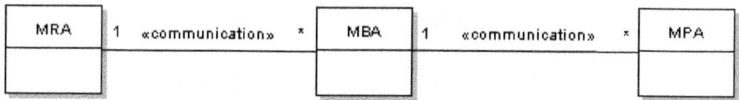

Fig. 5. Class diagram of multi-agent meeting system

In the following subsections we first describe the agent interactions for the meeting arrangement and detail the agent behaviors and, then, provide some implementation details of the agent-based system along with an experimental performance evaluation aiming at analyzing the MAS scalability.

5.1   Agent Interactions

The defined agents interact with each other to fulfill a meeting arrangement that can be constituted by one or more iterations (i.e. an iteration is an attempt to arrange a given meeting driven by the MRA requests). The interaction protocol is defined through the sequence diagrams reported in Figures 6-8 that show successful and unsuccessful cases. Figure 6 shows the 1-iteration successful interaction scenario in which a meeting is arranged with two participants (even though it can be generalized to n-participants). In particular, after the Request sent by the MRA to the MBA, the successful event flow is: the Propose event is sent by the MBA to the two MPAs that, in turns, accept it and send the AcceptProposal event to the MBA that finalizes the meeting and sends out the Confirm event to the accepting MPAs and MRA.

In Figure 7, the 2-iteration successful interaction scenario, in which a meeting is arranged with three participants, is reported. Differently from the previous interaction scenario, here the MPA_1 refuses the proposal by sending the RejectProposal event to the MBA that, in turn, send the AskForRequest event to the MRA to have information about new potential participants. After receiving such information the MBA therefore sends out a Propose event to MPA_3 that accepts it.

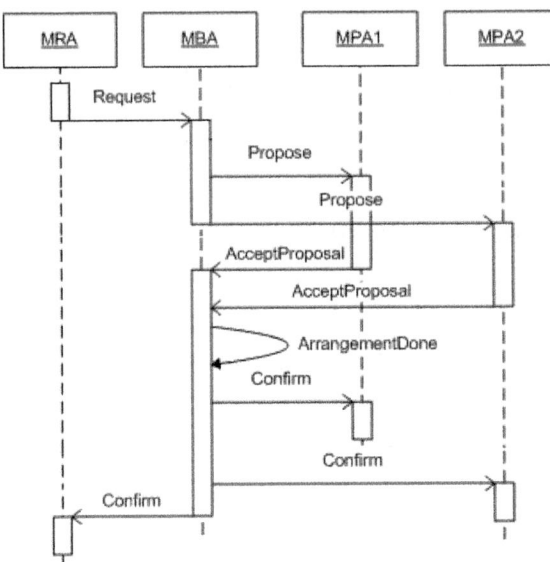

Fig. 6. Sequence diagram of agent interactions: successful case after 1-iteration

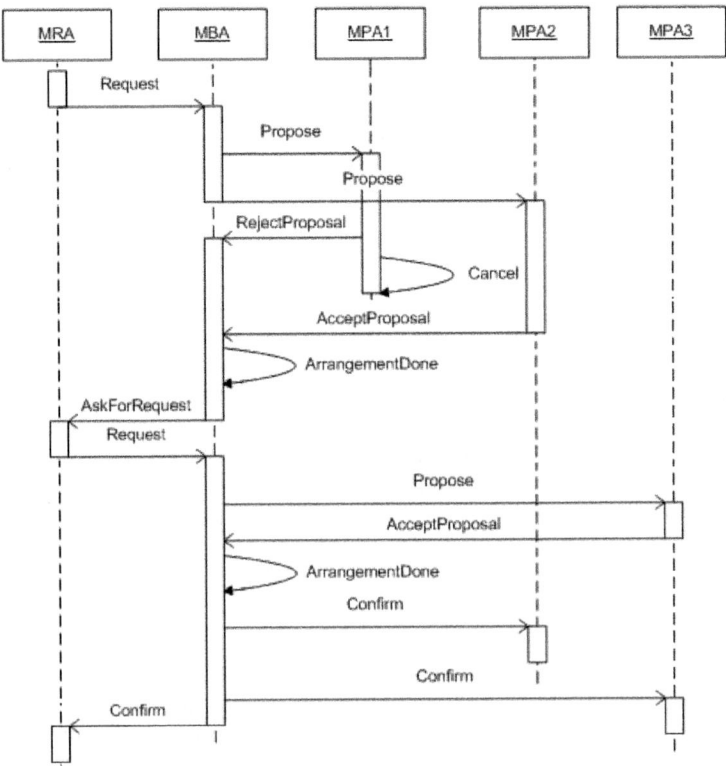

Fig. 7. Sequence diagram of agent interactions: successful case after 2-iterations

Finally, in Figure 8, the unsuccessful interaction scenario, in which a meeting is being arranged with three participants, is shown. MPA_2, MPA_3 and MPA_4 refuse the proposal so that after three additional requests (the maximum fixed number of attempts) the arrangement of the meeting fails.

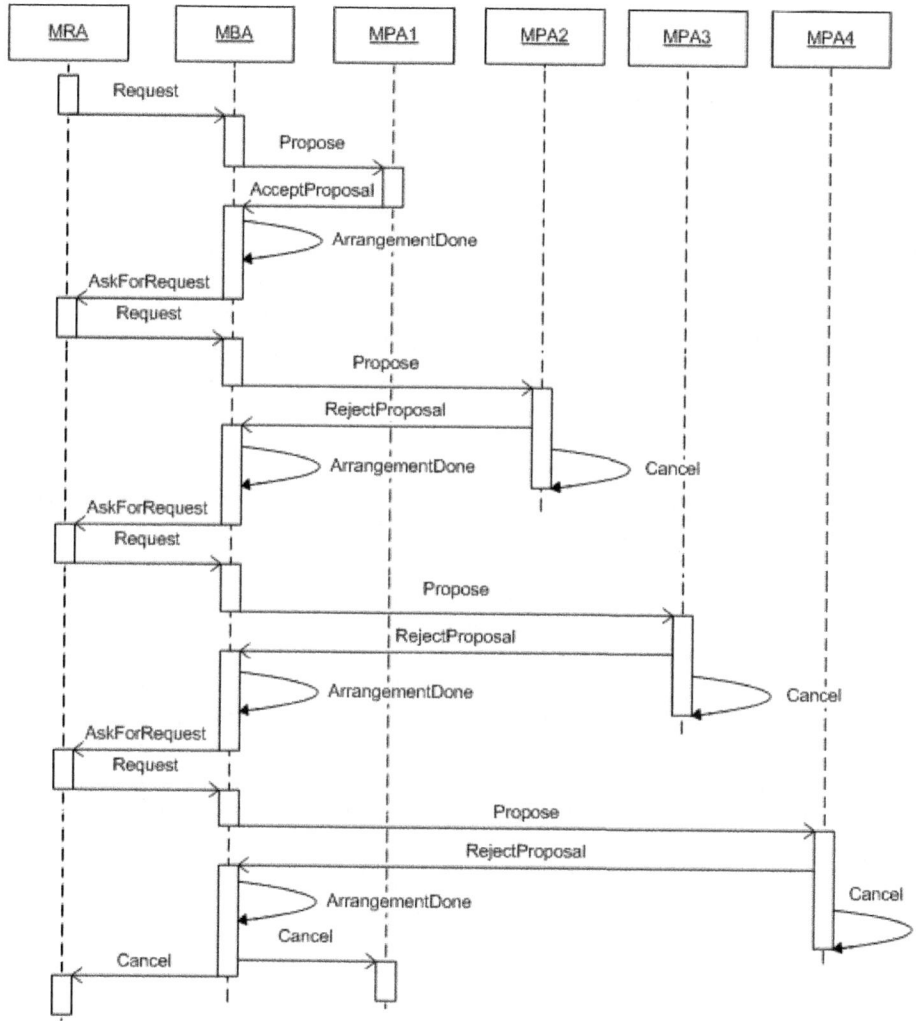

Fig. 8. Sequence diagram of agent interactions: unsuccessful case

5.2   Agent Behaviors

While the behaviors of the MRA (see Figure 9) and MPA (see Figure 10) are straightforward, more complexity is retained by the MBA behavior (see Figure 11). In particular, each behavior is described in terms of a DSC diagram, state variables and actions. Moreover, Table 2 summarizes the event-based interaction relationships

Table 2. Event-based interaction relationships among agents

SOURCE \ TARGET	MRA	MBA	MPA
MRA		Request	
MBA	Confirm, Cancel, AskForRequest	ArrangementDone	Propose, Confirm, Cancel
MPA		AcceptProposal, RejectProposal	

among agents, specifying the event source agent, which generates the event, and the event target agent, which receives and handles the event.

According to the MRA behavior (see Figure 9 and Tables 3-4), the MRA sends a Request event to the MBA (see action `sendRequest`) containing all needed information (potential participants, minimum number of participants, meeting topic, and chosen date) related to the appointment to arrange and waits for the meeting confirmation. As soon as the MRA receives the AskForRequest event, it will send out a new or modified Request (see action `sendRequest`). The reception of the Confirm event signals an arranged meeting (action `meetingDone`) whereas the Cancel event signals a failure in organizing a meeting (action `meetingCanceled`).

According to the MPA behavior (see Figure 10 and Tables 5-6), in the Started state, the MPA can receive the Propose even to check an appointment (see action `checkAppointment`) or to refuse it. As soon as it receives the Confirm event, the MPA finalizes the appointment set-up (see action `fixAppointment`).

As described above, the MBA manages the meeting arrangement requests sent by the MRA, and coordinates the MPAs. The MBA behavior (see Figure 11 and Tables 7-8) starts in the Negotiation composite state and acts as follows: upon the reception of the Request event, the MBA sends all the MPAs a Propose event containing the appointment to schedule (action `sendPropose`), starts a timer (action `initializeTimer`) and finally goes into the Arrange composite state. The MPAs send the MBA an AcceptProposal event to accept the appointment or a RejectProposal event to refuse it (see Figure 10). On the basis of the received responses, the MBA accepts (action `acceptParticipant`) or excludes (action `excludeParticipant`) the participants and, when it receives all the responses or when the timeout associated to the set timer expires (action `sendArrangementDone`), sends an ArrangementDone event to itself to carry out the final operations (see action `completeArrangement`) for the current appointment as follows:

- If at least M MPAs have accepted the appointment, the meeting organization is successfully done; then, the MBA sends a Confirm event to the MRA and to the accepting MPAs, which schedule the appointment in their rosters (see Figure 10).
- If the appointment has been accepted by less than M MPA and it is not yet reached the maximum limit of N requests of new participants sent to the MRA, the MBA issues a request of new participants to the MRA by sending it an AskForRequest event. Then, the MRA sends a new Request event to the MBA indicating new participants for the same appointment (see Figure 9). This way, the MBA can retry to schedule the appointment involving the new provided participants.

- If the appointment has been accepted by less than M MPA and it is reached the maximum limit of N requests of new participants sent to the MRA, the appointment is canceled and a Cancel event is sent to the accepting MPAs and MRA.

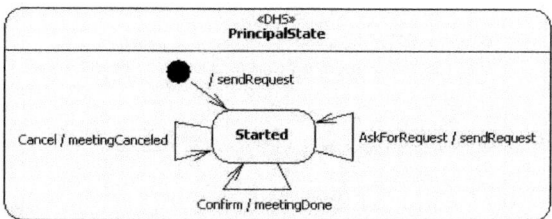

Fig. 9. The state diagram of the DSC-based behavior of the MRA

Table 3. Variables of the DSC-based behavior of the MRA

STATE	VARIABLES
ROOT	String meetingBroker
PrincipalState	Appointment currentAppointment

Table 4. Actions and functions of the DSC-based behavior of the MRA

ACTIONS
sendRequest

```
if (currentAppointment == null) {
 String description = getDescription();
 Calendar date = getDate();
 int n = getNumberOfParticipants();
 java.util.ArrayList<AID> participantsList = new java.util.ArrayList<AID>();
 for(int i = 1; i <= n; i++){
  String nickname = getNickname(i);
  participantsList.add(new AID(nickname, AID.ISLOCALNAME));
 }
 currentAppointment = new Appointment(participantsList, date, description);
 java.util.ArrayList<AID> target = new java.util.ArrayList<AID>();
 target.add(new AID(meetingBroker, AID.ISLOCALNAME));
 Request msg = new Request(self(), target, currentAppointment);
 generate(msg);
}
else {
 int n = getNumberOfParticipants();
 java.util.ArrayList<AID> participantsList = new java.util.ArrayList<AID>();
 for(int i = 1; i <= n; i++){
  String nickname = getNickname(i);
  participantsList.add(new AID(nickname, AID.ISLOCALNAME));
 }
 currentAppointment = new Appointment(participantsList,
  currentAppointment.getDate(), currentAppointment.getDescription());
 java.util.ArrayList<AID> target = new java.util.ArrayList<AID>();
 target.add(new AID(meetingBroker, AID.ISLOCALNAME));
 Request msg = new Request(self(), target, currentAppointment);
 generate(msg);
}
```

meetingDone (omissis)
meetingCancelled (omissis)

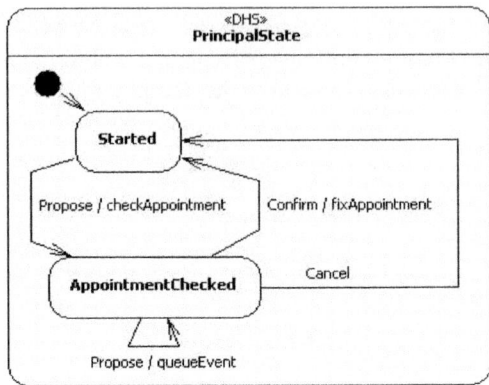

Fig. 10. The state diagram of the DSC-based behavior of the MPA

Table 5. Variables of the DSC-based behavior of the MPA

STATE	VARIABLES
PrincipalState	java.util.Hashtable myCalendar = new java.util.Hashtable() Appointment currentAppointment

Table 6. Actions and functions of the DSC-based behavior of the MPA

ACTIONS
checkAppointment

Propose p = (Propose) e;
currentAppointment = (Appointment) p.getData();
AID meetingBroker = p.getSource();
if(myCalendar.containsKey(getKey(currentAppointment.getDate()))){
  java.util.ArrayList<AID> target = new java.util.ArrayList<AID>();
  target.add(meetingBroker);
  RejectProposal msg = new RejectProposal(self(), target, null);
  generate(msg);
  java.util.ArrayList<AID> target2 = new java.util.ArrayList<AID>();
  target2.add(self());
  Cancel msg2 = new Cancel(self(), target2, null);
  generate(msg2);
} else{
  java.util.ArrayList<AID> target = new java.util.ArrayList<AID>();
  target.add(meetingBroker);
  AcceptProposal msg = new AcceptProposal(self(), target, null);
  generate(msg);
}

fixAppointment
myCalendar.put(getKey(currentAppointment.getDate()), currentAppointment);
queueEvent

java.util.ArrayList<AID> target = new java.util.ArrayList<AID>();
target.add(self());
e.setTarget(target);
generate(e);

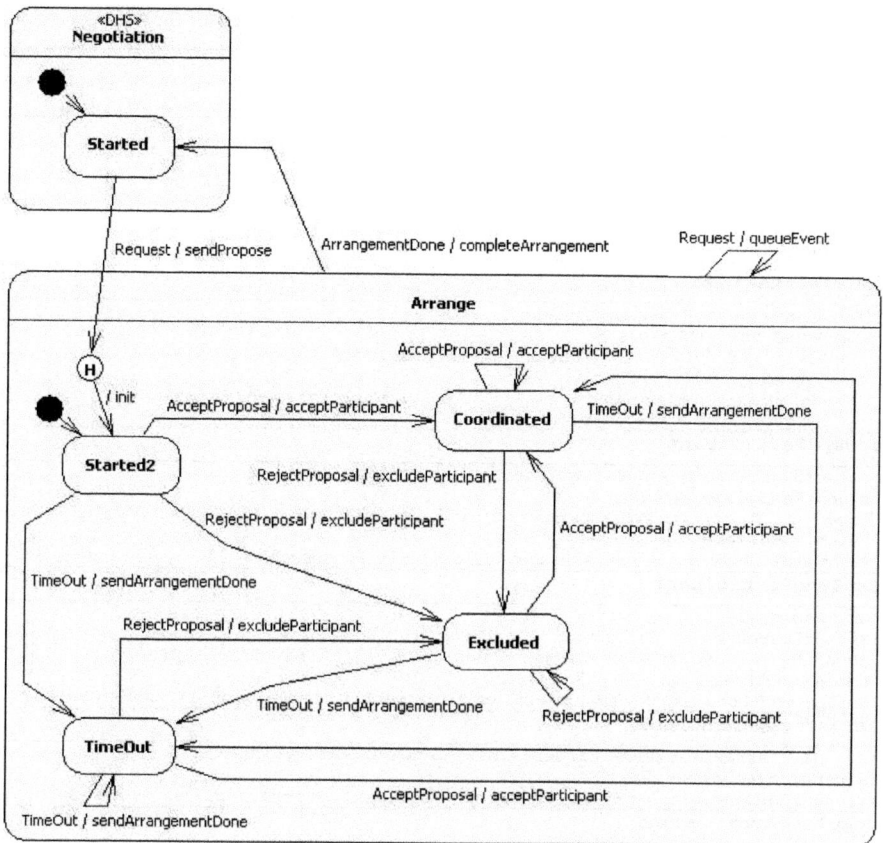

Fig. 11. The state diagram of the DSC-based behavior of the MBA

Table 7. Variables of the DSC-based behavior of the MBA

STATE	VARIABLES
ROOT	int contResponses
	int contRequestsToMeetingRequester
	WakerBehaviour timer
	AID meetingRequester
	int M, N
Arrange	ArrayList<AID> acceptedParticipants

After the completion of the completeArrangement action, the MBA goes back into the Negotiation composite state. The shallow history entrance (H) provides a powerful modeling solution when the Arrange composite state is to be re-entered due to a new Request related to the same appointment. In particular, when a new Request event is received, the MBA goes into the most recently left simple state of the

Table 8. Actions and functions of the DSC-based behavior of the MBA

ACTIONS
sendPropose

`Request r = (Request) e; Appointment app = (Appointment) r.getData();`
`contResponses = app.getParticipantsList().size();meetingRequester = r.getSource();`
`java.util.ArrayList<AID> target = new java.util.ArrayList<AID>();`
`for(int i=0; i < app.getParticipantsList().size(); i++)`
` target.add(app.getParticipantsList().get(i));`
`Propose msg = new Propose(self(), target, app); generate(msg);`
`initializeTimer(e);`

initializeTimer

`timer = new WakerBehaviour(myAgent, 30000){`
` protected void onWake() {`
`  java.util.ArrayList<AID> target = new java.util.ArrayList<AID>();`
`  target.add(self());`
`  TimeOut msg = new TimeOut(self(), target, null); generate(msg);`
` }}; myAgent.addBehaviour(timer);`

acceptParticipant

`acceptedParticipants.add(e.getSource()); contResponses--;`
`if(contResponses == 0){`
` java.util.ArrayList<AID> target = new java.util.ArrayList<AID>();`
` target.add(self());`
` ArrangementDone msg = new ArrangementDone(self(), target, null); generate(msg);}`

excludeParticipant

`contResponses--;`
`if(contResponses == 0){`
` java.util.ArrayList<AID> target = new java.util.ArrayList<AID>();`
` target.add(self());`
` ArrangementDone msg = new ArrangementDone(self(), target, null); generate(msg);}`

sendArrangementDone

`java.util.ArrayList<AID> target = new java.util.ArrayList<AID>();`
`target.add(self());`
`ArrangementDone msg = new ArrangementDone(self(), target, null); generate(msg);`

completeArrangement

`myAgent.removeBehaviour(timer);`
`if(acceptedParticipants.size() >= M){`
` java.util.ArrayList<AID> target = new java.util.ArrayList<AID>();`
` target.addAll(acceptedParticipants); target.add(meetingRequester);`
` Confirm msg = new Confirm(self(), target, null); generate(msg);`
` contRequestsToMeetingRequester = 0;`
` acceptedParticipants = new java.util.ArrayList<AID>();`
`} else{`
` if(contRequestsToMeetingRequester > N){`
`  java.util.ArrayList<AID> target = new java.util.ArrayList<AID>();`
`  target.addAll(acceptedParticipants); target.add(meetingRequester);`
`  Cancel msg = new Cancel(self(), target, null); generate(msg);`
`  contRequestsToMeetingRequester = 0;`
`  acceptedParticipants = new java.util.ArrayList<AID>();`
` } else{`
`  contRequestsToMeetingRequester++;`
`  java.util.ArrayList<AID> target = new java.util.ArrayList<AID>();`
`  target.add(meetingRequester);`
`  AskForRequest msg = new AskForRequest(self(), target, null); generate(msg);}}`

init
`contRequestsToMeetingRequester = 0;` `acceptedParticipants = new java.util.ArrayList<AID>();`
queueEvent
`java.util.ArrayList<AID> target = new java.util.ArrayList<AID>();` `target.add(self()); e.setTarget(target); generate(e);`

Arrange state, recovering exactly the same state variables and DSC status so continuing from the previous arrangement state without discontinuity. Moreover, if the Request event is received in the Arrange state, i.e. a Request from a different MRA is received, the MBA enqueues the Request.

5.3   MAS Implementation

The implementation of the meeting organization MAS is completely supported by the enhanced ELDATool features of visual modeling and automatic code generation. Figure 12 reports a screenshot of ELDATool containing the fully developed system described above. In particular, in the package explorer there are two folders: (i) *Meeting DSC* containing the set of graphical DSC agent behaviors (MeetingBroker.dsc, MeetingParticipant.dsc, MeetingRequester.dsc) and their related actions, events, functions, and guards; (ii) *Meeting_DSC_JADE_Implementation* containing the generated source code (src package). In the central panel, the MeetingBroker.dsc is visualized (the complete diagram is reported in Figure 11). Finally in the bottom panel, an excerpt of the generated code of the MeetingBroker is reported. The code of the DistilledStateChartBehaviour framework along with the generated source code of the meeting organization MAS is downloadable as (official) Jade add-on from [22].

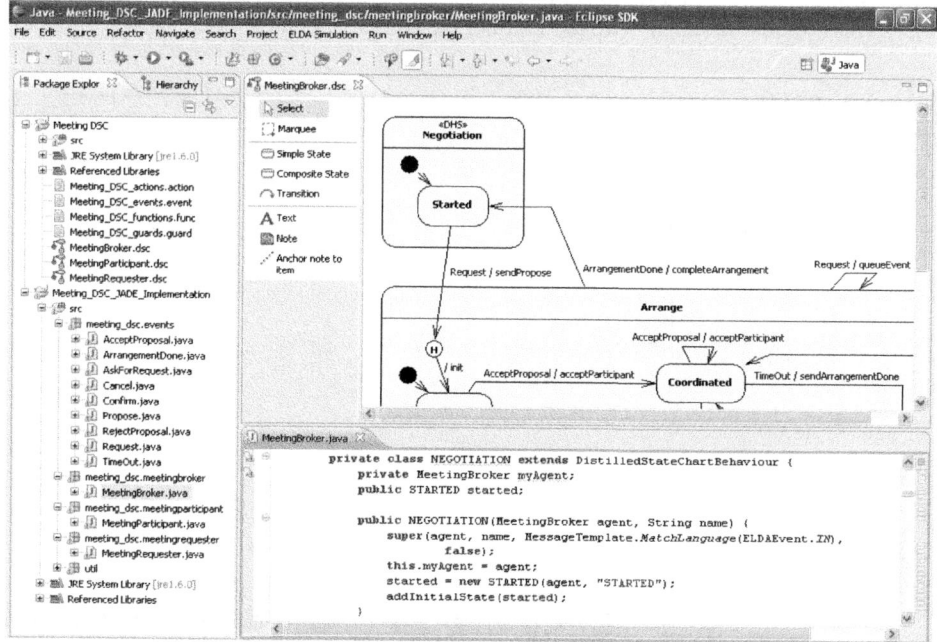

Fig. 12. A screenshot of the CASE tool showing the developed system

5.4   MAS Evaluation

The developed system was evaluated on a real experimental testbed composed of 50 workstations with the same hardware/software configuration (Windows XP Professional SP2 32-bit, CPU MD Athlon 64x2 dual-core 2.90GHz, RAM 4GB, JRE 1.6.0) interconnected by a 100Mbps switched Fast Ethernet. In particular, the goal of the evaluation was to compute the main application performance index, namely Meeting Arrangement Time (MAT), characterizing the speed with which the system replies to a user request, and analyze it by increasing the scale of the system. To this purpose, a supplemental monitoring agent-based architecture, which is able to collect statistical data about the application execution, was also developed and deployed atop the experimental testbed. The test runs were executed by varying the number of MRAs (and consequently the number of MBAs as there is a mapping 1-to-1 between MRAs and MBAs) and the number of MPAs. The number of MRAs was varied in the range [1..1000], whereas the number of MPAs was in the range [1..50]. In particular, each MPA was launched in its own JADE container, whereas all MRAs were launched in one different JADE container as well as all MBAs. Moreover, to avoid unbalance in the MPA behavior, only the successful case after 1-iteration was considered (see Section 5.1), so MPAs always agree to a meeting participation proposal as soon as they receive it.

The obtained results for the MAT index, averaged over 30 execution runs, are reported in Figure 13. As expected, MAT increases by increasing the number of MRAs and MPAs. In particular, the system with 1000 MRAs in parallel degrades its performance quadratically with the number of MPAs.

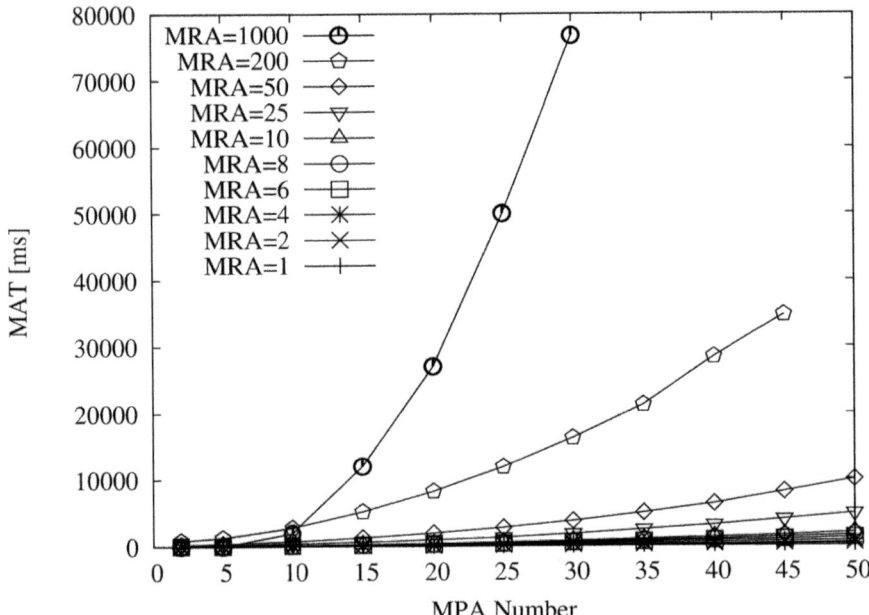

Fig. 13. Scalability evaluation of the system: meeting arrangement time by increasing the scale of the system

The MAS was also developed by using only the basic JADE framework without using the DistilledStatechartsBehaviour framework and evaluated on the same testbed with the same parameter setting. Performance evaluation results show an overlap of the performances of the DSC-based MAS and the JADE-based MAS so that the proposed framework does not introduce further overhead onto the system and system performances only rely on the JADE run-time infrastructure.

6   Conclusion

This paper has proposed programming techniques and tools based on Statecharts for the rapid development of JADE MASs. In particular, a new JADE behavior, named DistilledStateChartBehaviour, has been defined which is based on the Distilled StateCharts formalism providing hierarchical state machines including history mechanisms and features for enabling an automatic restoring of the agent execution state. The proposed DistilledStateChartBehaviour JADE add-on has been obtained on the basis of the HSMBehaviour that was purposely debugged and optimized. Moreover, the availability of a CASE tool, which supports the specification phase of JADE agent behaviors based on the DistilledStateChartBehaviour and their automatic translation into code, facilitates programming and enables rapid prototyping. As the JADE platform is one of the most used agent platform in the AOSE community to program and execute distributed agent systems, the paper proposal contributes to (i) enrich already existing agent-oriented methodologies having JADE as target platform with tools for further automating MAS development and (ii) foster a wider introduction and exploitation of Statecharts-based techniques for agents.

The effectiveness of the proposed approach for the development of MAS has been demonstrated through a case study concerning with a well-known agent-based meeting arrangement application. Specifically, the DSC-based modeling allows for a simplification of the MAS design and the availability of a visual tool supporting the development lifecycle of MAS allows for the automatic code generation so enabling rapid prototyping. Moreover, the exploitation of the DistilledStatechartsBehaviour facilitates the development of MAS in which agents interact through well-defined protocols as DSCs are a formalism well suited for defining agent protocols. This claimed effectiveness was directly experimented by also developing the MAS for meeting arrangement by means of the basic JADE framework. The developed DSC-based MAS and the basic JADE-based MAS have been also deployed and executed on an experimental testbed to analyze the system scalability. The obtained results show that scalability is only affected by the JADE run-time architecture as performances of the two developed systems overlap. Thus, the DistilledStatechartsBehaviour framework does not introduce any performance penalty.

Future work is geared at (i) integrating Statecharts-based modeling and the defined techniques within an MDD-driven agent-oriented methodology such as INGENIAS; (ii) defining a reverse engineering technique to obtain the DSC-based agent visual model from the agent source code compliant to the DistilledStateChartBehaviour.

References

1. Zambonelli, F., Omicini, A.: Challenges and Research Directions in Agent-Oriented Software Engineering. Autonomous Agents and Multi-Agent Systems 9(3), 253–283 (2004)
2. Ambler, S.W.: The Elements of UML 2.0 Style. Cambridge University Press (2005)
3. Harel, D., Gery, E.: Executable Object Modeling with Statecharts. IEEE Computer 30(7), 31–42 (1997)
4. Luck, M., McBurney, P., Preist, C.: A manifesto for agent technology: towards next generation computing. Autonomous Agents and Multi-Agent Systems 9(3), 203–252 (2004)
5. Bellifemine, F., Caire, G., Greenwood, D.: Developing Multi-Agent Systems with JADE. Wiley (2007)
6. Griss, M., Fonseca, S., Cowan, D., Kessler, R.: SmartAgent: Extending the JADE agent behavior model. In: Proc. of the Agent Oriented Software Engineering Workshop, Conference in Systems, Cybernetics and Informatics, Orlando, Florida (July 2002)
7. Fortino, G., Garro, A., Mascillaro, S., Russo, W.: Using Event-driven Lightweight DSC-based Agents for MAS Modeling. International Journal on Agent Oriented Software Engineering 4(2) (2010)
8. Boloni, L., Marinescu, D.C.: A component agent model – from theory to implementation. In: Müller, J., Petta, P. (eds.) Proc. of the Second International Symposium from Agent Theory to Agent Implementation (2000); Trappl, R. (ed.): Proc. of Cybernetics and Systems, Austrian Society of Cybernetic Studies, Vienna, pp. 663–639 (March 2000)
9. Bellifemine, F., Poggi, A., Rimassa, G.: Developing multi agent systems with a FIPA-compliant agent framework. Software Practice and Experience 31, 103–128 (2001)
10. Griss, M., Fonseca, S., Cowan, D., Kessler, R.: Using UML State Machines Models for More Precise and Flexible JADE Agent Behaviors. In: AAMAS AOSE Workshop, Bologna, Italy (July 2002)
11. Kessler, R., Griss, M., Remick, B., Delucchi, R.: A Hierarchical State Machine using JADE Behaviours with Animation Visualization. Technical report, University of Utah (2004)
12. Fortino, G., Russo, W., Zimeo, E.: A statecharts-based software development process for mobile agents. Information and Software Technology 46(13), 907–921 (2004)
13. Fortino, G., Garro, A., Mascillaro, S., Russo, W.: ELDATool: A Statecharts-based Tool for Prototyping Multi-Agent Systems. In: Proc. of the Workshop on Objects and Agents (WOA 2007), Genova, Italy, September 24-25 (2007)
14. Nwana, H., Nduma, D., Lee, L., Collis, J.: ZEUS: a toolkit for building distributed multi-agent systems. Artificial Intelligence Journal 13(1), 129–186 (1999)
15. Cost, R.S., Finin, T., Labrou, Y., Luan, X., Peng, Y., Soboroff, I., Mayfield, J., Boughannam, A.: Jackal: A Java-Based Tool for Agent Development. In: Working Notes of the Workshop on Tools for Developing Agents, AAAI 1998 (1998)
16. García-Magariño, I., Gómez-Sanz, J.J., Fuentes-Fernández, R.: Model transformations for improving multi-agent system development in INGENIAS. In: Gomez-Sanz, J.J. (ed.) AOSE 2009. LNCS, vol. 6038, pp. 51–65. Springer, Heidelberg (2011)
17. Cossentino, M.: From Requirements to Code with the PASSI Methodology. In: Henderson-Sellers, B., Giorgini, P. (eds.) Agent-Oriented Methodologies. Idea Group Inc., Hershey (2005)

18. Caire, G., Coulier, W., Garijo, F., Gómez-Sanz, J., Pavón, J., Kearney, P., Massonet, P.: The Message Methodology. In: Bergenti, F., Gleizes, M.-P., Zambonelli, F. (eds.) Methodologies and Software Engineering for Agent Systems The Agent-Oriented Software Engineering Handbook, vol. 11, pp. 177–194. Springer (2006)
19. Eshuis, R.: Reconciling statechart semantics. Science of Computer Programming 74(3), 65–99 (2009)
20. FIPA (Foundation for Intelligent Physical Agents), FIPA Agent Management Support for Mobility Specification, Document FIPA DC00087C (2002/05/10) (2002), http://www.fipa.org/
21. Fonseca, S., Griss, M., Letsinger, R.: Agent Behavior Architectures A MAS Framework Comparison, Technical report, N. HPL-2001-332, University of Utah (2001)
22. The JADE DistilledStateChartBehaviour add-on, documentation and software (2010), http://jade.tilab.com/

Fleet Organization Models
for Online Vehicle Routing Problems

Mahdi Zargayouna[1] and Besma Zeddini[2]

[1] Université Paris-Est, IFSTTAR, GRETTIA,
F-93166 Noisy-le-Grand, France
[2] IRSEEM-ESIGELEC, ITS Division
Saint Etienne du Rouvray
76801, France
hamza-mahdi.zargayouna@ifsttar.fr, zeddini@esigelec.fr

Abstract. Online vehicle routing problems with time windows are highly complex problems for which different artificial intelligence techniques have been used. In these problems, the exclusive optimization of the conventional criteria (number of vehicles and total traveled distance) leads to the appearance of geographic areas and/or time periods that are not covered by any vehicle because of their low population density. The transportation demands in these zones either cannot be satisfied or need to mobilize new vehicles. We propose two agent-oriented models that propose a particular dynamic organization of the vehicles, with the objective to minimize the appearance of such areas. The first model relies on a spatial representation of the agents' action zones, and the second model is grounded on the space-time representation of these zones. These representations are capable of maintaining an equilibrated distribution of the vehicles on the transportation network. In this paper, we experimentally show that these two means of distributing vehicles over the network provide better results than traditional insertion heuristics. They allow the agents to take their decisions while anticipating future changes in the environment.

Keywords: Vehicle Routing Problems, Multiagent Systems, Organization Models.

1 Introduction

Several operational distribution problems, such as the deliveries of goods to stores, the routing of school buses, the distribution of newspapers and mail etc. are instantiations of NP-Hard theoretical problems called the Vehicle Routing Problems (VRP). In its original version, a VRP is a multi-vehicle Traveling Salesman Problem: there exists a certain number of nodes to be visited once by a limited number of vehicles. The objective is to find a set of vehicles' routes that minimizes the total distance traveled. Besides their practical usefulness, the VRP and its extensions are challenging optimization problems with academic stimulating issues. One of the most widely studied variant of the problem is the time (and capacity) constrained version: the Vehicle Routing Problem with Time

N.T. Nguyen (Ed.): Transactions on CCI VII, LNCS 7270, pp. 82–102, 2012.

Windows (VRPTW henceforth) [1], in which the requests to be handled are not simply nodes, but customers. For each customer, the following information are provided: the concerned node, two temporal bounds between which she desires to be visited and a quantity (number of goods to receive, number of persons to transport, etc.). Every vehicle has a limited capacity, which should not be exceeded by the sum of the quantities associated with the customers it visits. The addition of time windows to the basic problem restrains considerably the space of valid solutions.

The VRP and the VRPTW can be divided in two categories: static problems and dynamic problems. The distinction between these two categories relies traditionally on the knowledge (static problem) or the ignorance (dynamic problem) before the start of the solving process of all the customers that have to be visited. The operational problems are rarely fully static and we can reasonably say that today a static system cannot meet the mobility needs of the users. Indeed, in operational settings, and even if all the customers are known in advance (before the execution start), there always exists some element making the problem dynamic. These elements include breakdowns, delays, no-shows, etc. It is thus always useful to consider a problem that is not fully static.

We rely on the multiagent paradigm for solving the dynamic VRPTW. An agent is a software system, that is situated in some environment and that is able to apply autonomous actions to satisfy its goals [2], and a MAS is a loosely coupled network of agents that interact to solve problems that are beyond the individual capabilities or knowledge of each one [3]. A multiagent modeling of the dynamic VRPTW is relevant for the following reasons. First, since it's a hard problem, choosing a design allowing for the distribution of computation can be a solution to propose short answer times to customers requests. Second, with the technological developments, it is reasonable to consider vehicles with onboard calculation capabilities. In this context, the problem is, *de facto*, distributed and necessitates an adapted modeling to take profit of the onboard equipments of the vehicles. Finally, the consideration of a multiagent point of view allows to envision new measures, new heuristics, not envisaged by centralized approaches. Even if the multiagent approach does not guarantee optimal solutions, it is often capable of finding satisfactory solutions in faster execution times [2].

The MAS that we propose in this paper simulate a distributed version of the so-called "insertion heuristics". Insertion heuristics are methods that consist in inserting the customers following their appearance order in the routes of the vehicles. The vehicle chosen to insert the considered customer is the one that has to make the minimal detour to visit her. Several MAS in the literature have been proposed to distribute insertion heuristics, but very few propose new measures for the insertion cost of a customer in the route of a vehicle, as an alternative to the traditional measure of its incurred detour. In the present work, we do propose two new measures, in the context of two new organization models. They are based on a space and on a space-time representation of the vehicle agents' action zones (the zone inside which all vehicle's actions take place). The objective is to allow the MAS to self-adapt exhibiting an equilibrated distribution of its vehicle agents, and to decrease this way the number of vehicles mobilized to serve the customers. Indeed, when providing an equilibrated distribution, the MAS is more reactive to customers' requests, which appear nondeterministically in space and time.

The remainder of this paper is structured as follows. In section 2, we discuss previous proposals for the dynamic VRPTW w.r.t our approach. We provide the formal definition of the problem in section 3. The architecture of the MAS is presenbted in section 4. In sections 5 and 6, we detail the models and the use of new measures for the insertion decisions of the vehicles. We report on our experimental results in section 7 and then conclude with a few remarks.

2   Related Work

2.1   Combinatorial Optimization

Exact approaches cannot meet operational settings of VRPTW, and upon the relatively small set of benchmarking problems of [1] - 56 problems of 100 Euclidean customers[1] each, only 45 have a known optimal solution up until today [4]. However, interested readers of optimization approaches can refer to, e.g. [5] for a survey. In fact, most of the proposed solution methods are heuristic or metaheuristic methods, which provide good results in non-exponential times, and which have presented good results with benchmark problems. For instance, large-neighborhood local search [6], simulated annealing [7,8], evolutive strategies [9] and ant colonies [10,11] present the best performances with static problems (where the set of transport requests is known *a priori*). For an extensive survey of the literature for the VRPTW approaches, the reader is invited to refer to, e.g. [12,13].

Generally speaking, most of the works dealing with the dynamic VRPTW are more or less direct adaptations of static methods. For instance, the large-neighborhood local search is adapted to a dynamic context in [14]. In [15], the authors propose to adapt the genetic algorithms to deal with the dynamic VRPTW. The proposed algorithm starts by creating a population of initial solutions and tries continually to improve their quality. When a new customer reveals, she is inserted in all current solutions in the position minimizing the additional cost. Upon the static methods, insertion heuristics are the most widely adapted in a dynamic environment (e.g. [16,17,18,19]). Insertion heuristics are, in their original version, greedy algorithms, in the sense that the decision to insert a given customer in the route of a vehicle is definitive. They are also combined with metaheuristics to improve the quality of the solutions. The advantage of using insertion heuristics is that they are intuitive and fast. However, when they are applied in a dynamic context, their solving process is said to be short-sighted. Indeed, the system doesn't know which customers will appear once it has assigned the known customers to the vehicles; and even if we could have an optimal assignment and scheduling of the known customers, a new coming customer

---

[1] Euclidean customers have cartesian coordinates, and the distance and the le travel times between each pair of customers are calculated following the Euclidean metric.

could make the old assignment sub-optimal, which would - in the worst case - necessitate a whole recomputation of all the routes. While preventing this reconsideration of previous decisions, insertion heuristics exhibit the fastest execution times but suffer a serious handicap.

Nevertheless, in their wide majority, agent-oriented approaches of the literature rely, at least partially, on insertion heuristics.

2.2   Multiagent Systems

In [20], the authors propose a multiagent architecture to solve a VRP and a multi-depot VRP. In [21], the authors propose a multiagent architecture to solve a dial-a-ride problem. The principle of these two proposals is the same: distribute an insertion heuristic, followed by a post-optimization step. In [20], the customers are handled sequentially. They are broadcasted to all the vehicles, which in turn propose insertion offers and the best proposal is retained by the customer. In the second step, the vehicles exchange customers to improve their solutions, each vehicle knowing the other agents of the system. Since vehicles are running in parallel, the authors envision to apply different heuristics for each vehicle, without changing the architecture. In-Time [21] is a system composed of *customer* agents and *vehicle* agents. The customer agent announces itself and all the vehicle agents calculate its insertion cost in their routes. Again, the customer agent selects the cheapest offer. The authors propose a distributed local search method to improve the solutions. Indeed, they allow a customer to ask stochastically to cancel its current assignment and to reannounce itself to the system, with the objective of having a better deal with another vehicle. MARS [22] models a cooperative scheduling in a maritime shipping company in the form of a multiagent system. The solution to the global scheduling problem emerges from the local decisions. The system uses an extension of the Contract Net Protocol (CNP) [23] and shows that it can be used for having good initial solutions to complex problems of tasks assignment. The MAS profits from an *a priori* structuring of the agents, since each vehicle is associated with a particular company and can handle the only customers of this company.

For the reasons that we have given in the introduction, we choose a multiagent modeling to solve the dynamic VRPTW. For their fast execution times and their adaptation to dynamic settings, we privilege a solving grounded on insertion heuristics. Thus, from a protocol and an architecture point of view, our system sticks with the multiagent systems we have just described, since we propose a distributed version of insertion heuristics. However, in these proposals, none have focused on the redefinition of the insertion cost of a customer. The traditional insertion cost of a customer in the route of a vehicle is based on the incurred detour of the vehicle. We propose two new insertion cost measures, focused on the space and space-time coverage of the transportation network by the vehicles. Our goal is to counterbalance the short vision of the traditional measures, by privileging an insertion process that is future-centered.

3   Problem Definition

In the following, we provide a formal definition of the VRPTW in order to define the parameters and the constraints of the system in an unambiguous way. It is noteworthy that although the objective in this definition is to minimize the routes global costs, the hierarchical and primary objective of minimizing the number of vehicles is traditionally used [4]. Indeed, the size of the vehicles fleet is not fixed when the system does not propose an exact solving of the problem. This size becomes a criterion to minimize.

Definition 1 (VRPTW). *An instance $I = (G, D, T, S, F, R, \kappa)$ of the VRPTW is defined as follows. Let $G = (V, E)$ a graph with a set of nodes $V = \{(v_i)\}, i = \{0, ..., N\}$ (node v_0 is the depot) and a set of arcs $E = \{(v_i, v_j) | v_i \in V, v_j \in V, v_i \neq v_j\}$. Let two matrices $D = \{(d_{ij})\}$ et $T = \{(t_{ij})\}$ of costs, of dimensions $N \times N$ (the arc (v_i, v_j) has a distance of d_{ij} and a travel time of t_{ij}), a M-array F of vehicles, and a N-array R of tuples (R for requests) $(q_i, s_i, [e_i, l_i])$ (node v_i has a demand q_i, a service time s_i and a time window $[e_i, l_i]$, $q_1 = (0, 0, [e_0, l_0])$). The window $[e_0, l_0]$ is the "scheduling horizon" of the problem. All the time windows have to be comprised between these two bounds. A vehicle has to be in i before l_i but can be in i before e_i, in which case it has to wait for the service start. Every request is supposed to be inferior to κ.*

Two decision variables are defined: $X = (x_{ijk})$ of dimension $N \times N \times M$ and $B = (b_i)$ of dimension N having the following interpretation:

$$x_{ijk} = \begin{cases} 1 \text{ if the vehicle k visits node } v_i \text{ immediately after node } v_j \\ 0 \text{ otherwise} \end{cases}$$

$b_i = t \Leftrightarrow v_i$ *is visited at t*

The objective function:

$$\min \sum_{i,j=0}^{N} d_{ij} \sum_{k \in F} x_{ijk} \tag{1}$$

Solving a VRPTW consists in finding X and B optimizing the objective function for all instance of I subject to the following constraints:

$$\sum_{k \in F} \sum_{j=1}^{N} x_{ijk} = 1 \; \forall v_i \in V \backslash v_0 \tag{2}$$

$$\sum_{j=1}^{N} x_{0jk} = 1 \; \forall k \in F \tag{3}$$

$$\sum_{i=0}^{N} x_{ijk} - \sum_{i=0}^{N} x_{jik} = 0 \; \forall k \in F, \forall v_j \in V \backslash v_0 \tag{4}$$

$$\sum_{j=1}^{N} x_{j0k} = 1 \; \forall k \in F \tag{5}$$

$$\sum_{i=0}^{N} q_i \sum_{j=0}^{N} x_{ijk} \leq \kappa \qquad \forall k \in F \tag{6}$$

$$x_{ijk}(b_i + s_i + t_{ij} - b_j) \leq 0 \; \forall k \in F, \forall (v_i, v_j) \in E \tag{7}$$

$$e_i \leq b_i \leq l_i \; \forall k \in F, \forall v_i \in V \tag{8}$$

$$x_{ijk} \in \{0, 1\}, \forall (v_i, v_j) \in E \; \forall k \in F \tag{9}$$

The function (1) expresses the system's objective: the minimization of overall cost. Constraints (2) restrict the assignment of every customer (but the depot v_0) to exactly one vehicle. Constraints (3) to (5) characterize the path to follow by a vehicle k: k has to leave the depot only once (3), for every served customer (if any), it has to leave it (4) and get back to the depot exactly once (5). Constraints (6) guarantee the non-violation of the capacity limits of the vehicles. Constraints (7) − (8) ensure the non-violation of time constraints.

4   The Multiagent Systems Architectures

Our systems are composed of a dynamic set of agents which interact to solve the dynamic VRPTW. A solution consists of a series of vehicles routes. Each route contains a sequence of customers with their associated visit time. We define three categories of agents. Customer agents, which represent users of the system (persons or goods), vehicle agents, which represent vehicles in the MAS and interface agents which represent an access point to the system (Web server, GUI, simulator, etc.). When a user logs in the MAS, the data she provides are verified (existing node, valid time windows, etc.) and, if the data are correct, a customer agent representing her is created.

In [24], we have designed, implemented and compared three possible architectures to model the dynamic VRPTW: a centralized architecture, a decentralized architecture and a hybrid architecture. The hybrid architecture has provided the best results in terms of robustness and execution times.

In the centralized approach, all the processing is performed by a central entity, which create vehicle plans and schedules. In the decentralized approach, vehicle agents exchange messages trying to insert the customers that reveal online. Each vehicle agent is responsible of the customers scheduling in its plan. The hybrid architecture (cf. Fig. 1) is a compromise between the centralized and the decentralized approach. Indeed, the vehicle agents don't exchange messages, they all interact with the new coming customer agent. Once created, the customer agent sends its request to all the available vehicles, collects bids from the vehicle agents and chooses the one offering the best cost. The process describes a CNP (Contract Net Protocol) [23]. If there is no vehicle agent that can insert the customer, a new vehicle is created. Finally, the customer agent informs the vehicles about its choice. The question is now to define the criteria to choose the best vehicle candidate for the insertion of the new customer.

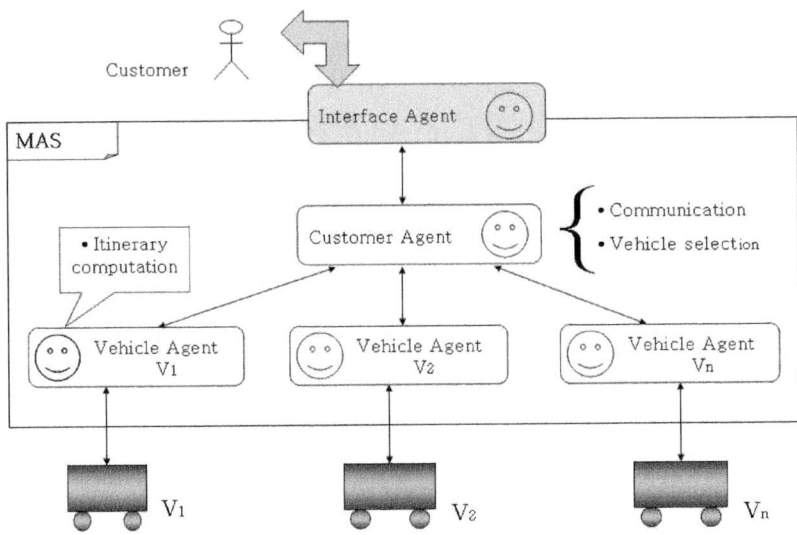

Fig. 1. MAS Architecture

We observe that the direct and exclusive focus on the conventional criteria for the VRPTW (the traveled distance and the fleet size) leads to the appearance of uncovered areas because of their low density. Indeed, the fact that we deal with a dynamic and nondeterministic problem can lead to the appearance of two different but non independent phenomena. The first is the concentration of vehicles in some geographical zones which are more attractive and may lead to the second phenomenon, which is the lack of service elsewhere. The idea behind the organization models - that we detail in the following - is that when the positioning of vehicles is made such as to cover as much territory as possible, the risk of customers whose demand is unsatisfied, and the obligation to mobilize new vehicles to serve them, decreases. The choice that we make to solve this problem is to use the multiagent paradigm coupled with insertion heuristics. In this context, we have only one lever to change the system's behavior, which is the way in which the vehicle agents calculate the insertion cost of a customer. These calculation methods are two dimensional: spatial and spatiotemporal. The two organization models that we propose have the objective of minimizing the number of used vehicles, while keeping the use of a "pure" insertion heuristics, i.e. without any further improvements or post-optimization.

Following the description above, the customer agent chooses between several vehicle agents the one with the minimal proposed insertion cost. The systems that are based on this heuristic use generally the measure of Solomon [1] as an insertion cost. This measure consists in inserting the customer which has the minimal impact on the general cost of the vehicle (which is generally function of the vehicle's incurred detour). This measure is simple and the most intuitive but has a serious drawback, since inserting the current customer might make lots of future customers' insertions infeasible, with the current number of vehicles. Its problem is that it generates vehicles' plans that are very constrained in time and space, i.e. plans that offer a few possibilities of insertion between each pair of adjacent planned customers. In this situation, the appearance of a new customer might oblige the system to create a new vehicle to serve it. Through the modeling of vehicle agents' action zones, we propose a new way to compute the customer's insertion cost in the route of a vehicle, and a new choice criterion between vehicles for the insertion of a given customer. We propose a new method that allows the customer to choose the vehicle agent "whose decrease in the probability to participate in future insertions is minimal", to serve the new customer. The logic of our models is different from the traditional models, which focus on the increase of the traveled distance, neglecting the impact of the current insertion decision on future insertion possibilities.

5   Spatial Organization Model

The objective of the spatial organization model is to allow the specialization of the vehicles to zones while maintaining a wide coverage of the network (cf. Fig. 2). Thus, we define action zones on the transportation network, to which the vehicles are attached. The attachment of vehicles to their zones is not encoded in their behavior, but has an effect on how they calculate their customers insertion costs. This computation should ensure that a vehicle agent plans its itinerary while being encouraged to stay in its zone[2]. Each zone is defined by a set of nodes and a centroid. In Fig. 2, vehicles V1 and V2 might be tempted to leave their zones to serve new customers, the mechanism that we propose should make it more expensive for them to do so.

Definition 2 (Spatial Action Zone). *Given $G = (V, A)$ the graph describing the network (cf. Definition 1), we define the zone $\zeta = (N_\zeta, A_\zeta)$ as a subgraph of G.*

Definition 3 (centroid of a Zone). *The centroid of zone ζ is a node $n^{*\zeta}$ of N that minimizes $\sum_{y \in N_\zeta} d_{n^{*\zeta}, y}$.*

---

[2] The segmentation of the network in geographical zones is treated as a graph partitioning problem and is left out of the scope of this paper. We assume that the definition of these zones is a system parameter, which is the responsibility of an expert.

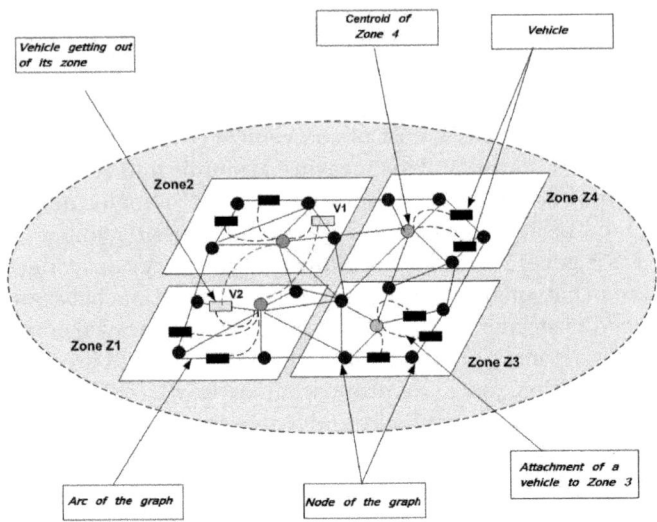

Fig. 2. Specialization and Attraction Zones

Each zone is defined by a centroid and a set of nodes (cf. Fig. 3). The centroid of a zone corresponds to the node which is the closest to all other nodes in the zone. At any point in time, each vehicle agent has a distance from its action zone. This distance is equal to the average distance of the nodes in its route from the centroid of its zone. It depends of the customers inserted in its route. If the vehicle has a node in its route that is outside its zone, the distance of this node is multiplied by a factor β (> 1) which is a system parameter. Since the insertion cost proposed by a vehicle agent to the customer depends of the vehicle distance from its zone (see definition 5), the penalty β discourages the vehicle from inserting customers that are located outside its action zone.

Definition 4 (Vehicle Distance from its Zone). *The distance of a vehicle v from its zone ζ_v at a given moment is equal to the average distance of the nodes in its route from the centroid of ζ_v:*

$$d_{v,\zeta_v} = \frac{\sum_{n^v \in Nodes(v)} d_{n^v, n^{*\zeta}}}{|Nodes(v)|} \tag{10}$$

with

$$\forall c \in N, d_{n^v,c} = \begin{cases} d_{n^v,c}, & if\, n^v \in \zeta_v \\ \beta \times d_{n^v,c}\; else \end{cases}$$

$Nodes(v)$ represents the nodes of the vehicle agent's route, $|\,Nodes(v)\,|$ is the number of nodes in $Nodes(v)$ and β is the penalty imposed to the vehicle distance, if its route integrates nodes which are outside its zone.

The objective of the new measure is to encourage vehicles to stay in the vicinity of network zones to which they are allocated. This is done by integrating in the insertion cost, besides the increase in the traveled distance, a factor that is function of the distance from the centroid, and a penalty if it had to leave its zone to satisfy a request. The insertion cost of a customer in the route of a vehicle agent becomes equal to the incurred detour to insert the new customer, multiplied by the variation of the vehicle agent's distance from its zone (we denote $v \succ c^*$ the vehicle v with c^* in its route).

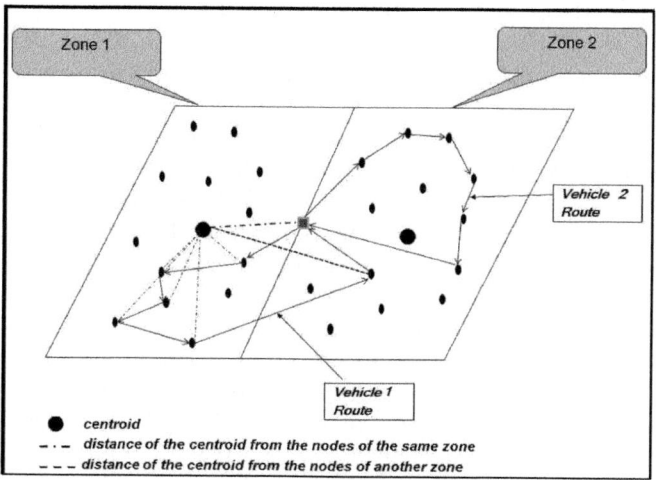

Fig. 3. Spatial Action Zones

Definition 5 (Insertion cost of a customer). *The insertion cost proposed by the vehicle for the insertion of the customer c^* is equal to:*

$$cost(v, c^*) = \frac{d_{v \succ c^*, \zeta_v}}{d_{v, \zeta_v}} \times (Dist_{v \succ c^*} - Dist_v) \tag{11}$$

$Dist_v$ is the total distance traveled by vehicle v. There exists several possible insertion positions of a customer c^* in the route of a vehicle agent. To each of these positions, there corresponds a value of $cost(v, c^*)$. The considered cost is the one for which $cost(v, c^*)$ is minimal.

The offer that a vehicle agent proposes to a customer for its insertion is then weighted by the difference between the old distance of the vehicle from its zone and its new one. The bigger β is, the more the vehicles are organized so that they stay in their zones. When a vehicle plans to quit it zone, it is penalized with an increase of its insertion cost and sees thus its competitiveness limited w.r.t the other vehicles that are candidates for the insertion of the considered customer. This penalty plays the role of an attractive force exerted on the vehicle. As if a sort of a spring were fixed to the centroid of the zone and to the vehicle.

Unlike ADART [25], our spatial action zones are not rigid. Indeed, a vehicle in our system has the right to quit its zone, with a penalty, while it can't at all in [25]. This choice is motivated by the fact that insertion heuristics consider only a very small subset of all the possible routes combinations for a given set of customers, and this is precisely why they are so fast. Narrowing this set even more, by completely preventing vehicles from leaving their zones, would limit the search space more and would lead, *In Fine*, to the mobilization of new vehicles to serve the unsatisfied customers.

6   Space-Time Organization Model

Even if it allows a better spatial coverage of the network, the spatial organization model has two major drawbacks. First, it assumes *a priori* geographical segmentation. This task requires a great calibration effort to specify the most efficient zones' segmentation. Second, it doesn't incorporate the temporal dimension of the problem, since a vehicle might not be able to serve a customer even if it is located in its zone, because of the time constraints. In the following, we propose to integrate the temporal dimension in the vehicle agents' action zones and to eliminate any *a priori* definition of these zones.

In the heuristics and multiagent methods of the literature, the hierarchical objective of minimizing the number of mobilized vehicles is considered in priority w.r.t the distance traveled by all the vehicles. The vast majority of the literature heuristics are as a consequence based on a two-phase approach: the minimization of the number of vehicles, followed by the minimization of the traveled distance [4]. The model that we propose in this section has the objective of minimizing the number of used vehicles.

To this end, our model allows vehicle agents to cover a maximal space-time zone of the transportation network, avoiding this way the mobilization of a new vehicle if a new customer appears in an uncovered zone [26]. A space-time pair $\langle i, t \rangle$ - with i a node and t a time - is said to be "covered" by a vehicle agent v if v can be in i at t. In the context of the dynamic VRPTW, maximizing the space-time coverage of vehicle agents results in giving the maximum chance to satisfy the demand of a future (unknown) customer. Through the new modeling of vehicle agents' space-time action zones, we propose a new way to compute the customer's insertion cost in the route of a vehicle.

6.1   Environment Modeling

The space-time action zone of a vehicle agent is composed of a subset of the network nodes, together with the times that are associated to them. We model the MAS environment in the form of a space-time network, inferred from the network graph. Each node of the graph becomes a pair $\langle space, time \rangle$, which represents the "state" of the node in a discrete time period. The space-time network is composed of several subgraphs, where each subgraph is a copy of the static graph, and corresponds to the state of the graph in a certain period of time (cf. Fig. 4). We index the nodes of a subgraph as follows: $\langle 0, t \rangle, \dots, \langle N, t \rangle$, with $t \in \{1, ..., h\}$, where $0, \dots, N$ are the nodes of the network and h the number of

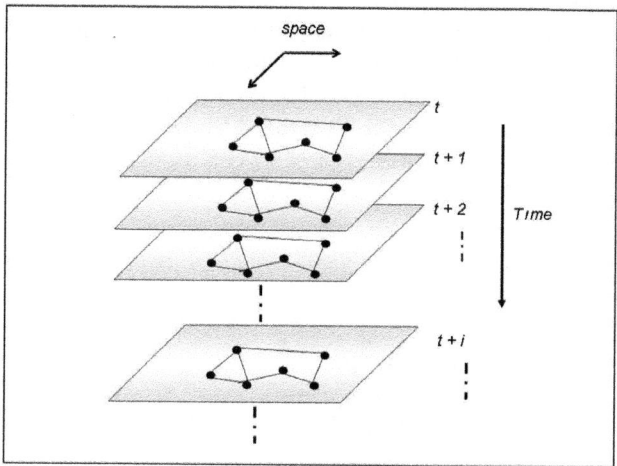

Fig. 4. Space-Time Network

considered discrete periods. The total number of nodes in the space-time network is equal to $h \times N$. The edges linking the nodes of a subgraph are those of the static graph, and the costs are the travel times as described in the problem definition.

6.2   Intuition of the Space-Time Action Zones

Consider a vehicle agent v that has an empty route. In order for this agent to be able to insert a new customer c - described by: n a node, $[e, l]$ a time window, s a service time, and q a quantity - l has to be big enough to allow v to be in n without violating its time constraints[3]. More precisely, the current time t, plus

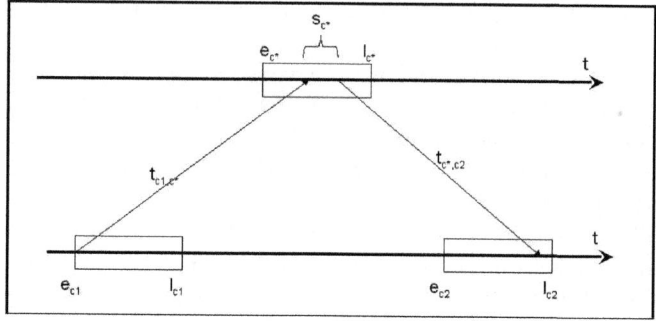

Fig. 5. Feasible insertion

---

[3] Note that we assume that only one customer is considered by the vehicle agents until it is inserted in one of their routes.

the travel time between the depot and n has to be less or equal to l (cf. Fig. 5). Starting from this observation, we define the action zone of a vehicle agent as agent as the set of pairs $\langle n, t \rangle$ of the space-time network that remain valid given its current route (n can be visited by the vehicle at t). The action zone of a vehicle agent with an empty route is illustrated by the triangular shadow[4] in the Fig. 6.

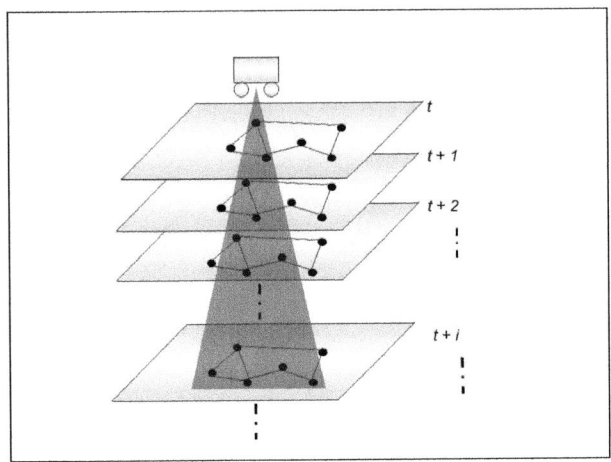

Fig. 6. Initial Space-Time Action Zone

When a vehicle agent inserts a customer in its route, its action zone is recomputed, since some $\langle node, time \rangle$ pairs become not valid because of its insertion. In Fig. 7, a new customer is inserted in the route of the vehicle. The action zone of the vehicle agent after inserting the customer is represented by the interior of the contour of the bold lines, which represent the space-time nodes which remain accessible after the insertion of the customer (the computation of the new action zone is explained later).

The associated cost to an offer from a vehicle agent v for the insertion of a customer agent c corresponds to the hypothetical decrease of the action zone of v following the insertion of c in its route.

The idea is that the chosen vehicle for the insertion of a customer is the one that looses the minimal chance to be candidate for the insertion of future customers. Thus, the criterion that is maximized by the society of vehicle agents is the sum of their action zones, i.e. the capacity that the MAS has to react to the appearance of customer agents, without mobilizing new vehicles.

To illustrate the action zones and their dynamics, we present the version of the measure that is related to an Euclidean problem, i.e. where travel times are computed following the Euclidean metric. The following paragraphs detail the measure as well as its dynamics.

---

[4] It is actually a conic shadow in a three-dimensional space.

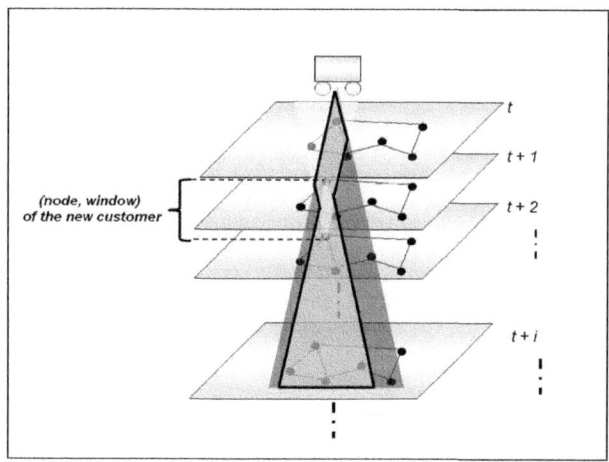

Fig. 7. Action Zone after the Insertion of a Customer

6.3   The Computation of Action Zones

In the Euclidean case, the transportation network is a plane, and the travel times between two points i (described by (x_i, y_i)) and j (described by (x_j, y_j)) is equal to

$$\sqrt{(x_i - x_j)^2 + (y_i - y_j)^2}(12) \tag{12}$$

Therefore, if a vehicle is in i at the moment t, it cannot be in j earlier than $t_i + \sqrt{(x_i - x_j)^2 + (y_i - y_j)^2}$.

We can compute at any time, from the current position of a vehicle, the set of triples (x, y, t) where it can be in the future. Indeed, considering a plane with an X-axis in $[x_{min}, x_{max}]$ and a Y-axis in $[y_{min}, y_{max}]$, the set of space-time positions is the set of points in the cube delimited by $[x_{min}, x_{max}], [y_{min}, y_{max}]$ and $[e_0, l_0]$ (recall that e_0 and l_0 are the scheduling horizon and are the minimal and maximal values for the time windows). Consider a vehicle in the depot (x_0, y_0) at t_0. The set of points (x, y, t) that are accessible by this vehicle are described by the following inequality:

$$\sqrt{(x - x_0)^2 + (y - y_0)^2} \leq (t - t_0)(13) \tag{13}$$

The (x, y, t) satisfying this inequality are those that are positioned inside the cone $\mathcal{C}$ of vertex (x_0, y_0, t_0) and with the equation $\sqrt{(x - x_0)^2 + (y - y_0)^2} = (t - t_0)$ (c.f Fig. 8). This cone represents the action zone of a vehicle agent, with an empty route, in the Euclidean case. It represents all the possible space-time positions that this vehicle agent is able to have in the future.

We use the action zone of the vehicle agents when a customer agent has to choose between several vehicle agents for its insertion. We have to be able to compare the action zones of different vehicle agents. To do so, we propose

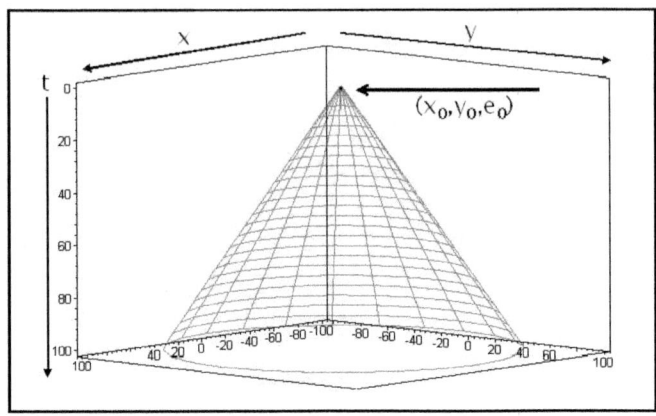

Fig. 8. Initial Action Zone

to quantify it, by computing the volume of the cone $\mathcal{C}$ representing the future possible positions of the vehicle:

$$Volume(\mathcal{C}) = \frac{1}{3} \times \pi \times (l_0 - e_0)^3 \tag{14}$$

This is the quantification of the initial action zone of any new vehicle agent joining the MAS. When a new customer agent appears, a vehicle agent computes its new action zone, the cost that it proposes to the customer agent is the difference between its old action zone and its new one. The new action zone computation is detailed in the following paragraph.

6.4 Dynamics of the Action Zones

Consider a customer c_2 (of coordinates (x_2, y_2) and with a time window $[e_2, l_2]$) that joins the system, and suppose that v is temporarily the only available vehicle agent of the system and has an empty route. The agent v has to infer its new space-time action zone, i.e. the space-time nodes that it can still reach without violating the time constraints of c_2. The new action zone answers the following questions: "if v had to be in (x_2, y_2) at l_2, where would it have been before? And if it had to be there at e_2 where would it be after $e_2 + s_2$?". The triples (x, y, t) where the vehicle agent can be before visiting c_2 are described by the inequality (15), and the triples (x, y, t) where he can be after visiting c_2 are describe by the inequality (16).

$$\sqrt{(x - x_2)^2 + (y - y_2)^2} \leq (l_2 - (t)) \tag{15}$$

$$\sqrt{(x - x_2)^2 + (y - y_2)^2} \leq (t - (e_2 + s_2)) \tag{16}$$

The new action zone is illustrated by the Fig. 9: the new measure consists of the volume of the intersection of the initial cone $\mathcal{C}$ with the union of the two new cones described by the inequalities (15) and (16) (denoted respectively by $\mathcal{C}_1$ and $\mathcal{C}_2$). The new measure of the action zone is equal to the volume of the intersection[5] of $\mathcal{C}$ with the union of $\mathcal{C}_1$ and $\mathcal{C}_2$.

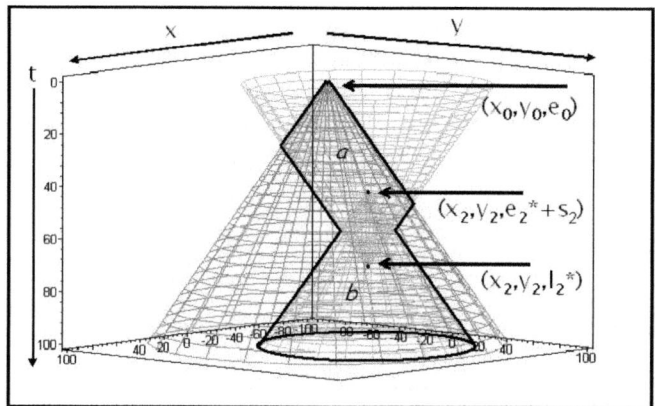

Fig. 9. Space-Time Action Zone after the insertion of c_2

The cost of the insertion of a customer in the route of a vehicle is equal to the measure associated with the old action zone of the vehicle minus the measure of the new action zone, after the insertion of the customer. The measured quantity represents the space-time positions that the vehicle cannot have anymore, if it had to insert this customer in its route. The retained vehicle agent is the one for which the insertion of the new customer causes the minimum loss in its space-time action zone. This corresponds to choosing the vehicle that looses the minimal chances to be candidate for future customers.

6.5   Coordination of Action Zones

The objective of the space-time organization model is to allow a better space-time coverage of the transportation network. This improvement is materialized by a minimal mobilization of vehicles when confronted to the appearance of new customers. With the mechanism described until now, every vehicle agent tries to maximize its own action zone independently from the other agents of the MAS. However, it would be more interesting to incite the agents society in its whole to cover the network in the most efficient way. More precisely, the fact that a vehicle looses space-time nodes that it is the only one to cover should be more costly than to loose nodes that are also covered by other agents.

---

[5] The complete computation of the volume of the intersection of these two cones is reported in the Appendix A of [26].

To this end, to every node of the space-time network, we start by associating the list of vehicles covering it. Then, to every creation of a new vehicle agent, the set of space-time nodes that are part of its action zone is computed. The vehicle proceeds then with the notification of these nodes that they are part of its action zone. Every node updates its list, containing the vehicles that are covering it, at each notification from a vehicle agent. Similarly, when the action zone of a vehicle agent loses a node, the node is notified and its list of vehicles is updated.

Now, when the insertion cost of a customer is computed, every vehicle agent starts by determining the space-time nodes that it would loose if it had to insert the new customer. Then, it interrogates each of these nodes about the "price to pay" if it were not covering it anymore. This price is inversely proportional to the number of vehicles covering this node. More precisely, the price to pay is equal to

$$\frac{1}{\mid v_{\langle n,t \rangle} \mid} \tag{17}$$

with $v_{\langle n,t \rangle}$ denoting the vehicle agents covering the space-time node $\langle n, t \rangle$ and $\mid v_{\langle n,t \rangle} \mid$ the number of such vehicles.

This way, more or less penalty is associated with the decisions of non-coverage of the network by the vehicles as time progresses. Thus, the vehicle agents are incited to cover the whole network in a coordinated way, improving by doing so the reactivity of the MAS.

7   Results

Marius M. Solomon [1] has created a set of different static problems for the VRPTW. It is now admitted that these problems are challenging and diverse enough to compare with enough confidence the different proposed methods. In Solomon's benchmarks, six different sets of problems have been defined: C1, C2, R1, R2, RC1 and RC2. The customers are geographically uniformly distributed in the problems of type R, clustered in the problems of type C, and a mix of customers uniformly distributed and clustered is used in the problems of type RC. The problems of type 1 have narrow time windows (very few customers can coexist in the same vehicle's route) and the problems of type 2 have wide time windows. Finally, a constant service time is associated with each customer, which is equal to 10 in the problems of type R and RC, and to 90 in the problems of type C. Short service times would represent problems where the loading and unloading of the transported entities is fast (transport of persons for instance). In every problem set, there are between 8 and 12 files containing 100 customers each.

We choose to use Solomon benchmarks, while following the modification proposed by [27] to make the problem dynamic. To this end, let $[0, T]$ the simulation time. All the time related data (time windows, service times and travel times) are multiplied by $\frac{T}{l_0 - e_0}$, with $[e_0, l_0]$ the scheduling horizon of the problem. The authors divide the customers set in two subsets, the first subset defines the customers that are known in advance, and the second the customers who reveals during execution. We do not make this distinction, since we consider no customers known in advance. For each customer, an occurrence time is associated, defining the moment when the customer is known by the system. Given a customer i, the occurrence time that is associated is generated randomly between $[0, \overline{e}_i]$, with:

$$\overline{e}_i = e_i \times \frac{T}{l_0 - e_0} \tag{18}$$

It is known that the behavior of insertion heuristics is strongly sensitive to the appearance order of the customers to the system. For this reason, we do not consider only one appearance order. We launch the process that we have just described ten times with every problem file, creating this way ten different versions of every problem file.

We have implemented three MAS with almost the same behavior, the only difference concerns the measure used by vehicle agents to compute the insertion cost of a customer. For the first implemented MAS, it relies on the Solomon measure (noted Δ Distance). The second relies on the space-time model (noted Δ Space-Time) and the third on the spatial model (noted Δ Space)[6]. We choose to run our experiments with the problems of class R and C, of type 1, which are the instances that are very constrained in time (narrow time windows). Our system is coded in JAVA and executed on a PC with a Core 2 Duo® 2.77 GHZ processor, with 4 GB of RAM.

Table 1. Results summary (Criterion: Fleet Size)

Problem	Δ Distance $\|$Fleet$\|$	Δ Space-Time $\|$Fleet$\|$	Δ Space $\|$Fleet$\|$
R1 25 customers	64	53	58
C1 25 customers	34	31	32
R1 50 customers	107	92	101
C1 50 customers	60	53	58
R1 100 customers	181	150	164
C1 100 customers	121	108	113

For each problem class and type, we have considered different customers numbers in order to verify the behavior of our models w.r.t to the problem size. To this end, we have considered successively the 25 first customers, the 50 first customers, and finally all the 100 customers contained in each problem file. Table 1 summarizes the results. Each cell contains the best obtained results with each problem class (the sum of all problem files). The results show, with the two classes of problems, that the use of the space-time model mobilizes less

---

[6] After several test runs, we set the penalty β to 1.2 and the geographical zones to four equal zones; these values have provided the best results. As we said earlier, the optimal definition of zones is a hard problem and is left out of the scope of this paper.

vehicles than the spatial model ($53 < 58, 31 < 32, 92 < 101, 53 < 58, 150 < 164, 108 < 113$). However, the spatial model behaves better than the traditional measure, whatever the number of considered customers ($58 < 64, 32 < 34, 101 < 107, 58 < 60, 164 < 181, 113 < 121$). These results validate the intuition of the models, which consists of maximizing the future insertion possibilities for a vehicle agent.

Once this result validated, it is interesting to check the results with respect to the total distance traveled by all the vehicles. Table 2 summarizes the results[7]. With respect to this criterion, the space model behaves better than the two others, while the behavior of the space-time model is less efficient, since it gives better results for the problems C1 with 25 customers and R1 with 100 customers, but is dominated by the traditional measure for the others. The fact remains that our results for both models provide better results than the traditional heuristic, provided the primary objective of the problem, which is to minimize the number of vehicles mobilized by the system.

Table 2. Results summary (Criterion: Total Traveled Distance)

Problem	Δ Distance Distance	Δ Space-Time Distance	Δ Space Distance
R1 25 customers	6372	6561	5732
C1 25 customers	3167	3152	3014
R1 50 customers	12036	12089	11307
C1 50 customers	6712	7093	6682
R1 100 customers	17907	17348	16680
C1 100 customers	16011	16512	15206

8   Conclusion

In the vehicle routing problems, the exclusive optimization of the conventional criteria leads to the appearance of geographic areas and/or time periods that are not covered by any vehicle because of their low population density. In this paper, we have proposed two agent-oriented organization models for the dynamic VRPTW based on the agents' action zones. The action zones of the vehicle agents reflect their coverage of the transportation network. We use these action zones to reduce the short-sighted behavior of traditional metrics. By optimizing the coverage of the environment by the vehicle agents, our models allow the MAS to self-adapt by exhibiting an equilibrated distribution of the vehicles, and to lessen this way the number of vehicles mobilized to serve the customers.

Our current works are oriented in two different directions. We envision to observe the behavior of our two systems following more qualitative criteria, such as the existence of emergent phenomena and their usefulness for the optimization process. Besides, like the quasi-totality of the state-of-the-art proposals, vehicle travel times are static. If the systems are implemented in urban zones or in time

[7] In Solomon's benchmarks, there is no unit associated with the distances.

periods which are subject to congestion, the vehicle routes might become not valid. To overcome this limitation, we envision to use an options mechanism on customers requests. An option is a reservation for serving a customer by a vehicle. The withdrawal of an option by a vehicle could take place when trafic predictions, which become more and more precise over time, result in the violation of the customer time windows by the vehicle.

References

1. Solomon, M.: Algorithms for the vehicle routing and scheduling with time window constraints. Operations Research 15, 254–265 (1987)
2. Wooldridge, M., Jennings, N.R.: Intelligent agents: Theory and practice. Knowledge Engineering Review 10(2), 115–152 (1995)
3. Sycara, K.P.: Multiagent Systems. AI Magazine 19, 79–92 (1998)
4. Nagata, Y., Bräysy, O., Dullaert, W.: A penalty-based edge assembly memetic algorithm for the vehicle routing problem with time windows. Computers & Operations Research 37, 724–737 (2010)
5. Jepsen, M., Petersen, B., Spoorendonk, S., Pisinger, D.: Subset-row inequalities applied to the vehicle-routing problem with time windows. Operations Research 56, 497–511 (2008)
6. Pisinger, D., Ropke, S.: A general heuristic for vehicle routing problems. Computers & Operations Research 34, 2403–2435 (2007)
7. Czech, Z.J., Czarnas, P.: A parallel simulated annealing for the vehicle routing problem with time windows. In: Proceedings of the 10th Euromicro Workshop on Parallel, Distributed and Network-based Processing, Canary Islands, Spain, pp. 376–383 (2002)
8. de Oliveira, H.C.B., Vasconcelos, G.C., Alvarenga, G.B.: A multi-start simulated annealing algorithm for the vehicle routing problem with time windows. In: Proceedings of the Ninth Brazilian Symposium on Neural Networks, p. 24. IEEE Computer Society, Washington, DC (2006)
9. Mester, D., Brysy, O.: Active guided evolution strategies for large scale vehicle routing problems with time windows. Computers & Operations Research 32, 1593–1614 (2005)
10. Gambardella, L.M., Taillard, E.D., Agazzi, G.: MACS-VRPTW: A multiple ant colony system for vehicle routing problems with time windows. In: Corne, D., Dorigo, M., Glover, F. (eds.) New Ideas in Optimization, pp. 63–76. McGraw-Hill, London (1999)
11. Barán, B., Schaerer, M.: A multiobjective ant colony system for vehicle routing problem with time windows. In: Applied Informatics, pp. 97–102 (2003)
12. Golden, B., Raghavan, S., Wasil, E.: The vehicle routing problem, latest advances and new challenges. Operations research/computer science interfaces, vol. 43. Springer (2008)
13. Desaulniers, G., Desrosiers, J., Solomon, M., Soumis, F., Cordeau, J.F.: The VRP with time windows. In: Vigo, D., Toth, P. (eds.) The Vehicle Routing Problem. SIAM Monographs on Discrete Mathematics and Applications, pp. 157–193. SIAM (2002)
14. Gendreau, M., Guertin, F., Potvin, J.Y., Sguin, R.: Neighborhood search heuristics for a dynamic vehicle dispatching problem with pick-ups and deliveries. Transportation Research Part C 14, 157–174 (2006)

15. Housroum, H., Hsu, T., Dupas, R., Goncalves, G.: A hybrid ga approach for solving the dynamic vehicle routing problem with time windows. In: Society, I.C. (ed.) Proceedings of the IEEE Conference on Information and Communication Technologies: from Theory to Applications, Damascus, Syria, pp. 3347–3352 (2006)
16. Madsen, O.B., Ravn, H.F., Rygaard, J.M.: A heuristic algorithm for a dial-a-ride problem with time windows, multiple capacities, and multiple objectives. Operations Research 60, 193–208 (1995)
17. Fu, L., Teply, S.: On-line and off-line routing and scheduling of dial-a-ride paratransit vehicles. In: Computer-Aided Civil and Infrastructure Engineering, vol. 14, pp. 309–319. Blackwell Publishers, Oxford (1999)
18. Horn, M.E.: Fleet scheduling and dispatching for demand-responsive passenger services. Transportation Research C 10, 35–63 (2002)
19. Diana, M.: The importance of information flows temporal attributes for the efficient scheduling of dynamic demand responsive transport services. Journal of Advanced Transportation 40, 23–46 (2006)
20. Thangiah, S.R., Shmygelska, O., Mennell, W.: An agent architecture for vehicle routing problems. In: Proceedings of the 2001 ACM Symposium on Applied Computing (SAC 2001), pp. 517–521. ACM Press, New York (2001)
21. Kohout, R., Erol, K.: In-Time agent-based vehicle routing with a stochastic improvement heuristic. In: Proceedings of the Sixteenth National Conference on Artificial Intelligence and the Eleventh Innovative Applications of Artificial Intelligence (AAAI 1999/IAAI 1999), pp. 864–869. AAAI Press, Menlo Park (1999)
22. Fischer, K., Muller, J., Pischel, M., Schier, D.: A model for cooperative transportation scheduling. In: Lesser, V.R., Gasser, L. (eds.) Proceedings of the First International Conference on Multiagent Systems (ICMAS 1995), pp. 109–116. AAAI Press / MIT Press, Menlo Park, CA, USA (1995)
23. Smith, R.G.: The contract net protocol: High-level communication and control in a distributed problem solver. IEEE Trans. on Comp. C-29, 1104–1113 (1980)
24. Zeddini, B.: Modèles d'Auto-Organisation Multi-Agent pour le problème du transport à la demande. PhD thesis, University of le Havre, Le Havre (France), 164 pages (2009) (in french)
25. Dial, R.B.: Autonomous dial-a-ride transit introductory overview. Transportation Research Part C: Emerging Technologies 3, 261–275(15) (1995)
26. Zargayouna, M.: Modèle et langage de coordination pour les systèmes multi-agents ouverts. Application au problème du transport à la demande. PhD thesis, University of Paris-Dauphine, Paris (France), 165 pages (2007) (in french)
27. Gendreau, M., Guertin, F., Potvin, J.Y., Taillard, E.D.: Parallel tabu search for real-time vehicle routing and dispatching. Transportation Science 33, 381–390 (1999)

Neural Smooth Function Approximation and Prediction with Adaptive Learning Rate

Villèvo Adanhounmè[1], Théophile K. Dagba[2], and Sèmiyou A. Adédjouma[3]

[1] International Chair of Mathematical Physics and Applications
(ICMPA-UNESCO Chair) Université d'Abomey-Calavi
072 BP 50 Cotonou, Republic of Benin
adanhounm@yahoo.fr
[2] Ecole Nationale d'Economie Appliquée et de Management
Université d'Abomey-Calavi
03 BP 1079 Cotonou, Republic of Benin
theophile.dagba@eneam.uac.bj
[3] Ecole Polytechnique d'Abomey-Calavi
Université d'Abomey-Calavi
01 BP 2009 Cotonou, Republic of Benin
semiyou.adedjouma@epac.uac.bj

Abstract. An algebraic approach for representing multidimensional nonlinear functions by feedforward neural networks is implemented for the approximation of smooth batch data containing input-output of the hidden neurons and the final neural output of the network. The training set is associated with the adjustable parameters of the network by weight equations which may be compatible or incompatible. Then in case the nonlinear and linear weight equations are compatible we obtain the exact solutions of these equations. Otherwise, we get the unique approximate solution with minimal norm such that the norm of the difference between the left and right handsides of these equations reaches the minimal value. This approach allows us to find a novel adaptive learning rate. Using the multi-agent system as the different kinds of energies for the plant growth and the multi-agent system as concentrations of different substances in the chemical reaction of higher order, one can predict the height of the plant and the concentrations of the substances respectively.

Keywords: function approximation, conjugate gradient method, adaptive training, multi-agent systems.

1 Introduction

Artificial Feedforward Neural Networks (FNNs) have been widely used in many application areas in recent years and have shown their strength in solving complex problems in Artificial Intelligence. Although many different models of neural networks have been proposed, multilayered FNNs are the commonest. Neural networks trained with back-propagation (BP) learning algorithm are often used for identification of nonlinear dynamic systems. The standard BP algorithm uses

N.T. Nguyen (Ed.): Transactions on CCI VII, LNCS 7270, pp. 103–118, 2012.

fixed learning rate. One of the important parameters in training a neural network is its rate speed. The selection of the learning rate to get the appropriate performance for a neural network involves a time consuming experimentation: a small learning rate causes small and slow changes to the weights in the network from one iteration to the next, and thus leads to a smooth learning curve; on the other hand, if the learning rate is large, the resulting larger and faster changes will help to speed up the learning process but this may cause instability. One way of attempting to improve the learning speed is by using adaptive learning rates where the rate is appropriately adjusted after every training cycle. Various adjustable learning rate algorithms have been proposed and studied ([1],[2]). In order to train an FNN, supervised training is the most frequently used technique. The training process is an incremental adaptation of connection weights that propagate information between neurons. The neurons are arranged in layers and connections between the neurons of one layer and those of the next exist. Also, one can use an algebraic training which is the approach for approximating multidimensional nonlinear functions by FNNs based on available input-output [3]. Typically, training involves the numerical optimization of the error between the data and the actual network's performance with respect to its adjustable parameters i.e. weights. Considerable effort has gone into developing techniques for accelerating the convergence of these optimization-based training algorithms ([4],[5],[6]). Another line of research has focused on the mathematical investigation of network's approximation properties ([7],[8],[9]). The latter results provide few practical guidelines for implementing the training algorithms, and they cannot be used to evaluate the properties of the solutions obtained by numerical optimization. The algebraic training approach provides a unifying framework that can be used both to train the network and to investigate their approximation properties. The data are associated with the adjustable parameters by means of neural network input-output. Hence the nonlinear training process and related approximation properties can be investigated via linear algebra.

Ferrari et al [3] studied the approximation of smooth batch data containing the gradient information and the final neural output of the network and showed that the linear system of output weight equations admits a unique solution under various assumptions. In this paper we focus on the application of approximation of multidimensional functions by feedforward neural networks as the approximation of smooth batch data containing input-output of the hidden neurons and the final neural output of the network. We obtain the exact input weights of the nonlinear system (compatible or not) which is a unique pseudosolution of the nonlinear system of input weight equations, without assumption a priori. Furthermore we determine the approximated output weight of the linear system of output weight equations by using the conjugate gradient method [10] which approaches the pseudosolution of the linear system, with adaptive learning rate. Doing so we generalize the solutions obtained in [3]. The novel learning rate has been tested against a variable learning rate and some fixed learning rates, and yielded improved performance.

The remaining part of the paper is organized as follows: in section 2 we propose the new algebraic training algorithm ; in section 3, the multi-agent systems as energies for the plant growth and for concentrations of different substances in the chemical reaction of higher order are introduced and simulation results of experiments are presented. The last two sections contain the discussion and the conclusion.

2   Framework

2.1   Background of the Algebraic Approach

The objective is to approximate smooth scalar functions of q inputs:

$$h, g_i : \mathbb{R}^q \to \mathbb{R} \quad i = 1 \cdots s \tag{1}$$

using a feedforward sigmoidal network. Typically, the functions to be approximated are unknown analytically, but a precise set of input-to-nodes samples $\{x^k, v_i{}^k\}_{k=1\cdots p}$ and a precise set of input-output samples $\{x^k, u^k\}_{k=1\cdots p}$ can be generated as follows

$$v_i{}^k = g_i(x^k) \quad , \quad u^k = h(x^k) \quad \forall \quad k \tag{2}$$

These sets of samples are referred to as training sets.
   We adopt the following assumptions:

- The scalar output y_i of the i-th neuron belonging to the hidden layer is computed as:

$$y_i = f[x^T w_i + \theta_i] \quad , \quad w_i = [w_{i1} \cdots w_{iq}]^T, \tag{3}$$

  where w_{ij}, $1 \le j \le q$ are the weights connecting q inputs to the i-th hidden neuron of the network, θ_i is the input bias of the i-th neuron and f the sigmoidal function of the hidden layer defined as follows

$$f(\tau) = \frac{e^\tau - e^{-\tau}}{e^\tau + e^{-\tau}}; \tag{4}$$

- The final scalar output of the network z is computed as a nonlinear transformation of the weighted sum of the input-to-node variables n_i with $i = 1 \cdots s$:

$$z = \nu^T f[wx + \theta] + \lambda \tag{5}$$

  where

$$f[n] = [f(n_1) \cdots f(n_s)]^T; \tag{6}$$

$$n = wx + \theta = [n_1 \cdots n_s]^T \tag{7}$$

$$w = (w_{ij})_{1 \le i \le s; 1 \le j \le q}; \quad \theta = [\theta_1 \cdots \theta_s]^T \tag{8}$$

and λ is the output bias.

Remark. In the general case, one can choose s hidden layer activation functions f_i, $1 \leq i \leq s$. The activation function for the output neuron is taken as the identity function. The computational neural network matches the training set $\{x^k, v_i{}^k, u^k\}_{k=1\cdots p}$ exactly if, given the input x^k, it produces $v_i{}^k$ and u^k as follows

$$y_i(x^k) = v_i{}^k; \quad z(x^k) = u^k \tag{9}$$

which leads to

$$v_i{}^k = f[(x^k)^T w_i + \theta_i] \tag{10}$$
$$u^k = \nu^T f[wx^k + \theta] + \lambda \tag{11}$$

where $\nu_i, 1 \leq i \leq s$ are the weights connecting s hidden neurons to the output neuron. Grouping the known elements $v_i{}^k$ and u^k from the training set in the vectors $v_i = [v_i{}^1 \cdots v_i{}^p]^T$ and $u = [u^1 \cdots u^p]^T$, the equations (10) and (11) can be written using matrix notation

$$v_i = f[n_i] \tag{12}$$
$$u = S\nu + \Lambda \tag{13}$$

which are referred to as weight equations, where

$$n_i = [n_i{}^1 \cdots n_i{}^p]^T; \quad n_i{}^k = (x^k)^T w_i + \theta_i; \tag{14}$$
$$f[n_i] = [f[n_i{}^1] \cdots f[n_i{}^p]]^T; \quad \Lambda = [\lambda \cdots \lambda]^T; \tag{15}$$

$$S = \begin{pmatrix} f[n_1{}^1] & f[n_2{}^1] & \cdots & f[n_s{}^1] \\ f[n_1{}^2] & f[n_2{}^2] & \cdots & f[n_s{}^2] \\ \cdots & \cdots & & \cdots \\ f[n_1{}^p] & f[n_2{}^p] & \cdots & f[n_s{}^p] \end{pmatrix}$$

2.2   The Proposed Algorithm

In this subsection we aim at solving the weight equations (12),(13) where the unknowns are w_i, ν. For this purpose, we need to define the pseudosolution of a system of linear equations, for which we will prove the existence and the uniqueness.

Let us consider the system (12) of linear equations

$$A(k)w_i = b_i, \quad w_i \in \mathbb{R}^q, \quad b_i \in \mathbb{R}, \quad i = 1, \cdots, s, \quad k = 1, \cdots, p, \tag{16}$$

where $A(k) = (x^k)^T$ are the $1 \times q$ matrixes, $b_i = f^{-1}(v_i{}^k) - \theta_i$, $f^{-1}(\xi) = \frac{1}{2}\ln\left(\frac{1+\xi}{1-\xi}\right)$, $\mathbb{R}^q$ and $\mathbb{R}$ are two $q, 1$-dimensional vector spaces respectively. For k fixed , $A(k)$ is constant and we put $A = A(k)$. So we consider i, k fixed.

Definition. A pseudosolution of the system (16) is the vector with the least norm belonging to the set of vectors w_i such that the error function $\Omega(w_i) = [b_i - Aw_i]^2$ can be minimized.

We consider the vector space $\mathbb{R}^q$ endowed with the inner product defined as follows $(\xi, \eta) = \xi^T \eta$. The following state holds [11].

Theorem 1. *The system of linear equations(16) admits a unique pseudosolution.*

Proof. Let us consider the error function Ω defined as follows

$$\Omega(w_i) = (b_i - Aw_i)^T (b_i - Aw_i), \quad w_i \in \mathbb{R}^q. \tag{17}$$

This function can reach its extremum only at the points where $d\Omega(w_i) = 0$ i.e.

$$A^T A w_i = A^T b_i. \tag{18}$$

First of all, we have to prove the compatibility of the system(18) , independently whether the system (16) is compatible or not. Taking into account the fact that matrix $A^T A$ is symmetric, we can write the homogeneous adjoint system associated with the system (18) in the form

$$A^T A \eta = 0, \quad \eta \in \mathbb{R}^q. \tag{19}$$

Then for every nonzero solution of (19) we can write the following relation

$$\eta^T A^T A \eta = (A\eta)^T (A\eta) = 0 \tag{20}$$

which leads to

$$A\eta = 0 \Longrightarrow \eta^T (A^T b_i) = 0. \tag{21}$$

This last relation means that the assumption of Fredholm's theorem (see Appendix) is satisfied; therefore the system (18) is compatible. The second step is to prove that the infimum of the function Ω is reached on the set

$$\Gamma = \{w_i \in \mathbb{R}^q : A^T A w_i = A^T b_i\}. \tag{22}$$

In fact, for $w_{i0} \in \mathbb{R}^q, w_{i0} + \delta w_i \in \mathbb{R}^q$ we have

$$\Omega(w_{i0} + \delta w_i) = \Omega(w_{i0}) - 2(\delta w_i)^T A^T (b_i - Aw_{i0}) + (A\delta w_i)^T (A\delta w_i) \tag{23}$$

which leads to

$$\Omega(w_{i0} + \delta w_i) \geq \Omega(w_{i0}), \quad w_{i0} \in \Gamma, \quad \forall \delta w_i. \tag{24}$$

Inversely the function $\Omega : w_i \mapsto \Omega(w_i)$ can reach its infimum only at the local extremum points where $d\Omega(w_i) = 0$ i.e. it follows the system (18) . Finally we obtain that the infimum of the function Ω is reached on the set Γ.

The last step of the proof is to point out the existence and the uniqueness of the pseudosolution. For this purpose we consider the sets $K \subset \mathbb{R}^q$ and $L \subset \mathbb{R}^q$ defined as follows

$$K = \{z \in \mathbb{R}^q : Az = 0\}, \quad L = \{A^T b_i \in \mathbb{R}^q, \quad b_i \in \mathbb{R}\}. \tag{25}$$

The condition $\xi \in L$ means that the system $A^T \chi = \xi, \forall \chi \in \mathbb{R}$ is compatible. In addition, according to Fredholm's theorem the last system is compatible if and only if $\forall z \in K, z^T \xi = 0$ which means that $K = L^\perp$. For the subsets L and $K = L^\perp$ of the Euclidean space $\mathbb{R}^q$ we can write the vector w_i uniquely as

$$w_i = w_{i0} + z$$

where $w_{i0} \in L, z \in K$. So, every vector $w_i \in \Gamma$ can be expressed in the form

$$w_i = w_{i0} + w_{i1} \quad w_{i0} \in L \quad w_{i1} \in K \tag{26}$$

because of

$$A^T A w_i = A^T A (w_{i0} + w_{i1}) = A^T (A w_{i0}) + A^T (A w_{i1}) = A^T b_i. \tag{27}$$

If η is another vector of Γ then $\eta = w_{i0} \in L$ because of the uniqueness of the orthogonal projection

$$\eta = (\eta - w_i + w_{i1}) + w_{i0}$$

where $(\eta - w_i) + w_{i1} \in K$. Therefore for all vectors of Γ the vector w_{i0} is the same.

For an arbitrary vector $w_i \in \Gamma$, we can write

$$\|w_i\|^2 = (w_{i1} + w_{i0})^T (w_{i1} + w_{i0}) = \|w_{i1}\|^2 + \|w_{i0}\|^2 \Longleftrightarrow \tag{28}$$

$$\|w_i\| \geq \|w_{i0}\| \tag{29}$$

since $w_{i1}^T w_{i0} = 0$. Therefore there exists the unique common vector w_i belonging to the sets Γ and L which has the minimal norm, i.e. the unique pseudosolution of the system (16) of the form

$$w_i = A^T z \tag{30}$$

where z is the solution of a system

$$AA^T z = b_i; \tag{31}$$

replacing A^T by x^k, b_i by $f^{-1}(v_i{}^k) - \theta_i$ we can write the pseudosolution of the system in the form

$$w_i = x^k z \tag{32}$$

where z is the solution of the equation

$$(x^k)^T x^k z = f^{-1}[v_i{}^k] - \theta_i. \tag{33}$$

Finally we get

$$w_i = \frac{f^{-1}[v_i{}^k] - \theta_i}{\langle x^k, x^k \rangle} x^k \tag{34}$$

for fixed k; that ends the proof.

As the weights w_i are known from the relation (34), S is the $p \times s$ known matrix. Without loss of generality we can choose $\Lambda = 0$ [1]. According to the previous theorem the system (13) admits a unique pseudosolution $\nu^\star$ and the minimizing function Ω takes the form $\Omega(\nu) = |u - S\nu|^2$. Then the sequence of solutions of (13) can be computed by the approximated method namely the conjugate gradient method for the minimization of $\Omega(\nu)$. Using the conjugate gradient method [10] described below, we construct the sequence $\{\nu^m\}_{m \in \mathbb{N}}$ convergent to the unique pseudosolution $\nu^\star$ of the system (13) such that

$$S^T S \nu^\star = S^T u \; ; \tag{35}$$

$$\nu^{m+1} = \nu^m + \alpha_m d^m; \quad m = 0, 1, 2, 3, \cdots \tag{36}$$

where ν^m is the current point, d^m a search direction and α_m the steplength. Various choices of the direction d^m give rise to distinct algorithms. A broad class of methods use $-d^m = \nabla \Omega(\nu^m)$ as a search direction and the steplength α_m is given by means of either the condition

$$\min_{\alpha_m > 0} \Omega\left(\nu^m - \alpha_m \nabla \Omega(\nu^m)\right) \tag{37}$$

or Wolfe's conditions [3]. The widely used gradient-based training algorithm, named batch back-propagation (BP) minimizes the error function using the following steepest descent method with constant, heuristically chosen, learning rate α:

$$\nu^{m+1} = \nu^m - \alpha \nabla \Omega(\nu^m). \tag{38}$$

Clearly, the behaviour of any algorithm depends on the choice of the steplength not less than the choice of the search direction. It is well known that pure gradient descent methods with fixed learning rate tend to be inefficient [4]. The proposed algorithm is an adaptive learning rate algorithm based on the conjugate gradient method. The motivation for this choice is that it provides the fast convergence of the approximation method. To obtain the learning rate we need to describe the conjugate gradient method applied to the minimization of the functional

$$\Omega(\nu) = |S\nu - u|^2, \quad \nu \in E^s, \quad u \in E^p \tag{39}$$

where E^n is the n-dimensional Euclidean space.

Choosing the initial approximated point ν^0 randomly we compute $d^0 = \Omega'(\nu^0)$. If $\Omega'(\nu^0) = 0$ then $\nu^0 = \nu^\star$ and the minimization of $\Omega(\nu)$ is solved. So suppose $\Omega'(\nu^0) \neq 0$. Then we set

$$\nu^1 = \nu^0 - \alpha_0 d^0, \quad \alpha_0 \geq 0 \tag{40}$$

where α_0 can be defined from the following condition

$$\xi_0(\alpha_0) = \min_{\alpha \geq 0} \xi_0(\alpha), \quad \xi_0(\alpha) = \Omega(\nu^0 - \alpha d^0). \tag{41}$$

Indeed, writing the variation of Ω

$$\Omega(\nu + h) - \Omega(\nu) = \langle \Omega'(\nu), h \rangle + \frac{1}{2} \langle \Omega''(\nu)h, h \rangle, \quad \forall \nu, h \in E^s \tag{42}$$

we obtain $\Omega'(\nu) = 2(S^T S\nu - S^T u)$, $\quad \Omega''(\nu) = 2S^T S$. For the differential of Ω the Cauchy inequality is satisfied

$$-|\Omega'(\nu)| \times |h| \le \langle \Omega'(\nu), h \rangle \le |\Omega'(\nu)| \times |h|. \tag{43}$$

If $\Omega'(\nu) \ne 0$ then for $h = \alpha \Omega'(\nu)$, $\quad \alpha \ge 0$ the right inequality becomes equality and the left inequality is satisfied .

As $\quad \langle \Omega''(\nu)d^0, d^0 \rangle = \langle 2S^T Sd^0, d^0 \rangle = 2\langle Sd^0, Sd^0 \rangle = 2|Sd^0|^2 \ge 0 \quad \forall d^0 \in E^s$ then ξ_0 is strongly convex and the quantity α_0 exists and can be determined. As

$$\xi_0'(0) = -\langle \Omega'(\nu^0), d^0 \rangle = -|\Omega'(\nu^0)|^2 < 0 \tag{44}$$

then $\alpha_0 > 0$ and we obtain

$$\xi_0'(\alpha_0) = 0 \iff \langle \Omega'(\nu^1), \Omega'(\nu^0) \rangle = 0. \tag{45}$$

If $\Omega'(\nu^1) = 0$ then $\nu^1 = \nu^\star$ and the minimization of $\Omega(\nu)$ is solved; thereafter $\Omega'(\nu^1) \ne 0$.

As $d^0 \ne 0$ then $\Omega''(\nu)d^0 \ne 0$; let us consider the set

$$\Gamma_1 = \{\nu \in E^s : \langle Ad^0, \nu - \nu^1 \rangle = 0\} \tag{46}$$

where $A = \Omega''(\nu)$, which represents the $(s-1)$−dimensional hyperplane passing through the point ν^1. Let us prove that the point $\nu^\star \in \Gamma_1$.

Indeed, given that the matrix A and its inverse A^{-1} are symmetric and taking into account (45) and $\Omega'(\nu^\star) = 0$ we can write

$$\langle Ad^0, \nu^\star - \nu^1 \rangle = \langle Ad^0, A^{-1}(2S^T u) - \nu^1 \rangle = \langle A^{-1}Ad^0, 2S^T u - A\nu^1 \rangle = -\langle d^0, \Omega'(\nu^1) \rangle = 0 \tag{47}$$

i.e. $\nu^\star \in \Gamma_1$.

Thereafter we will look for $\nu^\star \in \Gamma_1$. For this purpose we need to determine the arbitrary direction d^1 parallel to the hyperplane Γ_1 in the form , for example

$$d^1 = \Omega'(\nu^1) - \beta_0 d^0, \quad \beta_0 = \text{const} \tag{48}$$

and the parallelism condition of d^1 and Γ_1 yields:

$$\langle Ad^0, d^1 \rangle = 0 \iff$$
$$\langle Ad^0, \Omega'(\nu^1) - \beta_0 d^0 \rangle = 0 \iff \beta_0 = \frac{\langle Ad^0, \Omega'(\nu^1) \rangle}{\langle Ad^0, d^0 \rangle}. \tag{49}$$

As shown before, $\Omega'(\nu^1) \ne 0$ then $d^1 \ne 0$ and $Ad^1 \ne 0$. Setting

$$\nu^2 = \nu^1 - \alpha_1 d^1, \quad \alpha_1 \ge 0 \tag{50}$$

where the quantity α_1 can be determined from the condition

$$\xi_1(\alpha_1) = \min_{\alpha \ge 0} \xi_1(\alpha), \quad \xi_1(\alpha) = \Omega(\nu^1 - \alpha d^1), \tag{51}$$

we obtain

$$\xi_1'(0) = \langle \Omega'(\nu^1), -d^1 \rangle = \langle \Omega'(\nu^1), -\Omega'(\nu^1) + \beta_0 d^0 \rangle = -|\Omega'(\nu^1)|^2 < 0; \quad (52)$$

it follows that $\alpha_1 > 0$ and

$$\xi_1'(\alpha_1) = 0 \iff \langle \Omega'(\nu^2), d^1 \rangle = 0. \quad (53)$$

Taking into account the relations (45) and

$$\Omega'(\nu^1) - \Omega'(\nu^2) = A\nu^1 - 2S^T u - A\nu^2 + 2S^T u = \alpha_1 A d^1 \quad (54)$$

we obtain

$$\langle \Omega'(\nu^2), \Omega'(\nu^0) \rangle = \langle \Omega'(\nu^2), d^0 \rangle = \langle \Omega'(\nu^1) - \alpha_1 A d^1, d^0 \rangle = 0 \quad (55)$$

which produces

$$\langle \Omega'(\nu^2), \Omega'(\nu^1) \rangle = \langle \Omega'(\nu^2), d^1 + \beta_0 d^0 \rangle = 0. \quad (56)$$

Therefore the first two iterations of the gradient conjugate method for the minimization of Ω are described. Let us show that the vectors Ad^0, Ad^1 are linearly independent.

Indeed, let us consider two arbitrary constants γ_1, γ_2 and the relation $\gamma_0 Ad^0 + \gamma_1 Ad^1 = 0$. Acting on this relation, the inner product by d^0 and then by d^1 we get: $\gamma_0 = 0; \gamma_1 = 0$, which ends the proof. As mentioned before we suppose $\Omega'(\nu^2) \neq 0$. Now we adopt the following assumptions by induction:

- for $m \geq 2$ the elements $\nu^0, \nu^1, \cdots, \nu^{m-1}, \nu^m = \nu^i - \alpha_i d^i, \quad i = 0, 1, \cdots, m-1$ are obtained, where

$$d^i = \Omega'(\nu^i) - \beta_i d^{i-1} \neq 0, \quad \beta_i = \frac{\langle \Omega'(\nu^i), Ad^{i-1} \rangle}{\langle Ad^{i-1}, d^{i-1} \rangle} \quad (57)$$

and the positive quantities α_i can be determined from the conditions

$$\xi_i(\alpha_i) = \min_{\alpha \geq 0} \xi_i(\alpha), \quad \xi_i(\alpha) = \Omega(\nu^i - \alpha d^i), \quad i = 0, 1, 2, \cdots, m-1.$$

- $\langle Ad^i, d^j \rangle = 0, \quad i \neq j, \quad 0 \leq i, j \leq m-1,$
- $\langle \Omega'(\nu^i), d^j \rangle = 0, \quad 0 \leq j < i \leq m,$
- $\langle \Omega'(\nu^i), \Omega'(\nu^j) \rangle = 0, \quad i \neq j, \quad 0 \leq i, j \leq m;$
- $\Omega'(\nu^i) \neq 0, \quad i = 0, 1, \cdots, m$ and the vector system $\{Ad^0, Ad^1, \cdots, Ad^{m-1}\}$ are linearly independent.

Consider the set

$$\Gamma_m = \{\nu \in E^s : \langle Ad^i, \nu - \nu^{i+1} \rangle = 0, \quad i = 0, 1, \cdots, m-1\} \quad (58)$$

which represents the $(s-m)$−dimensional hyperplane.

From (2.2) it follows

$$\langle Ad^i, \nu^m - \nu^{i+1} \rangle = \langle d^i, A\nu^m - A\nu^{i+1} \rangle = \langle d^i, \Omega'(\nu^m) - \Omega'(\nu^{i+1}) \rangle = 0,$$
$$\forall i = 0, \cdots, m-1 \quad \text{i.e.} \quad \nu^m \in \Gamma_m \tag{59}$$

$$\langle Ad^i, \nu^\star - \nu^{i+1} \rangle = \langle Ad^i, A^{-1}(2S^T u) - \nu^{i+1} \rangle = \langle d^i, 2S^T u - A\nu^{i+1} \rangle$$
$$= -\langle d^i, \Omega'(\nu^{i+1}) \rangle = 0, \quad i = 0, \cdots, m-1, \text{i.e.} \quad \nu^\star \in \Gamma_m \tag{60}$$

Thereafter it is useful to search the element $\nu^\star \in \Gamma_m$; in this case we need to find the direction d^m parallel to Γ_m i.e. satisfying the conditions $\langle Ad^i, d^m \rangle = 0$, $i = 0, 1, \cdots, m-1$, which can be presented in the form

$$d^m = \Omega'(\nu^m) - \beta_m d^{m-1} \tag{61}$$

The relations (2.2), (2.2) and

$$\Omega'(\nu^i) - \Omega'(\nu^{i+1}) = A\nu^i - A\nu^{i+1} = \alpha_i Ad^i, \quad i = 0, 1, \cdots, m-1 \tag{62}$$

lead to

$$\langle Ad^i, d^m \rangle = \langle Ad^i, \Omega'(\nu^m) \rangle - \beta_m \langle Ad^i, d^{m-1} \rangle = \langle \Omega'(\nu^i) - \Omega'(\nu^{i+1}), \Omega'(\nu^m) \rangle \alpha_i^{-1} = 0,$$
$$i = 0, 1 \cdots, m-2 \tag{63}$$

for arbitrary β_m. The parallelism condition of the direction d^m and the hyperplane Γ_m is defined as follows

$$\langle Ad^{m-1}, d^m \rangle = 0 \iff \langle Ad^{m-1}, \Omega'(\nu^m) - \beta_m d^{m-1} \rangle = 0$$

which is equivalent to

$$\beta_m = \frac{\langle Ad^{m-1}, \Omega'(\nu^m) \rangle}{\langle Ad^{m-1}, d^{m-1} \rangle}. \tag{64}$$

Suppose that $d^m = 0$; then $\Omega'(\nu^m) = \beta_m d^{m-1}$ and $|\Omega'(\nu^m)|^2 = \beta_m \langle \Omega'(\nu^m), d^{m-1} \rangle = 0$ according to (2.2); this result contradicts the assumption. Therefore $d^m \neq 0$.

The following $(m+1) - th$ approximation can be written in the form

$$\nu^{m+1} = \nu^m - \alpha_m d^m, \quad \alpha_m \geq 0 \tag{65}$$

where the quantity α_m can be determined from the condition

$$\xi_m(\alpha_m) = \min_{\alpha \geq 0} \xi_m(\alpha), \quad \xi_m(\alpha) = \Omega(\nu^m - \alpha d^m). \tag{66}$$

As the function ξ_m is strongly convex then the quantity α_m exists and is unique. Taking into account the assumptions by induction we obtain

$$\xi_m'(0) = \langle \Omega'(\nu^m), -d^m \rangle = \langle \Omega'(\nu^m), -\Omega'(\nu^m) + \beta_m d^{m-1} \rangle = -|\Omega'(\nu^m)|^2 < 0. \tag{67}$$

i.e. $\alpha_m > 0$ and

$$\xi_m'(\alpha_m) = 0 \iff \langle \Omega'(\nu^{m+1}), d^m \rangle = 0 \tag{68}$$

which leads to

$$\langle \Omega'(\nu^m), d^m \rangle - \alpha_m \langle Ad^m, d^m \rangle = 0 \iff \tag{69}$$

$$\alpha_m = \frac{|\Omega'(\nu^m)|^2}{\langle Ad^m, d^m \rangle} \tag{70}$$

$$= 2\frac{\langle S^T S\nu^m - S^T u, S^T S\nu^m - S^T u \rangle}{\langle Sd^m, Sd^m \rangle} \tag{71}$$

since

$$\langle \Omega'(\nu^m), d^m \rangle = \langle \Omega'(\nu^m), \Omega'(\nu^m) - \beta_m d^{m-1} \rangle = |\Omega'(\nu^m)|^2, \tag{72}$$

$$\langle Ad^m, d^m \rangle = \langle 2S^T Sd^m, d^m \rangle = 2\langle Sd^m, Sd^m \rangle \tag{73}$$

Remark that

$$2\frac{\langle S^T S\nu^m - S^T u, S^T S\nu^m - S^T u \rangle}{\langle Sd^m, Sd^m \rangle} = \frac{\langle Sd^m, S\nu^m - u \rangle}{\langle Sd^m, Sd^m \rangle} \tag{74}$$

Finally we arrive at the following result:

we obtain the sequence $\{\nu^m\}$ convergent to the pseudosolution $\nu^\star$ and the learning rate α_m as

$$\nu^{m+1} = \nu^m - \frac{\langle Sd^m, S\nu^m - u \rangle}{\langle Sd^m, Sd^m \rangle} d^m, \tag{75}$$

$$\alpha_m = \frac{\langle Sd^m, S\nu^m - u \rangle}{\langle Sd^m, Sd^m \rangle}, \quad m = 0, 1, \cdots \tag{76}$$

where

$$d^0 = 2[S^T S\nu^0 - S^T u] \tag{77}$$

$$d^m = 2(S^T S\nu^m - S^T u) - 2\frac{\langle S^T Sd^{m-1}, S^T S\nu^m - S^T u \rangle}{\langle Sd^{m-1}, Sd^{m-1} \rangle} d^{m-1}, \tag{78}$$

and $m = 1, 2, \cdots$

3   Experiments and Results

Modelling has become a very important tool in the modern science and research. Scientists use modelling to test hypotheses, to evaluate the performance of systems, to explore some fields that are difficult to assess by experimentation. Many researches on plant growth modelling have been carried out in the past few years. Those works are based on various mathematical approaches. The method of finite elements is used in [15] where the authors propose a tool for the simulation of the behaviour of plants that are in the process of growing. De Reffye and his team

[16] have built a model based on the probability theory. Finite automata theory is used in [18] for the formulation of plant growth dynamics, and a Sequential Learning Neural Network (SLNN) is applied in [19] to agriculture. The method we propose in this paper has been applied in this section to train a feedforward neural network that predicts the height of the plant and the concentrations of substances in the chemical reactions of higher order.

3.1   Prediction of the Plant Height

Considering a plant growth model based on the received energy which must be equal to the spent energy according to energy conservation law, we have a multi-agent system which contains four agents:

- agent of energy received by the plant;
- agent of energy spent for the needs of photosynthesis process;
- agent of energy spent for the plant growth;
- agent of energy spent for nutritive substance transport.

In order to determine the plant height we use the mathematical modelling ([12],[13],[20]) of the plant growth that allows to define the plant height δ as follows:

$$\delta(t) = \sqrt{\frac{a}{b} \frac{e^{t\sqrt{ab}} - e^{-t\sqrt{ab}}}{e^{t\sqrt{ab}} + e^{-t\sqrt{ab}}}} \tag{79}$$

where a and b are positive parameters and there exists the following relations:

$$x_1(t) = 3(\delta(t))^2; \quad x_2(t) = 2(\delta(t))^2 \tag{80}$$

$$x_3(t) = (\delta(t))^2\left(1 - (\delta(t))^2\right); \quad x_4(t) = (\delta(t))^4 \tag{81}$$

and $x_j(t)$, $1 \le j \le 4$ is the energy for the arbitrary plant at a time t:

- $x_1(t)$ is the energy received by the plant by means of the light effect via photosynthesis at a time t;
- $x_2(t)$ is the energy spent for the needs of photosynthesis process at a time t;
- $x_3(t)$ is the energy spent for the plant growth at a time t;
- $x_4(t)$ is the energy spent for nutritive substance transport at a time t.

For simplicity reasons we choose $a = b = 1$, $p = 100$ and the data set gets the form:

$$\{x^k = [x_1(t_k), x_2(t_k), x_3(t_k), x_4(t_k)]^T; u^k = \delta(t_k); v_i{}^k; k = 1 \cdots 100\} \tag{82}$$

where $v_i{}^k$ are chosen randomly in the interval $[0, 1[$. Putting

$$w_i(t_k) = [w_{i1}(t_k), w_{i2}(t_k), w_{i3}(t_k), w_{i4}(t_k)]^T \tag{83}$$

the equation (34) can be written

$$w_{i1}(t_k) = \frac{3}{2} \frac{f^{-1}[v_i^k] - \theta_i}{(\delta(t_k))^6 - (\delta(t_k))^4 + 7(\delta(t_k))^2} \tag{84}$$

$$w_{i2}(t_k) = \frac{f^{-1}[v_i^k] - \theta_i}{(\delta(t_k))^6 - (\delta(t_k))^4 + 7(\delta(t_k))^2} \tag{85}$$

$$w_{i3}(t_k) = \frac{1}{2} \frac{\left(f^{-1}[v_i^k] - \theta_i\right)\left(1 - (\delta(t_k))^2\right)}{(\delta(t_k))^6 - (\delta(t_k))^4 + 7(\delta(t_k))^2} \tag{86}$$

$$w_{i4}(t_k) = \frac{1}{2} \frac{f^{-1}[v_i^k] - \theta_i}{(\delta(t_k))^4 - (\delta(t_k))^2 + 7} \tag{87}$$

Choosing $\theta_i = -1$ the 100×5 matrix S is known and choosing the initial approximated solution ν^0 randomly we can apply the equation (75).

The network consists of 3 layers. The input layer has 4 nodes. Since there are only 4 input nodes, the number of hidden nodes was chosen to be 5. Too few hidden nodes limit a network's generalization capabilities, while too many hidden nodes can result in overtraining or memorization by the network. The output layer consists of a single node representing the height of the plant in time period t. MATLAB is used for the implementation. The mean square error (MSE) is used to compare our adaptive rate algorithm with fixed rates algorithms. Simulations show that the choice of the proper initial weights is important for algorithms convergence. Results are shown on the table 1 where α is the learning rate, e the number of current epochs of training and n the total number of epochs to be trained (for instance $n = 200$).

3.2   Prediction of the Substance Concentrations in the Chemical Reactions of Second Order

Our method can also be applied to the prediction of the substance concentrations in chemical reactions of second order at the instant time. Without loss of generality we consider a chemical reaction of second order where two substances A, B act on each other. We have a multi-agent system containing three agents:

- agent of concentration of substance A;
- agent of concentration of substance B;
- agent of concentration variation due to the chemical reaction speed.

In order to determine the concentration we use the mathematical model [12] of the substance concentration in the chemical reaction of second order that allows to define the concentration δ as follows

$$\delta(t) = \frac{ab[e^{(b-a)\mu t} - 1]}{be^{(b-a)\mu t} - a} \tag{88}$$

where a, b are the initial concentrations of substances A and B respectively, μ is a coefficient and there exist the following relations:

$$x_1(t) = \delta(t); \quad x_2(t) = \delta(t); \tag{89}$$
$$x_3(t) = \mu(a - \delta(t))(b - \delta(t)) \tag{90}$$

and $x_j(t)$, $1 \leq j \leq 3$ is the concentration of a substance at a time t:

- $x_1(t)$ is the concentration of a substance A at a time t;
- $x_2(t)$ is the concentration of a substance B at a time t;
- $x_3(t)$ is the concentration variation due to the chemical reaction speed at a time t.

For simplicity reasons we choose $\mu = 3, a = 0.01, b = 0.002, p = 100$ and the data set gets the form:

$$\{x^k = [x_1(t_k), x_2(t_k), x_3(t_k)]^T; u^k = \delta(t_k); v_i^k; k = 1 \cdots 100\} \tag{91}$$

where v_i^k are chosen randomly in the interval $[0, 1[$. Putting

$$w_i(t_k) = [w_{i1}(t_k), w_{i2}(t_k), w_{i3}(t_k)]^T \tag{92}$$

the equation (34) can be written

$$w_{i1}(t_k) = \frac{\left(f^{-1}[v_i^k] - \theta_i\right)\delta(t_k)}{2(\delta(t_k))^2 + 9\left(0.01 - \delta(t_k)\right)^2\left(0.002 - \delta(t_k)\right)^2} \tag{93}$$

$$w_{i2}(t_k) = \frac{\left(f^{-1}[v_i^k] - \theta_i\right)\delta(t_k)}{2(\delta(t_k))^2 + 9\left(0.01 - \delta(t_k)\right)^2\left(0.002 - \delta(t_k)\right)^2} \tag{94}$$

$$w_{i3}(t_k) = 3\frac{\left(f^{-1}[v_i^k] - \theta_i\right)\left(0.01 - \delta(t_k)\right)\left(0.002 - \delta(t_k)\right)}{2(\delta(t_k))^2 + 9\left(0.01 - \delta(t_k)\right)^2\left(0.002 - \delta(t_k)\right)^2} \tag{95}$$

One can apply the same process used in the previous implementation.

Table 1. Comparison of different learning rates for the plant growth

Learning rate	MSE	Number of epochs	MSE	Number of epochs
$\alpha = 0.01$	0.001	116	0.01	14
$\alpha = 0.5$	0.001	8	0.01	8
$\alpha = (1 - \frac{e}{p})^2$	0.001	8	0.01	8
$\alpha_m = \frac{\langle Sd^{\overline{m}}; Sv^m - u \rangle}{\langle Sd^m; Sd^m \rangle}$	0.001	4	0.01	2

4   Discussion

Using the algebraic approach we obtain the weight equations which may , or may not, be compatible. The pseudosolutions for these equations are the generalization of the solutions obtained in [3]. The approach with these solutions can be used efficiently for the identification and control of dynamical systems, mapping the input-output representation of an unknown system and its control law [3]. Using the conjugate gradient method we contruct the sequence of output weights convergent to the pseudosolution, in other words we predict the height of a plant and the substance concentrations in a chemical reaction of the second order. The simulations show that the method with the adaptive learning rate is more stable and converge very fast. We can also apply this method to predict the size of a biological population.

5   Conclusion

The techniques developed in this paper match input-output information approximately or exactly by neural networks. The adjustable parameters i.e. weights are determined by solving algebraic equations and by using the conjugate gradient method. The algorithms used are derived basing on the exact and approximated solutions of input-output weight equations. Their effectiveness is demonstrated by training feedforward neural networks which produce the height of a plant and the substances concentrations in a chemical reaction of the second order. The experimentations show that our combination of the algebraic approach and the fast convergent conjugate gradient method is a useful approach to solve many complex problems.

Acknowledgments. Part of this work by the second author was carried out at the Institute of Computer Engineering, Control and Robotics, Wroclaw University of Technology in Poland. Thanks to Prof Jan Kazimierczak for his guidance, to Dr Olgierd Unold for many useful discussions, to Prof Ngoc Thanh Nguyen for advice and fruitful comments, and to Prof Czeslaw Smutnicki for granting unlimited access to the research facilities of the institute.

References

1. Iranmanesh, S.: A differential adaptive learning rate method for back-propagation neural networks. In: Proceeding of the 10th WSEAS International Conference on Neural Networks, Stevens Point, Wisconsin, USA, pp. 30–34 (2009)
2. Subavathi, S.J., Kathirvalavakumar, T.: Adaptive modified backpropagation algorithm based on differential errors. International Journal of Computer Science, Engineering and Applications (IJCSEA) 1(5), 21–24 (2011)
3. Ferrari, S., Stengel, R.F.: Smooth Function Approximation Using Neural Networks. IEEE Trans. Neural Netw. 16(1), 24–38 (2005)
4. Rumelhart, D., Inton, G.E., Williams, R.J.: Learning representations by back-propagating errors. Nature 323, 533–536 (1986)
5. Wolfe, P.H.: Convergence conditions for ascend methods. SIAM Review 11, 226–235 (1969)
6. Polak, E.: Optimization: Algorithms and Consistent Approximations. Springer (1997)
7. Jacobs, R.A.: Increased rates of convergence through learning rate adaptation. Neural Netw. 1(4), 295–308 (1988)

8. Rigler, A.K., Irvine, J.M., Vogl, T.P.: Rescaling of variables in back-propagation learning. Neural Netw. 3(5), 561–573 (1990)
9. Kolmogorov, A.N.: On the representation of continuous function of several variables by superposition of continuous functions of one variable and addition. Dokl. Akad. Nauk SSSR 114, 953–956 (1957)
10. Vassiliev, F.L.: Numerical Methods for the optimization problems, Nauk, Moscow (1988) (in Russian)
11. Beklemichev, D.: Cours de géometrie analytique et d'algèbre linéaire. Editions Mir, Moscou (1988)
12. Bavrine, I.I.: High mathematics. Instruction, Moscow (1980) (in Russian)
13. Dagba, T.K., Adanhounmè, V., Adédjouma, S.A.: Modélisation de la croissance des plantes par la méthode d'apprentissage supervisé du neurone. In: Premier colloque de l'UAC des sciences, cultures et technologies, mathématiques, Abomey-Calavi, Benin, pp. 245–250 (2007)
14. Dembelé, J.-M., Cambier, C.: Modélisation multi-agents de systèmes physiques: application à l'érosion cotière. In: CARI 2006, Cotonou, Benin, pp. 223–230 (2006)
15. Fourcaud, T.: Analyse du comportement mécanique d'une plante en croissance par la méthode des éléments finis. PhD thesis, Université de Bordeaux 1, Talence, France (1995)
16. De Reffye, P., Edelin, C., Jaeger, M.: La modélisation de la croissance des plantes. La Recherche 20(207), 158–168 (1989)
17. Rostand-Mathieu, A.: Essai sur la modélisation des interactions entre la croissance et le développement d'une plante, cas du modèle greenlab. Ph.D thesis, Ecole Centrale de Paris, France (2006)
18. Wu, L., Le Dimet, F.-X., De Reffye, P., Hu, B.-G.: A new Mathematical Formulation for Plant Structure Dynamics. In: CARI 2006, Cotonou, Benin, pp. 353–360 (2006)
19. Deng, C., Xiong, F., Tan, Y., He, Z.: Sequential learning neural network and its application in agriculture. In: IEEE International Joint Conference on Neural Networks, vol. 1, pp. 221–225 (1998)
20. Dagba, T.K., Adanhounmè, V., Adédjouma, S.A.: Neural Networks for Solving the Superposition Problem Using Approximation Method and Adaptive Learning Rate. In: Jędrzejowicz, P., Nguyen, N.T., Howlet, R.J., Jain, L.C. (eds.) KES-AMSTA 2010, Part II. LNCS (LNAI), vol. 6071, pp. 92–99. Springer, Heidelberg (2010)

Appendix

Theorem 2. *(Fredholm). The system (18) is compatible if and only if every solution of homogeneous adjoint system*

$$A^T A \eta = 0 \qquad \eta \in \mathbb{R}^q \tag{96}$$

satisfies the equation

$$\eta^T (A^T b_i) = 0 \tag{97}$$

A Multi-classifier Approach to Dialogue Act Classification Using Function Words

James O'Shea, Zuhair Bandar, and Keeley Crockett

Department of Computing and Mathematics
Manchester Metropolitan University
United Kingdom
`{z.bandar,k.crockett,j.d.oshea}@mmu.ac.uk`

Abstract. This paper extends a novel technique for the classification of sentences as Dialogue Acts, based on structural information contained in function words. Initial experiments on classifying questions in the presence of a mix of straightforward and "difficult" non-questions yielded promising results, with classification accuracy approaching 90%. However, this initial dataset does not fully represent the various permutations of natural language in which sentences may occur. Also, a higher Classification Accuracy is desirable for real-world applications. Following an analysis of categorisation of sentences, we present a series of experiments that show improved performance over the initial experiment and promising performance for categorising more complex combinations in the future.

Keywords: Dialogue Act, Speech Act, Classification, Semantic Similarity, Decision Tree.

Introduction

Collective Computational Intelligence is the form of intelligence that emerges from the collaboration and competition of many individuals. Whilst there is a natural tendency to focus on the machine aspects of multi-agent systems, ultimately these agents represent the beliefs desires and intentions (intentionality) of their human clients. It is difficult for the average human to express intentionality in the formal logic used by computers. Therefore Dialogue Management agents are required to bridge this gap, modeling user intentionality, conducting negotiations on the user's behalf and resolving conflict in the multi-agent system.

Dialogue Management (DM) is concerned with the communication between humans and computer-based systems using natural language. DM techniques support the production of Dialogue Systems (DSs) which will allow ordinary users to interact with increasingly powerful and complex applications in the future. Dialogue Act (DA) classification is an established element of research in the Natural Language Processing (NLP) approach to DM [1-6]. DA theory asserts that a sentence or spoken utterance can be separate into two components, the Propositional Content (i.e. what it is about) and the DA (i.e. what is it is saying about the propositional content) [7]. So

N.T. Nguyen (Ed.): Transactions on CCI VII, LNCS 7270, pp. 119–143, 2012.
© Springer-Verlag Berlin Heidelberg 2012

the propositional content "door is shut" can be in a question DA "Is the door shut?", an instruction DA "Shut the door!" or an assertion DA "The door is shut.", which mean quite different things.

This paper extends an investigation of the hypothesis that DAs can be classified into different categories solely by using function words. An initial study using the technique achieved a Classification Accuracy (CA) of 89.43% when classifying questions against a challenging mixture of non-questions [8]. Two research questions emerged from this work, "How can the CA be improved to the point where it is useful in real-world applications?" and "Can even more challenging combinations of questions and non-questions be classified effectively?"

More challenging combinations arise because questions and non-questions each come in a variety of forms. A generic classifier may be confounded by the fact that features suitable for discriminating between a particular form of question and a particular form of non-question could become obscured in the general mix. This paper extends the technique by investigating the production of specialist classifiers for particular combinations of forms of question vs. non-question DAs. A user utterance could be processed by a bank of specialised classifiers running in parallel which would collectively decide whether a question was present, and if so, its position in the utterance. This collective approach is also expected to be capable of dealing with complex utterances containing multiple, different CAs as classifiers are also under development to discriminate between instructions and non-instructions [9].

One example of the value of classifying DAs is in the use of questions, instructions and assertions to communicate with robots [10]. Another important application for DAs is in providing humans with advice in complex areas such as debt management and on workplace bullying and harassment procedures [11]. A new potential class of applications is also emerging, which may be described as Mandated Intentional Agents (MIAs). The concept of an Intentional Agent, acting according to its own beliefs, desires and intentions in the world, is an established concept in cognitive science [12]. An MIA is a machine-based agent which represents the beliefs, desires and intentions of a human client in the real world. One potential application would be buying and selling electrical power on behalf of a household connected to the smart grid [13]. Such an agent would be able to make advantageous deals on behalf of its human owner at any time of day or night as opportunities arose. The best method to instruct an MIA in such a complex task would be natural language dialogue.

The majority of current DSs use Pattern Matching (PM) or NLP to analyse and answer a user utterance. PM systems are considered to be the best for developing DSs that seem to be coherent and intelligent to users [14]. They support scalability to large numbers of users because they do not require pre-processing stages, but they are labour intensive to develop and maintain. NLP systems have a substantial theoretical basis but require a chain of computationally intensive and error-prone stages such as pos-tagging, syntactical repair and parsing. This rules them out for web-based systems that must service many users in real time.

Short Text Semantic Similarity (STSS) offers an alternative approach to PM and NLP. A user utterance (a unit of dialogue containing a communicative action [1]) is acquired as a Short Text (ST) and compared with a set of prototype STs. The ST with the highest similarity to the user utterance is taken to be its meaning and triggers a suitable response from the DS. However, current STSS algorithms have a weakness; they are oblivious to the DA performed by an utterance.

Latent Semantic Analysis (LSA) is a well-known method of measuring semantic similarity [15]. Taking the examples listed earlier, LSA scores all of the possible pairwise combinations of question, instruction and assertion as 1.0 – i.e. identical in meaning. Therefore devising an efficient method of classifying Dialogue Acts (DAs) will be a crucial first step in measuring the true semantic similarity between a pair of STs accurately.

The rest of this paper is organised as follows: section 1 briefly reviews prior work on function words, DA classifiers and evaluation methods. Section 2 describes the classes of the questions and non-questions used, how they were collected and how the training and testing files were composed. Section 3 outlines the experimental procedure, section 4 discusses the results and section 5 contains conclusions and recommendations for future work.

1   Prior Work

1.1   Features for DA Classification

Machine classification of DAs has used various techniques including n-gram statistical models [2], Bayesian networks [16] and Decision Trees (DTs) [3]. All of the approaches rely on extraction of features from the DA to present to the classifier.

The most common feature used is the n-gram. An n-gram is a sequence of contiguous symbols found inside a longer sequence. In DA classification it is usually a short string of words extracted from a marked up corpus [2, 4]. The importance of the n-gram is that any n-gram could be a predictive feature for classifying the text containing it.

Large numbers of n-grams are generated by any real-world corpus so a subset is used (in [3] sets of 10 or 300). N-grams have been used to code features for Hidden Markov Models [4]. Bigrams such as CanYou and IWant [16] have been used in Bayesian classifiers, which also combined them with the DAs of previous utterances in the dialogue [1].

Cue phrases have been used as features for a simple, efficient classifier described by Webb et al [2]. A cue phrase is a longer form of n-gram, selected on the basis of predictability for particular DA classes. In operation, the classifier examines an utterance for cue phrases and assigns the class of the highest predictive phrase it contains. This technique has the serious disadvantage that it ignores other potentially valuable information in the utterance.

In the LSA approach to DA classification [5], the features are terms in a "query" vector. A cosine measure is used to determine the vector of the closest matching "document" and the DA type of the match is assigned to the query. LSA normally removes function words [15], but it is not specified if this is the case with DA classification.

Keizer et al [16] used 13 surface features to train DTs in a comparison with a Bayesian network. Features included length, various starting bigrams, presence of particular words, positive/negative references and presence of particular grammatical classes. Keizer's work is interesting because it classifies DAs into two classes, forward-looking functions (acts that have an effect on following dialogue) or backward-looking functions (that relate to previous dialogue).

The closest work to this paper [3] uses a decision tree trained with a mix of features including the presence of a question mark, a count of the occurrences of the word OR, utterance length, a bigram of the labels of the last two DAs, n-grams of pos-tags for the utterance, n-grams of words in the utterance and the top 10 predictive individual words. A review by Verbree et al [3] also refers to the use of verb type and cites a number of uses of prosodic features.

These approaches have achieved good results, but they use complex and computationally intensive feature extraction which rules them out from future real-time applications. Also, Cue Phrases may discard considerable useful information.

1.2   Function Words

Words in the English Language can be divided into Function Words (a closed class of structural words such as articles, prepositions, determiners etc.) and Content Words (the open classes of nouns, verbs, adjectives and adverbs). "Stop word" lists contain words with a high frequency of occurrence - mostly function words with a few high frequency content words mixed in. There is no definitive list of stop words, although one by van Rijsbergen [17], which is often cited, contains 250 words. Others posted on the web contain over 300 [18]. A set of 264 function words (available from the authors on application) was compiled for this paper by combining stop word lists, removing the content words and then adding low-frequency function words from dictionaries.

Information Retrieval (IR) places a greater value on content words than function words in searching for documents. Spärck-Jones' [19] TD/IDF approach and Salton's [20] Vector Space Model increase the contribution of low frequency words to the similarity measurement. LSA removes 439 stop words [21], having "little or no difference on the SVD solution." [15] from the submitted terms or documents before comparing them. This list has not been published. Citeseer also removes stop words prior to performing word frequency calculation [22].

The STASIS [23] STSS measure used function words as well as content words because they carry structural information which is useful in interpreting sentence meaning [23]. However, STASIS can only detect matches between identical pairs of function words in the two STs. Recently an STSS algorithm which makes use of a corpus-based measure combined with string similarity, but filters out function words [24], has been reported to achieve good performance.

1.3   The Slim Function Word Classifier for Dialogue Acts

We classify DAs at a coarse level of granularity as we believe distinguishing between questions, instructions and assertions will be most useful in practical DSs [11] and

Robotics applications [10]. This work uses the Slim Function Word Classifier (SFWC) approach which takes a radically different view of the value of function words. The SFWC assumes that sufficient information is contained in the function words of an utterance alone to allow its DA to be classified [8]. Consequently, each function word in the utterance is replaced with a unique token and all content words replaced by the same wildcard. Table 1 shows an example of a tokenised question.

Table 1. Tokenisation of a typical question

Question	does wearing caps or hats contribute to hair loss
Tokenised form	56,0,0,156,0,0,212,0,0,300,300,300,300,300,300, 300, 300, 300, 300,300, 300,300,300,300,300

Processing a short text requires two stages. The first is the expansion of contractions. This uses a lookup table to replace contracted forms such as Don't with their full forms, i.e. Do not. Some contractions are ambiguous e.g. She'd could be She would or She had. At this stage of the work we take a brute force approach of replacing all the variants with a single form (e.g. 'd forms with would). Apostrophe usage in forming possessives is ignored and all possessives are treated as content words.

Second, the words comprising the sentence are successively looked up in a table of function words and numeric tokens (composed from the list described in 1.2). If the word is found it is replaced by the appropriate token (range 1 – 264). In this experiment the tokens are allocated in ascending order to the alphabetically sorted list of words, so that 1 represents the word "a" and 264 represents "yourselves".

If the word is not found it is replaced by the token 0 (indicating a content word). If the sentence contains fewer than 25 words, all empty slots are filled with a "no word present" token given the value 300. This particular value was chosen so that it would be easy for the DT algorithm to partition it from the word tokens.

Note that all punctuation, apart from the possessive apostrophe is stripped out as part of pre-processing. This means that the presence of a question mark – which has been used as a feature in some studies [3] is not used.

The brute force approach taken by the SFWC algorithm is particularly efficient in using only simple table lookup. It avoids complex pre-processing as parsing-based disambiguation would increase the computational load greatly. This virtue is emphasized because the same pre-processing steps will be required for data entered into real-world systems deployed on the web, which must be scalable to large numbers of users in real-time.

It should also be observed that the tokenisation generalises the sentences when they are preprocessed, i.e. two different questions could be based on the same skeleton of function words, so that after tokenisation (when all of the content words are replaced by zeros) they are represented by the same token string.

1.4   Evaluation Datasets

The normal method of evaluating classifiers is to measure their CA on test data which was not used to train the classifier. Comparing DA classifiers is difficult as there is no standard dataset for developing and testing them. The different datasets used are tagged with different numbers and types of DA [3], ranging from 2 [16] to 232 different tags [5]. The sizes of the datasets also vary, from 223,000 utterances in the Switchboard set [2] to one of 81 utterances for a DT classifier [16]. Variety is also an issue. One dataset of 2794 DAs was drawn from only two humans [4] and may not generalise beyond these two people. One example of very good performance was a CA of 89.27% for a classifier with over 40 DA categories using a large training set [3]. Results can be variable however; another study [6] achieved 92.9% on suggestions but scored 0 on queries.

The first stage of the present work used the particular task of discriminating between Questions vs. Non-questions. This was because prior empirical experience with DSs has shown this to be a non-trivial problem and because the task is appropriate to other agent-based applications such as robotics.

Data is required for training and testing Artificial Intelligence (AI) classifiers. In this case it was decided to collect a new dataset, principally because existing datasets are not appropriate for the instant messaging style dialogue expected in DS applications. Many datasets examined from the literature are terse, having been derived from telephone-based Automatic Speech Recognition systems and may be constructed to test aspects such as repair of misunderstood utterances. It was also decided to collect 3 types of utterance: straightforward questions, straightforward non-questions and difficult non-questions. It will be shown in section 2 that a representative range of question and non-question sub-categories can be constructed from this base set.

Choice of the size of the dataset was influenced by three interacting factors: the effort involved in collecting the data, the minimum size required to represent the domain and the execution time required to construct a decision tree. These factors were balanced by using n-fold cross validation. Under n-fold cross validation, the dataset is randomly divided into n folds. Working through the folds in sequence, one is held back for testing whilst the others are used for training. This allows all of the data to be used for training and testing a large set of classifiers, without any of the classifiers being tested on the data it was trained on. All of the following trees were trained using 60-fold cross validation on a set of 600 questions and 600 non-questions. Choice of 60-fold cross validation meant that over 1,000 training cases were used to construct each classifier (a rule of thumb recommended by Quinlan for Decision Tree classifiers [25]). Also, this allowed reasonable execution times for the training and testing of the classifiers. Finally, manually mining the Web for a pool of questions and non-questions to compose the datasets was feasible at this size. Some classifiers require fixed length records, so an upper limit of 25 words was set (determined empirically).

The first step was the collection of a pool of "straightforward" questions and non-questions. Questions were acquired from FAQ lists and non-questions were acquired from blogs. Both of these sources are capable of producing texts which are like the utterances used on messaging-style dialogue. 1,660 straightforward questions were collected from the highest user-rated FAQ lists from the Usenet news system and 2288 straightforward non-questions were collected from "blogs of note" commended blogs on blogspot.com.

Straightforward questions are those which are fairly easy to recognise as they often have distinguishing features such as a wh-cheft (what, who) or an auxiliary verb (can, is) at the beginning. The straightforward non-questions are sentences which are not questions and do not have one of the question's distinguishing features at the beginning. To increase the challenge of the dataset, difficult non-questions were included. A difficult non-question is defined as a non-question which starts with one of the question's distinguishing features. For example the word "What" is commonly used to start a question and in this role it is known as an interrogative introducer. For example:

> What alternative therapies exist and are they any good?

On the other hand, "What" can also be pronoun, in which case it is not indicative of a question. For example:

> What all men want is beer and sport.

In fact non-questions rarely start in this way and it was not practical to collect them from web sources, so a set of additional non-questions was synthesized. Despite their rarity, we have observed empirically that confusion of this type of utterance with questions reduces users' confidence in the agent. The approach of synthesising rare data is well-established [26]. Sometimes the synthetic non-questions are not valid sentences in their own right, but they would make sense as a terminating utterance in a dialogue sequence.

The dataset for the initial experiment [8] was composed in the approximate proportions 50% questions, 25% straightforward non-questions and 25% difficult non-questions (using random sampling). In fact the final proportions in the dataset were 591 questions and 615 non-questions. For each category, a randomly selected sample larger than the target size was taken. The sentences were then pre-processed and duplicates removed to create the initial dataset. Because there were more duplicates in the questions and fewer in the non-questions the classes were slightly imbalanced. Examples from the dataset are shown in table 2.

Table 2. Example training data

Category	Example
FAQ question	**Does wearing caps or hats contribute to hair loss?**
Blog non-question	**Sometimes the psoriasis treatment causes the hair loss.**
Synthetic non-question	**Which in many cases can be cured with a simple lotion.**

The pool of 1,660 straightforward questions and 2288 straightforward non-questions was also used as the source material for the new experiments reported in this study. However, in this case, after tokenisation the datasets were balanced so that exactly 600 of each were obtained. This involved an iterative process of adding or removing cases from the dataset followed by re-tokenising until all the duplicates were replaced.

It should also be noted that questions were balanced by non-questions derived from the same context. Contexts were highly varied including "IRS", "Immunisation", "Tattoo" and "Gasoline." The majority of non-questions were assertions (statements, clarifications and answers to previous questions) with some instructions.

1.5   Choice of Classifier

A good cross-section of classifiers has been evaluated for DA classification. These include   statistical [27] and n-gram models [2], Bayesian networks [16], Naïve Bayesian Classifiers [28], Kohonen Networks [29], Multi-Layer Perceptron [28], Backpropagation Artificial Neural Networks [30], Maximum Entropy [31],   C4.5 Decision Trees [3], Production Rules [32], Simple Heuristics [33], Hidden Markov Models [34], Partially-Observable Markov [35], K-Nearest Neighbour [30], Support Vector Machines [36], Learning Vector Quantisation [37] and Self Organising Maps [37].

Unfortunately, it is difficult to draw any conclusions about the relative performances of particular classifiers, because different studies use different features, different DA taxonomies and different corpora – so results are not comparable. The initial investigation conducted for this study [8] used 4 of the most common techniques, Decision Trees (C4.5), Naïve Bayes, Bayesian Classifiers and Multi-Layer Perceptrons (MLP).

DT induction is a highly effective method of machine learning for classification. One of the most well-established algorithms is C4.5 [25]. DTs partition the sample space recursively and the outcome is a set of rules induced from a training set of example instances previously labelled with their classes. The chief advantage of DTs over other classifiers is that the rules "explain" how they reach their decisions and (combined with pruning) provide a greater insight into the problem domain.

The starting point of a DT is one node with all examples labelled as belonging to one class. A node is 'impure' if the examples reaching that node are not all in the same class. During training impure nodes are successively partitioned to create new, purer nodes. The final, leaf, nodes are labelled with the appropriate class. Impure leaves, which may occur if the attributes have been tested exhaustively without reaching purity, are labelled with the majority class. An alternative pruning technique, Minimum Number of Objects (MNO) removes leaves with fewer than a specified number of cases and re-distributes them amongst leaves at the level above in the tree.

Bayesian techniques, such as Naïve Bayes and the Bayesian Network have long been of interest to NLP researchers due to their statistical origins. The Naïve Bayes classifier uses information extracted from a set of example instances to produce a probability estimate of the class of a new instance, assuming statistical independence between the attributes to make the estimate [38]. The Bayesian Network is an alternative to decision trees, which uses a Directed Acyclic Graph structure [38]. This structure is less constrained in allowing linkage between nodes than a pure tree. Also, the node does not contain a splitting rule; rather it contains a probability distribution that is used to predict the class probability for a particular instance. The proposed advantage of the Bayesian Network over the DT is that it retains information that is lost due to splitting in DTs. However, the Bayesian network is also sensitive to missing values and this is an issue in handling STs of varying lengths.

The Multi-Layer Perceptron (MLP) is an Artificial Neural Network (ANN), modeled on the biological structure of the brain [39]. Inputs are fed through a network of simple processing units with weighted connections to produce (in this application) a classification output. The MLP is trained using backpropagation, which uses a training set to modify the weights until the performance is optimised. Of the 4 techniques, the MLP is the least transparent in explaining its decisions; however it has the benefit of robustness to noise and missing values.

The initial evaluation of the classifiers was performed using the WEKA data mining tool. All comments about statistical significance are based on the standard test used by WEKA, the corrected re-sampled t-test. Table 3 shows the best Classification Accuracies obtained, using these classifiers at their default settings in WEKA. Results are also shown for the ZeroR and OneR classifiers, which provide a benchmark for the performance of the other classifiers. ZeroR shows the CA if all of the cases were labelled with the classification of the majority class, and helps the interpretation of unbalanced data. In this initial set of experiments, the dataset was slightly unbalanced, so that labeling all data with the majority class gives a CA of 50.99%. The OneR classifier shows the CA obtained using the single best classification rule that could be found. This is intended to be an indicator of the complexity of the domain. In this case a CA of 82.06 indicates that it is quite easy to classify four fifths of the cases, however it does not tell us how difficult it will be to improve on the classification of the remainder.

Table 3. Classification accuracies for baseline measures and popular classifiers

Classifier	ZeroR	OneR	Naïve Bayes	MLP	Bayes Net	C4.5
CA	50.99	82.06	55.98	69.14	77.87	88.73

Each increase in CA across the AI classifiers is statistically significant. All of the classifiers outperformed the ZeroR baseline significantly. C4.5 also outperformed the OneR classifier significantly, whereas each of the other techniques failed to reach the OneR level of performance.

A further set of experiments was conducted to investigate optimisation of the C4.5 decision tree, using two different methods of pruning, Confidence Interval (Conf) and

Minimum Number of Objects (MNO), starting from the baseline of 88.73% CA and a DT size of 118 nodes.

Optimising CA, confidence pruning achieved a best CA of 89.43% (Conf = 0.04) and MNO pruning achieved a best CA of 88.97% (MNO = 5). On the other hand, when optimising (minimising) tree size, confidence pruning achieved a size of 47 nodes (Conf = 0.0003) and MNO pruning achieved a size of 46 nodes (MNO = 13). These were the greatest reductions that could be achieved before a statistically significant reduction in CA from the baseline value of 88.73%. This degree of pruning is a good indicator that the DT classifier is generalising to model the domain effectively, rather than just memorising the training cases.

The high performance of DTs, combined with their efficiency and transparency, was conclusive in their choice for further experiments.

2   Classification of Questions and Non-questions

2.1   New Question Sub-classes

An investigation of question taxonomies revealed two useful approaches to categorising questions: Grammatical classification [40] and Domain-based classification [41] [42]. Additionally, the highest level of grammatical distinction between different types of sentences is between Simple and Multiple sentences.

2.1.1   Grammatical Classes of Questions Composed of Simple Sentences
A Simple Sentence contains a single independent clause. The standard grammatical classes of questions derived from simple sentences, with an example in each case [40] are listed below:

1. Yes-No
   Have you finished the book?
2. Wh-questions
   What is your name?
3. Option selection
   Would you like to go for a walk or stay at home?
4. Tag questions
   They forgot to attend the lecture, am I right?
5. Declarative questions*
   You've got the explosive?
6. Exclamatory*
   Hasn't she grown?
7. Rhetorical*
   Who cares?

* Without prosodic information the declarative question form would be interpreted as a declarative rather than a question. Declarative, exclamatory and rhetorical are all dependent on prosodic information for their correct interpretation. This can be resolved using the question mark. As Quirk observed [40] "… the question mark matches in writing the prosodic contrast between this sentence as a question and the same sentence as a statement." The exclamatory and rhetorical categories do not implicitly ask for information; uses include emphasis or giving an opinion. Given the text-based approach, declarative, exclamatory and rhetorical questions are not suitable for inclusion in this study.

2.1.2 Grammatical Classes of Questions Composed of Multiple Sentences

Grammar recognises two more sophisticated question categories which could be more challenging to the techniques developed in this work – these are questions embedded in Compound Sentences and Complex Sentences.

A Compound sentence contains two or more co-ordinated main clauses, for example:

> *I admire her reasoning but were her conclusions valid?*

A complex sentence has a single main clause and one or more subordinate clauses, for example:

> *Can you confirm which flight we are taking?*

The complex form allows questions to participate in indirect DAs, for example:

> *Please confirm which flight we are taking.*

is a directive (instruction) which seeks the same information as the question Which flight are we taking?

2.1.3 Domain-Based Classification

An example of domain-specific categorisation is the assessment of medical students. A list of categories, with examples, derived from Christensen [42] is shown below:

1. Information-Seeking Questions:
What were the blood values from the lab?
2. Diagnostic Questions:
What conclusions did you draw from these data?
3. Challenge (Testing) Questions:
What evidence supports your conclusion?
4. Hypothetical Questions:
If the liver function tests were normal, how would that have affected your treatment plan?
5. Action Questions:
What needs to be done to implement the plan for this patient?
6. Extension Questions:
What are the implications of your conclusions for the treatment of asthma among children in elementary school in our community?
7. Priority/Sequence Questions:
Given the patient's limited resources, what is the first step to be taken?

8.   Prediction Questions:
If your plan (conclusion) is appropriate, what do you expect to happen over the next month? Year?
9.   Generalisation Questions:
Based on your experience and the studies of the incidence of teenage pregnancy, what do you consider to be the most effective strategies for our local high school teachers and counsellors?

Of the above categories, 1,2,3,5 and 6 are questions comprised of simple sentences and 4, 7, 8 and 9 are complex questions. From the point of view of constructing a dataset for this study, there is nothing to be gained from discriminating between questions such as What were the blood values from the lab? and What evidence supports your conclusion?

Some other types of question were found during the investigation:

- indirect questions:
  Joan asked was he ready yet?
- directives containing questions:
  Please confirm which flight we are taking.
- assertives implying questions:
  I have received an invoice and I do not know what it relates to.
- leading questions:
  You did have the gun when you left, didn't you?

The leading question is a specialist form from the legal domain and is easily disposed of. Its distinguishing feature is that it implies a correct (or known) answer. Structurally these questions will fall into one of the categories described previously and therefore will be covered automatically (the example given is a negative form of tag question). The indirect questions don't necessarily increase the complexity of the recognition task over and above the existing categories. The problem is deciding what to do in response – how they would affect a Conversational Agent's intentionality within its task and problem domain. This is beyond the scope of the present work so this question form will not be included.

The Directive corresponds to Which flight are we taking? and the Assertive corresponds to Can you explain what the invoice I have received relates to?

In fact, both are indirect dialogue acts; they seek information but are prima facie, non-question. As such they will not be included in the current work (although the examples look promising in terms of the function words contained in the sentences).

2.2   Classes of Questions and Non-questions Used in Datasets

The classes described in section 2.1 indicate what should be represented in the combinations of questions and non-questions used in this chapter. However, a one-to-one mapping between the classes in 2.1 and the datasets used for training and testing is not required as some of the grammatical or domain-based categories are indistinguishable for the purposes of this study. The categories described in the following sections were derived for experimental purposes.

2.2.1 Straightforward Questions

The Straightforward question type is, effectively the question contained in a Simple Sentence. The term "Straightforward" has been adopted to indicate that although the question itself may be quite sophisticated or difficult to answer, the form of the question is likely to be the least challenging for a DA classifier.

These questions are short and to the point. They do not require resolution of references to prior dialogue and they do not contain pertinent information embedded in clauses separated from the main question clause. Good examples of this simplest form, such as "When was James Dean born?" can be found in the TREC factoid set. Such questions have a very obvious feature in the first word position – the presence of a Wh-cheft.

Straightforward questions cover the grammatical classes Yes-No, Wh-questions and Option selection from the simple sentences class and provide evidence for some questions from the multiple sentences class. For example, they will provide evidence that the first question in a compound question will be recognised. They also cover the domain-based classes Information-Seeking, Diagnostic, Challenge, Action and Extension.

2.2.2 Straightforward Questions with Preambles

It is possible to create a more difficult class of questions by shifting the first word (typically an auxiliary verb or a wh-cheft) of the question further down the sentence. This can occur in a form known as the "Pushdown" where a phrase or part of another clause, is moved to precede the main clause e.g. On what side of the road was he driving?

Introductory words and phrases, which do not qualify as clauses in their own right, can also be used with a question. They have a variety of purposes which don't actually contribute to the semantics of the sentence, for example for continuity, politeness, attention grabbing etc.

These words and phrases are accommodated in this study by adding a "preamble" of a few words to the start of the sentence. For the purposes of this study a preamble is any phrase of up to a maximum of 5 words and specifically does not contribute to the semantic content of the utterance. Thus examples include:

> *Actually*
> *Almost everyone asked*
> *And there is another thing*

So a question of this kind would be

> *And there is another thing, when was James Dean born?"*

These preambles look remarkably similar to Cue Phrases, however the two properties of a good preamble are that (i) it must "work" when placed in front of a question (like a cue phrase) and (ii) it must not provide evidence to the classifier that it is part of a question (contrary to a cue phrase). The middle phrase, *Almost everyone asked*, may appear to contradict these requirements. However, the key evidence for a question is in the word *asked*, a verb which will not be considered by the SFWC. When producing preambles for non-questions it was fairly straightforward to replace preambles of this type with equivalents that worked for non-questions but generated the same tokens. For example, *Almost everyone denied.*

Straightforward questions with preambles cover short Tag questions from the grammatical class and short versions of the Hypothetical, Priority/Sequence Prediction Questions and Generalisation questions from the domain-based classes.

2.2.3 Simulated Clauses

The need to represent the grammatical category of Questions in Multiple Sentences posed some problems. One source of data, the IRS FAQ set [43] contained some questions fitting this form:

> *For business travel, are there limits on the amounts deductible for meals?*

> *If I claim my daughter as a dependent because she is a full-time college student, can she claim herself as a dependent when she files her return?*

> *I received a Form 1099-MISC instead of a Form W-2. I'm not self-employed, I do not have a business. How do I report this income?*

The worst case of the last form of question is one that tends to occur in computer helpdesk applications, which contains a relatively long description of the current state of a computer followed by "...Can you help?"

Preliminary work revealed that attempting to collect examples of this data from real-world dialogue sources would be very heavily time consuming and have a low productivity. However, it was also clear that for this category, the questions were again straightforward questions with one or more clauses prefixing them. Therefore, for this set of experiments it was decided to prefix questions with non-questions to simulate the clauses. This may provide a harder classification task than real life because clauses that naturally precede a question may contain additional semantic features.

The IRS source is particularly interesting, because much of the previously reviewed work on DA classification concerned itself with problems involved with spoken dialogue such as dealing with incomplete utterances and channel management. However, when these are resolved the dialogue content is relatively simple. The IRS site reveals that even when these modal problems of dialogue have been resolved, the underlying problems of communicating in a real-world goal-oriented system are rich and complex.

Simulated clauses cover longer Tag and Multiple Sentences questions from the grammatical class, in particular the second question of a compound question.

They also cover longer versions of the Hypothetical, Priority/Sequence Prediction Questions and Generalisation questions from the domain-based classes.

2.2.4 Omitted Question Classes

The grammatical class Declarative was omitted because the only way it can be identified is with prosodic information. Prosodic information is beyond the scope of this study, which deals with text-based input. However, this information could be used in future DT classifiers.

Some questions composed of multiple sentences have also not been covered. In particular, a question in an Indirect DA could confuse a single DA classifier. However, it is anticipated that future multi-classifiers could cope with this, for example the sentence:

Please confirm which flight we are taking.

could be classified as Instruction containing a Question.

2.2.5 Straightforward vs. Difficult Non-questions

Two basic forms of non-question are required for this study, straightforward and difficult. Further sub-categories may be generated by applying the variants such as preambles and simulated clauses devised for the questions.

The problem of "Difficult non-questions" arises from testing by Donald Michie of early pattern matching systems developed by the MMU Centre for Conversational Agents. Simple patterns based on the occurrence of Wh-chefts break down when non-questions are framed using the Wh-chefts as pronouns or conjunctions. In particular, it is possible to construct valid non-questions with pronoun Wh-chefts or conjunctions as starting words.

An example taken from a hair / beauty blog site
(http://www.kaboodle.com/reviews/psoriasisnet-6) is:

When psoriasis develops on the scalp, hair loss sometimes follows.

and this needs to be represented in training and testing data used in the following experiments.

The term "difficult" is used because although sentences of this form do not have to be complex in a cognitive sense, the wh-cheft in the first position makes it more difficult for a DA classifier to deal with correctly. A straightforward non-question on the other hand does not contain features which suggest a question in the first few words.

As with the questions, varying forms of difficult non-questions can be generated from this starting point. Using this type of data calls for some fine judgment. The problem is that it is possible to construct some really taxing non-questions using wh-chefts as pronouns (and find other function word usages that cause problems). However, of their nature some of these are quite unnatural sounding and would be of very low frequency in a natural interaction. So the dilemma arises:

- Should these forms be included in a dataset at all when they are likely to occur with low frequency?
- If so should they be represented in proportion to their frequency of occurrence in the language?

The decisive factor for this work was "Loebner behaviour." This is most prominent in the logs of judging of the annual Loebner prize, although it has been observed to a lesser degree in logs from Conversational Agent tests conducted by the MMU Centre for Conversational Agents. When a human uses a Conversational Agent, the interaction tends to proceed without incident as long as the agent behaves like a human. As conversational partners (particularly in goal-oriented dialogue) both humans and Conversational Agents will make mistakes. As long as the agents make human-like mistakes things go reasonably well. However, even if a Conversational Agent is outperforming the equivalent human in terms of things like domain knowledge, once it makes the kind of mistake a human would not make the user tends to fasten on this to the exclusion of achieving the goal. Judges in the Loebner prize competition tend to be particularly vicious and relentless in this kind of behaviour. So exploring the issues of "difficult non-questions" is important if the product of the DA classifier is to be deployed ultimately in a Conversational Agent.

Having decided to include them, it is necessary to include them in far greater proportions than occur in real-life, otherwise the classifiers will not train properly. Therefore it should be born in mind that classifiers for exotic combinations that have a lower CA are not likely to degrade the general performance of overall DA classification significantly.

3   Experiments

Designing the experiments required the formulation of hypotheses followed by creation of suitable datasets, then the training and testing of decision tree classifiers. Again, these experiments were performed using WEKA and all of the comments about statistical significance are derived from the corrected re-sampled t-test. In the following experiments Classification Accuracy is the percentage of correctly classified DAs (both Question and Non-question) from the whole test data set.

3.1   Hypotheses

Table 4 shows a number of alternative hypotheses to be tested, for different combinations of question and non-question sub-categories. In each case the null hypothesis is that the classifiers do not score higher than chance in discriminating between questions and non-questions in the various combinations. Each hypothesis requires a series of experiments to be conducted to test it, so that when cross-validation and repeated runs from randomized starting points have been taken into account, in excess of 62,400 decision trees were constructed for the new experiments described in this paper.

Table 4. Experimental hypotheses

Experimental series	Hypothesis (H₁)
1	A decision tree using function words can achieve classification accuracy significantly higher than chance over the dataset of straightforward questions vs. straightforward non-questions.
2	A decision tree using function words can achieve classification accuracy significantly higher than chance over the dataset of straightforward questions with 1 word preambles vs. straightforward non-questions.
3	A decision tree using function words can achieve classification accuracy significantly higher than chance over the dataset of straightforward questions with 2 word preambles vs. straightforward non-questions.
4	A decision tree using function words can achieve classification accuracy significantly higher than chance over the dataset of straightforward questions with 3 word preambles vs. straightforward non-questions.
5	A decision tree using function words can achieve classification accuracy significantly higher than chance over the dataset of straightforward questions with 1-3 word preambles vs. straightforward non-questions.
6	A decision tree using function words can achieve classification accuracy significantly higher than chance over the dataset of straightforward questions vs. straightforward non-questions when both have 1 word preambles.

(The decision tree does not learn to classify more effectively by learning from features in 1-word preambles) |
| 7 | A decision tree using function words can achieve classification accuracy significantly higher than chance over the dataset of straightforward questions vs. straightforward non-questions when both have 2 word preambles.

(The decision tree does not learn to classify more effectively by learning from features in 2-word preambles) |

Table 4. (*Continued*)

8	A decision tree using function words can achieve classification accuracy significantly higher than chance over the dataset of straightforward questions vs. straightforward non-questions when both have 3 word preambles.
	(The decision tree does not learn to classify more effectively by learning from features in 3-word preambles)
9	A decision tree using function words can achieve classification accuracy significantly higher than chance over the dataset of straightforward questions vs. difficult non-questions.
10	A decision tree using function words can achieve classification accuracy significantly higher than chance over the dataset of straightforward questions vs. difficult non-questions when both have 1 word preambles.
11	A decision tree using function words can achieve classification accuracy significantly higher than chance over the dataset of straightforward questions vs. difficult non-questions when both have 2 word preambles.
12	A decision tree using function words can achieve classification accuracy significantly higher than chance over the dataset of straightforward questions vs. difficult non-questions when both have 3 word preambles.
13	A decision tree using function words can achieve classification accuracy significantly higher than chance over the dataset of straightforward questions vs. straightforward non-questions when both are preceded by difficult simulated clauses.

Experiment 1, in discriminating between straightforward questions and straightforward non-questions, is expected to pose the simplest discrimination task and set the upper bound of expected CAs for the following experiments. It also represents the kind of challenge a DS should face if the human user is complying with Grice's rules, in particular that dialogue should be clear, direct and to the point. [44].

Experiments 2-5 take the straightforward questions from the initial dataset and shift the first word position progressively further down the question. The preambles may contain a mix of function and content words, potentially obscuring an important feature. Experiment 5 provides a baseline generic classifier against which the performance of specialized classifiers 2-4 can be measured.

Experiments 6-8 correspond to experiments 2-4. These experiments were performed to check whether there were common features in the preambles which contributed to the classification, confounding the results of experiments 2-4.

Experiments 9-12 investigate how effectively the classifiers can work when features in the question first word position are counterbalanced by similar features in the non-question first word position. The difficult non-questions all start with a word which normally signifies a question when it appears in the first word position. Experiment 9 corresponds to experiment 1 and provides a baseline for comparing the effect of adding preambles in 10-12. Experiments 10-12 also correspond to experiments 6-8 by inserting a preamble in front of the original first word position.

3.2   Experimental Procedure

For each of the hypotheses listed above, a series of 4 experiments was conducted to determine the highest classification accuracy obtainable and the optimal level of pruning. The highest CA is an indicator of the performance of a trained classifier deployed in an application. The degree to which a decision tree classifier can be pruned before the CA drops significantly provides evidence about the degree to which the tree can generalise to model the problem domain.

Each experiment consists of a series of trials varying a DT pruning parameter. The first series of trials uses a standard initial set of confidence intervals to control the level of pruning, which establishes approximately where the optimum pruning level will be found. The second series of trials explores a range of pruning values about this initial approximation to establish optimal pruning. These two series usually establish both the maximum CA and the optimal pruning level; but if not, further series may be run based on the information obtained from them.

Confidence interval pruning is based on comparing the expected error rate for the original subtree with that for the replacement node. "Expected error rate" refers to the error rate that would be expected if the tree were run with an independently selected test dataset. The actual value is not known during tree construction, but the confidence interval defines the range it would be expected to fall in [25].

The third series of trials uses a standard initial set of values for Minimum Number of Objects (MNO) pruning. MNO pruning sets a minimum number of training cases for each leaf node. Again the fourth series of trials pins down the optimal pruning level for MNO pruning. Detailed results for series 1 are given in tables 5-8. In the tables a significant decrease in CA is marked with an asterisk.

Table 5. Experiment 1.1

Conf	0.25	0.2	0.15	0.1	0.05
CA	98.50	98.51	98.41	98.48	98.48
Tree Size	29-71	29-67	29-47	29-33	29-33

Table 6. Experiment 1.2

Conf	0.0005	0.0004	0.0003	0.0002	0.0001
CA	98.36	98.36	97.88*	97.89	98.77
Tree Size	25-31	25-31	21-31	21-31	17-31

Table 7. Experiment 1.3

Min	2	5	10*	15	20
CA	98.50	98.32	97.16	97.03	93.57
Tree Size	29-71	25-47	21-25	19-29	15-25

Table 8. Experiment 1.4

Min	5	6	7*	8	9
CA	98.32	98.28	97.80	97.62	97.21
Tree Size	25-47	25-49	25-35	21-35	21-35

Table 9. Best CA and pruning levels achieved for experiments in the series

Experiment	Baseline		Best Classifier		Best Pruned	
	%CA	Nodes	%CA	Nodes	%CA	Nodes
1	98.5	29-71	98.51	29-67	98.36	25-31
2	87.12	69-133	88.11	31-91	86.13	11-39
3	89.40	73-135	89.62	53-111	88.01	9-13
4	88.86	71-131	88.86	71-131	87.84	11-13
5	79.17	131-211	79.22	113-189	77.89	13-33
6	98.24	31-45	98.53	27-29	97.96	21-25
7	98.51	29-73	98.53	29-73	98.43	21-33
8	98.42	29-65	98.44	29-33	98.35	25-33
9	89.18	75-139	89.55	49-123	87.77	23-37
10	89.13	77-127	89.93	45-95	87.98	23-31
11	88.28	77-145	89.03	53-107	86.80	21-29
12	88.95	77-135	89.33	53-121	87.93	23-31
13	62.13	81-313	66.62	3-11	66.62	3-11†

The highest CA achieved was 98.51. The tree is performing significantly better than chance and by a very large margin. This provides good evidence to reject the null hypothesis and accept that the tree is a good classifier. The baseline range of tree sizes (Conf = 0.25, MNO = 2) was 29-71 so the smallest were quite compact. Pruning achieved a modest improvement in the lower limit (25) and a good reduction in the upper limit (31) before a significant reduction in CA. So the overall conclusion is that the decision tree is performing very well the most straightforward (but also the most likely) form of classification it will be required to make.

Table 9 contains summaries of all of the experiments. The first row of data is the summary of experiment 1 (tables 5 – 8 shown above). Each of the following rows is the summary of a corresponding series of trials for a particular experiment.

4   Discussion of Results

All of the results are statistically significant improvements in CA over the chance level of 50%, providing evidence to accept all of the alternative hypotheses. Comparing the corresponding experiments the following observations may be made.

The best result obtained for the initial experiment, classifying straightforward questions in the presence of a mix of straightforward and difficult non-questions (in approximately equal proportions) was 89.43%. Experiment 1 (CA = 98.51) showed an increase in CA of 9.08% when discriminating between straightforward questions and straightforward non-questions. Experiment 9 (CA = 89.55) showed a slight improvement in CA of 0.12 over the initial experiment but a decrease in CA of 8.96% compared with experiment 1. The average increase in CA over the initial experiment obtained by using separate classifiers was 4.6%. This difference is statistically significant.

Experiment 5 shows that when the straightforward questions have a mix of 1, 2 and 3 word preambles in equal proportions applied, the CA decreases by 19.34% from experiment 1. However, the decreases in CA from experiment 1, when classifiers are trained for the specific preamble lengths, are 10.4%, 8.89% and 9.65% for experiments 2, 3 and 4 respectively. So there is an average improvement of the individual classifiers for preambles vs. the generic version of 9.69%. All of these differences are statistically significant.

Experiments 6, 7 and 8 correspond to experiments 2, 3, and 4 respectively. They were conducted to see if the preambles themselves were providing features that contributed to the CA of the classifiers in experiments 2-4. Adding the preambles to both classes resulted in the CAs reaching values very close to experiment 1, where no preambles were used. Effectively the average decrease of 9.69% has been wiped out. The (statistically insignificant) differences were +0.02 for experiment 6, +0.02 for experiment 7 and -0.07 for experiment 8.

This is important because if the CA were significantly lower it would suggest that the preambles had contributed features assisting the classification process in experiments 2-4. In fact, the combined evidence from the experiments suggests that the preambles have an impact on classification accuracy, but that the classifiers are coping by learning to ignore them (to varying degrees). The results of experiments 6-8 suggest that although the preambles have an obscuring effect, they only add a little noise in terms of their own function word content.

Experiments 10, 11 and 12 combine the use of difficult non-questions with preambles applied to both questions and non-questions. When compared with the results for experiment 9, the differences were +0.38 for experiment 10, -0.52 for experiment 11 and -0.22 for experiment 12. Also the differences between experiments 10-12 and experiment 9 are only a little greater than the corresponding differences between experiments 6-8 and experiment 1, adding further weight to the inference that the preambles only add a little noise when inserted in front of both classes.

Pairwise comparisons of 10 with 6, 11 with 7 and 12 with 8 provide further insight on the impact of obscuring (or not obscuring) the first word feature in the presence of a preamble. Experiment 10 shows a decrease in CA of 8.6%, experiment 11 shows a decrease of 9.5% and experiment 12 shows a decrease of 9.11%. The average decrease is 9.07%, the decrease of 8.96 between experiment 1 and experiment 9 is very close to the average, in this case suggesting that adding the preambles has only made a small impact.

The final observations concern the results for experiment 13. The data for experiment 13 is created by concatenating two variable-length sentences. The closest equivalent is the use of mixed-length preambles in experiment 5.

The closest equivalent experiment is 5, which achieved a CA of 77.89%. At 66.62%, the CA of the simulated clauses was significantly lower. Although it exceeds chance performance by a statistically significant margin, it is still too low to be useful in a real-world classifier even after optimisation. Also, the optimisation process resulted in severe pruning of the DT classifiers generated. Consequently the final columns, marked with a †, repeat the values for the optimally pruned tree because it is not possible to prune it any further. Examining trees produced by this experiment shows they are dominated by a fairly simple split occurring at a word position approximately in the middle of the token string. This may simply be the best split that can be obtained when the discriminating features are smeared across the middle of the sentence by the concatenation process.

The decreases in CA for experiments 5 and 13 may be explicable by an increase in the complexity of the task, by dilution of the training data (1/3 as many training cases for each preamble in 5 and much worse in 13) or by a combination of the two. In any event, the individual classifiers clearly perform better than that for the mixed classes.

5   Conclusions and Future Work

The overall outcome of the experiments is encouraging. Four of the experiments produced classifiers with CAs of over 98% and one of theses categories represents the most likely question / non-question combination for dialogues where the participant follows Grice's rules. Of the remaining experiments, four produced classifiers scoring over 89% CA and 3 produced classifiers scoring over 88% CA. Only two of the experiments produced classifiers that had performance markedly below that required for use in real-world systems. In both these classifiers dilution of the training set may be a contributing factor in which case larger training sets may solve the problem. However, the final simulated clauses task may be too complex for this approach.

Future work may take a number of different directions. Before moving on to other dialogue acts it will be worthwhile developing the question classifiers further. The most obvious is an investigation of methods of combining the outputs of the current classifiers to produce a multi-classifier. This could involve a simple polling system or a more complex non-linear approach using Artificial Neural Networks for example. The second direction is to defer producing a multi-classifier until an investigation of optimisation of the specialised classifiers has been conducted, by optimising the feature extraction, for example. Finally, coping with sentences involving complex clauses with indirect and multiple dialogue acts may require a different method of presenting the tokenised sentences to a classifier. This could involve imposing a moving window with a limited size passing down the sentence from beginning to end, presenting each window position as a set of inputs to the classifier. This would also require a different training process.

Collectively, the experiments and directions for future work provide grounds to believe that Slim Function Word Classifiers can be improved to the point where they achieve CAs in excess of 95%.

References

1. Keizer, S.: A Bayesian Approach to Dialogue Act Classification. In: BI-DIALOG 2001 the 5th Workshop on Formal Semantics and Pragmatics of Dialogue, ZiF, Bielefeld (2001)
2. Webb, N., Hepple, M., Wilks, Y.: Dialogue Act Classification Based on Intra-Utterance Features. In: AAAI 2005. AAAI Press, Pittsburgh (2005)
3. Verbree, D., Rienks, R., Heylen, D.: Dialogue-Act Tagging Using Smart Feature Selection; Results On Multiple Corpora. In: IEEE Spoken Language Technology Workshop, pp. 70–73 (2006)
4. Venkataraman, A., Stolcke, A., Shriberg, E.: Automatic Dialog Act Labeling With Minimal Supervision. In: 9th Australian International Conference on Speech Science and Technology (2002)
5. Serafin, R., Di Eugenio, B., Glass, M.: Latent Semantic Analysis for dialogue act classification. In: The 2003 Conference of the North American Chapter of the Association for Computational Linguistics on Human Language Technology, Edmonton, Canada (2003)
6. Wermter, S., Lochel, M.: Learning Dialog Act Processing. In: 16th International Conference on Computational Linguistics, COLING 1996, pp. 740–745 (1996)
7. Searle, J.R.: Mind, Language and Society. Weidenfield & Nicholson (1999)
8. O'Shea, J., Bandar, Z., Crockett, K.: A Machine Learning Approach to Speech Act Classification Using Function Words. In: Jędrzejowicz, P., Nguyen, N.T., Howlet, R.J., Jain, L.C. (eds.) KES-AMSTA 2010. LNCS (LNAI), vol. 6071, pp. 82–91. Springer, Heidelberg (2010)
9. O'Shea, J., Bandar, Z., Crockett, K.: Using a Slim Function Word Classifier to Recognise Instruction Dialogue Acts. In: O'Shea, J., Nguyen, N.T., Crockett, K., Howlett, R.J., Jain, L.C. (eds.) KES-AMSTA 2011. LNCS (LNAI), vol. 6682, pp. 26–34. Springer, Heidelberg (2011)

10. Längle, T., Lüth, T.C., Stopp, E., Herzog, G., Kamstrup, G.: KANTRA — A Natural Language Interface for Intelligent Robots. In: Rembold, U., Dillman, R., Hertzberger, L.O., Kanade, T. (eds.) Intelligent Autonomous Systems (IAS 4), Amsterdam, pp. 357–364 (1995)

11. Crockett, K., Bandar, Z., O'Shea, J., McLean, D.: Bullying and Debt: Developing Novel Applications of Dialogue Systems. In: Knowledge and Reasoning in Practical Dialogue Systems (IJCAI), pp. 1–9. IJCAI, Pasadena (2009)

12. Biro, S., Hommel, B.: Becoming an intentional agent: Introduction to the special issue. Acta Psychologica 124, 1–7 (2007)

13. Vytelingum, P., Voice, T.D., Ramchurn, S.D., Rogers, A., Jennings, N.R.: Intelligent Agents for the Smart Grid. In: The 9th International Conference on Autonomous Agents and Multiagent Systems (AAMAS 2010), vol. 1, pp. 1649–1650 (2010)

14. Bickmore, T., Giorgino, T.: Health dialog systems for patients and consumers. J. Biomed. Inform. 39, 556–571 (2006)

15. Deerwester, S., Dumais, S.T., Furnas, G.W., Landauer, T.K., Harshman, R.: Indexing by Latent Semantic Analysis. Journal of the American Society of Information Science 41, 391–407 (1990)

16. Keizer, S., op den Akker, R., Nijholt, A.: Dialogue Act Recognition with Bayesian Networks for Dutch Dialogues. In: Third SIGdial Workshop on Discourse and Dialogue, Philadelphia, pp. 88–94 (2002)

17. van Rijsbergen, C.J.: Information Retrieval, Butterworths, Boston (1980)

18. Sanderson, M.: Stop Word List (1994),
    http://ftp.dcs.glasgow.ac.uk/idom/ir_resources/linguistic_ut
    ils/stop_words

19. Spärck-Jones, K.: A Statistical Interpretation of Term Specificity and its Application in Retrieval. Journal of Documentation 28, 11–21 (1972)

20. Salton, G., Wong, A., Yang, C.S.: A Vector Space Model for Automatic Indexing. Communications of the ACM 18, 613–620 (1975)

21. Deerwester, S., Dumais, S., Furnas, G.W., Harshman, R., Landauer, T., Lochbaum, K., Streeter, L.: Computer information retrieval using Latent Semantic Structure. In: Office, U.S.P. (ed.) Bell Communications Research Inc., United States of America (1989)

22. Bollacker, K.D., Lawrence, S., Giles, C.L.: CiteSeer: An Autonomous Web Agent for Automatic Retrieval and Identification of Interesting Publications. In: 2nd International ACM Conference on Autonomous Agents, pp. 116–123. ACM Press (1998)

23. Li, Y., Bandar, Z., McLean, D., O'Shea, J.: Sentence Similarity Based on Semantic Nets and Corpus Statistics. IEEE Transactions on Knowledge and Data Engineering 18, 1138–1150 (2006)

24. Islam, A., Inkpen, D.: Semantic Text Similarity using Corpus-Based Word Similarity and String Similarity. ACM Transactions on Knowledge Discovery from Data 2, 1–25 (2008)

25. Quinlan, J.R.: C4.5: programs for machine learning. Morgan Kaufmann Publishers, San Mateo (1993)

26. Quinlan, J.R.: Induction of Decision Trees. Machine Learning 1, 81–106 (1986)

27. Lesch, S., Kleinbauer, T., Alexandersson, J.: A new Metric for the Evaluation of Dialog Act Classication. In: Dialor 2005, the Ninth Workshop on the Semantics and Pragmatics of Dialogue (SEMDIAL 2005), Nancy, France (2005)

28. Kral, P., Cerisara, C., Kleckova, J.: Lexical Structure for Dialogue Act Recognition. Journal of Multimedia 2, 1–8 (2007)

29. Andernach, T., Poel, M., Salomons, E.: Finding Classes of Dialogue Utterances with Kohonen Networks. In: ECML/MLnet Workshop on Empirical Learning of Natural Language Processing Tasks, Prague, Czech Republic, pp. 85–94 (1997)
30. Levin, L., Langley, C., Lavie, A., Gates, D., Wallace, D., Peterson, K.: Domain Specific Speech Acts for Spoken Language Translation. In: 4th SIGdial Workshop on Discourse and Dialogue, Sapporo, Japan (2003)
31. Clark, A., Popescu-Belis, A.: Multi-level Dialogue Act Tags. In: 5th SIGDIAL Workshop on Discourse and Dialog, SIGDIAL 2004, Cambridge, MA (2004)
32. Prasad, R., Walker, W.: Training a Dialogue Act Tagger For Human-Human and Human-Computer Travel Dialogues. In: The 3rd SIGdial Workshop on Discourse and Dialogue, Philadelphia, Pennsylvania, vol. 2, pp. 162–173 (2002)
33. Webb, N., Hepple, M., Wilks, Y.: Error Analysis of Dialogue Act Classification. In: Matoušek, V., Mautner, P., Pavelka, T. (eds.) TSD 2005. LNCS (LNAI), vol. 3658, pp. 451–458. Springer, Heidelberg (2005)
34. Stolcke, A., Ries, K., Coccaro, N., Shriberg, E., Bates, R., Jurafsky, D., Taylor, P., Martin, R., Van Ess-dykema, C., Meteer, M.: Dialogue Act Modeling for Automatic Tagging and Recognition of Conversational Speech. Computational Linguistics 26, 339–373 (2000)
35. Bui, T.H., Poel, M., Nijholt, A., Zwiers, J.: A tractable DDN-POMDP approach to affective dialogue modeling for general probabilistic frame-based dialogue systems. In: International Joint Conference on AI, IJCAI 2007, India (2007)
36. Fernandez, R., Picard, R.W.: Dialog Act Classification from Prosodic Features Using Support Vector Machines. Speech Prosody (2002)
37. Jokinen, K., Hurtig, T., Hynnä, K., Kanto, K., Kaipainen, M., Kerminen, A.: Self-Organizing Dialogue Management. In: Isahara, H., Ma, Q. (eds.) The 2nd Workshop on Natural Language Processing and Neural Networks, NLPRS 2001, Tokyo, Japan, pp. 77–84 (2001)
38. Witten, I.H., Eibe, F.: Data Mining: Practical Machine Learning Tools and Techniques. Elsevier, San Francisco (2005)
39. Aleksander, I., Morton, H.: Introduction to Neural Computing. International Thomson Computer Press (1995)
40. Quirk, R., Greenbaum, S., Leech, G., Svartik, J.: A Comprehensive Grammar of the English Language. Addison Wesley Longman Ltd., Harlow (1985)
41. Flynn, R.: Question types - Glossary Definition - UsingEnglish.com (2002), http://www.usingenglish.com/glossary/question-types.html
42. Christensen, C.R., Garvin, D.A.: Education for Judgment: The Artistry of Discussion Leadership. Harvard Business School Press (1992)
43. IRS: Frequently Asked Tax Questions and Answers (2009), http://www.irs.gov/faqs/index.html
44. Saygin, A.P., Cicekli, I.: Pragmatics in human-computer conversations. Journal of Pragmatics 34, 227–258 (2002)

Building Group Recommendations
in E-Learning Systems

Danuta Zakrzewska

Institute of Information Technology Technical University of Lodz,
Wolczanska 215, 90-924 Lodz, Poland
dzakrz@ics.p.lodz.pl

Abstract. Building groups of students of similar features enables to
suggest learning materials according to their member needs. The paper presents an agent-based recommender system, which, for each new
learner, suggests a student group of similar profiles and consequently
indicates suitable learning resources. It is assumed that learners can
be characterized by cognitive styles, usability preferences or historical
behavior, represented by nominal values. Building recommendations by
using a Naïve Bayes algorithm is considered. The performance of the
technique is validated on the basis of data of learners, who are described
by cognitive traits such as dominant learning style dimensions or by usability preferences. Tests are done for real data of different groups of
similar students as well as of individual learners.

Keywords: e-learning, recommender agent, Bayesian classifier.

1 Introduction

The development of web-based education enables geographically distributed students to be involved in the same educational process. Such students are usually
characterized by different professional background and skills. They also vary in
learning needs and preferences. The performance of the educational process depends significantly on the extent to which an e-learning system is tailored to
individual learners' characteristics. Adaptivity of an educational software is a
very important feature, which can help in achieving educational goals [1]. In the
case of the big amount of students, adaptation of the system to individual needs
may be difficult, as even among learners studying the same subject at the same
university, it is impossible to define an average student and multiple versions of
the system have to be created [2]. What is more, designing different interfaces for
each user may be extremely costly [3]. Dividing students into groups of similar
preferences and, then, personalizing the system in compliance with their needs,
seems to be a good solution. Group recommendations enable new students to
choose colleagues, with whom they can learn together, by using the same course
resources.

In the paper, we consider a system, in which, agents are implemented in
order to provide, to each new learner, recommendations of student groups of

N.T. Nguyen (Ed.): Transactions on CCI VII, LNCS 7270, pp. 144–163, 2012.

similar profiles and consequently to indicate appropriate learning resources, or to refer the student to the tutor if any group of similar peers does not exist. Each student feature is supposed to be represented by a vector of nominal values, which can depict learner cognitive styles, usability preferences or historical behaviors. It is assumed that recommendations are based on computational intelligence methods. As the exemplary technique, Naïve Bayes algorithm is considered. The technique is very simple and ensures high accuracy of obtained results [4], even though the conditional assumption, on which it is based, is rarely fulfilled in the real world. The presented system was firstly introduced in the paper [5]. Currently, the proposed method is evaluated by using of 2 additional student models on the real data sets, namely the model of learning style preferences of 5 nominal values and the 3 valued model of usability preferences. As the considered models have their numerical equivalents, the presented approach is additionally compared with the one consisting in building group recommendations on the basis of the centroid minimum distance method [6].

The paper is organized as follows. In the next section a literature review concerning recommendations as well as data mining techniques in e-learning are presented. Then the recommender system architecture, together with computational intelligence technique are described. Next, the two cases of students modeled by cognitive traits and usability preferences are considered. For both of them, experiments, carried out on real students' data, are depicted in the following section. Finally, some concluding remarks are presented.

2 Related Work

In recent years, many researchers have examined possibilities of improving e-learning courses by using personalized recommendations of appropriate activities or learning materials. Those investigations have been focused mainly on the identification of learner requirements, so the system could suggest matching actions or learning resources that would support an educational process [7]. Zaïane presented how web usage mining could be used to enhance web-based learning environments. As the most useful methods, he mentioned association rule mining as well as sequential patterns mining, which can help in tasks such as identification of paths or frequently visited pages [7].

Student characteristics that decide on their requirements and preferences, and that can be the basis for adaptivity features of educational systems, have been investigated by different authors (see [8,9,10] for example). Santally and Alain proposed a framework for research in promoting personalization. They built algorithms for personalized instruction, which helps in deciding, which is the most appropriate learning object. They focused their investigations on psychological attributes of students [8]. Stash et al. considered adaptation to learning styles in hypermedia environments. They presented the tool "AHA", which aims at helping authors to associate an instructional strategy with the selected learning style [9]. Xu et al., in turn, presented multi-agent based educational system, based on learning activities and interaction history of students. By using fuzzy logic, the system made dynamic learning plans and students got personalized materials and advice [10].

Many of the researchers considered building student groups for recommendation purposes. They grouped students according to their behaviors, taking into account pages they visited or historical navigational paths. Tang and McCalla built clusters of students to find groups of similar learning interests. Then, they used collaborative filtering, taking into account knowledge level, to build recommendations for groups [11]. Talavera and Gaudioso clustered students according to their behaviors in unstructured collaboration spaces, defining attributes on the basis of the most often interactions with the system, such as number of messages, sessions, posts etc. They built descriptive group models and compared them with external features [12]. In [13], students were grouped according to their learning styles. In order to do that, different clustering techniques were considered and compared. Building groups on the basis of learning styles and usability preferences at the same time was investigated in [14]. Yang et al. [15] proposed learning resources recommendation system based on connecting similar students into small communities, where they could share resources and communicate with each other. After testing the system, authors concluded that such an approach not only enhanced the learning process, but also helped to reduce the isolation of distributed learners.

As the main technique used for student grouping, one should mention clustering, which was very often combined with other data mining techniques, such as collaborative filtering [11], sequential pattern mining [16] or association rules mining [6]. Shen et al. grouped students according to learning actions to discover their sequential patterns, for the purpose of web-based educational systems [16]. Romero et al., in [6], proposed the architecture for recommender systems based on web usage mining. The mining tool, which they presented, aimed at discovering patterns on the basis of student log files by using clustering, sequential pattern and association rule mining. Patterns were used to build recommendations providing personalized links and contents. Recommendations were made according to rules made on clusters. Each student was assigned to the cluster by using the centroid minimum distance method.

Hämäläinen and Vinni [17] used machine learning methods for modeling structures from educational data. They compared the accuracy of different classifiers for predicting the course outcomes. They gave general outlines for classifying educational data sets,which are small and of mixed types. Zaïane [18] used association rules mining to build models of on-line student behaviors. García et al. [19] combined association rules mining with collaborative filtering to build recommendations for courseware authors. They built the collaborative recommender system based on the client-server architecture. On the basis of student usage data, association rules were built and then evaluated, taking into account opinions of the both experts and teachers. The goal of the system was to improve the performance of the courses by making necessary modifications. A wide review of areas of interactions between data mining and building recommendations in e-learning can be found in [20].

Multi-agent architectures have often been used for building recommendations in e-learning environments. Zaïane [18] proposed an agent, which aimed at assisting on-line learning process by recommending learning activities or shortcuts in course web-sites. The recommendations were based on learners' historical activities. Andronico et al. [21] built their multi-agent system to suggest students educational materials in a mobile learning process. They considered learners' behavior and preferences while using different mobile devices including PDAs and cellular phones. Rosaci and Sarné, [22] in turn, proposed a multi-agent learning system called ISABEL,which considers both: student's profile and an exploited device. The recommendations were built on the basis of the time that the student spent on the particular Web site, taking into account the device used for navigating. Alexakos et al. [23] presented an agent based platform, for providing intelligent assessment services based on Bayesian Networks and Genetic Algorithms. They used the platform for assessment of students in a questioner-based examination process.

Bayesian modeling has been the subject of many investigations in e-learning, to mention such purposes as detecting learner misuse of the system [24] or predicting student attitude to learning, the amount learned and the perception of the system from the log data [25]. García et al. [26] applied Bayesian networks for detecting students' learning styles on the basis of their behaviors. Hämäläinen et al. [27] combined Bayesian networks with data mining to build a model, which describes learning process for students' guiding. Beck and Woolf [28], in turn, predicted the correctness of student's next response and the time of responding. They constructed an agent, which makes the prediction by using information about the student, the current topic, the problem, and the student's efforts to solve it.

3 Building Group Recommendations

In an intelligent e-learning system, where personalization is aimed at adjusting courses and environments to the needs of student groups, each learner should be the member of the group of peers of similar features. Application of unsupervised classification enables to find groups of students of similar preferences, taking into account several traits at the same time. Building group profiles representing most of their members' preferences allows to adapt the courses appropriately. In [13], a personalized e-learning system based on student groups was proposed. The system assumed that learning resources and information content could be adapted to groups' needs. The research, presented in [13], was limited to student clustering techniques examinations. As student characteristics, dominant learning styles and usability requirements were taken into account. Building group profiles and association rules for clusters was the matter of investigation in [29]. However, the research was limited to learning styles considered as student traits. Obviously, following investigations should concern appropriate assignments of learning resources to groups. What is more, new students, after their features are determined, should obtain a recommendation of the most suitable group and accordingly personalized learning materials and contents.

3.1 System Architecture

The recommender system is aimed at suggesting to each new student groups of peers with whom he or she can learn together by using the same learning materials. Recommendations are built assuming that the existing student groups consist of learners of similar features such as cognitive styles, usability preferences or whose historical behaviors were much alike. They are based on three data collections: of groups' members attributes, of learning materials equipped with flags indicating target learners and new student features. The system performs two tasks: assigning learning materials to groups and recommending groups together with materials to new learners.

There are three kinds of agents involved in the task realization: group, course and group recommendation agents. Each course has its agent. Its goal is to recommend learning materials to student groups. It is assumed that the materials are equipped in flags, indicating the attributes of students who should use them. Course agents take data from learning resource database and modify group data by assigning suitable learning materials. They use the Bayesian classifier and compute the respective probability. The highest probability value is chosen and suitable course materials are assigned.

Each group agent is in charge of finding out the group representation features, according to which course agents assign learning materials to groups. The recommendation agent aims at suggesting groups and learning materials to each new student, taking into account information obtained from group agents and course agents. If there is no group of features sufficiently similar to the ones of the student, the recommendation agent suggests that the student contact the tutor. The system is static at course level, however group structures as well as learning materials data can change in case of different courses. The system architecture is shown in Fig.1.

3.2 Methodology

We will assume that students are described by vectors of nominal attributes, which represent their traits such as cognitive styles, usability preferences or characteristics of their historical behaviors. We will also assume that there exist groups of students of similar features. For the purpose of building recommendations, on the basis of group member features, group representations should be determined.

Let us assume that each student ST is described by a vector of N attributes of nominal type:

$$ST = (st_1, st_2, ..., st_N) \; , \tag{1}$$

where st_i may take on k_i nominal values, $i = 1, ...N$. Then group representation can be defined as follows:

Definition 1. *Let GS be a group of objects described by vectors of N components of nominal type, each of which of M different values at most. As the group representation GSR we will consider the set of column vectors $gsr_i, i = 1, ..., N$*

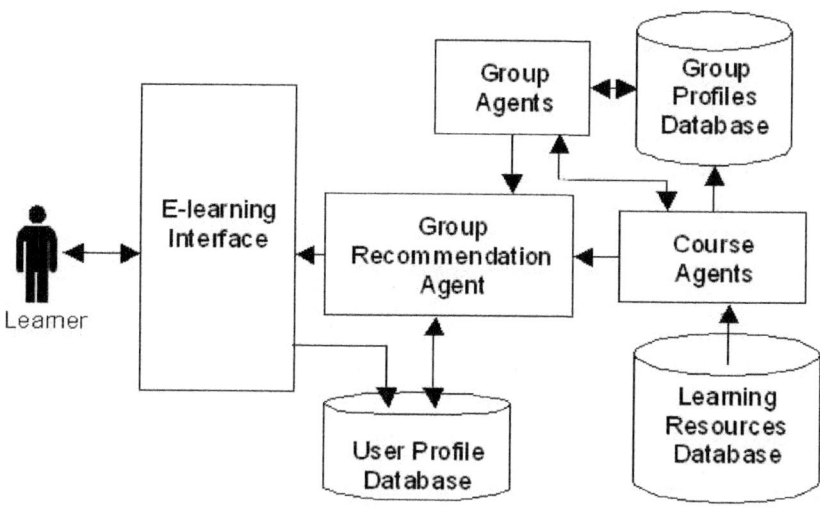

Fig. 1. The system architecture [5]

of k_i components, representing attribute values of GS objects where $M = max$ $\{k_i : i = 1, ..., N\}$. Each component of a vector $gsr_i, i = 1, ..., N$ is calculated as likelihood $P_{ij}, i = 1, ..., N; j = 1, ...k_i$ that objects from GS are characterized by the certain attribute value and is called the support for the respective attribute value in GS.

The above definition is the generalization of the group representation defined in [29], where learning styles were considered as student features. The group representation in a probabilistic form allows one to classify new learners to the closest groups and to choose the learning materials which are most suitable for the group. What is more, the group representation, defined that way, helps in looking at the group features comprehensively. The values of the biggest support indicate dominant attribute values for each group.

Having the group representation and the learner profile, the recommendation can be built, by using a computational intelligence technique. In the present study, we will take advantage of the probabilistic form of group representations and focus on using the Naïve Bayes model, which is the simplest form of Bayesian network for general probability estimation [30]. However, Bayesian networks are a very attractive method in cases with uncertainty, but they are too complex for small data sets and the model overfits easily. The Naïve Bayes model avoids the problem [17]. By application of the Naïve Bayesian algorithm, probability distribution of belonging to classes is obtained. The technique supports also uncertain cases, in which objects may not be assigned into any group or may be allocated into more than one class. Many advantages of the method were presented in [31]. Comparisons of the performance of the Naïve Bayes classifier and other techniques, like decision trees, neural networks, kNN, SVM or rule-learners, presented in [32], showed that Naïve Bayes technique outperformed other algorithms, especially in the speed of learning and classification, tolerance of missing values, explanation ability as well as model parameter handling. The Naïve Bayes model is based on maximum likelihood that uses the well known Bayes' formula.

Let us denote as $P(GL_j/ST)$ the probability that learner ST belongs to GL_j. Then it can be computed as follows:

$$P(GL_j/ST) = \frac{P(ST/GL_j)P(GL_j)}{\sum_{i=1}^{NG} P(ST/GL_i)P(GL_i)}, \tag{2}$$

where NG means number of student groups , $P(GL_j)$ is the probability of sampling and is computed as the proportion of students belonging to the group GL_j to the size of the entire set of students. $P(ST/GL_j)$ means conditional probability that a learner from GL_j is described by (1) and is determined by the respective values of vectors $gsr_i, i = 1, ..., N$ from Def.1. For any $j \in 1...NG$, $P(ST/GL_j)$ can be defined as:

$$P(ST/GL_j) = \frac{P(ST \cap GL_j)}{P(GL_j)}, \tag{3}$$

where $P(ST \cap GL_j)$ is computed as the ratio of number of students from the group GL_j described by (1) to the the size of the entire set of students. Maximal value of $P(GL_j/ST)$ for $j \in 1...NG$ indicates the group that should be recommended for students.

Naïve Bayes technique can be also used for assigning the most suitable course resources to the groups. Let us assume that each learning resource is equipped with flags indicating traits of students, for whom it is designed. Then learning materials can be described similarly to (1). Let NC be the number of available learning resources and let CR_i denote the learning material described by N nominal values:

$$CR_i = (cr_{i_1}, cr_{i_2}, ..., cr_{i_N}) , \tag{4}$$

where $i = 1, ..., NC$. Let us denote as $P(CR_i/GL_j)$ the probability that the material CR_i has features appropriate for students from the group GL_j. Then it can be computed as follows:

$$P(CR_i/GL_j) = \frac{P(GL_j/CR_i)P(CR_i)}{\sum_{k=1}^{NC} P(GL_j/CR_k)P(CR_k)}, \tag{5}$$

$P(CR_i)$ is the probability of sampling. $P(GL_j/CR_i)$ means conditional probability that the group GL_j is characterized by CR_i. For any $j \in 1...NG$, and $i \in 1...NC$, $P(GL_j/CR_i)$ can be computed by:

$$P(GL_j/CR_i) = \frac{P(CR_i \cap GL_j)}{P(CR_i)}, \tag{6}$$

where $P(CR_i \cap GL_j)$ is the probability that students in the group GL_j are characterized by attribute values of CR_i. Maximal value of $P(CR_i/GL_j)$ for $i \in 1...NC$ indicates the materials that should be assigned to the group GL_j.

3.3   Algorithm

Let us assume that there exist groups of students modeled by nominal values according to (1) and that the groups are described by their representations determined by Def. 1. Then as the group representative we will consider a vector of components equal to the nominal values for which the support is the biggest in the group. Let $R_j = (r_{j_1}, r_{j_2}, ..., r_{j_N})$ be the representative of the group GL_j, then for the student ST described by (1) and each group GL_j, we can define a recommendation error $Err_j, j = 1, ..., NG$ as follows:

$$err_{j_i} = \begin{cases} 1 & st_i = r_{j_i} \\ 0 & otherwise \end{cases} \tag{7}$$

$$Err_j = \sum_{i=1}^{N} err_{j_i}. \tag{8}$$

Let us assume also that there exist the set of learning materials described by nominal values equivalent to student features according to (4). Then for building group recommendations the following steps are neccessary:

```
[Input]:A set of NG groups GL_j, containing students
        described by N nominal attributes;
        a set of NC learning materials CR_i;
        attributes of the student ST;
        required maximal error value RE;
Step 1: For each group GL_j, j = 1, 2, ..., NG find their
        representations GSR_j, and representatives R_j;
Step 2: For each group GL_j find the best learning materials
        by using (5), (6), denote them by CR_j, j = 1, ..., NG;
Step 3: For the student ST find the group GL_k
        such that P(GL_k/ST) = max {P(GL_j/ST), j = 1, ..., NG}
        by using (2), (3);
Step 4: Compute the error Err_k by (7), (8);
Step 5: If Err_k < RE then recommend the k-th group
        and materials CR_k; else
        direct the student to the tutor.
```

4   Student Models

Many researchers agree on the importance of student modelling for the purpose of Web educational systems, but there is little agreement on which features can and should be used, or how to use them [33]. The traits, should be stable and are usually extracted by specially designed tests. For the purpose of the evaluation of recommendations' quality, we will consider two exemplary models: the one based on dominant learning styles and the one connected with usability needs.

4.1 Students' Characterized by Cognitive Styles

Brusilovsky [33] stated that student dominant learning styles can be used for web educational systems' personalization. We will apply Felder & Silverman [34] model, which has often been indicated as the most appropriate for the use in computer-based educational systems (see [35] for example).

In the considered model, Felder & Silverman distinguished 4 attributes, which indicate preferences for 4 dimensions from among excluding pairs: *active* vs. *reflective, sensing* vs. *intuitive, visual* vs. *verbal,* and *sequential* vs. *global*; or *balanced* if the student has no dominant preferences.The index has the form of the odd integer from the interval [-11,11], assigned for one of the dimensions from the pairs mentioned above. Each student, who filled ILS questionnaire, can be modeled by a vector SL of 4 integer attributes:

$$SL = (sl_1, sl_2, sl_3, sl_4) = (l_{ar}, l_{si}, l_{vv}, l_{sg}) \ , \tag{9}$$

where l_{ar} means scoring for *active* (if it has a negative value) or *reflective* (if it is positive) learning style, and respectively l_{si}, l_{vv}, l_{sg} are points for all the other dimensions, with negative values in cases of *sensing, visual* or *sequential* learning styles, and positive values in cases of *intuitive, verbal* or *global* learning styles.

A score from the interval [-3,3] means that the student is fairly well balanced on the two dimensions of that scale. Values -5,-7 or 5,7 mean that a student learns more easily in a learning environment which favors the considered dimension; values -9,-11 or 9,11 mean that learner has a very strong preference for one dimension of the scale and may have real difficulty learning in an environment which does not support that preference [36]. *ST* vector in that case can be presented as follows:

$$ST = SL = (ln_{ar}, ln_{si}, ln_{vv}, ln_{sg}) \ , \tag{10}$$

where

$$ln_{ar} = \begin{cases} a & l_{ar} = -11, -9, \\ ab & l_{ar} = -7, -5, \\ b & l_{ar} = -3, -1, 1, 3, \\ rb & l_{ar} = 5, 7, \\ r & l_{ar} = 9, 11; \end{cases} \tag{11}$$

$$ln_{si} = \begin{cases} s & l_{si} = -11, -9, \\ sb & l_{ar} = -7, -5, \\ b & l_{si} = -3, -1, 1, 3, \\ ib & l_{ar} = 5, 7, \\ i & l_{si} = 9, 11; \end{cases} \tag{12}$$

$$ln_{vv} = \begin{cases} vs & l_{vv} = -11, -9, \\ vsb & l_{ar} = -7, -5, \\ b & l_{vv} = -3, -1, 1, 3, \\ vrb & l_{ar} = 5, 7, \\ vr & l_{vv} = 9, 11; \end{cases} \tag{13}$$

$$ln_{sg} = \begin{cases} s & l_{sg} = -11, -9, \\ sb & l_{ar} = -7, -5, \\ b & l_{sg} = -3, -1, 1, 3, \\ gb & l_{ar} = 5, 7, \\ g & l_{sg} = 9, 11. \end{cases} \qquad (14)$$

According to Def. 1 the group representation takes the form of the matrix and may be defined as (compare [29]):

Definition 2. *Let GL be a cluster containing objects with ST data determined by equation (10). As the group representation we will consider the matrix $GLR = [glr_{ij}]_{1 \le i \le 5, 1 \le j \le 4}$, where the columns represent attributes from SL model and the rows nominal values of attributes. Each component of GLR is calculated as likelihood P that students from GL are characterized by the certain attribute value from SL model and is called the support for the respective SL attribute value in GL.*

$$GLR = \begin{bmatrix} P(ln_{ar} = a), & P(ln_{si} = s), & P(ln_{vv} = vs), & P(ln_{sg} = s) \\ P(ln_{ar} = ab), & P(ln_{si} = sb), & P(ln_{vv} = vsb), & P(ln_{sg} = sb) \\ P(ln_{ar} = b), & P(ln_{si} = b), & P(ln_{vv} = b), & P(ln_{sg} = b) \\ P(ln_{ar} = rb), & P(ln_{si} = ib), & P(ln_{vv} = vrb), & P(ln_{sg} = gb) \\ P(ln_{ar} = r), & P(ln_{si} = i), & P(ln_{vv} = vr), & P(ln_{sg} = g) \end{bmatrix}. \qquad (15)$$

As values from -11 to -5 (from 5 to 11) indicate the same preferred dimension value, the model can be simplified and the number of considered nominal values can be limited to 3. Then, the representation matrix GLR takes the form:

$$GLR = \begin{bmatrix} P(ln_{ar} = a), & P(ln_{si} = s), & P(ln_{vv} = vs), & P(ln_{sg} = s) \\ P(ln_{ar} = b), & P(ln_{si} = b), & P(ln_{vv} = b), & P(ln_{sg} = b) \\ P(ln_{ar} = r), & P(ln_{si} = i), & P(ln_{vv} = vr), & P(ln_{sg} = g) \end{bmatrix}. \qquad (16)$$

Both of the models will be considered during the experiments described in the Section 5.

4.2   Students' Characterized by Usability Preferences

In the second example of student models, usability preferences will be considered. As the most important design categories, deciding on Web sites usability, which should be evaluated by users, Marsico and Levialdi [37] mentioned information representation and appearance, access, navigation and orientation as well as the informative content architecture of the sites. Investigations presented in [14] showed that students put special attention to graphical attractiveness of Web sites and the efficiency of the system. The last feature is connected with a short time of loading the sites. Students also emphasized the importance of advanced search possibilities. Consequently, in the current research, 5 portal features are considered: informative contents, graphics, navigation, efficiency and search possibilities. Students were asked to score the importance of each of the feature, assigning from 1 to 5 scores. Values equal to 1 or 2 mean that a student does not put attention to the portal characteristic, 3 means that a learner does not distinguish the importance of considered feature from among the others, finally values 4 or 5 mean that the usability trait is important for the student. Taking into account the meaning of the score values, we can use two kinds of models of five attributes. The one of numerical values:

$$U = (u_1, u_2, u_3, u_4, u_5),\tag{17}$$

and the respective nominal model:

$$ST = UN = (un_1, un_2, un_3, un_4, un_5),\tag{18}$$

$$un_i = \begin{cases} nw & u_i = 1, 2, \\ o & u_i = 3, \\ w & u_i = 4, 5, \end{cases}\tag{19}$$

for $i = 1, \ldots, 5$.

In that case, cluster representation consists of vectors $[gsr_i]$, $i = 1, \ldots, 5$, of three components defined as follows:

$$[gsr_i]^T = [P(un_i = nw), P(un_i = o), P(un_i = w)].\tag{20}$$

5   Experiments

The goal of the experiments was to evaluate the performance of the system concerning group recommendations. We assumed that learning materials assigned to groups were consistent with their profiles, which were characterized by dominant attribute values. It means that the flags of learning materials coincided with the last ones. The evaluation can be done by comparison of classification results obtained by the system with memberships to the groups which match students best. The main criterion can be the fitness between student characteristics and the flags of learning materials, which are assigned to the recommended group. As student characteristics, we considered both the presented models of student dominant learning styles and usability preferences.

5.1   Data Sets

The first part of the tests was done for three different datasets of real students' attributes representing dominant learning styles of students who filled in an available online ILS self-scoring questionnaire [36] as was presented in SL model (see (10)). The first set contains data of 194 Computer Science students from different levels and years of studies, including part-time and evening courses. Those data were used for building groups of similar learners. The two other sets contain data of students, who were to learn together with their peers from the first dataset and whose data were used for testing the recommendation efficiency. The set A consists of 31 data of students studying the same master's course of

Information Systems in Management, the set B contained data of 56 part-time learners. Additionally the fourth set of artificially generated data was used to verify the presented method. It contained 2 kinds of data: instances being representatives of the groups and instances for which likelihood of group membership was the least for all the considered groups.

In the second part of the experiments, three other datasets of real students' attributes representing usability preferences were used. Computer Science students from Technical University of Lodz, filled in the questionnaire, where they scored the importance of 5 portal features : informative contents, graphics, navigation, efficiency and search possibilities as was depicted in Section 4.2. The first set of 103 students from different courses was used for group building. The two other sets of students' data: C of 22 learners and D of 23 learners studying the same master's course of Information Systems in Management, but representing different years of studies, were considered for group recommendations building. Students from the set C were characterized by 12 different vectors of attribute values. In the set D, 15 different patterns of attribute values were distinguished. Similarly to the first part of the tests, the fourth set of artificially generated data was created. As in the previous case, it contained instances being representatives of the groups and instances for which likelihood of group membership was the least.

Finally, appropriately to considered student characteristics, the datasets of different learning resources, which were expected to be the most suitable for groups were created. Flags of the resources, which indicated the target group features were used during the experiments.

5.2   Grouping

The groups of students were created as clusters of disparate structures and sizes, by application of different techniques, taking into account attributes of numeric types in both of the examined cases. For the purpose of the experiments, we considered clusters built by three well known algorithms: K-means, EM and Farthest First Traversal. Such an approach allows one to check the considered techniques for groups of different similarity degree and different structures.

K-means is one of the most known technique from among partitioning methods [38]. The algorithm consists in assigning data into the given number of clusters. At the beginning, clusters are randomly selected. In each iteration, observations are reassigned by moving them into the nearest cluster. New cluster centers are recalculated. The process is continued until all the observations are situated in the closest cluster. The method is simple and effective on large data sets, but its results depend significantly on initial assignments.

The goal of statistical models is to find the most likely set of clusters on the basis of training data and prior expectations. Expectation - Maximization algorithm (EM) uses the finite Gaussian mixtures model to generate probabilistic descriptions of clusters in terms of means and standard deviations [38]. Similarly to K-means method, parameters are recomputed until the desired convergence value is achieved.

Farthest First Traversal algorithm (FFT) is based on the strategy introduced in [39]. This divisive approach guarantees very good performance in comparison with agglomerative methods [40]. Similarly to K-means, it is very simple and requires the desired number of clusters as an input parameter.

During the tests, data were divided by each of the algorithm into 5 clusters: the number, for which most of the clustering schemes occurred to be the best from the point of view of cluster qualities (compare [41]), which ensured the similarity of group members. Group profiles were determined, by taking into account attribute values of the biggest support according to Def. 1.

5.3   Case 1 - Dominant Learning Styles

As learning materials were created according to existing group profiles, the precision of assignments of the resources to clusters will not be the matter of further investigations. In the cases of the sets A and B, the efficiency of group recommendations was examined in three steps. Firstly, it was checked if the suggested group is the best choice for the learner, taking into account the fitness between student features and flags of learning materials. Then, the classification accuracy measured by number of attributes, which take on the same value was calculated. Finally, qualitative analysis of group representations and student attributes was carried out.

During experiments both of the learning style student models were considered. At first, the 3 valued model with the respective representation matrix (16) was examined. In that case, students from the set A were represented by 16 different SL vectors. In the set B, 26 different SL attribute values were distinguished. Quantitative analysis of the quality of recommendations showed that in the worst case of groups built by FFT method, 3 students from the set A and 7 from the set B, could obtain better suggestions, which means, respectively, 3 and 7 wrongly classified instances. For those groups, the number of students of exact match was the smallest. For groups created by EM schema, the recommendations were the best, for all the students of the set A. In the set B, 2 students were wrongly classified. For those groups, the number of students of the exact match is also the greatest and amounts to 18.75% of all the students of the set A and to 15.38% of the learners of the set B. In that case, for both of the datasets, 1 attribute of the biggest number of learners differ from those consistent with suggestions. The detailed results of quantitative analysis for different group structures and for datasets A and B are presented in Table 1. Columns show, respectively, the percentage of students: for whom better suggestions can be done, of exact match, and whose 1,2,3 attributes are different from exact match.

Qualitative analysis was aimed at recognizing all the instances that were shown as wrongly classified by quantitative analysis. In the case of groups built by K-means and EM, the detailed examination of all the cases showed that incorrect classifications take place if the best group does not contain students of at least one dominant learning style dimensions consistent with those of the considered learners, or the likelihood of students of some characteristics is very small. For example, in the case of the set A, 1 wrong recommendation of groups built

Table 1. Quantitative analysis for the sets A and B and the 3 valued model

Set	Schema	Better choice	Exact match	1 attrib.	2 attrib.	3 attrib.
A	EM	0%	18.75%	56.25%	25%	0%
	K-means	6.25%	18.75%	43.75%	31.25%	6.25%
	FFT	18.75%	12.5%	43.75%	50%	6.25%
B	EM	7.70%	15.38%	50%	26.92%	7.70%
	K-means	15.38%	11.54%	34.62%	38.46%	15.38%
	FFT	26.92%	11.54%	34.62%	34.62%	19.22%

by K-means took place for the *reflective* learner and the likelihood of *reflective* students in the cluster of the best choice was equal to 0.05. The biggest number of *reflective* students are contained in the group number 4, which was recommended to him. In 2 cases, from the same dataset, connected with FFT schema and which were wrongly classified, the situation is similar: one of the student is *visual* and the cluster of the best choice contains no *visual* learners; while the second one is *verbal* and similarly, there are no *verbal* learners among the students, who belong to the group that should be the best for him. Concluding, in all that cases students may obtain better recommendations concerning learning materials, but from the point of view of suggestions of peers to learn together, the recommended group appeared to be the best. The analysis of the results of the set B and groups created by FFT algorithm showed also the big influence of the group size on recommendations. In 4 from the 7 incorrect indications, where likelihoods of some characteristics were of the similar range, the classifier indicated the group of the biggest size, instead of the one that seemed to be the best from the point of view of learning materials assignment.

In the case of the fourth set, almost all the cluster representatives were correctly classified. The only exception concerned cluster number 4 built by FFT method, where the learner, *balanced* in all the learning style dimensions, should be classified. Instead, similarly to the set B, the biggest cluster was recommended to the student. Recommendations for students, whose characteristics differ significantly from those of the majority of their peers differed markedly from exact match in most of the cases (in 3 and 4 attributes). It means that in such cases tutors should decide on recommendations.

Investigation concerning the 5 valued model was limited to the sets A and B. In that case, students from the set A were represented by 22 different SL vectors, while those from the set B were represented by 35 different SL vectors. In many cases, the results, obtained for the 3 valued model, showed that groups, which should be indicated as better choices from the point of view of the number of consistent attributes, have not contained any learners of at least one dominant learning style of the considered student. Such a situation took place often for the 5 valued model, as representation matrices for all the clusters contained on

Table 2. Quantitative analysis for the sets A and B and the 5 valued model

Set	Schema	Better choice	Exact match	1 attrib.	2 attrib.	3 attrib.
A	EM	13.64%	9.09%	27.27%	36.36%	18.18%
	K-means	9.09%	9.09%	22.73%	40.91%	22.73%
	FFT	9.09%	4.54%	31.82%	31.82%	22.73%
B	EM	14.29%	5.71%	37.14%	40%	14.29%
	K-means	0%	0%	31.43%	42.86%	17.14%
	FFT	11.43%	8.57%	17.14%	37.14%	22.86%

average 33% zero values (from 15% to 50%). As the result, a group in which all the considered student features were not presented has not been regarded as a better choice.

Quantitative analysis showed that the effects for 5 valued model were worse than in the case of the 3 valued one. For both of the sets and all of the group structures, the percentage of recommendations of exact match was lower significantly than in the previous model. What is more, the percentage of recommendations with 3 attributes different from exact match was higher. Besides, students for whom all the attribute values were different from exact match have been found for all the clustering schemas and both of the sets. The biggest number of such students took place for groups created by FFT algorithm. All the results for the 5 valued model are presented in the Table 2. Percentages of students without recommendations are shown in the Table 3. Similarly to the previous model, quantitative analysis showed that the Naïve Bayes classifier indicates bigger groups for the recommendations. The small likelihood that students of some characteristics are members of the group has also the big influence on the classifier value.

Table 3. Students without recommendations for the sets A and B and the 5 valued model

Set	EM	K-means	FFT
A	9.09%	4.54%	9.09%
B	2.86%	8.57%	11.43%

5.4   Case 2 - Usability Preferences

Similarly to the previously presented case, learning resources were created according to existing group profiles based on usability preferences of group members. Additionally, it was assumed that the resources were correctly assigned to clusters. In the cases of the sets C and D, the efficiency of group recommendations was examined in the same way as for the sets A and B. The results of the

Table 4. Quantitative analysis for the sets C and D and different group structures

Set	Schema	Better choice	Exact match	1 attrib.	2 attrib.	3 attrib.
C	EM	0%	25%	58.33%	16.67%	0%
	K-means	8.33%	41.67%	41.67%	8.33%	0%
	FFT	16.67%	8.33%	50%	25%	16.67%
D	EM	0%	20%	20%	33.33%	20%
	K-means	13.33%	20%	40%	13.33%	13.33%
	FFT	13.33%	6.67%	20%	46.67%	20%

quantitative analysis are presented in the Table 4. As previously, the columns show, respectively, the percentage of students for whom better suggestions can be done, of exact match, and whose 1,2,3 attributes are different from exact match.

The biggest number of students of exact match is obtained for K-means clustering schema for the set C and for both techniques K-means and EM for the set D. Also in that case, clusters built by the last method guarantee the best recommendations, as the number of better suggestions is equal to 0. Similarly to the previous case the worst recommendations were obtained for groups built by FFT method. In the set D, there were 2 students, without recommendations for groups created by K-means schema. One of the students could not also get suggestions for groups created by two other methods. Both of the learners should be directed to tutors.

The qualitative analysis showed that wrong classification takes place, when a student is characterized by the attribute value which does not occur in the cluster. Then, the respective likelihood is close to 0 and even if all the other features are similar to all the group members, the cluster will not be suggested. The big size of the group has also the influence on recommendations and may be the reason of wrong classifications. Additional tests carried out on cluster schemas of a number of clusters smaller than 5, showed that recommendations on big groups performed worse. Results obtained for groups created by FFT, confirmed the observation: 1 cluster of the big size (84%) resulted in the worst classification effects (see Table 4).

Artificially generated datasets performed similarly to the ones created for learning styles attributes. Almost all the cluster representatives were correctly classified, while the recommendations for the students from the set, where data diverge significantly from those of most of the learners, differed from the exact ones, which confirmed the necessity of tutors' decisions.

5.5   Comparison with Centroid Minimum Distance Approach

Existence of numerical student models equivalent to nominal ones allows to compare the presented approach with that based on a minimum distance to the cluster centroid. As grouping has been done by application of clustering technique taking into account attributes of numeric types, centroids of each cluster can be easily determined. Then, distances of the considered student attribute values and group centroids are computed. Finally, the group of the smallest distance is recommended.

As the group recommendation is connected with learning materials assignments, we require that student characteristics are consistent with the dominant features of the recommended group. To check if that reqiurement is fulfilled, numerical values of student attributes are changed to nominal ones. In the case of learning styles model they are replaced according to (10)-(13). Then an error, measured by the number of the student nominal attributes which are different from the recommended group representatives, is determined.

To compare the performance of Naïve Bayes classifier and centroid minimum distance approach (CMD), the effects for both of the techniques were analysed. As the performance of the considered classifier in the cases of both of the 3 valued models were better than that of the 5 valued model, the last one will be used for the comparison purpose. Table 5 presents results for both of the data sets and all the considered clustering algorithms. In the first column, percentage of students for whom CMD recommendation was better is shown, next column, in turn, presents percentage of students for whom Bayes classifier occurred to be better. Following 2 columns contain data for which recommendations were equivalent: the same (3rd column) or of the same error (4th column). In the last column percentage of students, who obtained CMD recommendations different than those of their peers of the same characteristics is shown.

It is easy to notice that performance of both of the methods is similar, however Bayes classifier gave better recommendations for more students than CMD approach, especially when they were clustered by EM method. Unlike the Bayes algorithm, CMD indicated groups not containing students of features consistent with those of the considered learner. Finally, in many cases CMD gave different recommendations to students of the same characteristics. The problem occured to be significant in the case of groups built by FFT algorithm.

Table 5. Comparison between centroid minimum distance approach and Bayes classifier

Set	Schema	CMD	Bayes	Equal.	Same err.	Diff. ass.
A	EM	6.45%	12.9%	67.74%	12.9%	6.45%
	K-means	3.23%	12.9%	70.97%	12.9%	0%
	FFT	6.45%	6.45%	77.42%	9.68%	19.35%
B	EM	3.57%	32.14%	64.29%	0%	1.79%
	K-means	0%	5.36%	75%	19.64%	1.79%
	FFT	1.79%	8.93%	80.36%	8.93%	3.57%

6   Concluding Remarks

The paper discussed building group recommendations for students, whose preferences are characterized by nominal attributes. The proposed agent-based recommended system uses group representations in the probabilistic form and Naïve Bayes classifier as the main recommendation tool. The technique was examined in the case of students described by dominant learning styles and usability preferences. Experiments done for datasets of real students and different group structures showed that in almost all the cases the system indicated the best possible choice of colleagues to learn with. The influence of the likelihood close or equal to 0 on Naïve Bayes classifiers occurred to be an advantage in many cases. Tests carried out for the simulation data showed big classification errors, in the case of students whose characteristics differed from those of their colleagues. Then, the recommendation agent may advise the students to contact their tutor.

The presented method was compared with the centroid minimum distance approach. Experiments showed that even for the worstly performed model, in most of the cases effects of the Naïve Bayes algorithm were better than those of the CMD. What is more, the last one recommended different groups to students of the same traits.

The proposed method of recommendation building can be used by educators during the process of course creating, suggesting learning resources or while building joint activities for student groups of similar features.

Future research will consist in further investigations of the recommendation tools, including different computational intelligence methods, examination of other attributes, broadening the range of learning resources and taking into account activity recommendations, as well as making the group creating process more dynamic, by including new learners each time the recommendation is accepted.

References

1. Liegle, J.O., Janicki, T.N.: The effect of learning styles on the navigation needs of Web-based learners. Computers in Human Behavior 22, 885–898 (2006)
2. Shneiderman, B.: Designing the User Interface. Addison-Wesley, Reading (1997)
3. Gonzalez-Rodriguez, M., Manrubia, J., Vidau, A., Gonzalez-Gallego, M.: Improving accessibility with user-tailored interfaces. Appl. Intell. 30, 65–71 (2009)
4. Zhang, H.: The optimality of Naïve Bayes. In: Proc. of the 17th FLAIRS Conf., Florida (2004)
5. Zakrzewska, D.: Building Group Recommendations in E-Learning Systems. In: Jędrzejowicz, P., Nguyen, N.T., Howlett, R.J., Jain, L.C. (eds.) KES-AMSTA 2010. LNCS (LNAI), vol. 6070, pp. 391–400. Springer, Heidelberg (2010)
6. Romero, C., Ventura, S., Delgado, J.A., De Bra, P.: Personalized Links Recommendation Based on Data Mining in Adaptive Educational Hypermedia Systems. In: Duval, E., Klamma, R., Wolpers, M. (eds.) EC-TEL 2007. LNCS, vol. 4753, pp. 292–306. Springer, Heidelberg (2007)
7. Zaïane, O.R.: Web usage mining for a better web-based learning environment. In: Proc. of Conf. on Advanced Technology for Education, Banff, AB, pp. 60–64 (2001)

8. Santally, M.I., Alain, S.: Personalisation in web-based learning environments. International Journal of Distance Education Technologies 4, 15–35 (2006)
9. Stash, N., Cristea, A., De Bra, P.: Authoring of learning styles in adaptive hypermedia: Problems and solutions. In: Proc. WWW Conf., N.Y., pp. 114–123 (2004)
10. Xu, D., Wang, H., Su, K.: Intelligent student profiling with fuzzy models. In: Proc. of HICSS 2002, Hawaii (2002)
11. Tang, T., McCalla, G.: Smart recommendation for an evolving e-learning system. International Journal on E-Learning 4, 105–129 (2005)
12. Talavera, L., Gaudioso, E.: Mining student data to characterize similar behavior groups in unstructured collaboration spaces. In: Workshop on Artificial Intelligence in CSCL. 16th European Conference on Artificial Intelligence, pp. 17–23 (2004)
13. Zakrzewska, D.: Cluster Analysis in Personalized E-Learning Systems. In: Nguyen, N.T., Szczerbicki, E. (eds.) Intelligent Systems for Knowledge Management. SCI, vol. 252, pp. 229–250. Springer, Heidelberg (2009)
14. Zakrzewska, D., Wojciechowski, A.: Identifying students usability needs in collaborative learning environments. In: Proc. of 2008 Conference on Human System Interaction, Krakow, pp. 862–867 (2008)
15. Yang, F., Han, P., Shen, R.-M., Hu, Z.: A Novel Resource Recommendation System Based on Connecting to Similar E-Learners. In: Lau, R., Li, Q., Cheung, R., Liu, W. (eds.) ICWL 2005. LNCS, vol. 3583, pp. 122–130. Springer, Heidelberg (2005)
16. Shen, R., Han, P., Yang, F., Yang, Q., Huang, J.: Data mining and case-based reasoning for distance learning. Journal of Distance Education Technologies 1, 46–58 (2003)
17. Hämäläinen, W., Vinni, M.: Comparison of Machine Learning Methods for Intelligent Tutoring Systems. In: Ikeda, M., Ashley, K.D., Chan, T.-W. (eds.) ITS 2006. LNCS, vol. 4053, pp. 525–534. Springer, Heidelberg (2006)
18. Zaïane, O.R.: Building a recommender agent for e-learning systems. In: Proc. of the 7th Int. Conf. on Computers in Education, Auckland, New Zeland, pp. 55–59 (2002)
19. García, E., Romero, C., Ventura, S., de Castro, C.: An architecture for making recommendations to courseware authors using association rule mining and collaborative filtering. Use Model. User-Adap. 19, 99–132 (2009)
20. Romero, C., Ventura, S.: Educational data mining: a survey from 1995 to 2005. Expert Syst. Appl. 33, 135–146 (2007)
21. Andronico, A., Carbonaro, A., Casadei, G., Colazzo, L., Molinari, A., Ronchetti, M.: Integrating a multi-agent recommendation system into a Mobile Learning Management System. In: Proc. of Artificial Intelligence in Mobile System 2003 (AIMS 2003), Seattle, USA, October 12 (2003)
22. Rosaci, D., Sarné, G.: Efficient personalization of e-learning activities using a mult-device decentralized recommender system. Comput. Intell. 26, 121–141 (2010)
23. Alexakos, C., Giotopoulos, K., Thermogianni, E., Beligiannis, G., Likothanassis, S.: Integrating e-learning environments with computational intelligence assessment agents. International Journal of Human and Social Sciences 1, 180–185 (2007)
24. Baker, R.S., Corbett, A.T., Koedinger, K.R.: Detecting Student Misuse of Intelligent Tutoring Systems. In: Lester, J.C., Vicari, R.M., Paraguaçu, F. (eds.) ITS 2004. LNCS, vol. 3220, pp. 531–540. Springer, Heidelberg (2004)
25. Arroyo, I., Woolf, B.P.: Inferring learning and attitudes from a Bayesian Network of log file data. In: Proc. of the 12th Int. Conf. on Artificial Intelligence in Education, pp. 33–40 (2005)
26. García, P., Amandi, A., Schiaffino, S., Campo, M.: Evaluating Bayesian networks' precision for detecting students' learning styles. Comput. Educ. 49, 794–808 (2007)

27. Hämäläinen, W., Suhonen, J., Sutinen, E., Toivonen, H.: Data mining in personalizing distance education courses. In: World Conference on Open Learning and Distance Education, pp. 1–11 (2004)
28. Beck, J.E., Park Woolf, B.: High-Level Student Modeling with Machine Learning. In: Gauthier, G., VanLehn, K., Frasson, C. (eds.) ITS 2000. LNCS, vol. 1839, pp. 584–593. Springer, Heidelberg (2000)
29. Zakrzewska, D.: Student Groups Modeling by Integrating Cluster Representation and Association Rules Mining. In: van Leeuwen, J., Muscholl, A., Peleg, D., Pokorný, J., Rumpe, B. (eds.) SOFSEM 2010. LNCS, vol. 5901, pp. 743–754. Springer, Heidelberg (2010)
30. Lowd, D., Domingos, P.: Naive Bayes models for probability estimation. In: Proceedings of 22nd International Conference on Machine Learning, Bonn, Germany (2005)
31. Murphy, K.P.: Naive Bayes classifiers,
    `http://www.cs.ubc.ca/~murphyk/Teaching/CS340-Fall06/reading/NB.pdf`
32. Kotsiantis, S.B.: Supervised machine learning: a review of classification. Informatica 31, 249–268 (2007)
33. Brusilovsky, P.: Adaptive hypermedia. Use Model. User-Adap. 11, 87–110 (2001)
34. Felder, R.M., Silverman, L.K.: Learning and teaching styles in engineering education. Eng. Educ. 78, 674–681 (1988)
35. Kuljis, J., Liu, F.: A comparison of learning style theories on the suitability for elearning. In: Proc. of IASTED Conference on Web Technologies, Applications, and Services, pp. 191–197. ACTA Press (2005)
36. ILS Questionnaire, `http://www.engr.ncsu.edu/learningstyles/ilsweb.html`
37. De Marsico, M., Levialdi, S.: Evaluating web sites: exploiting user's expectations. Intern. Journal of Human-Computer Studies 60, 381–416 (2004)
38. Han, J., Kamber, M.: Data Mining. Concepts and Techniques, 2nd edn. Morgan Kaufmann Publishers, San Francisco (2006)
39. Hochbaum, S.D., Shmoys, B.D.: A best possible heuristic for the k-center problem. Math. Oper. Res. 10, 180–184 (1985)
40. Dasgupta, S.: Performance Guarantees for Hierarchical Clustering. In: Kivinen, J., Sloan, R.H. (eds.) COLT 2002. LNCS (LNAI), vol. 2375, pp. 351–363. Springer, Heidelberg (2002)
41. Zakrzewska, D.: Validation of clustering techniques for student grouping in intelligent e-learning systems. In: Jozefczyk, J., Orski, D. (eds.) Knowledge-Based Intelligent System Advancements: Systemic and Cybernetic Approaches, pp. 232–251. IGI Global (2011)

Individual Semiosis in Multi-Agent Systems

Wojciech Lorkiewicz[1,2], Radoslaw Katarzyniak[1], and Ryszard Kowalczyk[2]

[1] Wroclaw University of Technology
Institute of Informatics
{wojciech.lorkiewicz,radoslaw.katarzyniak}@pwr.wroc.pl
[2] Swinburne University of Technology
Faculty of Information and Communication Technologies
{wlorkiewicz,rkowalczyk}@groupwise.swin.edu.au

Abstract. Underlying the importance of communication in highly distributed and autonomous systems, i.e., multi-agent systems, such communication should be autonomously managed by the system itself. As such, it should be managed on the individual level of each individual agent, and still result in a general consistent framework of communication. Such an approach, opposite to the centralised and controlled stance, poses additional problems and introduces new challenges for the system design. It is therefore crucial to design and develop agents that could cope with this new tasks and be able to emerge, align and maintain a common framework of communication. This research intends to fill the current gap and investigate the dynamics of the model of individual semiosis, i.e., narrowing the interaction pattern of Language Game Model to a case of a single teaching agent. In particular, the presented research studies both, analytically and using a simulated framework, the dynamics of the alignment process itself, depending on the internal behaviour of the agent, and the dynamics of the observed phase transition in the alignment process in case of deviations from common context settings.

1 Introduction

Language is an extensively used everyday tool. It allows individuals to gain, share and utilise information in a social setting. It is also a key capability of any autonomous agent that facilitates the exchange of knowledge and enables collaboration in a multi-agent environment. As such, the language constitutes the collective adaptation to the changing circumstances of the environment and advances the performance of certain social tasks.

Developing an arbitrary language in a highly distributed and dynamic population of autonomous agents is not a trivial task [9]. First of all, due to physical limitations the simplistic approach of central coordination is not possible. For instance, the global broadcast mechanism significantly increases the energy consumption and is not always available lowering its reliability. Further, due to the dynamic character and natural openness of the environment the communication mechanism cannot be completely known beforehand and as such imprinting the language at the design time is not possible. Moreover, the heterogeneity and

N.T. Nguyen (Ed.): Transactions on CCI VII, LNCS 7270, pp. 164–197, 2012.

autonomy of the individual agents implies that decisions are highly distributed as the internal structure of grounded symbols is shaped autonomously by the individual.

The superior goal of the resolution of language symbols meaning in a MAS, i.e. autonomous emergence and alignment of meaning, is the resultant formulation of consistent and common substance of symbols, i.e. conventionalised symbols. In short, in order to communicate successfully the agents must utilise a shared language, i.e. shared naming conventions. As it is only this shared convention that gives rise to coherent communication system.

Up to now several approaches of the horizontal transmission of language have been proposed in the literature. However due to its broad scope and complexity, the research is still far from exhaustion and numerous challenges are still in the scope of researchers[22]. Nevertheless, the most relevant research in this area was performed by Steels et al. introducing the Language Game Model (LGM) and formulating basic settings for the interaction between agents.

Vast amount of ongoing research focuses only on a limited set of models of the LGM and investigates the 'classical' scenarios, assuming significant feedback capabilities of the system and limiting the context sizes. Nevertheless, despite being neglected several more rational scenarios are still important and pose a crucial research question. In terms of real application (e.g. robotics, smart sensor networks) and common-sense (e.g. without telepathy) the incorporated models should assume a lack or a very limited feedback - as in the real world all of these properties are very hard to achieve and are currently manually enforced in all embodied experimental settings.

In the presented paper we try to fill this gap and study the dynamics of the semiosis process that utilises the fine-grained model of language acquisition in multi-agent setting. Limiting the original interaction pattern proposed in [20] to a single fixed speaker, i.e. teacher agent, and multiple hearers, i.e. learners, we model the settings of language acquisition, i.e. individual semiosis [9]. In particular, it is significant to analyse how different learning models (See Sec.4.4), different settings, i.e. population size, context size (See Sec.4), and different deviation intensities influence the process of individual semiosis.

From the pragmatic perspective such an approach focuses on an important design issue. In particular, in conditions of high autonomy and diversity of the individual units of the system, communication is the main basis for all manner of social activities, information exchange and collective actions. In addition, the dynamic nature of the outside world, i.e., changing conditions of the system, and the effects of interaction between individuals significantly modulate the used communication system. In such a setting *the developed framework enables an effective and rapid evaluation* when it is put to the task of selecting an appropriate method for establishing the joint (between the agents involved in the interaction) context. For instance, in a situation of a choice between multiple methods, with known costs of implementation and known quality (in setting the common context) for the selected type of environment, *the designer can make a qualitative assessment*. In particular, *make appropriate design decisions to ensure optimal cost while meeting all of the fundamental requirements of the correct execution of the process of semiosis in an artificial system. Consequently, a pragmatic outcome of the research is the development of basic criteria for the proper design of multi-agent system that ensures the intended dynamics of the process of semiosis.*

We focus solely on the individual semiosis case and model it using the Language Game Model (See Sec.3.1) of interaction and develop several aligning mechanisms (See Sec.4.4) based on the Cross-Situational Learning Model. We study how a population of distributed agents can acquire a lexicon from a distinguished source of naming conventions. In particular, we address a sub-problem of the problem of language alignment in a population of multiple, distributed and autonomous individuals (See Sec.2). We propose an original model (See Sec.4) to describe the internal organisation of an agent, teacher agent and the entire population (See Sec.4.1,4.2), interplay between individuals (See Sec.4.3), alignment strategies (See Sec.4.4), and describe the performance of the system (See Sec.4.5). Using developed simulation framework we show the dynamic behaviour of the model in both, the idealised case of no deviation (See Sec.5) and a more realistic settings of erroneous communications (See Sec.6). Finally, we present a brief analysis of the obtained results and short summary in section 8.

2   Semiosis in Multi-Agent Systems

The fundamental layer of language requires manipulation of grounded symbols [5]. In essence allowing to relate experienced sensory patterns to arbitrary established system of signs – language [13]. As opposed to classical definitions of categories, that follow the Aristotles existence of a mind-independent reality and absolute truths, we follow the cognitive linguistics approach to communication and adopt the phenomenological stance. As such, all individuals maintain a conscious and intentional relationship to the external world through their bodily experiences. In short, an observation is an individual perception that is introduced into the agent body and represented as embodied structures. Namely, it is assumed that the cognitive agent can store internally reflections of perceptually available objects $\mathcal{O}$. It means that each aspect of the external world is recognisable by the agent and can become a part of its empirically originated knowledge.

The internal organisation of the agent is strictly private and individual, consequently the embodied structures are not shared among the interacting agents and cannot be directly communicated. As such, for an agent to share its current viewpoint, it is necessary to utilise a language that is established within the population. Moreover, as the language and meaning goes beyond the individual, all the internal linguistic structures are influenced by the collective stance of the population, for instance due to multiple interactions. In particular, registering a given language symbol triggers a consistent, with the knowledge stance of the speaker, reaction within the hearer. Additionally, following the view of Lakoff and Johnson '(...) human language and thought are structured by, and bound to,

an embodied experience (...)' [8], agent's internal system of accessible concepts is
strictly related to the structure of the external world, i.e., the language symbol
is grounded in the embodied experience. Consequently, the agents must not only
be able to develop their individual linguistic structures but also align them to
the shape developed within the entire population. As such a group of individuals
engaged in communication activity can be considered as a 'dynamic distributed
cognitive system' [19], where different participants actively align their linguistic systems in order to collaborate, i.e. perform a certain distributed, social or
cognitive task.

In order to answer the general question, how a population of agents autonomously learn, adapt and optimise their semantics, it is crucial to identify
the needed components of autonomous emergence of language in an individual
artificial agent. This process can be decomposed into three tasks [5]: sensing,
pre-processing of the sensorimotor data, meaning construction, categorising collected data, and labelling, assigning an arbitrary representation of meaning. As
such the agent grounds, the process that interprets signs as referring to their real
world objects, the symbols. As the language should be elaborated beyond the
individual several additional problems arise. At first the collective language is
shaped by individuals, i.e. the meaning of a symbol in a given population results
from a certain convention and is a result of a common agreement, and at second
individual system is shaped by collective, i.e. a sign cannot function until the
audience distinguishes it.

The process of semiosis, i.e. a process where the entire population of autonomous agents establishes a common language[1] from scratch, is crucial in the
proper development of communication means for a highly distributed systems.

2.1 Models of Semiosis

As proposed in [9], developing a complete mechanisms of symbol meaning resolution in a multi agent system requires to deal with three basic problems, i.e.
individual language emergence, where a single agent or group of agents is resolving the meaning from the general population semantics, population language
emergence, where each single agent is forming the general population semantics,
and cross-population language emergence, where two or more populations align
their semantics.

Individual Semiosis. An individual agent is shaping and aligning its language
with a distinguished external source of meaning (Fig. 1). A group of learning
agents is interacting with a population of linguistically mature agents, i.e., agents
with predefined meaning of language symbols and assumed static language. The
sole purpose of such interplay is to learn how to correctly interpret the language
symbols utilised by the teachers by the means of agent's individual perceptions.
Used symbols, imposed by the mature population, can be correlated by the

---

[1] For the sake of simplicity we further assume that the term language relates to a
naming convention represented by a certain lexicon.

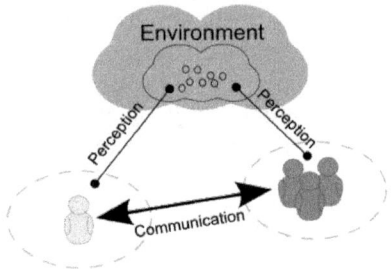

Fig. 1. Individual case of semiosis

learning agent with empirically perceived external states of the environment that are the populations source of grounded meaning. As such through numerous interactions the learning agent is capable of identifying the correct sources of meaning for each encountered language symbol.

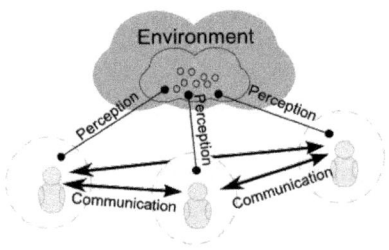

Fig. 2. Population case of semiosis

Population Semiosis. More generally the problem of shaping the meaning of language symbols can be deliberated without the distinguishing a predefined population agents (Fig. 2). The process of language emergence is then distributed among individual agents, each autonomously developing its own personal semantics and adapting it to the current state of the population. As such each agent is grounding the meaning of symbols, relating their representation with a referent from the external world, and aligns it, setting certain boundaries over the grounding mechanism, with the entire population. The former allows agent to autonomously perceive a dynamic environment, whilst the latter allows the population to reach a common agreement on the essence of used language symbols.

Cross-Population Semiosis. The third case of semiosis involves two or more mature populations, each having differently established semantics, predefined or differently developed as of the process of population semiosis. These populations are set together in a common environment where they interact with each

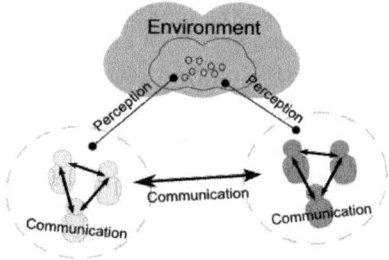

Fig. 3. Cross-Population case of semiosis

other. Treated as a whole the collated populations may have various meanings assigned to the same language symbols, and in order to communicate their semantics should be aligned, or may have different language symbols, as such both dictionaries should be related to each other. The straight forward incorporation of population semiosis mechanism might be inadequate, as it is necessary for the populations to sustain a high level of efficiency in communicating within original populations. The aligned languages share the same environment, common to all populations, that serves as a common background of reference and allows developing proper correlation between languages, as the existence and state of the external world is objective rather than subjective.

2.2   Individual Semiosis

The individual semiosis is the fundamental cases of the more general problem of language alignment in multi-agent systems. Additionally, being the narrowest situation of semiosis, it focuses solely on a single learning individual, i.e., independently of the state of other agents from the learning population. In particular, the alignment task is centred on each individual separately and depends only on the state of the single individual and the teacher (or teachers). This intuitive fact is significant, as it allows to further idealise the entire process, by neglecting the internal interactions within the learning population, and to focus solely on the communication between learners and teacher (or teachers).

From a general perspective this process can be viewed as a task of language acquisition, where a group of learning agents is aligning its linguistic structures with the mature population. As such, the main goal of the process is to reach both, a maximum possible coherence between the learning and the mature population, and to maximize the effectiveness of the communication. In such a setting each learning agent is faced with the task of aligning its individual linguistic system with the already utilised and established language. Following a basic simplification that word learning is, in principle, a rather simple task of mapping linguistic labels (words) onto a set of pre-established concepts (objects)[2], the agent needs to successfully resolve the meaning of utilised language symbols encountered during its interaction with other agents from the mature population. In other words, the learning agent (or more general learning population) needs to align its individual naming convention with the naming convention incorporated by the established mature population.

It is assumed that an agent is equipped with a given set of sensors that allow it to register certain signals from the environment - as such enabling the agent to autonomously perceive its surroundings. Additionally, each agent is capable of producing, i.e., uttering, and registering, i.e., hearing, distinguished linguistic signs - words. Moreover, due to the multi-modal nature of the agent and through the co-occurrence of sensor activation and linguistic sign occurrence each agent can correlate the utilised symbol with an external state of the environment [5]. Resultantly, through such numerous episodes individuals are able to fine-grain the relation between words and objects [19]. Further, based on this distributed mechanism of alignment the entire population is able to identify the consistent source of meaning for each of the language symbols and spread its successful usage.

3   Individual Semiosis and the Naming Game

Up to now several approaches of the horizontal transmission of language have been proposed in the literature. However due to its broad scope and complexity, the research is still far from exhaustion and numerous challenges are still in the scope of researchers [22]. Most recognized work in this area involves the interaction pattern defined by the Language Game Model and the alignment procedure defined by the Cross-situational learning. Both complimentary to each other and naturally intertwined propose a general and consistent language framework. This paper builds on the introductory research performed in this area [11], where the preliminary results were presented, and provides a significant extension and major revision of the individual semiosis game (See Sec.3.3).

3.1   Naming Game

The most promising approach addressing the problem of developing a shared lexicon in a population of agents is the language game model [19,20]. Steels et all introduced an intuitive and common-sense interaction pattern, i.e. a routinised game played by the agents, that represents a routinised way of interplay between the agents. Following the Wittgenstein's idea of Language as a Game,

Through a simple interaction and a simple learning mechanism, the agents develop a shared set of labels that reference, through the so-called meaning relation, to the states of environment - object from a given set of objects. The basic language game involves two agents - one speaker and one hearer - and a shared context of objects. Both agents perceive the context and the speaker selects one object as the topic and tries to produce an utterance based on its lexicon. The lexicon is typically an associative memory between meaning representations and forms, where each association has a score that indicates the effectiveness of the association based on past interactions. These lexicons, like the ontologies, are private and thus can differ from one agent to another. The speaker searches its lexicon for an association that corresponds to the meaning of the topic and that has the highest score. If such an association is found, the corresponding form is uttered. When hearing a form, the hearer searches, for this form, the association that has the highest score for those meanings that are in the context or that relate to the topic, if this is known. Typically, the success of the game is evaluated and if the game succeeds, the used association are reinforced - reinforcement, while competing associations are laterally inhibited - inhibition. If the game fails, the scores of the used associations are decreased. These adaptations ensure that successfully used elements tend to be reused again and again, while unsuccessful ones tend to get weaker.

The Naming Game (NG), assumed that both, speaker and hearer, perceive the same object in the environment, as the speaker uttering name of object was simultaneously pointing at it. The problem of referential uncertainty does not appear in the NG, as the speaker gives a direct feedback to the hearer by pointing the intended object. The hearer can then immediately distinguish the topic of the utterance, as the meaning. In such setting the experiments have proved that cross situational learning (CSL) [15,16] may become a viable learning strategy.

3.2   Cross-Situational Learning

Cross-Situational learning (CSL) is a simple mechanism for learning the meaning of words despite the implicit referential uncertainty (See [23]) that the learner is faced with. In particular, by combining the linguistic information across multiple exposures the learner is able to extract the true meaning of utilised words. As such, the CSL strategy perfectly fits in the routine described by the LGM.

CSL is based on the idea that robots can learn the meaning of a word solely based on co-variances that occur across different situations. In the early stage Smith et all [16] managed to prove that assuming words and meanings as atomic parts, uniform distribution of meanings, independent learning of words, the population convergence to a shared lexicon using CSL mechanism. Moreover they showed that when the size of context is relatively small in comparison to the size of lexicon the time needed to learn the vocabulary is $Mlog(M)$, where M is the number of words in the lexicon.

Unfortunately, basic CSL approach did not work in the early embodied experiments, basically due to the minimal environment few variations could be detected across different situations. The basic model of cross situational learning incorporates the elimination algorithm, that is approach to eliminate all inconsistent meanings across examples in hope that only a single one will prevail [16]. The elimination procedure is appropriate in the case of existing and stable language, however in case of bootstrapping a language the elimination procedure tends to lead to empty sets, as their is no consistency of meaning in the early stages of emergence. To overcome this limitation several modifications were proposed - enumeration approach, where the number of occurrence of each word are monitored, and adaptation, where additionally the relative frequencies of co-occurrence are monitored. The former, adaptation mechanism, outperforms the enumeration and elimination approaches, as it guarantees a convergence and reduced convergence time.

Additionally, there is an ample proof that humans can and do utilise the cross-situational learning to learn a lexicon [2,17,18,26,27]. The early experimental work by Yu and Smith (See [26,17]) provides empirical evidence of successful cross-episode learning in ambiguous situations in both humans and children. The authors exposed adults to a series of multiple ambiguous trials, each containing 4 unknown words and 4 possible referents for the words - episodes. They managed to show that utilising the statistical information across multiple exposures participants were able to learn more than half of the mappings in less than 6 minutes. Thus, humans can use CSL 'to learn word-object mappings by storing, computing, and continuously reducing a set of possible referents over time'. In the most recent research by Smith et al. [18], the authors show that humans do use cross-situational learning strategies in experimental conditions, moreover they tend to use various CSL strategies and switch between them according to the difficulty (level of referential uncertainty) of the task they are given. Interestingly, Yurovsky et al. [27] shows that participants utilising the CSL strategy can even break the constraint to learn one-to-two word-referent mappings - demonstrating the high robustness of learning.

3.3   Individual Semiosis Game

Due to the nature of individual semiosis agents' capabilities can be limited according to a particular type of the individual. In essence, as the sole purpose of the learner is only to learn the language utilised by the teacher its behaviour can be limited to basic registering functionalities, i.e., hearing and adapting. Moreover, there is no internal communication between the learners that would require such an agent to produce utterances. On the other hand, as the sole purpose of the teacher is to provide the learner with linguistic cues about the utilised naming convention its behaviour can be limited to basic production functionalities, i.e., uttering. Certainly, the learner is not involve in any adaptation and as such is not required to perceive external utterances. In short, we can limit the agents to an uttering teacher, and a registering and adapting learner agents (See Fig.4).

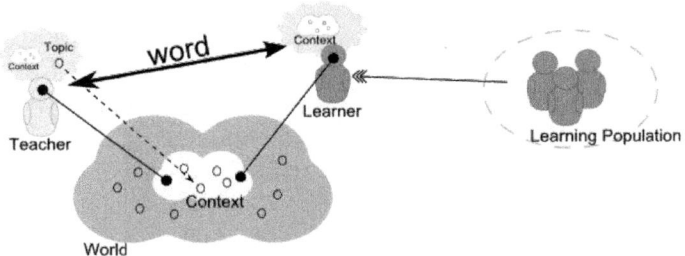

Fig. 4. Single episode in the individual semiosis game

3.4   Common Context Setting

Maintaining a common context between the interacting agents, in particular a joint attention scene, is a notoriously hard problem in embodied systems. Following Kaplan [7], we can state that 'joint attention is probably one of the hardest problems to be solved by developmental robotics research'. The development of joint attention between two robots relates strictly to a successive triggering and managing of multiple underlying parallel processes, i.e. attention detection, attention manipulation, social coordination, and intentional stance (See [7]).

The strict assumptions of NG require that both of the agents are able to share their perceptions of the environment and simultaneously focus on a particular part of the external world (See Fig.4). In essence, the set of registered objects must be identical in both agents. However, in practice this restrictive requirement can be loosened to a simpler form of joint topic scene, where the hearer shares only the topic with the speaker, whilst the co-occurring objects are uniformly sampled. Nevertheless, even with the simplified restriction it is technically challenging to establish and maintain such a situation in an embodied settings. Every joint scene requires a form of sharing some additional (besides the communication itself) coordination information between the interacting agents. Due to aforementioned problems current physical realisation, most commonly, assume a manually enforced common context settings introduced by the designers/experimenters. In particular, before each episode the interacting agents are coordinated by hand, e.g. camera views and sensors are physically aligned, and are set together in a joint attention scene.

However the manual enforcement of the setting is questionable for a proper operation of an autonomous embodied system. As such, there are several approaches to the problem of establishing and maintaining a joint attention scene. In particular, this line of research focuses on developing and implementing a procedure that would allow a distributed system to form a shared scene, i.e. only guaranteeing some threshold in deviation from the ideal joint attention scene. For example [4,6,14] propose several mechanisms of establishing a somewhat common context between multiple agents. However, as aforementioned, all of the state of the art solutions do not guarantee the level of coherence required by the NG - ideal synchronisation of the perception of interacting agents. Consequently, it is vital to study the behaviour of the individual semiosis game in settings that explicitly allows some extent of deviations from this highly constraining restriction.

Any deviation from the shared context settings may have twofold interpretation (See Fig.5). At first, an interaction with non-overlapping contexts represents a case where the communication involves an interplay between speaker and a hearer without joint attention, i.e. due to the imprecision of the mechanism of establishing joint attention. Secondly. such an interaction may result strictly from an erroneous behaviour of the speaker. For instance, when both agents share the current context, however, due to an error the speaker intends

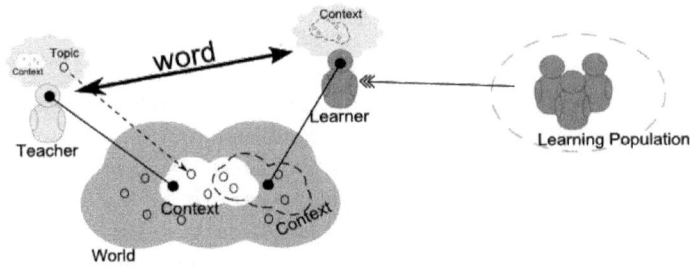

Fig. 5. Single episode in the individual semiosis game (without common context)

to communicate about part of the environment being outside of the current scope. However, despite of the origin it is crucial to investigate the behaviour of the system in case of common deviations from the idealistic restrictions on common context in the NG.

4   Model

We extend the original LGM model to a case of individual semiosis (See Fig.4). Additionally, we introduce the possibility of deviations from the basic assumption of shared context (See Fig.5).

We begin by introducing the notion of a system state, i.e., the state of the entire multi-agent system, as a 4-tuple S_t, as follows:

Definition 1. *For each* $t \in \mathcal{T} = \{t_1, \ldots, t_{NT}\}$ *a system state* S_t *in time point* t *is a tuple:*

$$S_t = \langle \mathcal{O}, \mathcal{P}_L, \mathcal{P}_{TH}, \mathcal{X}_t^O, \mathcal{X}_t^P, p_\epsilon \rangle, \qquad (1)$$

where[2]

- *set of identifiable objects* $\mathcal{O} = \{o_1, \ldots, o_{NO}\}$,
- *population of agents* $\mathcal{P}_L = \{a_1, \ldots, a_{NPL}\}$,
- *population of teacher agents* $\mathcal{P}_{TH} = \{A_1, \ldots, A_{NPT}\}$,
- *interaction* $\mathcal{X}_t^P \in \mathcal{P}_L \times \mathcal{P}_{TH}$,
- *context* $\mathcal{X}_t^O \in 2^{\mathcal{O}}$,
- *deviation intensity* $p_\epsilon \in [0, 1]$.

The system state resembles a general state of the entire multi-agent system in a given point of time. First, it depicts the identifiable objects $\mathcal{O}$, where each object o_i represents a self contained invariant in the external environment that

---

[2] By NT, NO, NPL and NPT we further denote the cardinality of a particular set of time points $\mathcal{T}$, set of objects $\mathcal{O}$, set of learning agents $\mathcal{P}_L$ and set of teaching agents $\mathcal{P}_{TH}$, respectively.

is available to agent's perception, i.e., is distinguished by agents' perception system. It is assumed that each agent is capable of analysing its low level stimulus by the means of object perception [12], i.e., a fixed and static set of objects. Second, it depicts the population of agents, both, all of the learning agents $\mathcal{P}_L$ and all of the teaching agents $\mathcal{P}_{TH}$. Each single agent is the most fine-grained autonomous entity present in the system. It is embodied in the environment and is a part of the interacting population. Depending on the role played in the interaction, two types of agents can be identified, learner agent(See Sec.4.2) and teacher agent(See Sec.4.1). In short, the main and sole purpose of the agent is to either learn (former) the utilised naming convention or to teach (latter) the utilised naming convention, i.e., the so-called mature language. In order to do so each agent needs to be equipped with an appropriate, dependant on its role, semantic infrastructure allowing it to properly utilise the language (See Sec.4.1 and Sec.4.2).

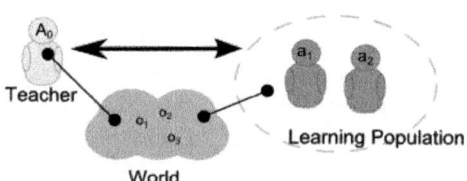

Fig. 6. Example of a system

Example 1. Let us assume a system of multiple agents – embedded in a spacious terrain consisting of objects $\hat{\mathcal{O}}$ – randomly allocated in the environment. Such agents ($\hat{\mathcal{P}}_{TH} \cup \hat{\mathcal{P}}_L$) can autonomously manoeuvre around, observe their surroundings, and from time to time interact with each other (sporadically due to spacious character of the terrain and individual movement). In particular, let us assume a system $\hat{S}$ (See Fig.6) consisting of:

- a single teacher agent $\hat{\mathcal{P}}_{TH} = \{A_0\}$,
- 2 learning agents $\hat{\mathcal{P}}_L = \{a_1, a_2\}$,
- and 3 distinguishable objects $\hat{\mathcal{O}} = \{o_1, o_2, o_3\}$.

Moreover, the system state defines two fundamental processes – model of the dynamics of the environment $\mathcal{X}_t^O$ (available through a context to each individual agent) and model of the interaction between the agents $\mathcal{X}_t^P$ (available through an interaction defined between the agents).

In particular, *interaction* for every time point t determines the currently interacting agents $(a, A) = \mathcal{X}_t^P$ (See Fig.7). In a more general settings, multiple agents can be involved in the interaction, i.e., n_l learning agents interacting with a teacher agent, we restrict the interaction process to a two agent only structure. However, as these interactions can still be decomposed to a form of multiple pair-wise games, i.e., in the aforementioned example n_l individual interactions, and for the sake of simplicity, we further assume a pair-wise only interaction limited to a single learner ($a \in \mathcal{P}_L$) and a single teacher ($A \in \mathcal{P}_{TH}$) pattern, i.e., $\forall_{t \in \mathcal{T}}\ \mathcal{X}_t^P = (a, A)$.

Further, at each discrete time point t the interacting agents are situated in a given *context* of their interaction $\mathcal{X}_t^O \subset \mathcal{O}$ – as a set of objects currently in agent's sight (See Fig.7). In particular, $\mathcal{X}_t^O$ models the current, available to interacting agents, state of the environment, i.e., each interacting agent engages in a joint attention scene and perceives the same part of the environment – current context $\mathcal{X}_t^O$. For the sake of simplicity, we further assume a fixed context size ($\forall_{t \in \mathcal{T}}\ \|\mathcal{X}_t^O\| = c$, where $c \in \mathbb{N}$) and equal probability of appearance in the context ($\forall_{o_i, o_j \in \mathcal{O}} Pr(o_i \in \mathcal{X}_t^O) = Pr(o_j \in \mathcal{X}_t^O)$).

In short, the system (state S_t) undergoes dynamic changes due to its embodiment in the external world and the internal interaction within the population. In particular, a learning agent $a \in \mathcal{P}_L$ sporadically meets and interacts with a teacher agent $A \in \mathcal{P}_{TH}$. For instance, the activity of the learning agent is in the close proximity of the teacher agent, that eventually allows the teacher to detected the learning agent and trigger the language game. If we take time into consideration, the Poisson process can model the time intervals between consecutive interactions. However, without loss of generality we can abstract from the exact values and focus solely on the content of events – learning episodes. Each such episode can be described as a random interaction and can be realised as a random variable with an uniform distribution over $\mathcal{P}_L$ (as the teacher A is fixed).

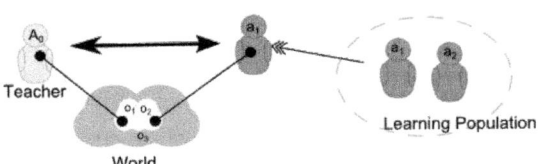

Fig. 7. Example of an idealised interaction at $t = 1$

Example 2. Following the example 1, let us assume that:

- at first episode the teacher interacts with a_1 $\hat{\mathcal{X}}_t^P = (a_1, A_0)$,
- at second with a_2 $\hat{\mathcal{X}}_t^P = (a_2, A_0)$,
- and at third with a_2 $\hat{\mathcal{X}}_t^P = (a_2, A_0)$.

Assuming the idealised settings (with a perfect mechanism for establishing common context) at each interaction the involved agents, both register the same set of objects $\hat{\mathcal{X}}_t^O \subset \hat{O}$ (See Fig.7). For example:

- at $t = 1$ $\hat{\mathcal{X}}_1^O = \{o_1, o_2\}$,
- at $t = 2$ $\hat{\mathcal{X}}_2^O = \{o_3, o_1\}$,
- and at $t = 3$ $\hat{\mathcal{X}}_3^O = \{o_1, o_3\}$.

Nevertheless, due to the imprecise nature of embodied realisation of the joint attention mechanism (See Sec.3.4), the requirement that both agents share the same set of objects at each episode ($\mathcal{X}_t^O = \mathcal{X}_t^{O,a} = \mathcal{X}_t^{O,A}$) does not always hold. In particular, the precision of the method of establishing the common context, can be described as the probability $Pr(\mathcal{X}_t^{O,a} \neq \mathcal{X}_t^{O,A}) = p_\epsilon$ that at a particular point of time t the agents would not be able to establish common context. For instance, for $p_\epsilon = 0.2$ roughly 80% of the interactions fulfil the strict requirement, whereas 20% does not. As such, we extend the classical settings of LGM by introducing sporadic impairments in initiating the joint attention scene between the interacting agents. The frequency of the impaired interactions is governed by the deviation intensity p_ϵ, i.e., probability that a particular interplay between agents is an impaired communication, that regulates the amount of deviation in the system. In short, depending on the intensity a certain interaction may fail to initiate the joint attention ($\forall_{a \in \mathcal{P}_L} \mathcal{X}_t^{O,a} \subset \mathcal{X}_t^O$). In such a case the context available to the agents differs between the teacher and the learner, i.e., $\mathcal{X}_t^{O,A} \neq \mathcal{X}_t^{O,a}$ (detailed description of the interaction scheme is presented in section 4.3).

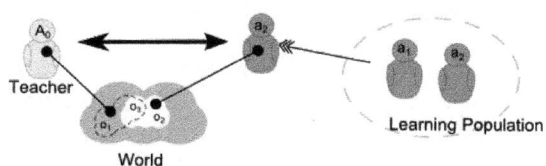

Teacher

World

Learning Population

Fig. 8. Example of interaction that deviates from common context at $t = 2$

Example 3. Following the previous example 2 we extend it to include impairments (See Fig.8):

- first interaction between the teacher A_0 and a_1: both were able to establish a common context $\hat{\mathcal{X}}_1^{\bar{O},a_1} = \hat{\mathcal{X}}_1^{\bar{O},A_0} = \{o_1, o_2\}$,
- second interaction (with a_2): due to a more complex situation (e.g. caused by a limited visibility), it deviates from common context setting - $\hat{\mathcal{X}}_2^{\bar{O},a_2} = \{o_2, o_3\}$ and $\hat{\mathcal{X}}_2^{\bar{O},A_0} = \{o_3, o_1\}$,
- third interaction (with a_2): it again follows a perfect synchronisation of the context - $\hat{\mathcal{X}}_3^{\bar{O},a_2} = \hat{\mathcal{X}}_3^{\bar{O},A_0} = \{o_1, o_3\}$.

4.1   Teacher

The sole purpose of the teacher agent is to provide linguistic clues to the learner allowing the latter to get insights into the utilised language. As such, its required linguistic capabilities can be strictly limited to a proper production mechanism only, i.e., allowing the agent to utter the name of a selected object. Moreover, the teacher always acts as a speaker in the game, and is equipped with a static lexicon at the design time. Consequently, its state can be limited to a production function only and its minimal semantic infrastructure can be defined as follows:

Definition 2. *Teacher agent's A state in a given system state S_t is a tuple:*

$$S_t^A = \langle \mathcal{O}, \mathcal{W}, \mathcal{L}_t^A, \phi_t, \eta_t \rangle, \tag{2}$$

where

- *set of identified objects* $\mathcal{O} = \{o_1, \ldots, o_{NO}\}$,
- *set of words* $\mathcal{W} = \{w_1, \ldots, w_{NW}\}$,
- *lexicon mapping* $\mathcal{L}_t^A : \mathcal{W} \times \mathcal{O} \rightarrow \{0,1\}$,
- *production function* $\phi_t : \mathcal{O} \times \mathcal{L}_t^A \rightarrow \mathcal{W}$,
- *selection strategy* $\eta_t : 2^{\mathcal{O}} \rightarrow \mathcal{O}$.

Each object is explicitly identified by the agent through a unique and strictly internal identifier (o_i), e.g., a certain pattern of the available sensor data. Words, on the other hand, are external representations identified by the population as dedicated communication signs, i.e. a distinguished form of externalised representation available to all agents. Each such sign $w_j \in \mathcal{W}$ is utilised to denote a particular object from the environment. Moreover, it can be used by the agent to convey this relation to other agents in a form of a linguistic clue.

The internal association between signs and objects forms the lexicon $\mathcal{L}_t$. Following the associationistic approach, it defines the mapping $\mathcal{L}_t^A$ that encapsulates the current state of agent's language, i.e., through the correlation strength $\sigma_{o_i,w_j}^A = \mathcal{L}_t^A(o_i, w_j) \in \{0,1\}$ between an object $o_i \in \mathcal{O}$ and a particular word $w_j \in \mathcal{W}$. As the teacher is equipped with a predefined lexicon and for the sake of simplicity it is further assumed that the lexicon $\mathcal{L}_t^A$ is a bijection between words and objects. In particular, the lexicon represents a binary relation that for a given object o defines only a single word w ($\mathcal{L}_t^A(o, w) = 1$) and neglects other words $w' \neq w$ ($\mathcal{L}_t^A(o, w') = 0$).

Based on the lexicon $\mathcal{L}_t^A$ each teacher is able to produce proper utterances by selecting the most adequate name w_j for a particular object o_i. We further assume a straight forward and well established relative mechanism of production [21]. In particular, as the teacher's lexicon is a bijection and the correlation strengths are binary, the association between a given object and a word is either 0 or 1. As such, for a given object o_i the production function ϕ_t selects the word w_j with the maximum correlation strength ($\phi_t(o_i, \mathcal{L}_t^A) = argmax_{w_k} \sigma_{o_i,w_k}^A$), and thus assigns w_j as referring to o_i if and only if $\mathcal{L}_t^A(o_i, w_j) = 1$.

Example 4. Following the aforementioned example, the teacher agent is able to register and distinguish all of the objects $\hat{\mathcal{O}} = \{o_1, o_2, o_3\}$ from the environment. For instance, the robot is equipped with a set of sensors, adequate to the nature of objects, and appropriate processing mechanisms that allow it to filter out the salient sensorimotor data. As such allowing it to establish, at least 3, internal reflections of sensorimotor invariants of the external world (o_i).

On the other hand the teacher is capable of producing words $\mathcal{W} = \{w_1, w_2, w_3\}$, e.g. is equipped with a distinguished light source that is able to produce different light colours and intensities - thus sub serving as an external representation available to all agents. As the teacher is a proficient language user it also has a particular knowledge that the internal reflection o_i relates to the word w_i - $\forall_{i \in \overline{1,3}} \mathcal{L}_t^{A_0}(o_i, w_i) = 1$ and $\forall_{i \neq j} \mathcal{L}_t^{A_0}(o_i, w_j) = 0$.

As aforementioned, each interaction is triggered by the teacher. It begins with the teacher selecting a particular object from its sight as the topic of its utterance. Such selection process models a particular modus operandi that the agents are utilising (See [10] for detailed deliberation) and a particular strategy depends on the actual task the system is faced with. For instance, the linguistic clue can be used by the agents to focus their individual attentions on a particular object from the environment, and further perform a certain mutual action upon it (See Fig.4). Nevertheless, due to general character of this research we focus on a broad strategy that models a rather generic motivation. As such, we further assume that the teacher uniformly samples the current context $\mathcal{X}_t^{O,A}$ for a topic object, i.e., $Pr(\eta_t = o | o \in \mathcal{X}_t^{O,A}) = 1/\|\mathcal{X}_t^{O,A}\|$. Not surprisingly, such a strategy is the most commonly and widely used – due to its generic character and its popularity in the research on the Language Game Model (See [22]).

Example 5. Following the aforementioned example, the teacher agent at first encounter registers $\{o_1, o_2\}$ and randomly selects a single object as the topic of its utterance, e.g. o_1. Then it recalls the appropriate representation for o_1, that is it searches for such a w that $\mathcal{L}_t^{A_0}(o_1, w) = 1$ ($w = w_1$ See Ex.4). Similarly, in all other encounters at time t_2 and time t_3 (See Ex.3).

Example 6. In particular, an exemplary teacher agent A_0 state consists of:

- internal reflections of sensorimotor invariants of the external world ($o_i \in \hat{\mathcal{O}} = \{o_1, o_2, o_3\}$),
- words $\mathcal{W} = \{w_1, w_2, w_3\}$,
- lexicon $\forall_{i \in \overline{1,3}} \mathcal{L}_t^{A_0}(o_i, w_i) = 1$ and $\forall_{i \neq j} \mathcal{L}_t^{A_0}(o_i, w_j) = 0$,
- production function $\phi_t(o_i, \mathcal{L}_t^A) = w_i$,
- selection strategy η_t – uniform selection among the context objects $\mathcal{X}_t^{O,A_0}$.

4.2   Learner

The sole purpose of the learner agent is to acquire the utilised naming convention through a series of linguistic clues provided by the teacher. As such, its minimal linguistic capabilities require a proper interpretation and update mechanisms, i.e., interpreting a name to a particular object and aligning the current state of its lexicon. In essence, learner's minimal required semantic infrastructure can be defined as the learner state, as follows:

Definition 3. *Agent's $a \in \mathcal{P}_L$ state in a given system state S_t is a tuple:*

$$S_t^a = \langle \mathcal{O}, \mathcal{W}, \mathcal{L}_t^a, \delta_t^a, \theta_t^a \rangle, \tag{3}$$

where

- *set of identified objects* $\mathcal{O} = \{o_1, ..., o_{NO}\}$,
- *set of words* $\mathcal{W} = \{w_1, ..., w_{NW}\}$,
- *lexicon mapping* $\mathcal{L}_t^a : \mathcal{W} \times \mathcal{O} \rightarrow [0, 1]$,
- *interpretation function* $\delta_t^a : \mathcal{W} \times \mathcal{L}_t^a \rightarrow \mathcal{O}$,
- *update function* $\theta_t^a : \mathcal{W} \times 2^{\mathcal{O}} \times \mathcal{L}_t^a \rightarrow \mathcal{L}_t^a$.

As aforementioned, we follow the associationist stance and define the lexicon as a mapping $\mathcal{L}_t^a$ (See Sec.4.1) between words and objects. However, due to the fact that each learner a needs to acquire the language utilised by the teacher, its lexicon $\mathcal{L}_t^a$ must be flexible and adaptable. As such, the value of correlation strength $\sigma_{o_i,w_j}^a = \mathcal{L}_t^a(o_i, w_j) \in [0, 1]$ between an object $o_i \in \mathcal{O}$ and a particular word $w_j \in \mathcal{W}$ changes over time due to the interaction the agent is experiencing. In particular, the higher the σ value is, the more definite the agent is that a certain word is an adequate name for a given object.

As such, each learner is able to interpret the received external utterance w, i.e. select the most adequate object o, according to its current state of the lexicon $\mathcal{L}_t^a$. As aforementioned, the straight forward and well established relative mechanism of interpretation [3] is assumed. In particular, for a given word $w \in \mathcal{W}$ the interpretation function δ_t^a selects an object $o \in \mathcal{O}$ with the maximum correlation strength $(\delta_t^a(w, \mathcal{L}_t^a) = argmax_{o_i}(\mathcal{L}_t^a(o_i, w)))$, and thus interprets w as referring to o, solely based on the internal relation between correlation strengths of competing word-object pairs.

The update function defines how the lexicon is aligned, based on the current state of the lexicon $\mathcal{L}_t^a$, the current context $\mathcal{X}_t^{O,a}$ and given word $\phi_t^A(\eta_t^A(\mathcal{X}_t^{O,A}), \mathcal{L}_t^A)$ uttered by the speaker agent A. In particular, it defines how the linguistic clue (produced by the teacher) affects and modifies learner's naming convention (See Sec.4.4), i.e., through proper modification in the association structure within the lexicon.

Example 7. Following the aforementioned example, each learning agent a_i is capable of distinguishing the objects $\hat{\mathcal{O}}$ and is capable of distinguishing individual words from the set of all available $\mathcal{W}$ uttered by the teacher. Due to the fact that the learner a is acquiring the language, its lexicon $\mathcal{L}_t^{a_i}$ must be flexible, e.g.:

Table 1. Exemplary lexicon

$\mathcal{L}_t^{a_i}$	w_1	w_2	w_3
o_1	.4	.3	.1
o_2	.2	.6	.2
o_3	.3	.2	.8

Based on these values the learner is able to determine its interpretation of a particular word w, e.g. utilising the maximum value approach. Moreover, as the learner is acquiring the language based on the learning episodes (See Sec.4.3) it needs a proper mechanism of modifying its lexicon (See Sec.4.4).

Example 8. In particular, an exemplary learning agent's a_i state consists of:

- internal reflections of sensorimotor invariants of the external world $o_j \in \hat{\mathcal{O}} = \{o_1, o_2, o_3\}$),
- words $\mathcal{W} = \{w_1, w_2, w_3\}$,
- lexicon $\mathcal{L}_t^{a_i}$ (See Tab.1),
- interpretation function $\delta_t^{a_i}(w) = argmax_{o \in \hat{\mathcal{O}}} \mathcal{L}_t^{a_i}(w, o)$,
- update function ψ^a (See Sec.4.4).

4.3   Interaction

Interaction between the agents is the only opportunity for an individual learner to gain information about the utilised language, i.e., the naming conventions utilised by the teacher.

In the assumed settings, the interaction is governed by the means of no feedback naming game routine adopted to the individual semiosis task (See Sec.3.3). At each time point $t \in \mathcal{T}$ a random learning agent $a_H : (a_H, A_T) = \mathcal{X}_t^P$ advances in a simple communication with the teacher agent A_T. Next, the teacher selects a single object o_T as the topic of its conversation, and further names it $w_T = \phi_t^{A_T}(o_T, \mathcal{L}_t^{A_T})$, based on its current lexicon state $\mathcal{L}_t^{A_T}$ and utilising its production function $\phi_t^{A_T}$. The uttered word w_T is then registered by the hearer a_H, i.e., it is registered and related to the current context of perception $\mathcal{X}_t^{O,a_H}$.

Based on the available information, i.e., the current context $\mathcal{X}_t^{O,a_H}$ and the uttered word w_T, the hearer a_H updates its lexicon $\mathcal{L}_t^{a_H} = \theta_t^{a_H}(w_T, \mathcal{X}_t^{O,a_H}, \mathcal{L}_{t-1}^{a_H})$. Further, the hearer is able to interpret the received utterance w_T according to its interpretation function $\delta_t^{a_H}$ and its current state of the lexicon $\mathcal{L}_t^{a_H}$ (updated), i.e., $o_I = \delta_t^{a_H}(w_T, \mathcal{L}_t^{a_H})$. As the agents do not have any additional means to verify the results of their interaction this step concludes the interaction between the agents.

Additionally, on the system level we can evaluate if the intended meaning o_T is the same as the learners interpretation o_I. In particular, the interaction can be considered as a success if the intended and interpreted meanings are the same – $o_T = o_I$ – and as a failure if the intended and interpreted meanings are different – $o_T \neq o_I$. As aforementioned, in the basic type of individual semiosis game the topic object o_T of the utterance is shared among both contexts, i.e., $o_T \in \mathcal{X}_t^{O,a_H} \cap \mathcal{X}_t^{O,A_T}$.

Example 9. Following the example, let us focus on a single episode that involves interaction between the teacher A_0 and a_1:

1. Both agents perform observation of the surrounding environment and register the same set of 2 objects $\hat{X}_{\hat{O}}(1) = \{o_1, o_2\}$.
2. The teacher randomly selects a single object as the topic of its utterance, e.g. $o_1 = \eta_t^{A_0}$.
3. The teacher names the object o_1 ($\mathcal{L}_t^{A_0}(w, o_1) = 1) \Rightarrow (w = w_1)$ and utters the word w_1.

4. The learner receives the utterance w_1 and updates its lexicon based on current observation $\theta_t^{a_1}(w_1, \hat{X}_{\hat{O}}(1))$.
5. The learner interprets the utterance $o_T = \delta_t^{a_1}(w_1)$.
6. Finally the success of the game is evaluated - whether o_T is the object o_1.

However, it can sporadically happen that some of the interactions involve a modified routine. As aforementioned, it is possible that the teacher A_T can produce an utterance with the selected topic being outside of the hearer's a_H current context of perception $o_T \notin \mathcal{X}_t^{O,a_H}$. In essence, the teacher provides a linguistic clue for an object that is outside of the current scope of the attention of the learner - as such introducing a inherent deviation in the interaction. Moreover, due to the lack of any additional communication schemes involved in the interplay the hearer has no other means of predicting the correct, nor the incorrect, behaviour of the teacher. Resultantly, when such a game occurs, i.e., involving deviation, the hearer is not aware of it, and is forced to update the strengths of incorrect associations, i.e., treating the deviated episode as a proper episode of the game.

Depending on the deviation intensity $p_\epsilon \in [0,1]$, i.e., defined as the probability of deviation in a single interaction (See Sec.4), the teacher's selection strategy complies either with the idealised procedure or a modified procedure. With probability p_ϵ it happens that the teacher selects an object in its current sight that is outside of the learners current context ($o_D \notin \mathcal{X}_t^{O,a_H} \wedge o_D \in \mathcal{X}_t^{O,A_T}$). Following the generic approach of selection, the teacher uniformly samples all of the objects that are currently out of the hearer's scope $\mathcal{O} \setminus \mathcal{X}_t^{O,a_H}$ and selects the deviated topic object o_D. Further, the deviated topic is named and the uttered word is used as a linguistic clue that is received by the hearer. While the procedure from the point of view of learning agent is unchanged, inevitably, the inappropriate associations are enforced by the hearer. Consequently, such a behaviour is affecting the current, additionally future, interactions and introduces errors in the correlations within the lexicon.

Example 10. We modify the aforementioned example according to the alternate interaction protocol. In this case,

1. Both agents (teacher and a_2) observe the surrounding environment and register different sets of objects $\hat{X'}_{\hat{O}}^2(2) = \{o_2, o_3\}$ and $\hat{X'}_{\hat{O}}^T(2) = \{o_3, o_1\}$.
2. The teacher further selects the object that is outside of the scope of the learner - o_1 - as the topic of its utterance (as we focus on the worst case scenario).
3. The learner receives the utterance w_1 and updates its lexicon based on current observation $\theta_t^{a_2}(w_1, \hat{X}_{\hat{O}}(1))$.
4. The learner interprets the utterance $o_I = \delta_t^{a_2}(w_1)$.
5. Finally the success of the game is evaluated - whether o_I is the object o_1.

Having this in mind, we should stress that it is significant to analyse how such a situation affects the entire process of language alignment. In particular, as such sporadic deviations from joint attention settings are common to embodied implementations of individual semiosis it is crucial to investigate the margin of robustness against different learning models, different configurations, i.e. population size, context size, and different intensities of deviation.

4.4   Alignment Strategies

As the agents do not receive any direct feedback concerning the outcomes of the game – the interpreted meaning and the heard word pair (w_T, o_I) is regarded as the most probable one – there is a need of a particular learning scheme that would allow an individual to infer the proper associations from a series of such interaction (See Sec.3.2). Following the cross-situational learning, i.e., learning from co-occurrences between words and objects, implies that after each interaction the hearer updates its lexicon $\mathcal{L}_t^a$ by modifying internal correlations $\sigma^a(o, w_i)$ between words and objects. In general, the idea behind such procedure requires that the update function θ_t^a should dampen the correlation $\sigma^a(o, w_i)$ between the received word w_i and all objects currently not perceived by the agent $o \notin \mathcal{X}_t^{O,a}$. On the other hand, all the correlations between the received word w_i and currently perceived objects $o \in \mathcal{X}_t^{O,a}$ should be enforced, while leaving all of the correlations with other words unchanged.

Certainly, in settings that involve context consisted of multiple objects, a single interaction is typically not sufficient to determine the utilised naming convention. In particular, presumably all objects from the context are equally probable intended meanings. We note, that an object can dominate the correlation between a certain word only if it occurred, with this word, more times then with any other object.

In this paper we assume that each individual is aligning itself with the teacher according to one of the possible alignment strategies [2] $\kappa^a : \theta_t^a(w, \mathcal{X}_t^{O,a}, \mathcal{L}_t^a) = \mathcal{L}_{t+1}^a$ - Elimination, Frequency, Damping.[3] For each of the meta strategies we investigate two concrete learning algorithms:

Elimination. Elimination strategy assumes the idealised situation, that each exposure of a certain word is accompanied by the presence of the object it denotes. As such, the true meaning of a particular word lies in the intersection of the contexts it was uttered with. However, instead of utilising the pure elimination strategy, where only the intersections are taken into account, we modify this approach by still keeping track of the co-occurrences while eliminating the frequencies of not available word-object $(o - w)$ pairs.

$$\kappa_{eliminationPure}^a : \begin{cases} if o \in \mathcal{X}_t^{O,a} \wedge w = \phi_t^A(o, \mathcal{L}_t^A) \Rightarrow \sigma'(o, w) = \sigma(o, w) \times 1 \\ if o \notin \mathcal{X}_t^{O,a} \wedge w = \phi_t^A(o, \mathcal{L}_t^A) \Rightarrow \sigma'(o, w) = \sigma(o, w) \times 0 \\ \qquad\qquad else \qquad\qquad\qquad\quad \Rightarrow \quad \sigma'(o, w) = \sigma(o, w) \end{cases} \quad (4)$$

---

[3] For the sake of simplicity let us assume that the lexicon decodes the strengths of all $o - w$ correlations $\sigma(o, w)$, whilst updated lexicon $\mathcal{L}_{t+1}^a$ decodes the updated strengths of all $\sigma'(o, w)$ correlations.

$$\kappa_{elimination}^{a} : \begin{cases} if o \in \mathcal{X}_t^{O,a} \wedge w = \phi_t^A(o, \mathcal{L}_t^A) \Rightarrow \sigma'(o,w) = \sigma(o,w) \times 1 \\ if o \notin \mathcal{X}_t^{O,a} \wedge w = \phi_t^A(o, \mathcal{L}_t^A) \Rightarrow \sigma'(o,w) = \sigma(o,w) \times \lambda \\ \qquad\qquad else \qquad\qquad\qquad \Rightarrow \quad \sigma'(o,w) = \sigma(o,w) \end{cases} \quad (5)$$

where $\lambda \in (0,1)$ is the more flexible elimination rate.

Example 11. Let us assume $\hat{X'}_{\hat{O}}^i(1) = \{o_1, o_2\}$, $\hat{X'}_{\hat{O}}^i(2) = \{o_2, o_3\}$, and $\hat{X'}_{\hat{O}}^i(3) = \{o_1, o_3\}$ as the history of learning episodes. Utilising the pure elimination strategy the learner a_i:

- from the first episode $\theta_t^{a_i}(w_1, \{o_1, o_2\})$ correlates w_1 only with objects $\{o_1, o_2\}$, as this is the first encounter of the word,
- after the second episode $\theta_t^{a_i}(w_2, \{o_2, o_3\})$ correlates w_2 only with objects $\{o_2, o_3\}$, again as it is the first encounter of the word,
- finally after the third episode $\theta_t^{a_i}(w_1, \{o_1, o_3\})$ correlates w_1 with objects $\{o_1, o_3\} \cap \{o_1, o_2\}$, as the word is already correlated with objects $\{o_1, o_2\}$.

Frequency. Frequency strategy is based on counting the co-occurrences of particular word-object pairs. As such, at each interaction the agent increases the strength of all correlations $\sigma(o,w)$ between the currently available objects and currently uttered word.

$$\kappa_{frequency}^{a} : \sigma'(o,w) = \nu_{o,w} \times (\nu_w)^{-1}$$

$$\begin{cases} if o \in \mathcal{X}_t^{O,a} \wedge w = \phi_t^A(o, \mathcal{L}_t^A) \Rightarrow \nu_{o,w} = \nu_{o,w} + 1 \\ \qquad\qquad else \qquad\qquad\qquad \Rightarrow \quad \nu_{o,w} = \nu_{o,w} \end{cases} \quad (6)$$

where ν_w is the weighted number of occurrences of the word w - as such $\nu *_{o,w} \times (\nu *_w)^{-1}$ is the weighted frequency of $o - w$.

$$\kappa_{freqadaptive}^{a} : \sigma'(o,w) = \nu *_{o,w} \times (\nu *_w)^{-1}$$

$$\begin{cases} if o \in \mathcal{X}_t^{O,a} \wedge w = \phi_t^A(o, \mathcal{L}_t^A) \Rightarrow \nu *_{o,w} = \nu *_{o,w} + (\sigma(o,w)/max_{o \in \mathcal{X}_t^{O,a}}(\sigma(w,o))) \\ \qquad\qquad else \qquad\qquad\qquad \Rightarrow \qquad\qquad \nu *_{o,w} = \nu *_{o,w} \end{cases}$$

$$(7)$$

where $\nu *_w$ is the weighted number of occurrences of the word w - as such $\nu *_{o,w} \times (\nu *_w)^{-1}$ is the weighted frequency of $o - w$.

Example 12. Let us assume $\hat{X'}_{\hat{O}}^i(1) = \{o_1, o_2\}$, $\hat{X'}_{\hat{O}}^i(2) = \{o_2, o_3\}$, and $\hat{X'}_{\hat{O}}^i(3) = \{o_1, o_3\}$ as the history of learning episodes. Utilising the frequency strategy the learner $agent_i$:

- from the first episode $\theta_t^{a_i}(w_1, \{o_1, o_2\})$ establishes the frequency of correlations $\mathcal{L}_t^{a_i}(w_1, o_1) = 1$, $\mathcal{L}_t^{a_i}(w_1, o_2) = 1$, $\mathcal{L}_t^{a_i}(w_1, o_3) = 0, \ldots, \mathcal{L}_t^{a_i}(w_3, o_3) = 0\}$,

- after the second episode $\theta_t^{a_i}(w_2, \{o_2, o_3\})$ establishes the frequency of correlations $\mathcal{L}_t^{a_i}(w_1, o_1) = 1$, $\mathcal{L}_t^{a_i}(w_1, o_2) = 1$, $\mathcal{L}_t^{a_i}(w_1, o_3) = 0$, $\mathcal{L}_t^{a_i}(w_2, o_1) = 0$, $\mathcal{L}_t^{a_i}(w_2, o_2) = 1$, $\mathcal{L}_t^{a_i}(w_2, o_3) = 1 \ldots$, $\mathcal{L}_t^{a_i}(w_3, o_3) = 0\}$,
- finally after the third episode $\theta_t^{a_i}(w_1, \{o_1, o_3\})$ establishes the frequency of correlations $\mathcal{L}_t^{a_i}(w_1, o_1) = 1$, $\mathcal{L}_t^{a_i}(w_1, o_2) = 0.5$, $\mathcal{L}_t^{a_i}(w_1, o_3) = 0.5$, $\ldots$, $\mathcal{L}_t^{a_i}(w_3, o_3) = 0\}$.

Damping. Damping strategy is based on the Frequency strategy, where an additional decrease of co-occurrences between non exhibited pairs is performed. As such, at each iteration not only the agent updates it's frequencies, but also dampens the co-occurrences of currently uttered word and currently non-available objects.

$$\kappa_{frequencyDamping}^a : \sigma'(o, w) = \nu_{o,w} \times (\nu_w)^{-1}$$

$$\begin{cases} if\, o \in \mathcal{X}_t^{O,a} \wedge w = \phi_t^A(o, \mathcal{L}_t^A) \Rightarrow \nu_{o,w} = \nu_{o,w} + 1 \\ if\, o \notin \mathcal{X}_t^{O,a} \wedge w = \phi_t^A(o, \mathcal{L}_t^A) \Rightarrow \nu_{o,w} = \nu_{o,w} - \beta \\ \qquad else \qquad\qquad\qquad\qquad \Rightarrow \quad \nu_{o,w} = \nu_{o,w} \end{cases} \tag{8}$$

$$\kappa_{ICSL}^a : \sigma'(o, w) = \nu_{o,w} \times (\nu_w)^{-1}$$

$$\begin{cases} if\, o \in \mathcal{X}_t^{O,a} \wedge w = \phi_t^A(o, \mathcal{L}_t^A) \Rightarrow \nu_{o,w} = \lambda \times \sigma(o, w) \times \frac{\gamma'}{\gamma} + (1 - \lambda) \times \frac{\gamma'}{C} \\ if\, o \notin \mathcal{X}_t^{O,a} \wedge w = \phi_t^A(o, \mathcal{L}_t^A) \Rightarrow \qquad \nu_{o,w} = \sigma(o, w) \times \frac{\delta'}{\delta} \\ \qquad\qquad else \qquad\qquad\qquad \Rightarrow \qquad \nu_{o,w} = \nu_{o,w} \end{cases} \tag{9}$$

where $\gamma = \sum_{o \in \mathcal{X}_t^{O,a}} (\sigma(o, w))$, $\gamma' = \mu + \gamma \times (1 - \mu)$, $\delta = 1 - \gamma$ (μ being the learning rate), $\delta' = 1 - \gamma'$, and $\lambda = \sqrt{1 - (1 - \gamma)^2}$ (For details See [3]).

Example 13. Let us assume damping level o 0.1, and $\hat{X}'^i_O(1) = \{o_1, o_2\}$, $\hat{X}'^i_O(2) = \{o_2, o_3\}$ and $\hat{X}'^i_O(3) = \{o_1, o_3\}$ as the history of learning episodes. Utilising the elimination strategy the learner a_i:

- from the first episode $\theta_t^{a_i}(w_1, \{o_1, o_2\})$ establishes the frequency of correlations $\mathcal{L}_t^{a_i}(w_1, o_1) = 1$, $\mathcal{L}_t^{a_i}(w_1, o_2) = 1$, $\mathcal{L}_t^{a_i}(w_1, o_3) = 0$, $\ldots$, $\mathcal{L}_t^{a_i}(w_3, o_3) = 0\}$,
- after second episode $\theta_t^{a_i}(w_2, \{o_2, o_3\})$ establishes the frequency of correlations $\mathcal{L}_t^{a_i}(w_1, o_1) = 1$, $\mathcal{L}_t^{a_i}(w_1, o_2) = 1$, $\mathcal{L}_t^{a_i}(w_1, o_3) = 0$, $\mathcal{L}_t^{a_i}(w_2, o_1) = 0$, $\mathcal{L}_t^{a_i}(w_2, o_2) = 1$, $\mathcal{L}_t^{a_i}(w_2, o_3) = 1 \ldots$, $\mathcal{L}_t^{a_i}(w_3, o_3) = 0\}$,
- finally after the third episode $\theta_t^{a_i}(w_1, \{o_1, o_3\})$ establishes the dampened frequency of correlations $\mathcal{L}_t^{a_i}(w_1, o_1) = 1$, $\mathcal{L}_t^{a_i}(w_1, o_2) = 0.4$, $\mathcal{L}_t^{a_i}(w_1, o_3) = 0.5$, $\ldots$, $\mathcal{L}_t^{a_i}(w_3, o_3) = 0\}$.

4.5   Measures

In order to formulate the dynamics of the alignment process, we need to identify a major axis of comparison, i.e. define a numerical summary of the current state of the learning population.

The most obvious measure is the frequency of successful communications between agents. In particular, it resembles the observed ability of the system to transfer information from the teacher to the learner. In order to keep track of the effectiveness of the communication we calculate the success rate μ_{SR}, as follows:[4].

$$\mu_{SR(N)} = \sum_{t \in \mathcal{T}|_N} \mathcal{I}_{\{o_T = \delta_t^a(\phi_t^A(o_T, \mathcal{L}_t^A), \mathcal{L}_t^a)\}} \tag{10}$$

In particular, at each interaction the teacher produces a name w of the selected topic o_T - $w = \phi_t^A(o_T, \mathcal{L}_t^A)$ - that is further received by the learning agent (hearer). Hearer can further interpret the name w as a particular object $o = \delta_t^a(w, \mathcal{L}_t^a)$. Then if they are identical $o = o_T$ the game is considered as a success and $\mu_{SR(N)}$ is increased, otherwise it is a failure and $\mu_{SR(N)}$ is decreased.

Example 14. Let us assume a series[5] of 14 interactions between a teacher and multiple learners - $(1,1,1,0,1,0,0,0,1,1,0,1,1,1)$ - and a window of calculation $N = 10$:

- after first interaction the success rate is equal to $\mu_{SR(10)}(1) = 1$,
- after 10 interactions the success rate is equal to $\mu_{SR(10)}(10) = 0.6$,
- after first 11 interactions $\mu_{SR(10)}(11) = 0.5$,
- and after all 14 interactions is equal to $\mu_{SR(10)}(10) = 0.6$.

Despite its simplicity the frequency of successful communications does not take into consideration the coherence between other names. Due to this restriction, we formulate an additional measure resembling the naming convention spread among the entire learning population and reflecting the coherence of names among all existing objects. As such, we introduce language coherence μ_{LC}, as the probability that a randomly selected agent assigns the same name for a randomly selected object from the environment as the teacher, as follows:

$$\mu_{LC} = E_{a \in \mathcal{P}_L, o \in \mathcal{O}}[\delta_t^a(\phi_t^A(o, \mathcal{L}_t^A), \mathcal{L}_t^a) = o] \tag{11}$$

The lowest possible coherence, i.e. $\mu_{LC} = 0$, reflects a state of no language coherence in the system, as none of the learners uses the same name for any of the objects as the teacher. The highest possible coherence, i.e. $\mu_{LC} = 1$, represents the state of full coherence, where all learners share teacher's naming convention.

Example 15. Following the example with system $\hat{S}$ consisting of 2 learning agents, with 3 distinguishable objects $\hat{O} = \{o_1, o_2, o_3\}$ that the teacher names w_1, w_2, and w_3 respectively, we can calculate the language coherence in an exemplary case. Let us assume that all agents agree on the interpretation of $w_1 \sim o_1$ and

---

[4] $\mathcal{I}$ is the identity function, i.e. $\mathcal{I}_{x=x} = 1$ and $\forall_{x \neq y} \mathcal{I}_{x=y} = 0$.
[5] It is assumed that a 1 - represents successful communication, whilst 0 represents the unsuccessful interaction.

$w_2 \sim o_2$, and vary on the interpretation of w_3. In such a case the language coherence is equal to $\mu_{LC} = \frac{6-2}{6} \approx 67\%$, as out of 2 agents and 3 objects (6 elements in total) two of them have different understanding of a particular object.

5   Individual Semiosis Simulations

Using a developed simulation framework we have tested the behaviour of the individual semiosis. All of the presented results are an average of more then 50 consecutive runs and represent the general behaviour of the system. The baseline settings for the experiments include population of 10 learners, a single teacher, context of size 2 objects and the deviation intensity set to 0.

In the following subsections we investigate the idealised situation assuming the existence of a perfect mechanism for establishing common context setting between interacting agents. As such, the early results and analysis focuses solely on the behaviour of different learning mechanisms in the individual semiosis game. In particular, we research the dynamics of the language coherence and basic limits in number of iterations needed to reach a particular consistency of the system.

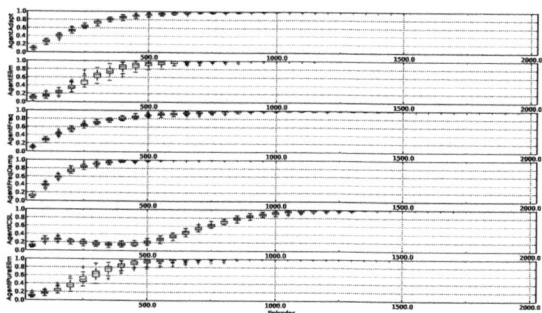

Fig. 9. Language coherence dynamics in case of different types of learners, with context size set to 2, population size set to 10 agents, and 10 objects

In the idealised settings of individual semiosis (deviation intensity $p_\epsilon = 0$) all of the incorporated learning strategies allow the learning population to reach a full lexicon coherence with the teacher (Fig. 9). Having roughly the same initial distributions (Fig. 9 - starting point at around $\mu_{LC} = 0.1$) the system undergoes a sudden increase of coherence that gradually flattens out and stabilises at it's maximum - both in case of the coherence measure (μ_{LC}) and the success measure (μ_{SR}). Certainly, at the point where all of the learning agents utilise the same naming conventions as the teacher there are no further forces that could destabilise the system. As such, the full coherence state is an absorbing state that the system is thriving to achieve and can never escape from it.

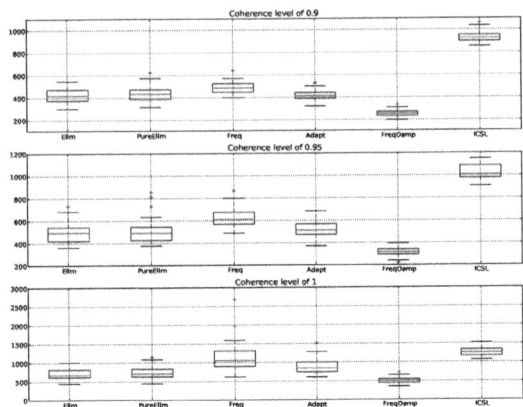

Fig. 10. Number of iterations to reach a particular language coherence level in case of different types of learners, with context size set to 2, population size set to 10 agents, and 10 objects

In particular, it is interesting to estimate the number of iterations needed for the system to reach a particular level of consistency (Fig. 10). From the figure (Fig. 9) we can read that most of the strategies already after 400 iterations, i.e. roughly 40 interactions per learning agent, reach a consistent level of at least 80% of coherence. Such a coherence resembles the fact that the whole population of learning agents, treated as a whole, is 80% similar to the teacher - which is already a high level as we can notice analysing the success rate measure (Fig. 11). The only strategy that seems to perform weaker is the ICSL. In particular, due to its weak and conservative modifications in the early stages, ICSL requires substantially more iterations to reach high levels of coherence, i.e. level of 80% at roughly 800 iterations (around 80 interactions per learning agent). Consequently, in comparison with all other strategies ICSL requires twice the number of interactions to settle at a particular spread of naming convention.

It should be noted that the observed behaviour of the system is maintained at higher consistency levels, i.e. 90%, 95% and 100% (Fig. 10). Interestingly, the strategy involving frequentist approach extended with a damping mechanism ($\eta^a_{frequencyDamping}$) results in the quickest establishment of a particular consistency, roughly requiring 100 iterations (on average 10 iterations per agent) less.

The registered language coherence dynamics (Fig. 9) depicts three basic types of dynamic behaviour. First, both of the elimination strategies undergo a three stage evolution: short, early and slow increase (convex curve), followed by a relatively longer and significantly steeper raise (changing the curvature - inflection point), that further flattens out (concave curve) and settles at the maximum value. Second, all of the frequency based approaches follow a simpler two stage evolution: relatively longer and significantly steeper raise (concave curve), that further flattens out at maximum values, without the early stage of slow increase and without the change of curvature. Third, ICSL strategy undergoes a four stage evolution: an early decrease (concave curve), that further flattens out (changes curvature - inflection point) and is followed by a long and steady increase (convex curve that changes curvature), that again flattens out (concave curve) and settles at the maximum value.

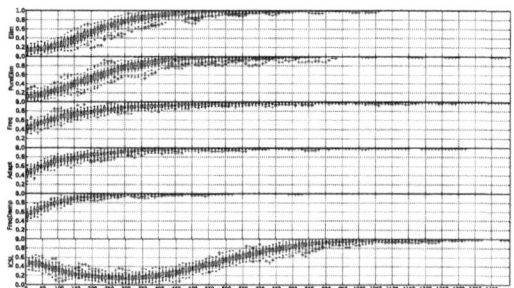

Fig. 11. Success rate dynamics in case of different types of learners, with context size set to 2, population size set to 10 agents, 10 objects, and success rate window N set to 50

As aforementioned, all of the incorporated strategies allow the learning population to reach and maintain successful communication with the teacher (Fig. 11). It should be noted that all of the presented graphs assume a window of 50 iterations, i.e. the frequency of success in the last 50 iterations. As such, the value at iteration $t = 100$ represents the $\mu_{SR(50)}(100)$, that is the frequency of successful communications from $t \in [50, 100]$, and is evaluated from 50 consecutive runs of the simulation. The frequency based approaches reach a frequency of success larger then 50% just after 100 iterations. Success rate greater than half is reached by the elimination based approaches after 200 iterations and for the ICSL after 600 iterations. Again the ICSL strategy seems to require substantially more iterations to reach a particular level, in comparison to the other tested strategies. Not surprisingly, the damping approach ($\eta^a_{frequencyDamping}$) results in the quickest establishment of a particular success rate.

Cross analysing the obtained results ((Fig. 9) and Fig. 11) we can correlate the dynamic behaviour of the success rate measure with the dynamics of the language coherence measure. In particular, we can notice that it is easier to reach a successful communication than to establish a certain coherence between the agents. As such, we can notice that a high level of success rate l_{SR}

does not actually require an equally high level of language coherence $l_{LC} < l_{SR}$ (i.e. after early dynamics of the system). Such a behaviour can be easily explained by the fact that after reaching a particular coherence of the system, and due to the random character of context and interaction processes, it is more probable that the interaction will involve an already established name. Consequently, if the agents communicate with already established names more often then the resultant success is more frequent. On the other hand, in such a situation it is less probable that the communication involves names that are not yet established - that could result in a unsuccessful communication. Moreover, the aforementioned situation is also highly probable to result in a proper modification in the learners lexicon, i.e. settling on a proper name, and as such result again in successful communication.

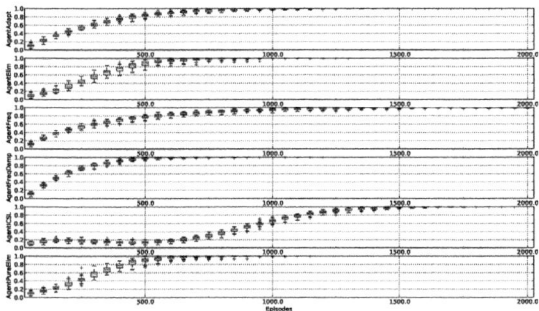

Fig. 12. Language coherence dynamics in case of different types of learners, with context size set to 3, population size set to 10 agents, and 10 objects

Increasing the size of the context results in a stretch of the dynamics graphs presented for the baseline settings (context size of 2). In particular, for context size of 3 (Fig. 12) the aforementioned consistency level of 80% requires roughly 100 more interactions, i.e. 10 iterations per agent. Similarly, for context size of 4 (Fig. 13) requires roughly 250 more iterations than the baseline behaviour. Certainly, the exact amount of change, i.e due to the increase of context size, varies depending on a particular strategy.

Summarising, the performance of the damping strategy seems to perform better in comparison to all the other approaches, mostly the pure elimination and simple frequency approaches. This intuitive fact can be easily attributed to the mixture of strong assumption of the idealised settings, i.e. context sharing between the learner and teacher, and to the very severe punishment of inconsistent word-object pairings. As such, the learner is able to very quickly dampen the wrong associations and focus only on a limited set of the inconclusive ones.

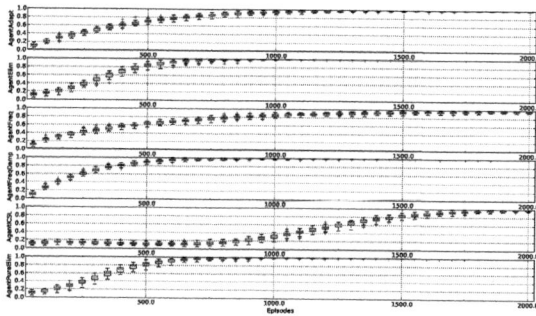

Fig. 13. Language coherence dynamics in case of different types of learners, with context size set to 4, population size set to 10 agents, and 10 objects

6   Deviation from Common Context Setting

More interesting and certainly more substantial is the study of different learning strategies in more realistic settings, i.e. where sporadic deviation from the common context setting are highly probable. Intuitively, the presence of deviation, represented as a inadequate samples received by the hearer, should result in general inability of the system to reach and maintain an agreement. On the other hand, small disturbances, i.e. only sporadic presence of deviation, should still be marginal and allow the system to reach and maintain a coherent naming convention. As such it is interesting and important to analyse to what extent the presence of 'invalid' samples affects the behaviour of the system.

All of the graphs present the dynamics of the language coherence in case of changing intensity of deviations. In particular, we depict (on the X axis) the intensity of deviations as $1 - p_\epsilon$, i.e. the higher the value the less deviation, and the lower the value the more deviation, and depict (on Y axis) the language coherence at a particular iteration (depicted on all graphs). The idea behind such a assumption lies in the fact that the value $1-p_\epsilon$ depicts the quality of the method of establishing common context.[6] As such, this quality has a particular and crucial physical interpretation. In all cases the baseline parameters are assumed - 10 agents, 10 objects and context size of 2.

First, we can notice that for small intensity of deviation (less then 40%) the language coherence is still able to reach its maximum even after only 3000 iterations (figure omitted). Then the continuing increase of intensity results in continuing decrease of the performance of the alignment process, and finally for high values of intensity (above 90%) the system is completely unable to align itself despite the utilised method. Increasing the number of iterations to 10000 (Fig. 14) we can notice that both the area of agreement ($\mu_{LC} > 0.2$) and area of disagreement ($\mu_{LC} < 0.8 <$) are increased in size. Moreover, after increasing the number of iterations even more, to 30000 iterations (Fig. 15), we can notice that again, both the area of agreement and area of disagreement are even further

---

[6] Consequently, we will use the term intensity to depict p_e and quality to depict $1-p_e$.

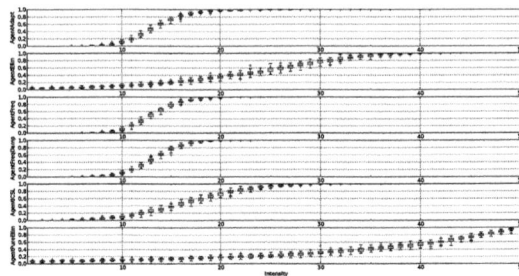

Fig. 14. Language coherence (Y axis) after 10000 iterations against different deviation probabilities (X axis) in case of different strategies

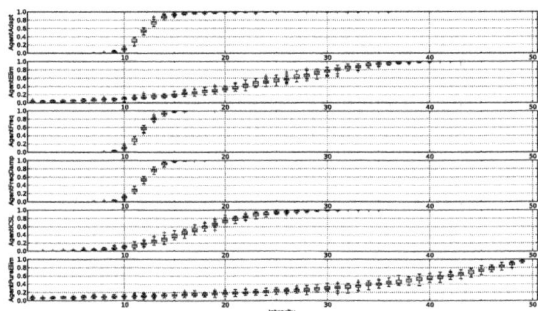

Fig. 15. Language coherence (Y axis) after 30000 iterations against different deviation probabilities (X axis) in case of different strategies

increased. Not surprisingly the more general observation is that the distinction between the two phases becomes more strict with the increase number of iterations. As such, in the limit of number of iterations the system undergoes a rapid phase transition from the agreement state (maximal language coherence) to disagreement state (minimal language coherence). However, it should be underlined that in all of the presented cases the learners managed to align themselves to the teacher even with the deviation intensity greater then 50%, i.e. more then every second sample was an incorrect sample.

Second, we can notice two types of the behaviour of the system after 30000 (Fig. 15) iterations. For the frequency based strategies we can distinguish three areas of the system: for low quality (less than 20%) of common context the system maintains minimal coherence levels, for high quality (above 35%) maintains maximal coherence, and for medium-low quality (between (20 − 35%)) undergoes the change of behaviour. We can notice that in case of this type of strategies the sharp transition effect (in the limit) is noticeable. Such behaviour is also shared by the ICSL strategy, the only difference is the significantly smaller areas of agreement and disagreement. For the elimination based approaches we can distinguish two areas of the system: for high quality values (more than 80%for pure elimination, and more than 98% for elimination) the system maintains high coherence, whilst for other values with the decrease of quality the coherence decreases nearly linearly.

Third, we can investigate the points of the transition between the agreement-disagreement areas. For the frequency based approaches the transition is noticeable between quality of $20 - 30\%$, that is deviation intensity of $70 - 80\%$.[7] For the ICSL strategy the transition is between quality of $25 - 40\%$. Finally, for the pure elimination strategy between $60 - 90\%$, whilst for the elimination strategy between $40 - 60\%$. Consequently, we can easily notice that frequency based approaches are significantly more robust to any form of deviation, then all of the other tested mechanisms.

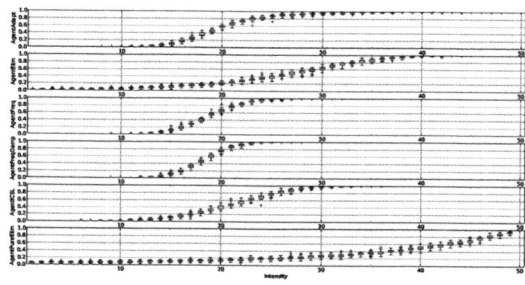

Fig. 16. Language coherence (Y axis) after 10000 iterations against different deviation probabilities (X axis) in case of different strategies, with context size 3

Additionally we have tested the behaviour of the transition effect against different context sizes, i.e. more complex structure of the learning episodes. First of all we have studied the behaviour of phase transition between agreement and disagreement. For this purpose we have tested the distributions of final language coherence against different intensities of deviation after 10000 iterations for context size of 3 (Fig. 16), 4 (Fig. 17) and 5 (Fig. 18).

As the size of the context determines the indeterminacy of the learner it drastically influences the point of transitions between the phases. In particular, the intuitive behaviour is noticeable as the increase of context size results in drastic decrease of the agreement area, i.e. lowering the transition point (Fig. 16,17,18). After 10000 iterations the increase of context size from 2 objects to 3 objects results in nearly a 1/8 decrease in the agreement area, whilst the increase to 4 objects results in nearly a 1/3 decrease. Additionally, we should underline the fact that even with the higher indeterminacy the system managed to cope with deviation intensities larger than 50%.

---

[7] As this class of strategies is fundamental for the process of semiosis we further investigate the transition analytically in the next section.

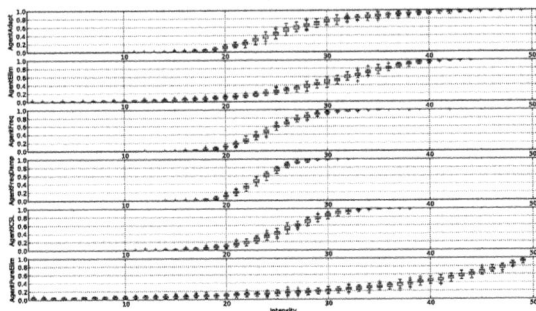

Fig. 17. Language coherence (Y axis) after 10000 iterations against different deviation probabilities (X axis) in case of different strategies, with context size 4

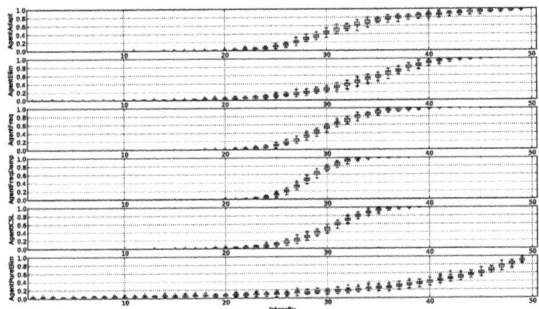

Fig. 18. Language coherence (Y axis) after 10000 iterations against different deviation probabilities (X axis) in case of different strategies, with context size 5

7   Analysis and Discussion

Analysing the obtained results we can notice that despite the distinct learning procedures utilised by the learners the influence of changing intensity of deviation on the behaviour of the alignment process is analogous (despite minor differences). This fact is due to the similarity of the underlying mechanisms in the learning process. As all of the proposed learning strategies follow the idea of cross-situational learning they try to estimate the correct word-object mappings through the registered co-occurrences of particular o-w pairs. Resultantly the influence of the sporadic introduction of 'invalid' samples has a similar effect on all of the tested strategies.

Common-sense suggests that the sporadic introduction of misleading samples should not disrupt the ability of the learner to grasp the language utilised by the teacher. Certainly, as the the 'deviated' samples are not common they can are treated as noise and filtered out easily. Additionally, the common-sense suggests also that frequent introduction of misleading samples should disrupt the ability of the learner to grasp the teacher's convention. Reversing the previous argument, as the 'deviated' samples are frequent then the correct ones tend to be treated as noise and are not properly enforced by the learners. Certainly this concludes that the observed and noted behaviour of the system seems to reflect perfectly the intuitively expected results. However, it seems against the common-sense that the learner is able to grasp the convention utilised by the teacher even in a case where more then half of the received samples are 'deviated'.

This interesting fact can be easily tracked for the basic type of agent - Frequent Learner (Sec. 4.4). Such a learner implicitly assumes that the o-w pair (o, w) with the highest frequency of co-occurrence is the adequate one, whilst all of the other $\forall_{o_i \in \mathcal{O}, o_i \neq o}(o_i, w)$ o-w pairs (concerning the word w) are incorrect. In particular this implies that the learner, in order to learn the proper naming convention (the one utilised by the teacher) needs to develop higher frequency values for the correct o-w pairs. As such, the probability that the learner will increase the proper association (o, w) is $P(o, w) = (1 - p_\epsilon) \times (p_o^c \times s_o^c)$, where $p_o^c = Pr(o \in \mathcal{X}_t^O ||| \mathcal{X}_t^O || = c)$ is the probability that object o appears in the current context and $s_o^c = Pr(o = \eta_t^A(t)|o \in \mathcal{X}_t^O \wedge || \mathcal{X}_t^O || = c)$ is the probability that object o is selected as topic from the current context. On the other hand the probability that the learner will increase the association between any other object then o and the word w is $P(o_i, w) = (1 - p_\epsilon) \times (p_{o_i, o}^c \times s_o^c) + p_\epsilon(p_{o_i, \neg o}^c \times s_o^{O-c})$, where $p_{o_i, o}^c = Pr(o_i \in \mathcal{X}_t^O \wedge o \in \mathcal{X}_t^O ||| \mathcal{X}_t^O || = c)$ is the probability that both o and o_i appear in the context, $p_{o_i, \neg o}^c = Pr(o_i \in \mathcal{X}_t^O \wedge o \notin \mathcal{X}_t^O ||| \mathcal{X}_t^O || = c)$ is the probability that object o_i appears in the context where there is no object o and $s_o^{O-c} = Pr(o = \eta_t^A(t) ||| \mathcal{X}_t^O || = c)$ is the probability of selecting object o as topic from objects outside of the current context. Further, if $P(o, w) > P(o_i, w)$ then on average the correct o-w pairs are more frequent and if $P(o, w) < P(o_i, w)$ then on avarage the incorrect o-w pairs are less frequent. Resultantly, in the former case the learner agent is able to learn the correct convention, whilst in the latter it is unable. These formulas can serve as a criterion for the system of learning agents to successfully align with a teacher agent, i.e. for a population of agents to incorporate a naming convention utilised by the teacher.

Further, the point where the probability of increasing a correct association is equal to the probability of increasing the incorrect association ($P(o, w) = P(o_i, w)$) represent the point of the phase shift, i.e. shift from the agreement to the disagreement. Assuming a system with 10 objects, 10 agents, context size 2, we can estimate[8] the aforementioned point to be roughly 78%. We can notice that the analytically obtained value is perfectly in-line with the simulation results (Fig 15).

8   Conclusions

This paper focuses on the studies of the key sub-process of the process of semiosis in artificial systems, namely individual semiosis. Utilising the multi-agent perspective and incorporating the strict language game model we show that a

---

[8] Due to limited space we do not provide detailed calculations.

population of agents can agree on a shared language. Moreover, we show that in a more relaxed settings, where the strict rule of common context is lessened to a case that allows sporadic deviations, the interacting population can still agree on a shared naming convention. Most importantly, we managed to pinpoint the phase transition in the alignment process that depends on the intensity of deviations happening in the system. As such, allowing to reason about the flexibility of learning strategies, for instance what are the requirements imposed on the system to maintain the ability to learn the naming convention utilised by the hearer.

In particular, the developed framework provides background that enables an effective and rapid evaluation of methods for establishing the joint context. For instance, allowing *the designer to make a qualitative assessment* in a situation of a choice between multiple methods. Consequently, the results provide ground for *making appropriate design decisions* that ensure optimal cost while meeting all of the fundamental requirements of the correct execution of the process of semiosis in an artificial system. As aforementioned, a pragmatic outcome of this research is the development of basic criteria for the proper design of multi-agent system that ensures the intended dynamics of the process of semiosis.

Moreover, it is interesting to study the possibility of the learner to infer, from the past interaction and current state of context perception, that a particular interplay involves deviation settings triggered by the teacher, i.e., due to the inability of the system to reach a joint attention between interacting partners. Such an extension should greatly increase the ability of the system to cope with the sporadic deviations from the basic interaction scheme. Allowing the learning population to align the language even in more frequent deviation.

Acknowledgments. This paper was partially supported by Polish Ministry of Science and Higher Education under grant no. N N519 407437.

References

1. Bloom, P.: How children learn the meanings of words. The MIT Press (2002)
2. Blythe, R.A., Smith, K., Smith, A.D.M.: Learning Times for Large Lexicons Through Cross-Situational Learning. Cognitive Science 34(4), 620–642 (2010)
3. DeBeule, J., DeVylder, B., Belpaeme, T.: A cross-situational learning algorithm for damping homonymy in the guessing game. In: Proceedings of ALIFE X. MIT Press (2006)
4. Droeschel, D., Stckler, J., Holz, D., Behnke, S.: Towards Joint Attention for a Domestic Service Robot Person Awareness and Gesture Recognition using Time-of-Flight Cameras. In: Proc. of the IEEE Int. Conference on Robotics and Automation (ICRA), Shanghai, China, pp. 1205–1210 (2011)
5. Harnad, S.: The symbol grounding problem. Physica D: Nonlinear Phenomena 42(1-3), 335–346 (1990)
6. Ito, M., Tani, J.: Joint attention between a humanoid robot and users in imitation game. In: Proc. of the 3rd Int. Conf. on Development and Learning (ICDL 2004), La Jolla, U.S.A. (2004)

7. Kaplan, F., Hafner, V.: The Challenges of Joint Attention. Interaction Studies 7, 67–74 (2004)

8. Lakoff, G., Johnson, M.: Philosoph in the Flesh: the Embodied Mind and its Challenge to Western Thought. Basic Books (1999)

9. Lorkiewicz, W., Katarzyniak, R.P.: Representing the Meaning of Symbols in Autonomous Agents. In: Intelligent Information and Database Systems, pp. 183–189. IEEE (2009)

10. Lorkiewicz, W., Kowalczyk, R., Katarzyniak, R., Vo, B.: On Topic Selection Strategies in Multi-Agent Naming Game. In: AAMAS 2011, pp. 499–506 (2011)

11. Lorkiewicz, W., Katarzyniak, R., Kowalczyk, R.: Deviating from Common Context in Individual Semiosis in Multi-Agent Systems. In: Wang, Y., Li, T. (eds.) ISKE2011. AISC, vol. 122, pp. 229–238. Springer, Heidelberg (2011)

12. Rosch, E., Mervis, C., Gray, W., Johnson, D., Boyes-Braem, P.: Basic objects in natural categories. Cogn. Psychol. 8, 382–439 (1976)

13. Saussure, F.: Course in General Linguistics. Open Court Pub. Co. (1986)

14. De Silva, P.R.S., Tadano, K., Lambacher, S.G., Herath, S.: Unsupervised approach to acquire robot joint attention. In: Proc. of the 4th International Conference on Autonomous Robots and Agents, pp. 601–606. IEEE (2009)

15. Siskind, J.M.: A computational study of cross-situational techniques for learning word-to-meaning mappings. Cognition 61(1-2), 39–91 (1996)

16. Smith, K., Smith, A.D.M., Blythe, R.A., Vogt, P.: Cross-Situational Learning: A Mathematical Approach. In: Vogt, P., Sugita, Y., Tuci, E., Nehaniv, C.L. (eds.) EELC 2006. LNCS (LNAI), vol. 4211, pp. 31–44. Springer, Heidelberg (2006)

17. Smith, L., Yu, C.: Infants rapidly learn word-referent mappings via cross-situational statistics. Cognition 106, 1558–1568 (2008)

18. Smith, K., Smith, A.D.M., Blythe, R.A.: Cross-Situational Learning: An Experimental Study of Word-Learning Mechanisms. Cognitive Science 35, 480–498 (2011)

19. Steels, L.: Language as a Complex Adaptive System. In: Schoenauer, M., Deb, K., Rudolph, G., Yao, X., Lutton, E., Merelo, J.J., Schwefel, H.-P. (eds.) PPSN VI. LNCS, pp. 17–26. Springer, Heidelberg (2000)

20. Steels, L.: Language Games for Autonomous Robots. IEEE Intelligent Systems (2001)

21. Steels, L.: The Naming Game. The Electricity Journal 11(9), 30–33 (2004)

22. Steels, L.: Modeling the Formation of Language in Embodied Agents: Methods and Open Challenges. In: Evolution of Communication and Language in Embodied Agents, pp. 223–233. Springer, Heidelberg (2010)

23. Quine, W.V.O.: Word and Object. MIT Press, Cambridge, MA (1960)

24. Vogt, P.: The emergence of compositional structures in perceptually grounded language games. Artificial Intelligence 167(1-2), 206–242 (2005)

25. Vogt, P.: The physical symbol grounding problem. Cognitive Systems Research 3(3), 429–457 (2002)

26. Yu, C., Smith, L.B.: Rapid Word Learning under Uncertainty via Cross-Situational Statistics. Psychological Science 18, 414–420 (2007)

27. Yurovsky, D., Yu, C.: Mutual Exclusivity in Cross-Situational Statistical Learning. In: Love, B.C., McRae, K., Sloutsky, V.M. (eds.) Proceedings of the 30th Annual Conference of the Cognitive Science Society, pp. 715–720. Cognitive Science Society, Austin (2008)

Evaluation of Multi-Agent Systems:
Proposal and Validation of a Metric Plan

Pierpaolo Di Bitonto, Maria Laterza, Teresa Roselli, and Veronica Rossano

Department of Computer Science, University of Bari
Via Orabona 4, 70125 Bari, Italy
{dibitonto,marialaterza,roselli,rossano}@di.uniba.it

Abstract. In the MAS evaluation research field there are still few works devoted to evaluating systems' efficacy, and none of these aimed to measure the adequacy of the MAS in terms of rationality, autonomy, reactivity and environment adaptability. A reliable evaluation method should be general enough to estimate the success of the multi-agent paradigm in different domains, measuring the performances of each single agent and then of the entire MAS. Moreover, it should be able to relate these measures to the environment complexity, that embodies the complexity of the problem solved by the MAS. In this paper a method for evaluating static multi-agent systems is presented and its validation described. The main novelties of the method are that it allows the MAS to be evaluated in the context of the environment in which it will operate, and its adequacy to the environment to be judged from the viewpoints of both the designer, wishful to measure the quality of the designed MAS, and the evaluator, wishful to verify the adequacy of several MASs in a specific context. A validation of the method is described, carried out by evaluating two MASs: the GeCo-Automotive system and a Multi-Agent Tourism Recommender system.

Keywords: Multi-agent system, Goal-Question-Metric, MAS evaluation.

1 Introduction

In the last few years the growing employment of Multi-Agent Systems (MASs) in several domains, including logistics, networking, automation, simulation and robotics, has provided the impetus for much research into new tools and methodologies for their design and implementation. Although researchers in the MAS field have proposed a huge number of solutions, there are still few works addressing valid methods for evaluating MASs.

MAS evaluation is a complex process that should take into account several dimensions, considering a MAS not only as an aggregation of single agents, but also as a system in which the agents must interact in order to solve problems.

A reliable evaluation method should be general enough to estimate the success of the multi-agent paradigm in different domains, measuring the performances of each agent and of the entire MAS, and should be able to relate these measures to the

N.T. Nguyen (Ed.): Transactions on CCI VII, LNCS 7270, pp. 198–221, 2012.

environment complexity. In fact, the environment complexity embodies the problem that needs to be solved by the MAS.

Against this background, the aim of our research is to define a method for evaluating static multi-agent systems consisting of a metric plan based on the Goal-Question-Metric paradigm [1] and a set of guidelines to interpret the results of the GQM application.

The metric plan allows measurement of the complexity of the environment where the agent acts, as well as the level of rationality, autonomy, reactivity, and adaptability to the environment exhibited by the MAS. The paper presents a MAS evaluation method that is an evolution of the first proposal described in [2]. The newest version is more detailed than the previous one, because it splits MAS characteristics and environment complexity into different evaluation dimensions. By comparing each MAS dimension with the relative environment complexity, the evaluator can gain a more accurate evaluation of the adequacy of the MAS to the environment.

One of the main novelties of the proposed method is that it merges two different approaches, namely intra-agent and inter-agent, to the analysis of multi-agent systems. The intra-agent approach analyses the MAS agent as an individual system, highlighting the internal structure, the beliefs, the goals, and the perceptions related to its environment. The inter-agent approach considers each single MAS agent as a part of a society and analyses its interaction with the other agents of the system and its environment. Moreover, a strong point of the proposed method is that it can be used for two evaluation purposes: on one hand, to estimate the adequacy of the MAS from the designer point of view, allowing this specialist to check whether the implemented MAS is adequate to cope with the problem constraints, and on the other, to estimate the adequacy of a MAS from the evaluator point of view, verifying which MAS, among a set of similar systems, is the best suited to solve a specific problem. In order to validate the method's independence of the problem domain and to investigate the efficacy of its application according to the different evaluation goals (designer vs. evaluator), two MASs have been evaluated: GeCo-Automotive [3] and a Multi-Agent Recommender for Tourism [4]. The former aims at developing an ICT environment to manage small-medium sized company knowledge about automotive spare parts; this MAS is evaluated from the designer point of view, since the authors are the designers of the system. On the other hand, the Multi-Agent Recommender for Tourism [4], that aims to promote tourism in Argentina, is evaluated from the evaluator point of view in order to measure the adequacy of this system to a specific context in which the evaluator wishes to use it. It is important to notice that, the Multi-Agent Recommender for Tourism, developed by Casali et al. [4], is evaluated only to show how the defined GQM could be applied in order to verify if a MAS is adequate to a specific environment problem.

The paper is organized as follows: section 2 discusses some related works about the evaluation of multi-agent systems; section 3 presents the defined metric plan, using the GQM paradigm; section 4 describes the guidelines to interpret the metric plan measures, relating these measures to the environment complexity; sections 5 and 6 describe the application of the defined method to the two MASs. Finally, some conclusions and future research directions are outlined.

2   Related Works

Analysis of the literature shows that several approaches have been proposed to evaluate MAS quality. The first proposed approaches stem directly from the field of software engineering because the agent-based paradigm was originally considered as an evolution of object-oriented programming (the agents are often implemented using object-oriented programming languages). In this perspective, the aspects evaluated are only related to the software quality of each single agent. Higher level characteristics such as MAS organizational models or interaction among agents are still not considered. The most popular metrics collected in the suite of metrics for O.O. design are those proposed by Chidamber and Kemerer [5]. These metrics, based on object-oriented programming key concepts (class, method, inheritance, coupling), measure the software quality in terms of coupling between object classes, depth of the inheritance tree and so forth [6]. For example, the metric coupling between object classes measures how many classes each class is coupled with. It allows estimation of both the reusability and the software code efficiency, because a high coupling value between classes will mean that there is low modularity and reusability. These metrics seem too low-level to be meaningful for agent-based systems [7], but the next, higher level approaches allow estimation only of some aspects of MAS such as the architecture and communication among agents, considered mainly as distributed systems. For example, in [8], Król and Zelmozer focus attention on the structural performance of multi-agent platforms. In particular, they consider only Java RMI implementations and define metrics such as the connection cost metric, serving to predict how well different implementations are suited to various network configurations and environments. In [9] the intent is to propose a set of metrics for measuring the communication among MAS agents in order to detect reasons for an unbalanced communication. But, as emphasized in [10], the current trend in the MAS evaluation field should go beyond the hardware and software implementations. For this reason, the authors propose an approach that captures the messages exchanged by the application agents and extracts useful information serving to draw a communication graph. On the basis of this graph they calculate the value of metrics such as the degree of communication, the number of agents involved in communication, the network mean traffic, and so on. Following this trend, the newest research works have aimed at defining metrics for measuring higher level characteristics of MASs. In their recent work [11], Lass et al. survey existing metrics employed to estimate MASs, provide an evaluation framework for applying them and use this framework to compare the performances of some distributed algorithms. They classify the metrics as environment/host metrics and system metrics. The first ones describe the MAS environment (i.e. the physical world in the case of a robot, or users, services and other MAS agents in the case of a software agent) and allow the environment complexity to be measured. The second ones measure macroscopic aspects of the MAS as a whole, and therefore describe the overall behavior of the MAS. The evaluation framework consists of three main steps: selection, collection and application. In the selection step the evaluator chooses the metrics to be used to evaluate the MAS. In the collection step the measures are collected. Finally, in the application step, the measures collected are used to assess whether the MAS meets the evaluation objectives, or is better than another one. Because of the huge number of existing metrics and ways to apply them, the authors suggest the use of Basili's GQM approach [1] to decide which metrics are most usefully measured in their MAS. The work lacks a ready-to-use metric plan that could be adopted to measure and compare them. Moreover, although evaluating MASs seems to be very important in order to be able to predict the MAS performance and to design systems suited to various environments, MAS characteristics such as rationality, autonomy, reactivity and the environment's adaptability are still not evaluated and no approaches have yet been described in literature that are able to evaluate both the characteristics of the agents in the MAS and the characteristics of the overall MAS. For all these reasons, in [2] we proposed a MAS evaluation method that differs from the other approaches cited in literature in four principal ways. Firstly, it proposes the use of high-level metrics to evaluate the MAS, and emphasizes the measurements of agent characteristics such as rationality, autonomy, reactivity and adaptability to the environment. Secondly, the defined method merges two MAS evaluation perspectives: inter-agent and intra-agent. The inter-agent evaluation considers the overall MAS (cooperation and communication among agents), whereas the intra-agent evaluation considers the internal structure of each single agent (in terms of its ability to learn, planning capabilities, and so on). Thirdly, it provides a metric plan for assessing MASs. Fourthly, the method allows a MAS to be evaluated from the viewpoints of both the designer, wishful to measure the quality of the designed MAS, and the evaluator, wishful to verify the adequacy of several MASs in a specific context.

3   The Metric Plan

In [2], a metric plan based on the GQM approach is described. This means that the MAS assessment can be made independently of its specific implementation and context of use. The plan has five goals. The first assesses the complexity of the environment where the MAS operates, while the other four allow assessment of important features of an agent or of the whole MAS, namely the autonomy, reactivity, rationality and adaptability to the environment. For each of the five goals, questions and metrics are defined to allow assessment to be made of the complexity of the environment, or the MAS feature under study (in this paper the questions are not reported for the sake of brevity). These questions and metrics make it possible to evaluate firstly the agents as single units and then the MAS as a whole. In [9], Russell and Norvig define the environment as the problem that the agent is there to solve. When the problem is complex, the single agent approach may be insufficient, or unable to solve it. In such cases, it may be better or necessary to solve the problem via a multi-agent approach, using a set of agents that interact among themselves or with other system components to find the solution. In these cases, the environment is the complex problem to be solved, and the MAS is the solution. In the real world, complex problems are continually being posed. Although different problems may have a different complexity, it should be noted that even the same problem can be considered at different complexity levels. In this way, problem solving depends not only on the type of problem but also on the choice of the level of complexity at which it needs to be solved. For example, let us consider the problem of teaching English. It could be solved using a MAS that considers the students' knowledge level to be determined entirely by the results of questionnaire tests. Otherwise, the choice may be to use a MAS that takes into account the results of a questionnaire test as the basis for further reasoning which may lead to identification of the students' "true" knowledge of the language. Evaluating a MAS that solves the problem of teaching English independently of the environment would be meaningless. For this reason, the evaluation must relate the values obtained in the assessment of the MAS characteristics (autonomy, reactivity, rationality and adaptability) to the complexity of the environment. One of the problems encountered in defining the metric plan was the different definitions used in literature not only to refer to the environment but also to the internal characteristics of the MAS. To avoid the risk of ambiguity in defining the metric plan, a definition of both the characteristics and evaluation lines considered for each goal is provided, as well as the measurements to be made (or calculated) to estimate them.

3.1   Goal 1: The Environment Complexity

According to Russell and Norvig [12] an environment can be classified on the basis of various lines: its observability, the effect the agent's actions have on the environment, the time, the number of agents, the way the environment is perceived by the agents and the way it evolves. The number and subjectivity of these lines makes it difficult to characterize the environment. It is easy to identify which environment is the most complex, but if it presents other combinations of these properties it will be difficult to define its complexity. Moreover, these properties are not always enough to characterize the environment and the effect the agents' interactions will have on it. In the defined method the complexity of the agent and of the MAS environments is assessed on the basis of three different parameters, namely: **Inaccessibility**, **Instability**, and **Complexity of the Interaction**.

The parameters are measured for each single agent (intra-agent perspective) and for the entire MAS (inter-agent perspective). Thus, the agent environment complexity (metric: *AgEnvCompl*) is the mean of the values obtained for each parameter measured from the intra-agent perspective, and the MAS environment complexity (metric: *MASEnvCompl*) is the mean of the AgEnvCompl values measured from the inter-agent perspective.

Inaccessibility. The Inaccessibility parameter expresses the difficulty in gaining complete access at any instant to the resources in its environment. Such resources include the environment components (e.g. web services, DBMS, etc.) or data (e.g. metadata, ontologies, etc.). The more difficult the access to the resources, the more complex the environment. In such circumstances it is necessary to adopt strategies to deal with this inaccessibility. For example, when driving a taxi, environment resources include pedestrians that may suddenly cross the road under the taxi wheels. If the light is poor, the pedestrians are less visible so the taxi driver must have the lights on full beam and pay even closer attention to avoid running them down. In the proposed assessment method, the environment inaccessibility is evaluated using the metrics: **CompInacc** and **ResInacc**, that assess the inaccessibility of the agent environment components and data; and **AgInacc** and **MASInacc**, that represent the inaccessibility of the agent and the MAS environment, respectively.

- *CompInacc* assesses the inaccessibility of the agent environment components (DBMS, other MAS agents with which it interacts, etc.). For each component CompInacc is 1 if the inaccessibility is high, 0.5 if it is medium, 0 if low. The agent overall value is the mean of the measured values.
- *ResInacc* assesses the inaccessibility of the agent environment data (metadata, ontologies, etc). For each type of datum, ResInacc is 1 if the inaccessibility is high, 0.5 if it is medium, 0 if low. The overall value is the mean of the measured values.

In the intra-agent perspective the environment inaccessibility is evaluated using the AgInacc, that is the mean of the previous metrics.

Finally, in order to evaluate the MAS environment inaccessibility (inter-agent perspective), *MASInacc* is used. This is the mean of the *AgInacc* measures for all the MAS agents. The value of *MASInacc* can range between [0-1]. If $MASInacc \in [0\text{-}0.3]$ then the value is low, if $MASInacc \in [0.3\text{-}0.6]$ it is medium, and if above, the MAS environment inaccessibility is high.

Instability. The Instability parameter expresses the way the environment evolves, and how fast. In other words, the difficulty in perceiving changes in the environment. The faster and more unpredictably the environment changes, the more complex it is. In such cases, the agent must have mechanisms to perceive these rapid changes. The environment instability is assessed using the metrics: **Time**, **Dynam** and **NumEffeAct**. **AgInstab** and **MASInstab** represent the measures from the intra-agent and inter-agent perspectives, respectively.

- *Time* is the time taken to pass from one state to another. This passage can be continuous or intermittent. Clearly, an environment that evolves continually is more complex than one that evolves intermittently at set times. The evaluator identifies the agent environment (components, data, other agents) and sees whether the passage from one state to another occurs continually or intermittently. If it occurs continually, the evaluator will assign a value of 1, otherwise 0. The Time overall value is the mean of measured values for all the environment resources.
- *Dynam* is the speed at which the environment passes from one state to another, in other words the rapidity of change. The passage may be static, in the sense that the environment does not change while the agent is thinking or acting, or dynamic if the environment is changing even while the agent is thinking or acting. If the environment is dynamic it is necessary to keep it under observation while the agent is deciding how to act or it is acting, and also to take account of time. If the environment is dynamic, the value 1 is assigned to each environment component and data, otherwise 0. The Dynam overall value is the mean of the measured values for all the environment resources.

- *NumEffeAct* assesses how unpredictable changes of the environment are as a result of actions taken by the agents. If an agent's actions can have different effects, then the environment will be more unpredictable and so more complex. Let us consider the case in which an agent proposes teaching materials to a student. Of all the material available, the agent chooses to propose some dealing with the solution of second degree equations. The proposal of this material can have different effects on the student's learning depending on whether s/he already has some knowledge of the topic and on other unpredictable factors. For each agent, the evaluator lists the main possible actions and for each action, the possible different effects. If the action can have several effects the action will be scored 1, otherwise 0. The NumEffeAct overall value is the mean of the measured values for all the agent's actions.

From the intra-agent perspective the environment instability is measured by *AgInstab* metric, that is the mean of the previous metrics.

Finally, the MAS environment instability (inter-agent perspective) is measured by *MASInstab*, that is the mean of the *AgInstab* values. The value of *MASInstab* can range between [0-1]. If *MASInstab*∈ [0-0.3] then the value is low, if *MASInstab*∈ [0.3-0.6] it is medium, and if above, the instability of the MAS environment is high.

Complexity of the Interaction. The Complexity of the Interaction expresses how complex the interactions between agents are in the MAS. The more complex they are, the more needful it is to make predictions and activate coordination mechanisms or competitive strategies. Three metrics are used to assess the complexity of interaction: *CompGrad*, *CoopGrad* and *Tr&RepMod*. *AgComplInt* and *MASComplInt* represent the measures from the intra-agent and inter-agent perspectives, respectively.

- *CompGrad* is the degree of competition between the agent and the other MAS agents. The evaluator checks whether the agent competes with another agent to solve the problem; if so, the value 1 is assigned, if not 0. The agent overall value is the mean of the measured values.
- *CoopGrad* is the degree of cooperation between the agent and the other MAS agents. The evaluator checks whether the agent cooperates with another agent or not, and assigns the value of 1 if so, 0 if not. The agent overall value is the mean of the measured values.
- *Tr&RepMod* assesses the need to use trust and reputation models to verify the reliability of the data and behavior of the components in the environment. If it is necessary to use such models the value of 1 is assigned to the metric Tr&RepMod, if not, 0.

From the intra-agent perspective the complexity of interaction is measured by *AgComplInt* metric, that is the mean of the previous metrics.

Finally, the MAS complexity of interaction (inter-agent perspective) is measured by *MASComplInt*, that is the mean of the *AgComplInt* values. The value of *MASComplInt* can range between [0-1]. If *MASComplInt* ∈[0-0.3] then the value is low, if *MASComplInt* ∈[0.3-0.6] it is medium, and if above, the complexity of interaction is high.

3.2   Goal 2: The Rationality

Russell and Norvig in [12] define the rationality of an agent as its ability to take actions that can maximize its success. This ability varies according to the performance metrics, the perception sequence, the knowledge of the environment and the actions the agent can accomplish. In the defined metric plan the degree of rationality was evaluated according to two parameters: **Mode of Choice of the Actions** and **Maximization of the Success**. The parameters are measured for each single agent (intra-agent perspective) and for the entire MAS (inter-agent perspective).

Thus, the agent rationality degree (metric: *AgRatio*) is the mean of the values obtained for each parameter measured from the intra-agent perspective, and the MAS rationality degree (metric: *MASRatio*) is the mean of the AgRatio values measured from the inter-agent perspective.

Mode of Choice of the Actions. This parameter expresses the degree of rationality in choosing the actions to be performed. It is assessed using the metrics: *AgType*, *PlaConstr*, *LearAb* and *InsMod*. Then the metrics *AgModChAct* and *MASModChAct* are calculated.

- *AgType* is the type of agent (simple, stimulus-response, and goal-based agent). Different types have different degrees of rationality. For example, an agent of stimulus-response type shows no rationality because its actions are pre-established by the designer: each sequence of perceptions corresponds to a specific action or series of actions. Instead, a goal-based agent needs to achieve goals and so, at each turn, will choose the actions to be executed to achieve the goal or goals. The evaluator assesses the agent type, and if it is of simple or stimulus-response type the metric AgType will be assigned the value 0, whereas if it is goal-based it will be scored 1.
- *PlaConstr* assesses the agent's ability to build plans of action. If it can do so this is an index of a greater rationality and the value assigned will be 1, 0 if not.
- *LearAb* evaluates the agent's ability to learn. An agent that can learn is considered more rational, then the value of 1 will be assigned, otherwise 0.
- *InsMod* is the agent's possession of an internal model of the actions and intentions of the other MAS agents. An agent that takes into account these factors is more rational, so the metric will be scored 1, otherwise 0.

From the intra-agent perspective the degree of rationality in choosing the actions is measured by the *AgModChAct* metric, that is the mean of the previous metrics.

Finally, the MAS degree of rationality in choosing the actions to be performed (inter-agent perspective) is measured by *MASModChAct*, that is the mean of the *AgModChAct* values. The value of *MASModChAct* can range between [0-1]. If *MASModChAct* $\in$ [0-0.3] then the value is low, if *MASModChAct* $\in$ [0.3-0.6] it is medium, and if above, the rationality is high.

Maximization of the Success. The Maximization of the Success parameter expresses the ability to maximize the expected result of the actions. It is measured by the metric *AgMaxSucc* (from the intra-agent perspective).

- *AgMaxSucc* measures the gap between the expected result of the agent's actions and the result obtained. To calculate this metric, for each agent n intervals of observation lasting t seconds are defined. For each interval, the agent's perception sequence is derived, as well as the knowledge of the environment possessed. The possible agent's actions are defined as a function of the state it is in and the expected results on the environment in the observation interval. These results must be expressed in numerical terms. After establishing the expected result, the actual result on the environment caused by the agent's action is observed. These two outcomes are compared using the following expression: (|val.expect-val.obtain.|)/base where base is a numerical value that can normalize the value on a scale from 0 to 1. It is important to choose an optimal but realistic estimate of the agent's performance as the expected value. The base value depends on the choice of the range of expected and obtained results. After calculating the discrepancy, the value of AgMaxSucc is calculated as the mean discrepancy on the basis of the number of intervals considered. If the obtained result is equal to the expected result, the value of AgMaxSucc is 0, indicating maximum success.

Finally, the MAS ability to maximize the success (inter-agent perspective) is measured by *MASMaxSucc*, that is the mean of the *AgMaxSucc* values. The value of *MASMaxSucc* can range between [0-1]. If *MASMaxSucc* $\in$ [0-0.3] then the value is low, if *MASMaxSucc* $\in$ [0.3-0.6] it is medium, and if above, the ability level is high.

3.3   Goal 3: The Autonomy

According to Wooldridge [13], autonomy is the property that most strictly characterizes the agent. This refers to its ability to act without the need for human intervention or actions by other agents. In the defined metric plan the degree of autonomy was evaluated according to two parameters: **Proactivity** and **Autonomy in the Organizational Structure**. Like the previous ones, these parameters are measured using both perspectives: intra-agent and inter-agent.

Thus, the agent autonomy value (metric: *AgAuto*) is the mean of values obtained for each parameter measured from the intra-agent perspective, and the MAS autonomy value (metric: *MASAuto*) is the mean of the AgAuto values measured from the inter-agent perspective.

Proactivity. A key element of autonomy is proactivity, in other words the ability to "take the initiative" rather than simply acting in response to the environment. Proactivity includes the agents' capacity to exhibit behaviour directed both to satisfying their goals, and to anticipating future situations, making predictions.

The Proactivity parameter is assessed using the metrics *MoreRol*, *NegAg*, *DiaErPrAb* and *ComAutAb*. The metrics *AgProact* and *MASProact* allow the proactivity to be estimated from the intra and inter-agent perspectives, respectively.

- *MoreRol* measures whether the agent can play several roles to solve the problem and whether this passage from one role to another was pre-established by the designer or is decided autonomously by the agent depending on particular factors in the environment. It is assigned value 0 if the agent plays only one role or, although it plays more than one role, the passage from one to the other is pre-established, and the value 1 if it passes autonomously from one to another.

- *NegAg* is the agent's ability to negotiate the assignment of tasks or resources with the other MAS agents; if it can it is more autonomous than one that does not possess this ability. The value 1 is assigned if it can negotiate, 0 if not.
- *DiaErPrAb* is the agent's ability to diagnose errors and/or problems during execution of the tasks; an agent that can diagnose errors and/or problems is more proactive than one that cannot. The evaluator assesses whether the agent has diagnostic powers and if so, assigns the value of 1, 0 if not.
- *ComAutAb* is the agent's ability to undertake and autonomously conduct communication with the other MAS agents. If the agent can do so, it will be assigned the value of 1, if not then 0.

From the intra-agent perspective the proactivity value is measured by the *AgProact* metric, that is the mean of the metrics described above.

Instead, the MAS proactivity value (inter-agent perspective) is measured using the metric *MASProact*, that is the mean of the *AgProact* values. The value of *MASProact* can range between [0-1]. If $MASProact \in [0\text{-}0.3]$ then the value is low, if $MASProact \in [0.3\text{-}0.6]$ it is medium, and if above, the proactivity value is high.

Autonomy in the Organizational Structure. The parameter Autonomy in the Organizational Structure expresses the degree of autonomy of action within the MAS organization. To assess this parameter two metrics were used: **PosStr**, and **SharTask**. The metrics **AgAutoOrg** and **MASAutoOrg** represent the autonomy of the agent and of the MAS in the organizational structure, respectively.

- *PosStr* assesses whether the agent occupies a subordinate position in the MAS or not. If it does then it will be less autonomous. For each agent, if it occupies a subordinate position as compared to another MAS agent, the evaluator will assign value 0, if not, then 1. The value of the metric PosStr is the mean of the obtained measures.
- *SharTask* evaluates whether the agent shares tasks with the other MAS agents. If so, its actions will be less autonomous than those of an agent that does not do any sharing. The evaluator lists the main agent's tasks and for each task the value 0 will be assigned if the agent shares the task with other agents, 1 if not. The value of the metric SharTask is the mean of the assigned values.

From the intra-agent perspective the autonomy in the organization is assessed by *AgAutoOrg*, and is the mean of the previous metrics. The total value of the MAS agents for autonomy in the organization (*MASAutoOrg*) is the mean of the *AgAutoOrg* measures. This value can range between [0-1]. If the value $\in [0\text{-}0.3]$ then the autonomy is low, if the value $\in [0.3\text{-}0.6]$ it is medium, and if above, the autonomy in the organizational structure is high.

3.4   Goal 4: The Reactivity

Most of the proposals for classifying agents present in the literature [14] consider a reactive agent to be an agent that lacks internal states programmed to make the action to be accomplished according with a perception sequence. In the metric plan, reactivity is considered as the ability to perceive the environment and respond in a timely fashion to changes in it. This quality is assessed by taking into account the **Effectiveness of Acquisition of Perceptions** and the **Rapidity of Response in a Timely Fashion**. Both the parameters are measured for each single agent (intra-agent perspective) and for the entire MAS (inter-agent perspective).

The agent reactivity level (metric: *AgReact*) is the mean of the values obtained for the assessment parameters. The mean of the *AgReact* values for all the MAS agents is the reactivity value of the entire MAS (metric: *MASReact*).

Effectiveness of Acquisition of Perceptions. The parameter *Effectiveness of Acquisition of Perceptions* expresses how well the surrounding environment is perceived. This ability is measured with the metric *AgEffAcqPerc*.

- *AgEffAcqPerc* assesses the agent's ability to use the sensors to perceive the relevant components and data in the environment. To measure this ability, firstly the relevant components and data are identified. For example, to solve a problem where it is important for the agent to perceive a user query, the relevant datum is the query. Then, the agent's sensors are examined and which environmental components or data are perceived by the sensors is verified. If the agent perceives all the relevant components and data, a value of 1 will be assigned to metric *AgEffAcqPerc*, otherwise 0.

The value of *MASEffAcqPerc* indicates the whole MAS efficacy of perception of its environment, being the sum of the values obtained for the metric *AgEffAcqPerc* divided by the agents making up the MAS. This value ranges between 0 and 1.

Rapidity of Response in a Timely Fashion. This parameter measures how fast each single agent, and the whole MAS, can respond to environmental needs. The metrics defined for assessing this parameter are: *PercQual*, *DefBeh*, *InsMod*, and *ComMin*; the metrics *AgRapRespTimFash* and *MASRapRespTimFash* represent the rapidity of the agent and of the overall MAS, respectively.

- *PercQual* measures how well the perceptions are processed, working on the assumption that an agent that can process its perceptions of the environment to a refined degree will take time to do this and will therefore be slower than an agent that does not. The same applies when assessing the MAS as a whole. For each agent, the evaluator identifies its sensors and checks whether they process crude perceptions, for example by choosing the most significant perceptions or aggregating large perception sequences. If this processing occurs the value 0 will be assigned, otherwise 1.
- *DefBeh* ascertains whether the agent's reactions were pre-established by the designer. Such agents have faster reactions to the environment than agents that

need to reason before acting. If the actions are pre-established by the designer, the value 1 is assigned to the metric, 0 otherwise.

- *InsMod* assesses the agent's possession of an internal model of the actions and intentions of the other MAS agents. An agent that takes these into account is slower to react than an agent that does not. If the agent possesses such a model, metric InsMod is given value 0, otherwise 1.
- *ComMin* is the minimization of communication; in other words the agent's ability to carry out tasks or goals with minimal communication with other agents, since this would increase the response times. For this purpose, n intervals of time are defined, each interval lasting time t with the number gr of goals achieved in interval t. Then the mean number of messages exchanged to achieve the goal is calculated. If this value is equal to or less than the previously defined expected value, *ComMin* has a value of 1, otherwise 0.

From the intra-agent perspective, the value for the agent rapidity is calculated using the metric *AgRapRespTimFash*; this is the mean of the values assigned to the three parameters.

The speed of the whole MAS response (MASRapRespTimFash) is the mean of the AgAutoOrg measures. This value ranges from 0 to 1. If the value 0 is assigned it means that the MAS is slow to respond to the environment, whereas 1 shows maximum rapidity of response.

3.5   Goal 5: The Adaptability to the Environment

Since the environmental conditions can change rapidly, the agent (and the entire MAS) must be able to adapt to these changes. This involves being able to modify the plan of actions to be undertaken to achieve the goal and in some cases, also the possibility of changing the short term goal if pursuit of this would lead to failure to achieve the main goal.

The adaptability is evaluated by taking into account the **Ability to Respond to new External Stimuli** and the **Ability to Manage Different Situations**.

These parameters are measured for each single agent (intra-agent perspective) and for the entire MAS (inter-agent perspective). At the end of the assessment both the agent and the MAS adaptability level can be calculated. The first (*AgAdapt*) is the mean of the values obtained for each evaluation parameter from the intra-agent perspective; the second (*MASAdapt*) is the mean of the AgAdapt values measured from the inter-agent perspective.

Ability to Respond to New External Stimuli. The parameter represents the ability to respond to changes of the environment. This capacity has been evaluated using the metrics *CorrChangReact* and *RightRol*; the metrics *AgAbRespExtStim* and *MASAbRespExtStim* allow calculation of the agent's and MAS ability to respond to changes in the environment, respectively.

- *CorrChangReact* evaluates the correlation between the agent's reactions and the changes in the environment. The evaluator identifies which components belong to the agent's environment. It observes and verifies, during the problem resolution process, the harmony between the change of the environment and the agent's reactions during the time t intervals defined. If there is a high relationship the evaluator assigns the value 1 to the metric CorrChangReact, otherwise 0. For example, in taxi-driving an environment component could be an avalanche sliding down the street. An agent that is able to respond to new external stimuli should change the path of the taxi.

- *RightRol* is the agent's ability to change roles during problem resolution according to changes in the environment. If the agent has this ability the value 1 is assigned to the metric, otherwise 0.

Finally, the agent's ability level (***AgAbRespExtStim***) is the mean of the parameter values; instead, ***MASAbRespExtStim*** calculates the MAS ability to respond to new external stimuli. This value is the mean of the metric AgAbilRespExtStim of all MAS agents and can range from 0 to 1. If the value $\in [0\text{-}0.3]$ then the ability to respond to changes of the environment is low, if the value $\in [0.3\text{-}0.6]$ it is medium and if above, this ability is high.

Ability to Manage Different Situations. This parameter measures the ability to cope with different and unpredictable situations. It is evaluated using ***LearAb***, ***EurFinAb***, and ***ExcManAb***. ***AgAbManFiffSit*** and ***MASAbManDiffSit*** measure the agent's and MAS ability to cope with different and unpredictable situations.

- The *LearAb* metric is the same one used to evaluate the agent's rationality. It is alsoused in the adaptability to the environment evaluation because if an agent is able to learn, it can use its experience to manage unusual and unpredictable situations.
- *EurFinAb* calculates the agent's effectiveness in finding suitable heuristics for achieving the goals (for goal-oriented agents) or performing tasks (for non goal-oriented agents). Its value is calculated by comparing the average number of messages sent by the agent to obtain useful information (*vmr*) and the number of messages sent by the agent in the environment expected by the evaluator (*va*). If $vmr > va$ the metric EurFinAb has a value of 0, otherwise it will be 1.
- *ExcManAb* measures the agent's effectiveness in handling exceptions. This effectiveness is calculated by comparing the number of exceptions managed by the code of each single agent (*nem*) and the number of exceptions the agent is expected to manage (*ea*). If $nem \geq ea$ ExcManAb has a value of 1, otherwise 0.

Finally, the agent's capacity to manage different situations (***AgAbManFiffSit***) is the mean of the previous measures, while the MAS capacity (***MASAbManDiffSit***) is the mean of the values assigned for AgAbManFiffSit to all MAS agents. The value of *MASAbManDiffSit* ranges from 0 to 1. If *MASAbManDiffSit* $\in [0\text{-}0.3]$ then the value is low, if *MASAbManDiffSit* $\in [0.3\text{-}0.6]$ it is medium and if above, the value is high.

4   Guidelines for Interpreting the Metric Plan Measures

The metric plan illustrated above allows the complexity of the MAS environment and several MAS characteristics to be measured, but does not enable assessment of its adequacy to the environment where it operates. For this purpose, it is necessary to define some guidelines to compare the evaluation of the environment with that of the MAS, and to go into the details of the parameters considered for both the MAS environment evaluation and the entire MAS itself.

Rationality (Goal 2) vs. Environment Complexity (Goal 1). In an environment with a high level of inaccessibility it is difficult to have access to the resources, and so it would be better for the MAS to use planning and learning strategies and to be able to keep an internal state of the environment. In the case of environments with a medium or low inaccessibility level, a medium and low level of rationality when choosing the actions is acceptable.

Moreover, in an environment in which the resources are difficult to access it would be difficult for the MAS to maximize the success. For this reason a medium level of this ability is acceptable. In any case, according to the importance that this ability has in the domain where the MAS will be used, the evaluator can decide if a low level is acceptable. On the contrary, if the environment is characterized by a low level of inaccessibility, it should be high.

In addition, even in an environment with a high level of instability it would be better if the MAS used planning and learning strategies (high value of Mode of Choice of the Actions), because in this way it can face environment evolutions. Nevertheless, if the response time is a critical factor for the environment, a medium level of rationality when choosing the actions is acceptable. Instead, an environment with a low level of instability does not impose constraints as regards this value.

As to the maximization of the success value, it should be high in an unstable environment because this means that the results obtained by the MAS are close to the expected ones. However, since it is difficult to obtain this in an unstable environment, a medium value is acceptable. On the contrary, for a stable environment a high value is expected.

When the value of the interaction complexity is high, a high value of rationality in choosing the actions to be performed will be necessary. Otherwise, both values could be low. Moreover, in a complex environment it would be better to have a high level of ability to maximize the success.

Autonomy (Goal 3) vs. Environment Complexity (Goal 1). In an environment with a high level of inaccessibility it is difficult to have access to the resources, so a medium/high level of proactivity can facilitate access to the resources in order to be able to adopt strategies to deal with the lack of accessibility. For example, if a MAS agent is not able to access a web service due to Internet connection problems, a proactive attitude can allow the necessary information to be found in the cache memory. A medium/high level of proactivity is also necessary in the case of a high level of complexity of interaction, because in an environment in which the agents have to cooperate or compete, proactivity is important. Otherwise, if the environment has a medium or low level of inaccessibility or complexity of interaction, low levels of proactivity are acceptable. Finally, the autonomy of the MAS agents in the organizational structure is not related to the inaccessibility level, nor to the degree of complexity of the interaction, because it depends on the MAS organization structure.

Reactivity (Goal 4) vs. Environment Complexity (Goal 1). The effectiveness of acquisition of perceptions is related to all the complexity parameters of the environment and is one of the necessary conditions for the MAS to be able to react to its environment. For this reason, its value should always be high. Instead, the ability to respond in a timely fashion is not related to the inaccessibility, nor to the interaction complexity, but depends on the instability values. If the instability is high a high rapidity value is necessary.

Adaptability (Goal 5) vs. Environment Complexity (Goal 1). In an environment with a high level of inaccessibility, regardless of the environment instability level unpredictable situations could occur, so the ability of MAS agents to respond to new external stimuli should be high. If the inaccessibility is medium, the ability to respond to new external stimuli can also be medium and so on. The ability to manage different situations is related to both the environment inaccessibility, because this ability supports the agent in gaining complete access to the resources, and the instability, because an increased instability level will mean that an increased number of different situations needs to be managed. For the same reason, the ability to manage different situations and the inaccessibility are also related and so should have the same values.

Moreover, the ability to manage different situations is related to the instability because an increased instability will result in an increased number of different situations to be managed. If the instability is high, a high value for the ability to manage different situations is needed, if it is medium a medium value is sufficient, and so forth. The capacity to respond to external stimuli is not related to the interaction complexity, whereas the ability to manage different situations is.

An environment with a high level of complexity has complex interactions (collaborative or competitive) that do not depend on the behavior of each single agent, but also on the community of agents. For this reason a good capacity to manage different situations is needed. The higher the complexity, the higher this capacity should be.

5   Evaluation of GeCo-Automotive System

GeCo-Automotive MAS has been evaluated from the designer point of view. The evaluation goal was to verify the adequacy of the MAS to the environment it was designed for.

5.1   GeCo-Automotive System

The GeCo-Automotive MAS aims at developing an ICT environment to manage small-medium-sized company knowledge about automotive spare parts. It is an ICT environment prototype integrating functionalities for the analysis and management of the human resources, skills, management of training activities and of documentation. The GeCo-Automotive environment was designed to respond to the knowledge and training requirements of the different professional figures involved in the automotive sector, providing personalized solutions for the work context, skills and tasks of each individual user. The system architecture (shown in Fig. 1) includes two repositories, two components and two static agents: (I) the Learning Object Repository (LOR) named e-TER that manages the Learning Objects [15], their description, and relative publication; (II) the Document Management System (DMS) is a set of tools, software and hardware, that allows management of digital documents (experience or good practices), building and sharing within an organization; (III) the Document Repository (DR) that contains the documents; (IV) the Skill Gap Analysis (SGAS) component that allows the user to self-assess her/his knowledge and to be evaluated by colleagues, on the basis of these evaluations the SGAS component builds the user model; (V) the Learning Management System (LMS) component manages the use of LOs, choosing them according to their content and the user model; (VI) a Classifier Agent that classifies teaching and documentary resources; (VII) a Search Agent that selects the teaching and documentary resources.

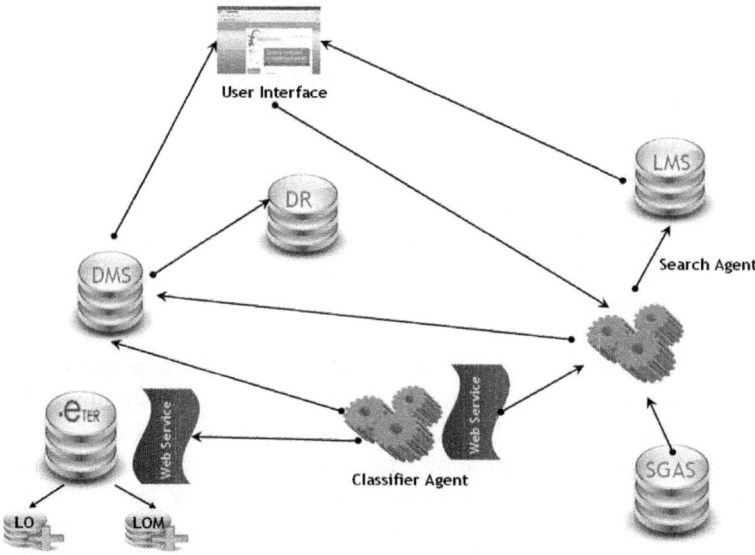

Fig. 1. Geco-Automotive architecture

The sensors of the classifier agent, even if in an embryonic state, are two web services that allow the agent to perceive the resources within repositories, whereas the agent actuator is the web service that sends the research agent the set of classified resources. In the same way, the research agent sensors are web services through which the agent perceives the user model built by the SGAS component, the classification of the resources built by the classifier agent, the association of teaching resources - user competences built by the LMS, and the set of user interface functions that allows the agent to perceive the queries inserted by the user. The agent actuator is the set of interface functions that the agent uses to propose the resources in response to searches by the user.

The MAS acts in the following way. The classifier agent accesses, by web services, e-TER and the DMS, then it catalogs all the resources on the basis of their descriptions and of previously defined taxonomies. In particular, the documents are classified on the basis of the document descriptions produced by the DR. The LOs are classified on the basis of the taxonomy of the resources, defined according to the LOM Educational category [3].

The catalogued resources are available through web services to the search agent that can make semantic searches for the resources. The search agent selects from the set of available resources those that best suit the user's specific needs. To provide this service, it uses the knowledge about the user (stored in the user model built by the SGAS component), the organization of the resources (expressed using decision rules inside the knowledge base of the agent itself), and its perception of the user's query gained by processing the syntax.

5.2   Environment Complexity Evaluation

The classifier agent environment is composed of different components (the Document Management System that manages the documents, the Repository e-TER that contains the LOs, and the search agent) and data (document and LOs metadata and related ontologies). The inaccessibility, measured as the difficulty in gaining complete access to each single component at any moment, is low, whereas the inaccessibility of data, measured in terms of the incompleteness of the metadata, is medium because the information could otherwise be very incomplete, in view of the fact that some metadata are optional. The total inaccessibility value of the classifier agent environment is medium.

The search agent environment is composed of different components and data. The components are the Skill Gap Analysis component, the Learning Management System, the classifier agent, the interface and the Document Management System. The data are the user's domain knowledge, the user's query, the document and LO ontologies. The inaccessibility of the components in this case, too, is low. Instead, the data inaccessibility is medium, because even if the ontologies are completely accessible, the user's query might not be very clear and the user's knowledge might not be available. Moreover, the user's knowledge may vary during the interactions, and would be accessible only if the user does the assessment test. Thus, the inaccessibility of the search agent is medium, as is the inaccessibility of the MAS environment.

The classifier agent environment evolves in a discrete, static way because it does not change during the cataloguing process. Moreover, the main action of this agent, namely cataloguing all the resources on the basis of both their descriptions and previously defined taxonomies, has only one effect on the environment. Thus, the instability environment value is low. The search agent environment also evolves in a discrete way, but it is dynamic because users can continuously modify their knowledge independently of their use of the system. The effects of the agents' actions can be multiple, because, according to the user profile, the search agent selects different types of resources. Overall, the instability of the search agent environment is medium, as is the instability of the MAS environment.

The GeCo-Automotive classifier agent does not compete with the search agent during the resolution process, nor collaborate, because the relationship is limited to sending the resources to the other agent using a web service. Moreover, in the classifier agent environment it is not necessary to use trust and reputation models to verify the reliability of the component behaviors, but it would be necessary to verify the reliability of the metadata describing both LOs and documents. Thus, the value of the interaction complexity of the agent environment is low.

Also, the search agent environment does not compete, nor collaborate, because the agent does not interact with the classifier agent during the search process to find the resource best suited to the user's learning gap. The search agent receives the classified resources from the other agent. In this environment, trust and reputation models are necessary to evaluate the reliability of the information about the user's knowledge. The complexity of interaction of the search agent environment is low.

Overall, the Complexity of the Interaction of the MAS environment is low.

5.3   Evaluation of the GeCo-Automotive Characteristics

Application of the metric plan showed a minimal level of rationality for both the classifier agent and the search agent in choosing the actions. Both agents have simple reflexes, do not build plans of actions to reach their goals, are unable to learn and do not possess an internal model of the actions and intentions of the other agent. The ability to maximize the expected result was measured for the classifier agent as the percentage of correctly classified resources in the time interval considered, and for the search agent as the percentage of proposed resources that satisfy the user's needs. The classifier agent showed a high level of ability to maximize the success, whereas the search agent had a medium value. Overall, the MAS rationality is low.

The MAS agents show the same level of autonomy. They not make diagnoses of errors or problems occurring during the performance of their tasks, nor can they autonomously undertake or maintain any communication. They have fixed roles in the MAS, defined a priori by the designer, and no ability to negotiate. The only values revealing autonomy are those relative to their non subordinate position in the MAS structure and lack of sharing of tasks with other agents. Overall, the MAS autonomy value is low.

The evaluation of the MAS reactivity demonstrated a very high reactivity level. The two agents do not perform any processing of the perceptions, carry out actions defined during the design phase, do not have an internal model of the environment and play a single role in the MAS. In addition, they do not communicate between themselves while carrying out their activities. This results in maximum rapidity of the reactions. The MAS classifier and search agents of the GeCo-Automotive system present poor adaptability to the environment. For both agents the only value showing a degree of adaptability is that of the management of exceptions.

To conclude, the evaluation of the environment complexity points out that the complexity of the classifier agent environment is low, while the complexity of the search agent environment is medium; overall, the MAS environment shows a medium complexity value.

6   Evaluation of the Multi-agent Tourism Recommender System

The goal of the evaluation of the Multi-agent Tourism Recommender System [4] using the proposed metric plan is to measure the adequacy of the MAS for a specific environment assumed by the evaluator. The aim of this evaluation is to show how the proposed method could be applied by an evaluator in order to verify if a MAS is adequate to a specific environment problem. In the following sections, the evaluator makes a set of assumptions both on the environment and the MAS.

6.1   Multi-Agent Tourism Recommender System

The Multi-agent Tourism Recommender system [4] is a knowledge-based system prototype that is aimed at promoting tourism in Argentina. For this reason it suggests the best tourist packages (a package consists of transport, accommodation, cost, activities to do during the holiday, etc.) for Argentinian destinations according to the user's needs and preferences.

The Multi-agent Tourism Recommender architecture is inspired by the different components of a tourism chain. It includes the following components: (I) the Package Repository (PR) that contains the tourist packages; (II) the Destination Ontology (DO) that contains information about the destinations and the resources available in them (geographical coordinates, types of resources, etc.); (III) a set of n Provider Agents (P-Agents) that supply the tourist packages to the T-Agent; (IV) a Travel Assistant Agent (T-Agent) that selects the packages best suited to the user's needs and preferences.

In this paper the prototype system architecture, that includes only two P-Agents, is considered. The agent sensors of a P-Agent are the set of functions and procedures that allows tourist packages to be acquired from external sources. Instead, the actuators are the functions that allow the agent to send the packages (each single package is a message) to the T-Agent. In the same way, the T-Agent sensors are the set of functions that allows the agent to receive the packages, the preferences and restrictions expressed by the user. The actuators, instead, are the set of functions that allows the agent to propose the tourist packages to the users using the interface.

The MAS acts in the following way. The P-Agents supply all the available tourist packages to the T-Agent, that identifies the packages that satisfy user's preferences and restrictions. To do this, the T-Agent accesses both the PR and the DO and, apart from the Travel Assistant role, also has that of Repository Maintenance in the MAS to update its information about the packages (before beginning the recommendation task), and an Interface role (during the recommendation task), to manage the user interface. When the T-Agent requests information, the P-Agents send it all the current packages they can offer. The communication between the agents is message-driven. The T-Agent's overall aim is to maximize the satisfaction of tourists' preferences. Thus, it acquires user preferences and restrictions from the interface, accesses the PR in order to relate the packages to the domain knowledge and infers which packages should be recommended.

6.2   Environment Complexity Evaluation and Prevision

It is assumed that the P-Agents receive the tourist package from the T-Agent and from a set of external sources. The environment data are the tourist packages, that are always accessible; the evaluator should assume, however, that the P-Agents environment components are not completely accessible to the agents. Instead, the T-Agent components (P-Agents, Destination Ontology, package repositories) are completely accessible but the user's preferences are not; in this case the inaccessibility value of T-Agent environment is medium, as is the MAS environment value.

If the packages are supplied by the provider agents at discrete time intervals, these agents' environment is discrete and, assuming that new packages cannot be available to the P-Agents while they supply the packages to the T-Agent, the environment is static. The only actions that the P-Agents can perform are those of acquiring the packages from the sources and supplying them to the T-Agent. For these reasons the P-Agents environment has a low level of instability. Moreover, the evaluator assumes that the T-Agent environment also evolves in a discrete and static way, because it is presumed that the user's preferences will not change the user's request during the agent process. The T-Agent actions have only one effect on the environment: to recommend the tourist packages. The T-Agent environment instability value is also low. Thus, the instability level of the entire MAS is low.

As regards the interaction complexity, the evaluator assumes that the P-Agents do not compete nor collaborate during the recommendation process, and they do not compete nor collaborate with the T-Agent. In this case, the value for competition or collaboration is null. In addition, if the sources of P-Agent packages in the considered environment were unreliable, it would be necessary to use trust and reputation models to verify the reliability of the sources. Assuming that the components and data in the T-Agent are reliable, it is possible to assign a low level to the interaction complexity of both P-Agents and the T-Agent. Thus, the Complexity of the Interaction of the entire MAS environment is low.

6.3   Evaluation of the Multi-Agent Recommender System Characteristics

The application of the metric plan to the Multi-Agent Recommender System shows that the P-Agents have a low level of rationality when choosing the actions in the environment assumed by the evaluator. Even if the P-agents have a high level of ability to maximize the success of the process they have simple reflexes, do not build plans of actions to reach their goals, are unable to learn and do not have an internal model of the actions and intentions of the T-agent. The T-Agent, instead, shows a very high grade of rationality in choosing the actions to be performed. It is a graded BDI agent and therefore an intentional agent, and it is able to build plans of actions. Overall, the MAS rationality value is medium.

Since there is no evidence that the two P-Agents are able to make a diagnosis of errors or problems occurring during the performance of their task, the evaluator assumes that they do not have this ability. They have fixed roles in the MAS, defined a priori by the designer, no ability to negotiate, but they can send messages at any moment. Therefore, their proactivity level is low. Moreover, each P-Agent ignores the other P-Agents, and has a subordinate position in the MAS structure with respect to the T-Agent and does not share its tasks with others. The level of autonomy in the organizational structure of the MAS is high. The P-Agents autonomy value in the MAS is medium.

For the T-Agent, too, the evaluator assumes that it cannot make a diagnosis of errors or problems occurring during the performance of its tasks. Like the P-Agents, it can autonomously engage in communication and has several roles in the MAS; its main role is to provide tourists with recommendations about Argentinian packages, but it also has a repository maintenance role. Moreover, it has not the ability to negotiate. For these reasons, the T-Agent proactivity level is medium. The T-Agent does not have a subordinate position in the MAS and it does not share its tasks, therefore its autonomy value in the MAS structure is high. The T-Agent shows a medium level of autonomy. Overall, the autonomy level of the MAS is medium.

Since the only task of the P-Agents is to provide the packages, it can be assumed they are able to perceive all the relevant components and data. In addition, it is assumed that the two P-Agents do not process the perceptions, i.e. the tourist packages. They carry out actions defined during the design phase, do not have an internal model of the actions and intentions of the other MAS agents, nor communicate between themselves while carrying out their activities; they only communicate with the T-Agent aiming to provide the tourist packages. Therefore, the P-Agents are very good at responding in a timely fashion. Overall, the P-Agents show a high reactivity level. The T-Agent, too, is able to perceive all the relevant components and data environment, but it is less rapid in responding to the environment than the P-Agents. Even if the T-Agent has minimal communication with the P-agents when asking for the packages, it processes the received messages (the packages) using a set of actions that are not predefined by the designer. It is an intentional agent, since it is able to build different plans of actions according to the messages received. Therefore, the agent shows a low value for rapidity to respond in a timely fashion. Overall, the T-Agents have a low reactivity level. For these reasons, the reactivity of the entire MAS is medium.

In [4] there is evidence that the P-Agents are able to respond to the packages requests of the T-Agent and they cannot change roles during the packages recommendation process. In this context, if there were changes of the environment, for example, and the T-Agent cannot receive the packages because it has not finished the internal deductions process, the P-Agents would send the messages anyway.

Thus, the P-Agents have a low level of ability to respond to new external stimuli. The P-Agents ability to manage different situations is also low because they do not learn, and are not able to find heuristics for performing the tasks. The adaptability of the P-Agents to their environment is low. The T-agent, instead, shows a high level of ability to respond to new external stimuli, because it is able to consider new user preferences and to build suitable plans of actions; it shows a medium ability level to manage different situations, because it is able to find heuristics for achieving its goals and to handle exceptions, but it is unable to learn. Overall, the adaptability level of the T-Agent to its environment is medium.

On the whole, the value of adaptability to the environment of the entire MAS is medium.

7   Conclusions

The paper proposes a method for evaluating MAS that, unlike other evaluation approaches presented in the literature, uses high level metrics that highlight characteristics like autonomy, reactivity, environment adaptability, thus allowing the agents to be distinguished from the objects (of the O.O. paradigm). Moreover, it merges the inter-agent and intra-agent characteristics evaluations, supplying a ready-to-use GQM.

The defined metric plan has numerous applications. It can be used by a MAS designer as a guideline during the building process or by an evaluator who wishes to compare different MAS in order to choose the one best suited to solve a specific problem. Considering the high level of abstraction of the approach, only the metrics need to be contextualized to the specific MAS to be evaluated. This flexibility is possible because the MAS evaluation is related to the environment in which it operates. Thus, during the analysis phase the defined metric plan supports the designer's definition of the problem that the MAS should solve, helping to define all the abilities that each single MAS agent should have in order to be able to cope with the problem. This is possible because the metric plan allows comparisons between the agents' capacities and the environment complexity. During the test phase it supports the evaluator aiming to understand whether the agent and the MAS have all the characteristics necessary to deal with the problem to be solved. Moreover, the defined metric plan helps the evaluator to find out which are the key characteristics (or desired qualities) to be considered during the evaluation of different MASs.

In order to validate the method's independence of the problem domain and to investigate the efficacy of its application according to the different evaluation goals, two applications of the defined metric plan have been described in this paper. The MASs considered are: GeCo-Automotive and the Multi-agent Tourist Recommender. The first is aimed at developing an ICT environment to manage small-medium-sized company knowledge about automotive spare parts, suggesting learning activities and best practices to employees of companies in the automotive sector; the second is aimed at promoting tourism in Argentina, suggesting the best tourist packages for Argentinian destinations according to the tourist's needs and preferences. The goal of the application of the method to GeCo-Automotive system has been to verify the MAS's adequacy to the environment complexity for which it was designed. In fact, the authors are the MAS designers. This evaluation allowed us to make some observations about both the agents' and MAS's suitability to the environment complexity. In particular, application of the method to the GeCo-Automotive MAS and its environment allowed us both to observe specific weaknesses of the single agents in terms of poor rationality, autonomy, reactivity and adaptability to the environment, and to assess whether the evaluation parameter values are suitable for the MAS environment complexity. The evaluation of the MAS using the metric plan highlighted the fact that the considered environment has a medium level of complexity. The rationality level of the MAS is appropriate because it depends on its ability to maximize the success of the process. The agents' autonomy, instead, is not adequate to the environment because it is related to each agent's independence during the execution of its tasks and does not depend on its ability to diagnose errors or problems. The reactivity level and the environment adaptability are acceptable. The estimated value of the adaptability to the environment is higher than the expected value, which is an important point in view of the need to face rapid evolutions of the environment. Thus, the analyzed MAS is adequate to its environment, even if the agents' autonomy level needs to be improved by increasing their proactivity.

Instead, the goal of the Multi-agent Tourism Recommender System evaluation was to show that the metric plan can be used to verify a MAS's adequacy to a specific environment assumed by an evaluator. In this case, the metrics highlighted the fact that the MAS is adequate to the considered environment, even if an improvement of the environment adaptability ability of the P-Agent would be desirable.

In fact, the rationality level of the MAS is medium but adequate to the environment complexity, that has been assumed as low. This value of rationality is due mainly to the T-Agent's capacity to choose and build plans of action during the recommendation process. The autonomy and reactivity values are sufficient for the defined environment, but the adaptability is not. When going into the details of the agent evaluations, it was noted that the P-Agents are not able to respond to new external stimuli and to manage different situations. Both capacities are useful in the given environment, where the providers acquire the packages from different sources and supply them to the T-Agent. Moreover, those capacities would be useful to face unpredictable situations of source inaccessibility and they would be helpful as a means of designing a synchronous Exchange of packages among the P-Agents and T-agent. Therefore, the results of this evaluation also provided a useful basis for reflections on further developments of multi-agent recommender systems working in the environments studied.

References

1. Basili, V., Caldiera, G., Rombach, H.: The Goal Question Metric Approach. In: Marciniak, J.J. (ed.) Encyclopedia of Soft. Eng., vol. 2, pp. 528–532. John Wiley & Sons, Inc. (1994)
2. Di Bitonto, P., Laterza, M., Roselli, T., Rossano, V.: An Evaluation Method for Multi-Agent Systems. In: Jędrzejowicz, P., Nguyen, N.T., Howlet, R.J., Jain, L.C. (eds.) KES-AMSTA 2010. LNCS, vol. 6070, pp. 32–41. Springer, Heidelberg (2010)

3. Di Bitonto, P., Plantamura, V.L., Roselli, T., Rossano, V.: A taxonomy for cataloging LOs using IEEE educational metadata. In: 7th IEEE International Conference on Advanced Learning Technologies, pp. 139–141. IEEE Press, Los Alamitos (2007)
4. Casali, A., Von Furth, A., Godo, L., Sierra, C.: A Tourism Recommender Agent: From theory to practice. J. of Inteligencia Artificial 12, 23–38 (2008)
5. Chidamber, S.R., Kemerer, C.F.: A Metrics Suite for Object Oriented Design. J. IEEE Transactions on Software Engineering 20, 476–493 (1994)
6. Jang, K.S., Nam, T.E., Wadhwa, B.: On measurement of Objects and Agents, http://www.comp.nus.edu.sg/~bimlesh/ametrics/index.htm
7. Klügl, F.: Measuring Complexity of Multi-agent Simulations – An Attempt Using Metrics. In: Dastani, M.M., El Fallah Seghrouchni, A., Leite, J., Torroni, P. (eds.) LADS 2007. LNCS (LNAI), vol. 5118, pp. 123–138. Springer, Heidelberg (2008)
8. Król, D., Zelmozer, M.: Structural Performance Evaluation of Multi-Agent Systems. J. of Universal Computer Science 14, 1154–1178 (2008)
9. Gutiérez, C., García-Magariño, I., Gómez-Sanz, J.J.: Evaluation of Multi-Agent System Communication in INGENIAS. In: Cabestany, J., Sandoval, F., Prieto, A., Corchado, J.M. (eds.) IWANN 2009. LNCS, vol. 5517, pp. 619–626. Springer, Heidelberg (2009)
10. Ben Hmida, F., Lejouad Chaari, W., Tagina, M.: Performance Evaluation of Multiagent Systems: Communication Criterion. In: Nguyen, N.T., Jo, G.-S., Howlett, R.J., Jain, L.C. (eds.) KES-AMSTA 2008. LNCS (LNAI), vol. 4953, pp. 773–782. Springer, Heidelberg (2008)
11. Lass, R.N., Sultanik, E.A., Regli, W.C.: Metrics for Multi-agent Systems. In: Madhavan, R., Tunstel, E., Messina, E. (eds.) Performance Evaluation and Benchmarking of Intelligent Systems. LNCS, pp. 1–19. Springer, US (2009)
12. Russell, S., Norvig, P.: Artificial intelligence: A modern approach. Prentice-Hall, Englewood Cliffs (1995)
13. Wooldridge, M., Jennings, N.R.: Intelligent agents: Theory and practice. The Knowledge Engineering Review 10, 115–152 (1995)
14. Nwana, H.S.: Software Agents: An Overview. The Knowledge Engineering Review 11, 205–244 (1996)
15. Wiley, D.A.: Connecting learning objects to instructional design theory: A definition, metaphor and taxonomy. J. of Instructional Use of Learning Objects 2830, 1–35 (2000)

Egress Modeling through Cellular Automata Based Multi-Agent Systems

Jarosław Wąs

AGH University of Science and Technology
al. Mickiewicza 30, 30-059 Kraków, Poland
jarek@agh.edu.pl

Abstract. The article discusses evacuation models based on a multi-agent approach. It contains reflections associated with several evacuation experiments carried out by the author, as well as a practical approach towards the creation of computer simulations using Cellular Automata based Multi-agent Systems. The article describes the results of large room evacuation experiments with a comparison of practical and theoretical approaches.

1 Introduction

Public safety has become an important subject of research in recent years. One of the most important issues is to ensure the safety of people at different sites, for instance: buildings, stadiums or shopping centers. Modern computer systems have the potential to build and test many scenarios in ensuring crowd safety in different facilities.

Over the recent years, one can observe a growing interest in the possibilities of exact mapping of crowd behavior. Therefore in modeling, a trend can be observed to depart from the general models (for example Pauls model, based on hydrodynamics) and turn towards accurate methods: specific models. A convenient approach is to design an evacuation model on the basis of a multi-agent system. This approach provides an opportunity to build crowd behavior based on different technologies: from queuing systems to sophisticated non-homogeneous cellular automata. Pedestrian traffic principles in these models vary from the very simple rules (i.e. functional analogy) to complex rules based on artificial intelligence. Classification of behaviors is shown in Fig. 1.

An interesting approach to estimating the parameters of large area evacuation was presented by Lämmel, Rieser and Nagel [12]. They proposed the use of a queuing system, implemented in a multi-agent framework. In this approach, each agent represents a pedestrian and is placed in FIFO queues. The queues are arranged in links (routes) of a network across the concerned area. Three key parameters describing flow are distinguished:

- free-flow speed - the free speed travel time of an agent in a link
- flow capacity - parameters of outflow from the link
- storage capacity - the maximal number of agents on the link

N.T. Nguyen (Ed.): Transactions on CCI VII, LNCS 7270, pp. 222–235, 2012.
© Springer-Verlag Berlin Heidelberg 2012

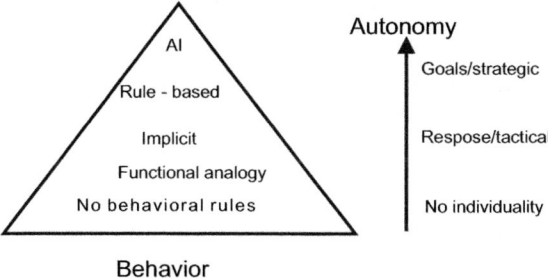

Fig. 1. The representation of behavior in pedestrian dynamics models according to [4]

More accurate results can be gained using non-homogeneous Cellular Automata (CA) [21]. Non-homogeneouos CA allow to represent different types of cells (like obstacles, exits, bottleneck cells etc.), different transition rules for different cells or different set of states for a cell [7]. In this approach, pedestrians are considered to be hopping particles in a cellular automaton (simple behavior) [21] or autonomous mobile agents, in more sophisticated CA-based models [8], [6]. The most popular construction of movement algorithm in non-homogeneous CA is using a potential field (with Point Of Interests defined for pedestrians/agents) for cells belong to class "movement space" (avoiding cells represented walls, obstacles etc). More precise description of this type of CA can be found in [21] or [7]. In the model non-homogeneous CA was used, because in the author opinion, the method is very efficient and its accuracy is acceptable [21]. Another possibility in egress modeling is the application of the continuous method, when evacuees are represented as self-driven particles across a continuous space (it is also a kind of MAS [13]).

Currently, the most serious challenge in crowd dynamics modeling is correct calibration and validation of created models. One can observe a necessity to collect various data for calibration and validation of pedestrian dynamic modeling.

2   Evacuation Experiments – Real Data

The variety of evacuation models developed in recent years, urges the necessity of their validation [9], [3], [17], [18]. We need both the data obtained during the actual evacuation as well as data obtained in controlled laboratory conditions. For each public facility, different drills and scenarios should be prepared in case of potential evacuation. Drills and different scenarios are connected with the evacuation experiments.

Drill - an exercise in which predetermined response actions are implemented.
Exercise - a scenario-based event to train and prepare for implementing emergency actions.
Evacuation experiment - a scenario-based event to collect evacuation data and/or to provide qualitative analysis of pedestrian behavior.

Pedestrian behavior can vary in different scenarios. The following types of pedestrian behavior can be distinguished:

- normal situation - free pedestrian flow
- non-competitive evacuation
- competitive evacuation
- panic situation

Previous studies indicate that competitive evacuation is disadvantageous because it often brings about the effect of "faster-is-slower" in bottlenecks[9,10]. Experiments constitute a very valuable source of information on evacuation situations. However, the experiments of competitive evacuation with the participation of a large number of pedestrians are connected with a risk. Currently the largest group in which the author carried out the tests involving competitive evacuation was a population of 31 persons, all the result have been presented in [15].

The author has also carried out experiments devoted to non-competitive evacuation with large groups (population 250-500 persons). A part of the experiments has been described in [14].

It has been observed that the following factors have an impact on traffic parameters: - the structure of the population (age, health, etc.), - time of day when the experiment is carried out, - motivation of the experiment participants, - level of knowledge of the environment (building layout), - participation of disabled persons in the experimental group.

Crowd control ability played a significant role in the carried out experiments, whilst the proper flow of information was a key factor influencing the performance of evacuation Fig. 3. In order to ensure crowd control (good flow of information) the following measures were undertaken:

- good technical conditions (such as a proper sound system),
- short and clear messages in communication,
- training of participants.

On the figures: Fig. 2, Fig. 3, Fig. 4 one can observe three consecutive phases of evacuation. Fig. 2 presents a response to an evacuation alert. Characteristic behavior can be observed: collecting things, putting on outerwear etc.

Pedestrians allocated in a lecture room before evacuation are presented in the Fig. 3. Participants were asked to take a sit according to initial allocation.

Pedestrians during evacuation are seen in Fig. 4. Crowd is divided into two main lanes (according to two accessible emergency exits).

It should be stressed that in real evacuation situations run time is only a part of the total evacuation process Fig. 5. The so-called times of "pre-evacuation" (reaction time etc.) play a key role in ensuring effective and safe evacuation [23].

3   Model Development

The basic question raised when a model is being created is where the model will be used. The answer to this question implies the use of specific technology. In the case

Fig. 2. Evacuation experiment - response to an evacuation alert, collecting things, and putting on outerwear

Fig. 3. Evacuation experiment - pedestrians before the final evacuation stage: the movement phase

Fig. 4. Evacuation experiment - pedestrians during the evacuation: the movement stage

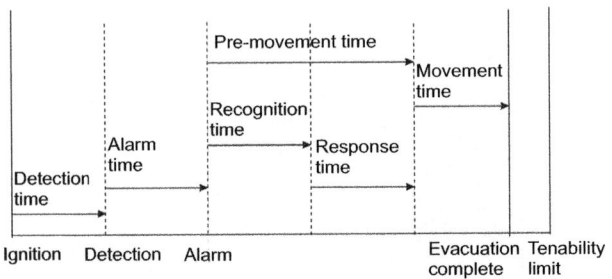

Fig. 5. Evacuation process (according to Proulx [19])

of large areas or the necessity of coarse estimation, queue system is a very good solution. The main limitation of this method is the lack of a precise description of the relationship between specific flow and crowd density. If the goal is to help architects and building designers to gain proper flow parameters of pedestrian flow, one can choose models based on CA [22]. However, in the case of accurate and detailed analysis of a building, one can chose continuous methods (Social Force), although MAS models based on Cellular Automata are more effective.

In this study, focus will be given to Multi-agent-systems based on non-homogeneous Cellular Automata. One of the major benefits of CA models is high efficiency [11] and the ability to simulate pedestrians behavior in large facilities in real time.

3.1 Formalization

In [2] a system called Situated Cellular Agents (SCA) was proposed. The system is denoted by the following three-tuple:

$$< Space; F; A > \tag{1}$$

where:
Space - is the single layered structured environment,
    A - is the set of situated agents,
    F - is the set of potential fields generated by Points Of Interest (POI).
An agent $a \in A$ is denoted:

$$< s; p; \tau >, \tag{2}$$

where:
$s \in \Sigma_\tau$ - denotes the agent state (one of the values specified by its type),
    $p \in P$ - is the site of the *Space* where the agent is situated,
        τ - is the agent type.
    In evacuation models, space is represented as a discrete lattice. A set of agents is allocated across this lattice and fields are connected with distance from emergency exits.

Currently, one can observe the tendency to create accurate, microscopic simulations of pedestrian egress [5,1,20]. Pedestrians are represented with consideration to their characteristics, such as age, weight, gender or physical fitness. An important feature is also the knowledge of the environment.

3.2   Space Representation and Pedestrian Representation

An important issue when creating a model is the choice of space representation; in discrete models, the choice of a lattice. The most popular is a square lattice, but sometimes a hexagonal grid is selected. Another possibility is an irregular lattice. It is used in the case when image recognition techniques are used [21].

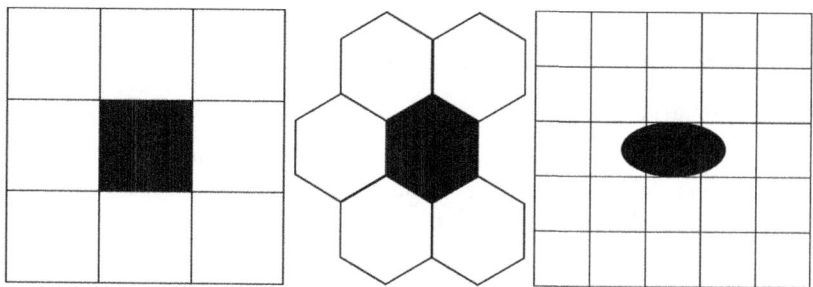

Fig. 6. Different representations of pedestrian on a discrete lattice

Another important issue is the choice of pedestrian representation. One can chose the simplest solution: one cell is occupied by one pedestrian. Pedestrian on a square grid can be represented as an occupied cell or in a more accurate way as an ellipse whose center coincides with the center of the cell fig. 6.

Pedestrians are represented as cellular agents [2] situated on a lattice with a potential field [16]. Exit cells are the source of potential.

Square Lattice. In the further consideration, we assume a square grid, where pedestrians will be represented as an occupied cell.

For each cell $c_i \in Lattice$, it is possible to determine a set of neighborhood cells (for Moore radius equals 1) with a better (i.e. lower) C_{output} potential and cells with a worse (i.e. higher) C_{input} potential. The third group of cells is c_i, but they are not taken into consideration in context of bottleneck [14]. The ratio of the number of C_{output} neighbor cells to the number of C_{input} neighbor cells determines the level of capacity (level of bottleneck) of a given cell $r_{BN}(c_i) = \frac{|C_{output}|}{|C_{input}|}$. If this ratio $r_{BN}(c_i) < 1$ we have a situation of a *bottleneck*. In this case, we take into account the probability of a local blockade p in the cell c_i to calculate the next configuration on the *Lattice*.

The local blockade parameter p is introduced, because flow in real situations is blocked in different classes of situations: for instance making others' passage possible (small values of p) or rivalry during panic (bigger values of p).

$$p = dens_{BN}(c_i) \cdot (1 - r_{BN}(c_i)) \cdot p_{glob} \qquad (3)$$

where:
$dens_{BN}(c_i)$ - crowd density around the cell c_i,
which is the bottleneck described by the equation:
$$dens_{BN}(c_i) = \frac{\sum_{c \in \eta(c_i)} s(c)}{|\eta(c_i)|}$$
$r_{BN}(c_i)$ - the level of the bottleneck,
p_{glob} - global blockade probability, which depends on situation (the level of pedestrian determination).

3.3   Decision Modeling at Different Levels

Agents in evacuation models can make decisions/actions at different levels:

- strategic level, for instance the choice of an evacuation route,
- tactical level, for instance overtaking groups of pedestrians,
- operational level, for instance avoiding obstacles.

Operational Level. The most efficient mechanism for movement in the model is to apply the potential field in which pedestrians move in accordance with the gradient of potential. The potential field mechanism provides a solution to any decision at *the operational level*; an agent has a possibility to avoid any obstacles.

Tactical Level. At the tactical level, pedestrians should have the possibility to avoid local congestion, for instance, in a wide corridor. Thus, one can modify potential field in the neighborhood of local congestions in the movement algorithm. Another possibility is to allow pedestrian to move, in the case of a congestion, according to the same value of potential (if all cells with a better value of potential are occupied). It should be stressed that the implementation of tactical mechanisms is essential to ensure proper validation of the model.

Strategic Level. At the strategic level, the most significant mechanism is the cost function. In recent years, the author has tested several different cost functions. Quite sufficient for the purposes of evacuation modeling is a simple cost function. A set of possible s states of an agent a is denoted as $\Sigma_\tau = /Wait, GoTo/$.

In the state $GoTo$, their movement rules are realized according to a cost function. The cost function is defined as follows (for each of the exits $e_j \in E$):

$$cost(c_i, e_j) = w_{dist} dist(c_i, e_j) + w_{dens} dens(e_j) + w_{fragrance} f(e_j) + w_{troughput} t(e_j) \qquad (4)$$

where:

$w_{distance}, w_{density}$ – weights of density and distance,

$w_{fragrance}$ – weight of fragrance,

$w_{throughput}$ – weight of throughput,

$f(e_j)$ – normalized fragrance of an exit e_j, $f(e_j) \in [0; 1]$,

$t(e_j)$ – normalized throughput of an exit e_j, $t(e_j) \in [0; 1]$,

$dist(c_i, e_j)$ – distance from c_i cell to any exit cell e_j,

$dens(e_j)$ – crowd density in neighborhood $N(e_j)$ around exit e_j, expressed by (5).

$$dens(e_j) = \frac{\sum_{c_i \in N(e_j)} s(c_i)}{|N(e_j)|} \qquad (5)$$

where:

$|N(e_j)|$ – number of cells in neighborhood N of exit e_j

The concepts of fragrance and throughput must be further clarified:

Fragrance of an exit measures how attractive particular exit is for pedestrians [16]. When more pedestrians move towards an exit, it becomes more attractive for the remaining persons.

Throughput of an exit tells how wide the particular exit is [16]. Exit cells can be treated as cluster members, when they keep direct contact with other exit cells. Two cells are in contact, when they belong to each other's Moore neighborhoods of radius 1.

3.4   Movement Algorithm

The movement algorithm of a particular pedestrian for one time step can be described as follows:

1. For the selection of exit, towards which an agent will direct, evaluate components of the cost function: distance, crowd density around the exit, fragrance and throughput of the exit.
2. Select the exit for which the cost function has a minimum value.
3. Determine potential field related to the selected exit e_j .
4. Check the value of potential generated by exit e_j in the occupied cell.
5. Determine the set of cells belonging to Moore neighborhood of The occupied cell. Determine the subset of vacant cells whose potential value is not lower than the potential of cell which you occupy.
6. Is this subset non-empty? If yes, move to a randomly selected cell of this subset and stop. Otherwise, follow to the next step.
7. Determine the new subset of vacant cells whose potential value equals the potential value of the cell which you could occupy.
8. Is this subset non-empty? If yes, move to the randomly selected cell of this subset and stop. Otherwise, you cannot move - you have to stay in a current cell.

4   Simulations

On the basis of the presented assumptions, a model has been implemented and several simulations have been executed. Space was discretized into a square lattice. Agents, according to cost function, are given a task to evacuate through two available exits. Black cells represent walls and obstacles, while white cells represent the movement space. Pedestrians are represented as circles placed in a cell. In the right side of the figure 7 one can observe evacuation times (movement times) and gained evacuation exits for each pedestrian. Clusters of grey cells represent two available emergency exits.

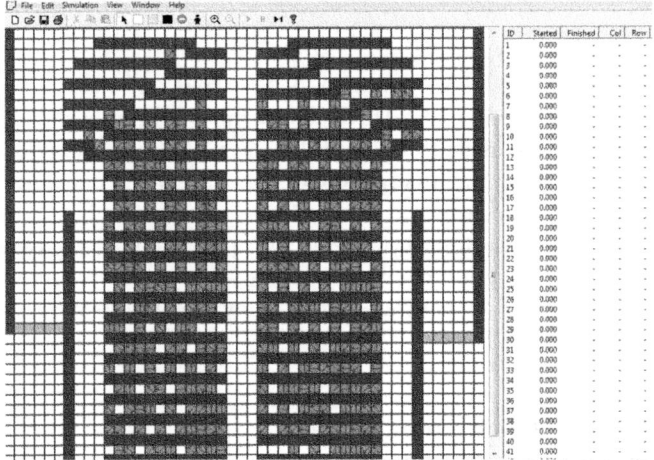

Fig. 7. Agents allocated in the lattice

In the detailed view, one can notice values of potential field in each cell 8. The potential field is a base element for movement algorithm of each pedestrian (It is connected with mentioned above distance criterion). When a cell possesses fewer outputs than inputs, such a cell becomes a bottleneck cell. In all exits, counters of pedestrians are placed. In a particular time-step we can ditinguish two states of pedestrian movement possibilities: {blocked} or {free}.

5   Validation

Certain evacuation experiments were prepared and executed. A group of students (average age about 19-20 years) allocated randomly in a big lecture room was evacuated. Two emergency exits were available. The experiment situation was classified as a controlled evacuation (non-competitive evacuation). The level of pedestrian determination was rather low.

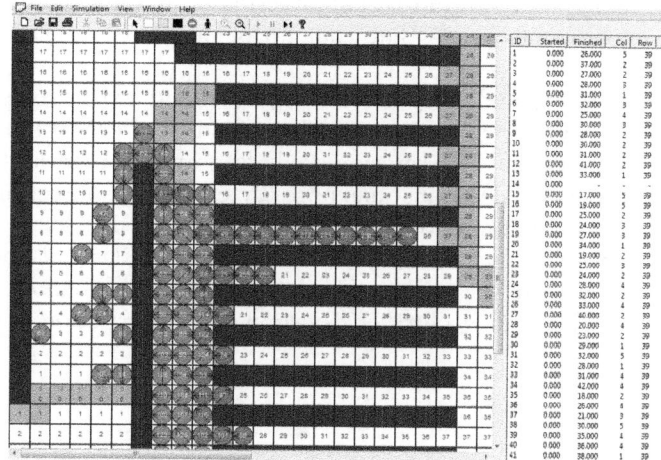

Fig. 8. The detailed view on a simulation

The following stage of the research was the feedback from evacuated persons. Thus, all participants were asked to fill in a questionnaire. One of the most important questions was about the exit selection criteria. The two main criteria were as follows: distance to an exit and density in the neighborhood of an exit. The results are presented Figure 9. The most important criterion turned out to be:*distance to an exit* (94% answers). Avoiding *density* (overcrowded exits) was the crucial criterion for 6 % of participants. Other criteria such as following others or exit throughput were crucial for less then 1% persons.

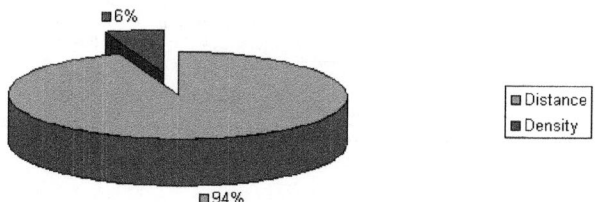

Fig. 9. Statistics of preferences in evacuation exit choice - data from the questionnaire

5.1   Criteria Selection in Cost Function – Discussion

The simulations showed that the main and most significant criterion for choosing the direction of movement must be a distance from the exit. If the value of distance in the simulation $w_{distance}$ was less than 0.95-0.96, one can observe the frequent changes of aim (and actual direction of movement) of pedestrians. Carried out experiments prove that changes of decision era rare during real evacuation.

Additional criteria like: density in exits neighborhood, exit throughput or fragrance, in fact defining quality of traffic flow (fluidity of crowd movement). In practice, it turned out that the criterion used "fragrance" causes additional fluctuations in traffic, i.e. pedestrians unexpectedly change the direction of motion and a stampede was sometimes observed. Therefore it was decided to exclude the application of this criterion for the modeled situation. Similarly, it appeared that the criterion of density in the exit neighborhood and exit throughput give almost identical results. Therefore, to further development, the criterion of density was chosen.

5.2   Results

The comparison of the actual experiment and computer simulation (exemplary view is shown in Fig. 10) shows the same dependency between the number of evacuated people and passing time. When we take into account only distance weight $w_{dist} = 1$, the plot varies a little from experiments results. We can observe some differences in evacuation times when we use $w_{dist} = 0.97$ an additional weight $w_{dens} = 0.03$.

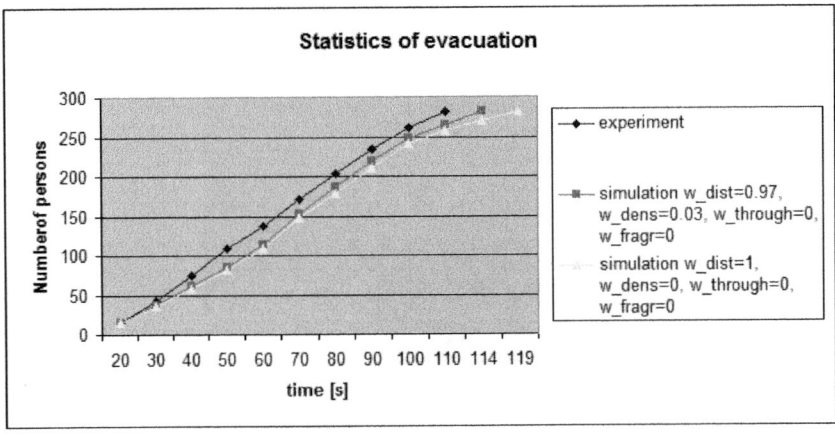

Fig. 10. Evacuation times: simulation vs. experiments

It is also interesting to take into consideration the number of people who chose the particular emergency exit shown in Table 1. A set of entrance parameters was chosen in correspondence to the situation, probability of global blockade for non-competitive behavior $p_{global} = 0.01$.

Table 1. Choice of emergency exits: simulation vs. real data

	Number of people who chose the left emergency exit	Number of people who chose the right emergency exit	Total number
Real data	149	133	282
Simulation $w_{distance} = 0.97$ $w_{density} = 0.03$ $w_{fragrance} = 0$ $w_{troughput} = 0$	144	138	282
Simulation $w_{distance} = 1$ $w_{density} = 0$ $w_{fragrance} = 0$ $w_{troughput} = 0$	142	140	282

6   Summary

At the strategic level of the decision-making process the evacuee is focused on the selection of the evacuation route. Constructing decision functions (illustrating the decision-making process) is associated with an evacuation drill and the base scenario. For standard scenarios, it is sufficient to apply a simple cost function. The main criterion is distance to an available evacuation exit; an additional criterion in some scenarios (large room evacuation) can be avoiding of the local density of emergency exits, exits throughput or pedestrian fragrance. For certain values of distance criterion, distribution of other criteria is not so important. For model simplicity in large room evacuation, only density in an exit neighborhood can be an additional criterion.

The carried out experiments prove that the weight of distance w_{dist} should equal above 95% of all criteria weight. Qualitative validation shows that if distance value has not high enough, pedestrians tend to change their decision very often, which results in model oscillations.

At the tactical level, it is important to implement local congestion avoidance mechanism. It makes it possible to obtain a good representation of reality and proper results of qualitative validation.

At the operational level of agent decision process, it is better to use probabilistic rather than deterministic elements. For example, a more realistic effect gives a random rule "to avoid an obstacle turn left or right" then deterministic rule "to avoid an obstacle always turn right".

It should be emphasized that during the creation of sophisticated models crowd behavior (using cognitive modeling or emotion modeling etc), in particular for large objects, it is important to ensure the accuracy of physical movement (bottleneck characteristic, fundamental diagrams, etc.). Thus, it is preferred to use a framework such as non-homogeneouos cellular automata for creating highly complex systems modeling the behavior of the crowd.

Acknowledgment. The research is partially supported within the FP7 project SOCIONICAL, No. 231288.

References

1. Averill, J.D., Song, W.: Accounting for Emergency Response in Building Evacuation: Modeling Differential Egress Capacity Solutions. NISTIR 7425, 13 p. (April 2007)
2. Bandini, S., Manzoni, S., Vizzari, G.: Situated Cellular Agents: a Model to Simulate Crowding Dynamics. IEICE - Transactions on Information and Systems E87-D(3), 669–676 (2004)
3. British Standards 9999 Code of practice for fire safety in the design, management and use of buildings BSI (October 2008)
4. ISO/TR 13387 Fire Safety Engineering - Part 8: Life Safety - Occupant Behavior, Location and Condition, International Organization for Standardization (1999)
5. ISO/TR 16738:2009 Fire-safety engineering – Technical information on methods for evaluating behaviour and movement of people (2009)
6. Song, W., Yu, Y., Wang, B., Fan, W.: Evacuation behaviors at exit in CA model with force essentials: A comparison with social force model. Physica A 371, 658–666 (2006)
7. Dudek–Dyduch, E., Wąs, J.: Knowledge Representation of Pedestrian Dynamics in Crowd: Formalism of Cellular Automata. In: Rutkowski, L., Tadeusiewicz, R., Zadeh, L.A., Żurada, J.M. (eds.) ICAISC 2006. LNCS (LNAI), vol. 4029, pp. 1101–1110. Springer, Heidelberg (2006)
8. Gloor, C., Stucki, P., Nagel, K.: Hybrid Techniques for Pedestrian Simulations. In: Sloot, P.M.A., Chopard, B., Hoekstra, A.G. (eds.) ACRI 2004. LNCS, vol. 3305, pp. 581–590. Springer, Heidelberg (2004)
9. Kirchner, A., Klüpfel, H., Nishinari, K., Schadschneider, A., Schreckenberg, M.: Simulation of competitive egress behavior: Comparison with aircraft evacuation data. Physica A 324 (2003)
10. Nilsson, D., Frantzich, H.: Measurement Techniques for Unannounced Evacuation Experiments. In: Pedestrian and Evacuation Dynamics. Springer (2010)
11. Gajer, M.: Task scheduling in real-time computer systems with the use of an evolutionary computations technique. Electrical Review, R. 86, NR 10/2010, 293–298 (2010)
12. Lämmel, G., Rieser, M., Nagel, K.: Bottlenecks and congestion in evacuation scenarios: A microscopic evacuation simulation for large-scale disasters. In: Proc. of 5th Workshop on Agents in Traffic and Transportation, at AAMAS 2008, Estoril, PT, pp. 54–61 (2008)
13. Nakajima, Y., Yamane, S., Hattori, H., Ishida, T.: Evacuation guide system based on massively multiagent system. In: Proceedings of the 7th International Joint Conference on Autonomous Agents and Multiagent Systems: Demo Papers (AAMAS 2008), pp. 1653–1654. International Foundation for Autonomous Agents and Multiagent Systems, Richland (2008)
14. Wąs, J., Kułakowski, K.: Multi-agent Systems in Pedestrian Dynamics Modeling. In: Nguyen, N.T., Kowalczyk, R., Chen, S.-M. (eds.) ICCCI 2009. LNCS, vol. 5796, pp. 294–300. Springer, Heidelberg (2009)
15. Wąs, J.: Experiments on Evacuation Dynamics for Different Classes of Situations. In: Pedestrian and Evacuation Dynamics 2008, Part 1, pp. 225–232 (2008)

16. Gudowski, B., Wąs, J.: Some criteria of making decisions in pedestrian evacuation algorithms. In: Computer Information Systems and Industrial Management Applications. IEEE (2007)
17. Kuligowski, E., Gwynne, S.: What a user should know when choosing and evacuation model. Fire Protection, 30–40 (Fall 2005)
18. Kuligowski, E.D., Peacock, R.D.: Review of building evacuation models. Technical Report 1471, NIST (2005)
19. Proulx, G.: Response to fire alarms. Fire Protection Engineering 2(30), 8–14 (2007)
20. Sharma, S.: AvatarSim: A multi-agent system for emergency evacuation simulation. J. Comp. Methods in Sci. and Eng. 9 (April 2009)
21. Schadschneider, A., Seyfried, A.: Validation of CA Models of Pedestrian Dynamics with Fundamental Diagrams. Cybern. Syst. 40(5), 367–389
22. Topa, P.: Network Systems Modelled by Complex Cellular Automata Paradigm. Cellular Automata - Simplicity Behind Complexity InTech (2011)
23. Rinne, T., Tillander, K., Grönberg, P.: Data collection and analysis of evacuation situations. VTT Tiedotteita - Research Notes (2010)

Author Index

GPSR Compliance

The European Union's (EU) General Product Safety Regulation (GPSR) is a set of rules that requires consumer products to be safe and our obligations to ensure this.

If you have any concerns about our products, you can contact us on ProductSafety@springernature.com

In case Publisher is established outside the EU, the EU authorized representative is:

Springer Nature Customer Service Center GmbH
Europaplatz 3
69115 Heidelberg, Germany

Batch number: 09490872

Printed by Printforce, the Netherlands